The Osborne/McGraw-Hill

Guide to IBM® PC Communications

David Kruglinski

Osborne/McGraw-Hill
Berkeley, California

Published by
Osborne/McGraw-Hill
2600 Tenth Street
Berkeley, California 94710
U.S.A.

For information on translations and book distributors outside of the U.S.A., please write to Osborne/McGraw-Hill at the above address.

The Osborne/McGraw-Hill Guide to IBM® PC Communications

234567890 DODO 8987654

ISBN 0-88134-126-6

Judy Ziajka, Acquisitions Editor
Cindy Hudson, Project Sponsor
David Ushijima, Technical Editor
Ted Gartner, Copy Editor
Judy Wohlfrom, Text Design
Yashi Okita, Cover Design

Trademarks

The boldface companies hold the corresponding trademarks. An ® denotes a registered trademark, and **sm** denotes a service mark. All others are trademarks.

Adventure International: Adventure ®
Altos Computer Systems: Altos ®
American International Communications: TLX-A-SYST ®
Anchor Automation: Signalman
Volksmodem
Apple Computer, Inc.: Apple ®
Applied Digital Data Systems, Inc.: Viewpoint
Ashton-Tate: dBASE II ®
Associated Press: Associated Press ®
AT&T: Picturephone ®
Sceptre⋆VideoTex Terminal
Atari, Inc.: Lunar Lander
Bank of America, NT&SA: VISA ®
Bizcomp: Bizcomp ®
PC: IntelliCom
PC:IntelliModem
Business Week/McGraw-Hill: Business Week ®
BYTE Publications, Inc.: BYTE ®
C.D. Anderson & Co.: The Desk Top Broker
Cappcomm Software: SmarTelex ®
Centronics Data Computer Corp.: Centronics ®
COMP-U-CARD of America, Inc.: COMP-U-STORE
CompuServe, Inc.: CompuServe ®
Consumer Information Service ®
InfoPlex
VIDTEX
Contex, Inc.: SOFTEX
Control Data Corp.: Control Data
PLATO ®
Control Data Publishing Co.: Homelink
Cornerstone Computer Co.: PCE-Mail

TRADEMARKS

Corvus Systems, Inc.: Corvus
Transporter
Custom Software: Remote Access
CXI: *PCOX*
Cygnet Technologies: CoSystem ®
DCA, Inc.: *IRMA* ®
IRMALETTE ®
IRMALINE ®
Dialog Information Services, Inc.: Dialog (sm)
Knowledge Index (sm)
Digisoft Computers, Inc.: Mail-COM
Digital Equipment Corp.: DEC
Digital Research: CP/M ®
Dow Jones & Co., Inc.: Barron's
Dow Jones Corporate Earnings Estimator
Dow Jones Current Quote
Wall Street Journal Highlights Online
Dow Jones Market Analyzer
Dow Jonew Market Manager
Dow Jones Market Microscope
Dow Jones News/Retrieval ®
Dynamic Microprocessor Associates, Inc.: ASCOM
Eagle Computers: Eagle ®
Firstworld Travel Corporation: Firstworld Travel Club
Forbes, Inc.: Forbes
General Electric Company: QuickCom
Graphnet Systems, Inc.: Graphnet
GTE Telenet Communications: Telemail ®
Hayes Microcomputer Products, Inc.: Hayes ®
Smartmodem
Henco Software: INFO X
IBM Corporation: IBM ®
Independent Publications, Inc.: NewsNet
Information Access Company: Newsearch
Intelligent Technologies International: Cluster-Net ®
Intelligent Technologies
Intertec Data Systems Corp.: Superbrain
PC Exchange
IT&T Worldcom: Timetran
ITT: Dialcom ®
Janadon, Inc.: Hostcomm ®
Kaypro Corporation: Kaypro
Lotus Development Corporation: 1-2-3
Management Contents: Management Contents ®
MCI Communications Corp.: MCI
Mead Data Central, Inc.: LEXIS ®
LEXPAT ®
NEXIS ®
Media General Financial Services, Inc.: Media General DataBank ®
Microcom, Inc.: MNP
Microcomputer Information Services: Microcom puter Index
MicroPro International Corp.: MailMerge ®
Wordstar ®
Microsoft Corporation: Microsoft ®
Multiplan
XENIX ®
Mobil Oil Corporation: Mobil ®
MSA Software Company: PeachCalc
Peachpak
PeachText
Executive Peachpak

Newsweek, Inc.: Newsweek ®
NorthStar Computers: North Star
Official Airline Guides, Inc.: Official Airline Guide ®
PC World Communications, Inc.: PC World
Plantronics: Colorplus
Plantronics
Prime Computer, Inc.: Prime
Quadram Corporation: Quadboard
Quadram
Quantum Software Limited: Qubulletin
Radio Shack, A Division of the Tandy Corporation:
Radio Shack ®
TRS-80 ®
Rixon, Inc.: Rixon ®
Saturn Consulting Groups, Inc.: VTERM
Shepard's/McGraw-Hill: Shepard's ®
Standard & Poor's Corporation: Standard & Poor's (sm)
Systems Development Corp.: ORBIT ®
Telelearning Systems: TeleLearning ®
Telenet Communications Corp.: Telenet
Teletype Corporation: Teletype
Televideo Systems, Inc.: TeleVideo ®
Texas Instruments, Inc.: Magic Wand
TI ®
Tymeshare, Inc.: OnTyme
Tymnet ®
The Headlands Press, Inc.: Freeware ®
PC-Talk.III ®
The New York Times Company: The Information Bank ®
The New York Times ®
The Reader's Digest Association, Inc.: Reader's Digest
The Telex Corp.: Telex
The Source Telecomputing Corp.: Castlequest
Cineman
Chat
Genindex
MusicSource
Radio Source
Sourcelink (sm)
Sourcemail (sm)
Source*Plus (sm)
The Source (sm)
Trak
Uninet, Inc.: Uninet ®
U.S. News & World Report: US News & Washington Letter
U.S. Postal Service: E-COM ®
Vector Graphic: Vector
Ven-Tel: PC Modem Plus ®
Viewdata Corporation of America, Inc.: Viewtron
West Publishing Company: WESTLAW ®
Western Union Telegraph Co.: EasyLink (sm)
Mailgram ®
TWX
Woolf Software Systems: Move-It
World Book, Inc.: World Book ®
Xerox Corporation: Xerox ®
Zenith Radio Corporation: Zenith
Zilog, Inc.: Zilog ®
Z-80 ®

To Michele

CONTENTS

Acknowledgements

Special thanks go to the software publishers, product manufacturers, and service providers who made their products available. Particularly helpful were Stan Knight of Hayes, Bill Louden of CompuServe, JoAnne Kennedy of Dow Jones, Mary Bulterman of Viewdata, Judith Staby of American International Communications, Don Withrow of Janadon, and Steve Raymond of the *Seattle Sun.*

Osborne/McGraw-Hill's Dave Ushijima contributed his editing skill and patience, and Cindy Hudson prodded ever so gently to maintain the schedule. Seattle communications consultant Mike Rose and Chuck Wilde of Aton International, Santa Clara, California, both helped decipher the IBM mainframe world and its connection with the PC. Rod Shearer, Michael Crowson and Dave Emerson generously lent equipment at the right times.

DK

About the Author

David Kruglinski, author of *Data Base Management Systems,* has worked with data bases and communications on both mini- and microcomputers and on timeshare systems for the last seven years. Kruglinski is president of TENON Software Services, Inc., a Seattle-based dealer and distributor of software for business applications. He also contracts as a consultant. Kruglinski received his master's degree in Electrical Engineering in 1970.

ONE

AN OVERVIEW OF PC COMMUNICATIONS

For the moment, set aside thoughts of computers, modems, communication programs, and other technicalities. Instead, think about human communication. Before personal computers became available, you had many options in one-way, two-way, and multi-way communication. With one-way communication, you cannot converse with the producer of the information. Examples of one-way communication are

Books
Magazines and newspapers
Records and audio tapes
Videocassettes and videodisks
Broadcast and cable TV
Movies and theater
Radio
Junk mail
Billboards and signs

Two-way communication allows you to initiate a conversation and converse with a second party. Examples of two-way communication are

Mail

Telephone

Telex/telegram

Last, multi-way communication allows you to interact with other members of a group. Face-to-face meetings have been the traditional means, but here are some more recent developments:

Video conferencing

Citizens band radio (CB)

Amateur radio

Notice that most of these communications media are electronic. People have been captivated by "instantaneous" communication ever since Samuel Morse introduced the telegraph in 1844. Each new electronic medium has had profound effects on society. Television became available only after World War II, but a recent news item underscored its importance today: a group of small children were offered the hypothetical choice of living without television or living without their fathers. One third said they'd rather have television.

Philosophers as well as advertising executives have intently studied the media and drawn some interesting conclusions. Marshall McLuhan went so far as to say "the medium is the message." But while media experts are good at analyzing a medium once it becomes popular, they can't predict the success of a new one. That depends on the promoters' aggressiveness and on the consumers' acceptance. In recent times, only the Picturephone and quadraphonic sound have failed to gain acceptance; other new forms of electronic media have been wildly successful. Study what follows and draw your own conclusions.

A New Method of Communicating

It sneaked up on the world without a Samuel Morse or an Alexander Graham Bell. It's here in full force and poised for explosive growth, but the public's perception is molded by a few newspaper stories, an ad showing Senator Howard Baker at a terminal, and a movie about a teenager using a remote computer to play "global thermonuclear war."

What is it? What is this new medium? It doesn't even have a name. **Videotex** is the closest word there is, but there are a few other terms used to describe it, such as

- Computer networking
- Data communications
- Personal computer communications
- Electronic mail
- Electronic publishing
- On-line database
- Information utility
- Viewdata

There's just no single word for the whole thing because there are so many different aspects to it.

As you'll see in Chapter 5, **videotex** is generally used to describe home-oriented, local services, usually with color graphics, as provided by newspaper publishers. Some writers apply the same term to one-way systems that use cable TV (more commonly called **teletext** in the United States). Though some of the larger national information utilities such as The Source (described in Chapter 4) refer to themselves as "videotex services," the term *videotex* will not be used to refer to information utilities in this book.

The IBM PC's Role In Personal Computer Communication

Think about the telephone system for a minute. You know there's a big network with wires on poles, microwave towers, exchanges, and operators. You can use this network to speak to anyone in the world; you can order a pizza, check the time, or arrange a date. Your link with this network is your own telephone, which used to be plain, simple, and owned by the phone company. Now you can buy your own phone with Mickey Mouse ears or an automatic dialer or one that is wireless and operates by remote control.

In the world of computer communication, your IBM PC is equivalent to your telephone. The PC is the instrument that you use to access an international network of computers and a vast store of information. With your phone you dial a friend and talk; with your PC you dial a computer and exchange data.

People have been connecting to remote computers for years. Business initiated the trend, but hobbyists were there too. Now business use is expanding quickly and home use has just begun. Early computer communication systems involved **terminals** connected to mainframe computers or minicomputers. These terminals were at first printing machines with keyboards. (The most notable is the Teletype Model 33.) Quieter printing terminals were soon introduced, followed by **video terminals**, which vaguely resembled personal computers. The **dumb terminals** were nothing more than "glass teletypewriters." They printed text one line at a time on a TV-like screen. New lines appearing at the bottom of the screen caused the old text to scroll up, displacing the top line. Later **smart terminals** were introduced. These terminals accepted commands to clear the screen, to insert or delete text, to position text on the screen, and to protect areas of the screen from accidental modification. Neither smart nor dumb terminals did anything useful unless they were connected to a computer.

The invention of the personal computer made many video terminals obsolete. The personal computer could do everything a terminal could do and a lot more. Today a fully configured IBM PC costs about $3000, while a terminal costs between $250 and $1000, but that price gap is narrowing quickly. A stripped-down PCjr costs about $700, and low-priced PC "clones" are appearing. While an ordinary terminal works with many information utilities, the PC works better, and it runs word processor programs, electronic spreadsheets, and all the other software you see advertised in magazines.

Most business-oriented information services still assume you have a teletypewriter that simply prints lines of text one after the other. However, there is a movement to take advantage of the personal computer's intelligence, allowing the PC and a remote or **host** computer to perform as though they were one big system. You could maintain a stock portfolio, for instance, on your PC's disk and then use a special program to automatically dial Dow Jones to get the current price quotations for each stock.

The first large-scale commercial home videotex system requires subscribers to buy a special $900 terminal that attaches to a color TV set. This terminal can be duplicated by a properly equipped PC. As a PC owner, you can participate in the videotex revolution as well as connect your computer to the established information utilities.

Using Your PC For Information Retrieval

Jacques Vallee has said in his book *Network Revolution: Confession of a Computer Scientist* (Berkeley: And-Or Press, 1982) that the words and numbers that are loaded into a computer are data; if someone asks a question about that data, the answer is information. Other authors such as Alvin Toffler (*The Third Wave,* New York: William Morrow & Co., 1980) and John Naisbitt (*Megatrends: Ten New Directions Transforming Our Lives,* New York: Warner Books, 1982) tell us that we've become an information society with more white-collar knowledge workers than blue-collar manufacturing workers.

Most of the half million subscribers to remote computer services are there for one-way access to information. The technology has already been perfected and forms a billion-dollar industry. It's not off in the future; it's here today. Businesspeople have led the way, often paying $100 per hour to get the information they need. Since businesses exist to make money, you can bet that their access dollars are well spent.

In an information society, information is a valuable commodity. The more information you have, the better off you are. Consider the case of a real estate agent who subscribes to a centralized multiple-listing service. A computer terminal in the office allows the agent to display a list of all the homes in a given area with certain characteristics. The agent doesn't need to be a computer scientist to use the system; it is a simple matter to obtain, for example, listings of all three-bedroom homes with prices under $70,000. In addition, the agent can compile a list of all the homes that were sold in the last month to compare the selling prices to the asking prices, or a list of homes that have been withdrawn from the market.

The multiple-listing information service is an example of a private information utility that is bought and paid for by a local association of real estate agencies. Only members of the association have access to the information, but the system works just like any other host computer system. A user dials the computer's number and enters a password. A user with a PC at home could access the system as though he or she were in the office.

There is an almost unlimited amount of information available to business and professional people from computer-based information utilities. Often there is a choice between competing services. The following is a list of categories from a typical information utility. The actual information consists of billions of characters stored in over a thousand databases.

Advertising and marketing
Agriculture and nutrition
Bibliographies
Business and economics
Chemistry
Current affairs
Directories
Education
Energy and environment
Foundations and grants
Industry newsletters
Law and government
Materials sciences
Medicine and biosciences
Newspapers
Patents
Science and technology
Social sciences and humanities

You have the equivalent of the world's largest library available through your PC with a convenience factor unmatched in any library. Everyone knows what it's like to pore through the card catalog and then wander through the stacks looking for a book that has already been checked out. If you use the library, can you compete against someone using computerized information retrieval?

Many information services are geared to businesses willing to spend $50-$100 per hour during regular business hours, but there are services available for the non-business subscriber at a lower cost. A substantial subset of the high-priced services can be used in the evenings and on weekends for about $25 per hour, telecommunications charges included. Off-peak rates are less for the same reason that off-peak long-distance telephone rates are less: the service providers need to utilize expensive equipment 24 hours a day. Here are some examples of $25-per-hour services from the same companies offering high-priced business information in prime time:

$25-per-hour Service

Books in Print An index of 700,000 books from 12,000 publishers

International Software Database An index of 11,000 programs

Microcomputer Index An index of 40 microcomputer publications

Standard & Poor's News Features about 10,000 publicly held U.S. corporations

ERIC Education information

Engineering Literature Index Engineering information

GPO Publications Reference File Information available from the Government Printing Office

Magazine Index A list of 438 popular U.S. magazines

Medline Medical database

Newsearch 1000 articles per day from 5 major newspapers

Complete text of the *Wall Street Journal* and *Barron's*

There is another group of service providers offering more general business and consumer information. Costs are $12-$35 per hour during business hours and $6-$12 per hour at other times. Here are some examples:

$6 - $12-per-hour Service

Quotes on stocks, options, and bonds
Employment opportunities

Legislative reports and analyses
Airline schedules
Hotel, restaurant, and entertainment guides
Weather
Sports scores
Electronic magazines
Feature reports
Health information
Microcomputer newsletters
World Book Encyclopedia

The information utilities providing these services are described in full detail in Chapter 4.

If even $6 per hour puts you off, there are some absolutely free databases set up as electronic yellow pages. Fees are paid by advertisers, and, as you would expect, the information is commercial in nature. However, the system operators do give some information of general interest. In one system you can learn about industrial sites around the world, but you can also find out the cost of living in Afghanistan compared to New York. Another service allows employers to post job openings and job seekers to post resumes. The seekers can scan the openings and the employers can scan the resumes, all with controlled confidentiality. The employers bear most of the cost, but job seekers must pay a nominal connecting charge.

The videotex services offered by the newspaper publisher Knight-Ridder are shaking up the communications industry by providing access to information for $12 per month plus $1 per hour in telephone charges. The orientation is local, but services such as Dow Jones stock market quotes, the *American Academic Encyclopedia* (Danbury, Conn.: Grolier, 1980), late-breaking news, and the J.C. Penney catalog are available. This service now reaches only a few parts of the country, but it could spread quickly.

The dissemination of information by computers is not limited to big electronic publishers. You can start your own information utility, using your PC with a host communication program (see Chapter 6). While the big companies have hundreds of subscribers connected at the same time, you are restricted to one caller at a time. If your subscribers aren't local, they pay long-distance charges.

Using Your PC for Electronic Mail

Information retrieval is an example of one-way communication. The PC also works well with two-way and multi-way communications. **Electronic mail** is a common form of two-way communication, and business has been using it in a limited way for years. High technology companies like Microsoft successfully use electronic mail for in-house communications. Microsoft employees do not send written memos or make phone calls; they send messages electronically from terminal to terminal. Everyone from secretary to president has a terminal and is fully committed to using it. Suppliers and customers are also tied into the system.

Companies with offices nationwide can use the services of one of the big information utilities for a public or private electronic mail system. There are nearly a dozen firms competing for the business. This area is expanding rapidly with some companies providing printed mail delivery service to addressees without terminals. Delivery is via courier service (fast and expensive) or by U.S. mail (usually providing next-day service for a $2 charge). A link to and from telex machines is also provided.

How does electronic mail work? Think of the mailbox outside your house. When you hear the letter carrier deliver the mail, you check the box, collecting and reading any mail. Outgoing mail may be placed in the box for the carrier to pick up or it may be dropped in a mailbox. Now imagine an electronic mailbox in a central computer. You've signed up with an electronic mail company, and you've received an account number that defines your mailbox. If somebody, knowing your account number, sends you a message, the text of the message is deposited in your mailbox where it stays until you remove it. You're free to connect, or **log in**, to the central computer anytime to check your mail. If you have messages waiting, you can display them on the screen, print them on your printer, or save them on your PC's disk.

Sending mail is the same. You must know the addressee's account number, just as you must know the street address for regular mail. Many systems allow you to send the same message to a number of people. Billing is either by connect time at the usual information utility rates ($8 an hour and up) or by the message ($1 for 7500 characters).

Why use electronic mail? Remember the last phone call you made. Was the person there? Did you leave a message? Did the person return the call when you weren't available? You get the idea. Letters have their disadvantages too. First they are handwritten, typed, or word processed. Then they must be folded, stuffed in addressed envelopes, stamped, and mailed. They are delivered several days later, and finally they are opened and distributed to the recipients.

Electronic mail would work very well if everyone had a terminal. However, only 6 percent of office workers now have terminals, and far fewer homes are so equipped. Telecommunications companies recognize electronic mail as a huge market and are investing millions to promote the service. MCI has taken the initiative, but everyone is waiting for AT&T to make its move. Even the U.S. Postal Service has made an attempt, but politics may prevent its success.

As of the start of 1984, all of the various electronic mail services are not interconnected; you as a Source subscriber can't send a message to a CompuServe subscriber unless you also have a CompuServe password. It's only a matter of time before these systems are interconnected in the way, for example, ITT's and Western Union's telex services are linked. An international committee is already defining the standards to enable this to happen.

Using Your PC for Conferencing

Electronic mail is easy to understand; it's much like phone calls and letters, only it's more efficient. **Computer conferencing**, on the other hand, is something new. It allows a group of people anywhere in the world to exchange ideas. Maybe all the conference members are connected at the same time, but more often they are not. A computer conference can go on for hours, days, or even years with each person's cumulative contribution always available to the group.

One trend identified by John Naisbitt in *Megatrends* is **networking**. Naisbitt is speaking not in the computer sense, but in the human sense. Naisbitt defines networking as people talking to one another, sharing ideas, information, and resources. As hierarchies break down both inside and outside of business, new horizontal structures are taking their place. Quality circles are replacing the supervisor-worker relationships, and many professional workers report to more than one supervisor. More and more decisions are reached by consensus. Before computer conferencing, networking was supported by face-to-face meetings or perhaps by an occasional video conference. Computer conferencing fits in very well with the concept of networking and is starting to catch on.

Citizens band radio is an example of networking at a very local level. People used CBs to discuss immediate problems such as the whereabouts of the next speed trap. The fad has died down but not out, possibly because of the randomness of participation. It did show that many classes of people were willing to exchange ideas with a group of peers, given a convenient and low-cost medium.

The most widespread use of computer conferencing is found in local **computer bulletin boards** (CBBs). These are single microcomputers, often Apple IIs and IBM PCs, that are equipped with communications paraphernalia and special programs. They are operated by computer clubs, computer stores, or individuals. Other computer owners can call in to scan messages or leave their own messages.

Because so many personal computers are owned by hobbyists, many conferences are microcomputer-oriented. Messages like "How do I get PC Talk to work at 450 bps?" or "Does anyone have a FORTRAN compiler to trade for a C compiler?" are fairly common. There are also a few sexually explicit CBBs around, presumably broken down into preference categories. So far there haven't been many CBBs devoted to other subjects like social work and gardening. When the social workers and gardeners get PCs, this will change.

Computer conferencing didn't start on CBBs. It started on a large government computer network in the late 1960s. Murray Turoff, co-author of the classic book *Network Nation: Human Communication Via Computer* (Reading, Mass.: Addison-Wesley, 1978), applied the concept to the administration of the 1971 wage-price freeze. What emerged was a centralized information exchange that enabled the Office of Emergency Preparedness to answer questions from thousands of callers per day. The experimental OEP system evolved into a powerful computer conferencing system called EIES, which is still on-line today. EIES and other similar systems are more sophisticated and more structured than CBBs, and they run on large mainframe computers that allow many people to use the system simultaneously. These high-powered conferencing systems have developed a following among the computer intelligentsia who enjoy suspending time and space.

If you want to start your own computer conference, one option you have is to dedicate a PC to the task, either 24 hours a day or on some fixed schedule. This works well for local networks such as clubs or service organizations. A computer bulletin board can be as public or private as necessary. Alternatively, you can start a conference on EIES or another information utility. Here's an idea for you: if enough members of your family have PCs, you can set up a permanent family conference as an alternative to the photocopied Christmas newsletter.

Other Uses for PC Communication

Information retrieval, electronic mail, and computer conferencing are the mainline PC communication applications, but they are by no means the only ones. Edison thought his phonograph would be used for relaying telegraph messages. Maybe the ultimate use of PC communication hasn't been thought of yet, but there's no shortage of ideas in the meantime.

Transaction processing is a growing area for PC communications. You can use your PC not only to get stock quotes, but also to actually buy and sell stocks through a discount brokerage house. After your PC looks up the airline schedules and lists, for example, the schedule of all of the flights to Phoenix, you can make a reservation through a designated travel agent. If your bank is connected to an information service, you can make balance inquiries, transfer funds between accounts, and pay bills electronically. You can even buy merchandise such as televisions and calculators from electronic "stores," charging everything to your credit card.

This method of doing business is bound to catch on because it saves money. No highly paid operators are necessary to enter data into the computer; you do it yourself. A warehouse with a computer terminal is cheaper to operate than a department store in a shopping mall. Don't look for a cash-dispensing computer peripheral yet; you'll still have to leave home for the actual stuff.

Teaching is another profession that will be substantially affected by computers. Computer-aided instruction (CAI) has been around for years, but it has been unsuccessful because of its high cost and technical problems. The PC is changing that. Several education services based on the PC have appeared. Lessons are **downloaded** (transferred) over the phone from a remote computer into the student's own machine. The student can then work on his or her own machine, contacting instructors through the network when assistance is needed. The PC's graphics are used for digitized pictures and special effects. The computer relieves students of the fear of embarrassment, but the key to the system's success is the availability of a human instructor to answer questions and monitor progress. One side effect is that youngsters adapt to the keyboard and display as a normal means of communication.

Entertainment is also available over the wires. The information utilities allow you to run game programs, but using games that run on the PC directly may be cheaper. Some of the remote games let you play against unseen human opponents nationwide. You'll never know, though, if your opponent is really human or simply someone's programmed PC. One new enterprise permits the downloading of games into a special cartridge for a fee comparable to the cost of a regular game cartridge.

Finally, the PC can earn its keep by doubling as a terminal to a local mainframe or minicomputer. Programs transform the PC into any number of popular terminals such as the DEC VT-100 or the IBM 3270 series. PCs can also talk directly to other PCs, to Apples, and to other machines either locally or over phone lines in order to exchange data and programs.

Some Classification and Terminology

PC communication neatly falls into two categories: **asynchronous** and **synchronous**. These are technical-sounding terms, but you need to learn them. The categories have nothing to do with the content of the communication, but rather with the medium. It's like AM and FM radio.

One type of PC communication that will not be covered in this book is **local networking**. Local networking ties multiple PCs together for the sharing of disks and printers. It's a separate technology that works only over limited distances. Hardware and software are being developed rapidly, and there are few standards.

If you are accessing information networks over phone lines or if you are connecting your PC to another microcomputer or to a minicomputer, you are using **asynchronous communication**.This means that the computers are transmitting one character at a time; but, more important, it means you must equip your PC with an asynchronous serial port (communications adapter) and an asynchronous modem, a device that connects your PC to the phone line. Fortunately, these are the most common and least expensive computer devices. Chapter 3 will survey the equipment you need, and Chapters 8 and 9 will go into the details of asynchronous communication.

Synchronous communication allows you to connect your PC to most IBM mainframes. Characters are transmitted in bursts using complex procedures. Often one communications line is connected to several computers or terminals, and the bursts, or messages, are coded according to their sources and destinations. You need a synchronous serial port and a special modem if phone lines are used. Often the connections are direct, using a special coaxial cable. Synchronous communication is used mainly in businesses where PCs are used to extend the power of a large mainframe computer. Chapter 10 covers the details of synchronous communication.

TWO

DATA COMMUNICATIONS HISTORY

As you leaf through this chapter, you'll see some drawings of old-fashioned telegraph apparatus. You may wonder what they have to do with PC communication. When you connect your PC to another computer, you're using 140-year-old technology. The electrical signals coming out of the PC are **digital** (on or off), just like the original telegraph signals. Technical terms like **mark, space,** and **duplex** are all over a hundred years old. Remember that both the telegraph and the PC allow the sending and receiving of messages in written form.

This chapter traces the history of the telegraph and telephone, which will help you understand data communication theory because the early devices were electro-mechanical. You can look at the drawings and visualize what was happening, an easier task than understanding the invisible processes inside a computer. Don't worry, you won't have to sit through the story of the computer's invention, nor will you be forced to endure another explanation of bits and bytes.

History will not only teach you the theory, but it will also help you predict the future of PC communications. The telegraph, the telephone, radio, and television were at one time new communications media. Study the social acceptance patterns of those media and draw your own conclusions about how people will respond to the new communications media.

The First Practical Electrical Telegraph

People have always wanted instant communication. In the late 1700s, **semaphore** systems were developed in France to relay military information. Windmill-like gadgets on high buildings served as visual signals to the station in the next town. All stations had to be manned by skilled operators during daylight hours, an expensive proposition. Information was valuable even then, and the system was credited with winning several battles.

The early 1800s saw an explosion of electrical knowledge. Great minds were making new discoveries every day, but because of poor communications, few people knew about the discoveries. Static electricity was known for a long time, and at least one person tried to use it for sending messages. Volta's invention of the battery in 1800 presented more possibilities. At last it was possible to have electricity in a useful, low-voltage form controlled by an on/off switch. Unfortunately, electromagnetism had not been discovered, and this limited what people could do with electricity.

A German, S.T. von Soemmering, noticed that when electricity was passed through an acid solution, bubbles appeared because of the decomposition of water into hydrogen and oxygen. You probably remember the principle from high school chemistry. Soemmering used this electrolytic effect in his 1809 telegraph system (Figure 2-1). The **sender** was 26 electrical contacts connected to a 26-wire cable corresponding to the 26 letters of the alphabet. Two wires from the battery could be manually connected to any two of the contacts. The **receiver** was an aquarium tank with 26 upright wires in the bottom, each connected to the corresponding conductor from the cable. If the battery wires touched the "T" and the "H" sender contacts, bubbles would rise from the "T" and "H" wires at the receiver. If the negative battery wire touched the "T", two parts of hydrogen would rise from the "T" wire and one part of oxygen would rise from the "H" wire. The convention was that the first of two letters got the negative wire, resulting in double bubbles.

Another amazing feature of Soemmering's telegraph was the "alarum," a device that saved the receiving operator from having to stare at the aquarium all day. Two additional contacts and conductors led to two special alarum wires in the receiver tank. As shown in Figure 2-1, the bubbles from the alarum wires (a) would collect in the inverted spoon (b), eventually causing the spoon to float upward. The rising spoon, connected through lever (c), caused the arm (d) to slope downward, allowing the weight (e) to slide off the rod and drop. The

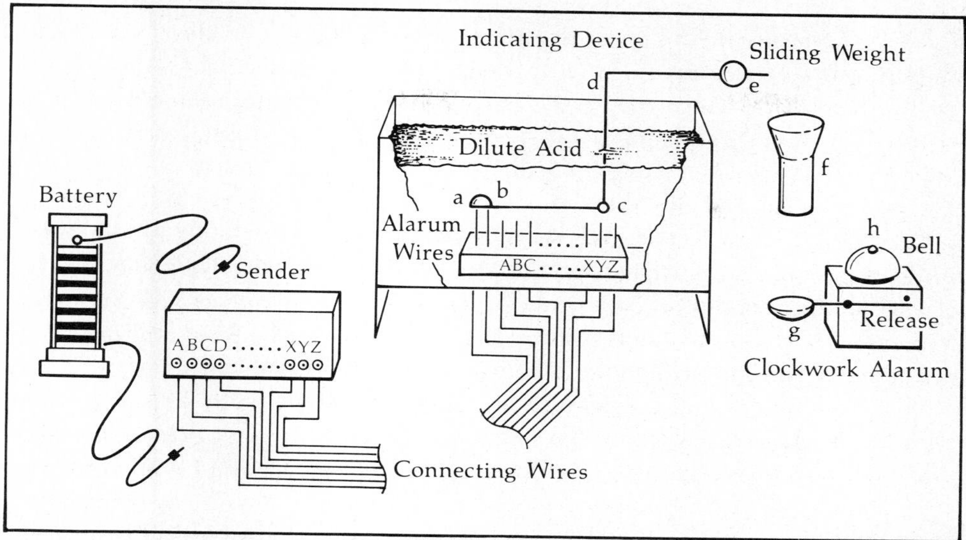

Figure 2-1. Soemmering telegraph system with "alarum"

falling weight passed through a funnel (f) onto a release lever (g), which activated the clockwork bell (h). Do you suppose Rube Goldberg got any ideas from this?

Soemmering thus invented the first **parallel** data communications scheme and also the first **relay**. One positive voltage and one negative voltage on two of 26 parallel conductors defined two characters in sequence. As for the relay, a tiny amount of signaling energy was able to release a large amount of stored energy to ring the bell.

The Soemmering telegraph was demonstrated over two miles of wire, but it never became practical because so many conductors were required. The device did receive a lot of attention, and other inventors were inspired to make improvements.

Cooke and Wheatstone

We are taught that Samuel Morse invented the telegraph and that the first message, the famous "What hath God wrought?", was sent between Washington and Baltimore in 1844. Although Morse did some pioneering work on the telegraph, two Englishmen, W.F. Cooke and Charles Wheatstone, had a working 13-mile telegraph set up on the British railways in 1839. The telegraph was used to order taxis, keep trains from colliding, and to catch pickpockets who tried to escape by train.

Andre Ampere's invention of the **galvanometer** took the bubbles out of data communication, replacing them with the movement of a needle. Just as a compass needle is deflected by the earth's magnetic field, the galvanometer needle is deflected by the magnetism created by a current flowing in an adjacent coil of wire. Ampere suggested using a needle for telegraphy in 1820, and Cooke and Wheatstone developed the idea.

Figure 2-2 shows Cooke and Wheatstone's receiving instrument, the **five-needle telegraph**. Each needle could point to the left or right depending on the polarity of the current flowing through its associated coil. Two deflected needles would define one of 20 often-used letters as specified by five hand-operated keys at the other end of the line. This was another **parallel** scheme; it required five data conductors plus a return wire to complete the circuit. This telegraph was much more efficient than Soemmering's 26-wire system. Each conductor could have a positive current (+), a negative current (−), or no current (0).

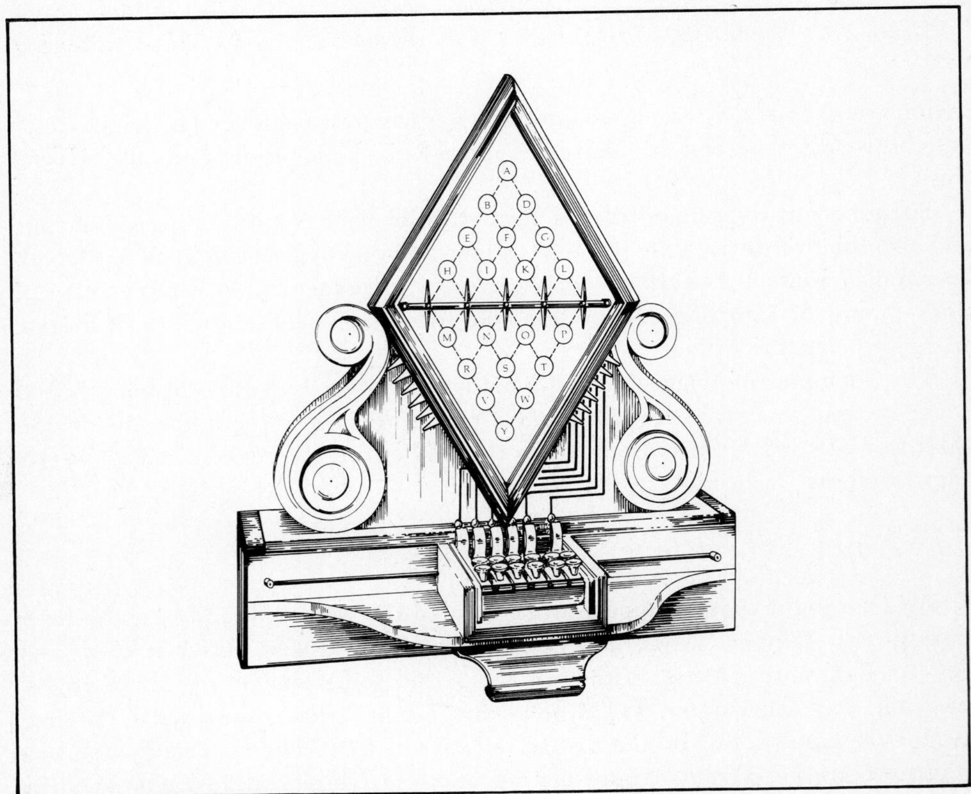

Figure 2-2. Cooke and Wheatstone's five-needle telegraph

Assuming that a positive current swings a needle to the right, the code for the letter "T" is 00−0+; "H" is +−000. Because each conductor can have three current values, this is a trinary scheme, as opposed to a binary scheme, which permits only two values.

Operators used the two-of-five code for letters, but they used a series of movements of a single needle for numbers. This idea, together with the high cost of six-conductor cable, soon reduced the five-needle telegraph to two needles and then to one. The single-needle telegraph shown in Figure 2-3 used sequences of left and right needle deflections to define letters and numbers. This **serial** data transmission method defines a "T", for instance, as one counter-clockwise deflection followed by three clockwise deflections. The sender was a switch that applied positive, negative, or no current to the two-wire line. The unique code was devised by Cooke and Wheatstone, but the Morse code was later retrofitted to the English system.

Five-needle telegraph technology remains today in the parallel interface between the PC and most printers. A character is specified by a combination of voltage states on eight wires. Voltage levels are +5 volts and 0 volts—a binary system.

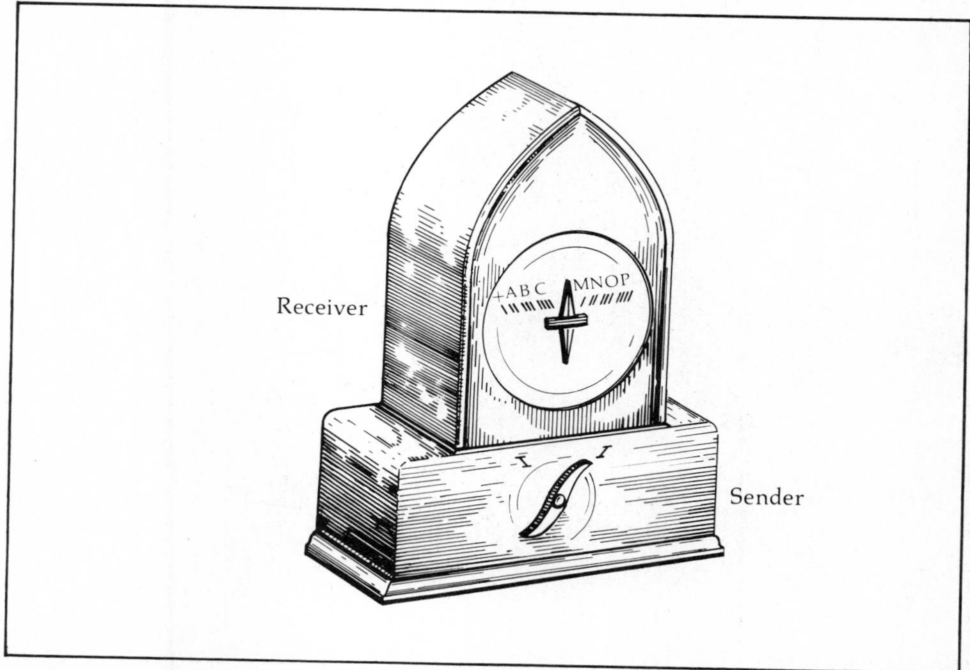

Figure 2-3. Single-needle telegraph

Early Telegraph Systems In the United States

Samuel F.B. Morse started thinking about electrical communication in 1832. By 1835 he had built a machine more like a word processor than the simple key-and-sounder systems that were so successful later. Messages were assembled from a kind of type, pieces of metal with teeth corresponding to letters of the alphabet. As a row of this type moved past a projection, the teeth would cause a mercury contact to interrupt an electrical current, sending a coded signal corresponding to the letters. The receiver consisted of a pencil

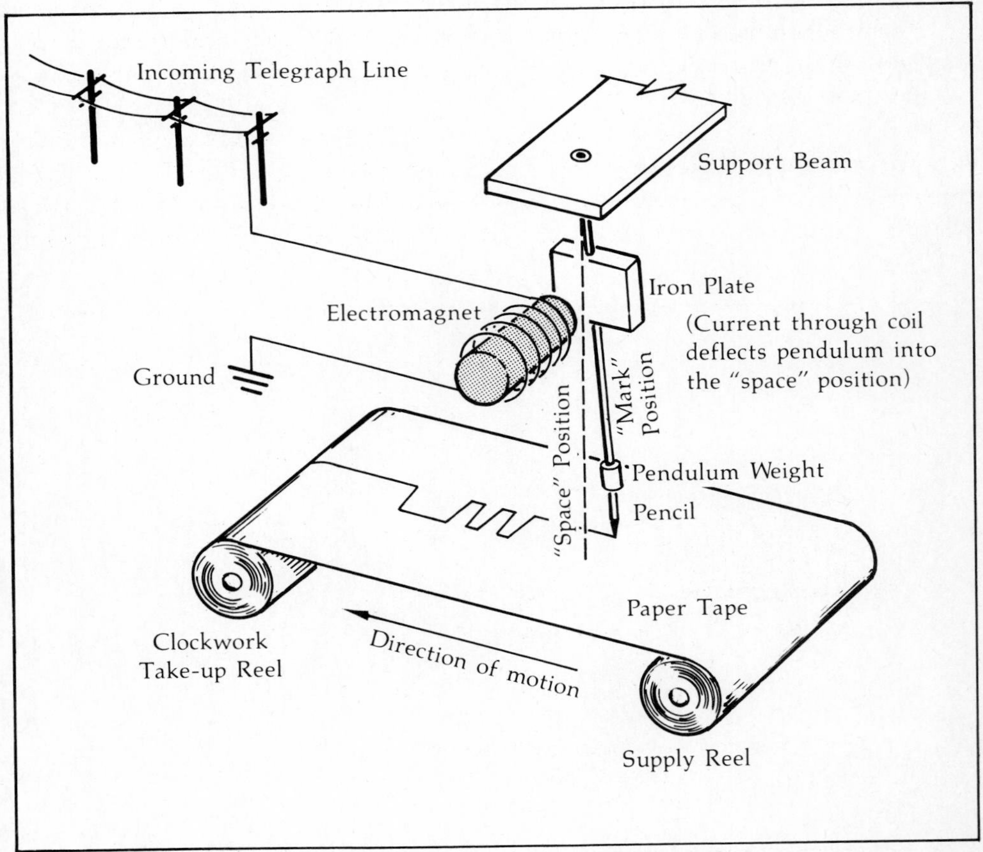

Figure 2-4. Morse's original telegraph receiver

attached to a pendulum activated by an electromagnet, as shown in Figure 2-4. Incoming signals moved the pencil, writing wavy lines on a slowly moving paper tape.

The machine was slow and unreliable, but Morse's real problem was that he didn't know the basic laws of electricity. He could not transmit more than a few feet because he didn't understand voltage and resistance. Over the next few years, Morse raised the voltage, replaced the toothed type with a switch called a **key**, and replaced the swinging pencil with a pen that went up and down with the current and drew short and long lines—dots and dashes.

Morse received some government money to build a line between Washington, D.C. and Baltimore and started service in 1844. During the first few weeks of operation, there were almost no paying customers, but then word spread and people with imagination took over. When the line was extended to New Jersey, lottery players sent numbers from Philadelphia to the west bank of the Hudson by telegraph and then by carrier pigeon into New York. Stock traders had a field day before the rest of the world caught on to this new, instantaneous communications method.

The printed dots and dashes quickly yielded to the **sounder** because operators found they could interpret the clicking sounds more efficiently than they could read paper tape. Figure 2-5 shows a typical Morse telegraph system. The sounder is just an electromagnet on a sounding box; when the current flowed,

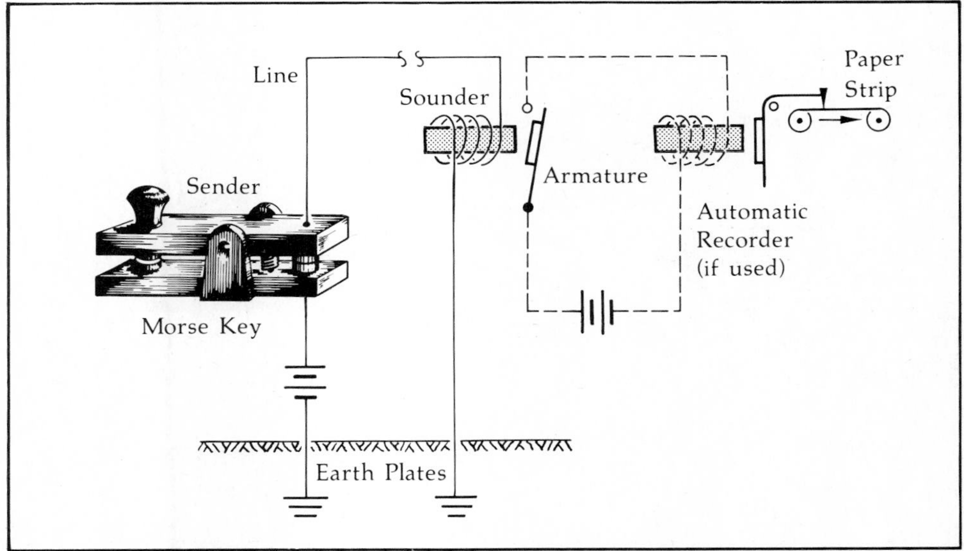

Figure 2-5. Typical Morse telegraph system

the metal bar, or armature, pulled in. The **Morse code**, shown in Figure 2-6, was actually devised by Morse's associate Alfred Vail, and it is still in use worldwide with some minor variations.

There was explosive growth in the U. S. telegraph industry starting in 1844. By 1852 the whole country east of the Mississippi was wired by competing small companies using over 18,000 miles of wire. The telegraph was used in commerce—farmers determining grain prices, merchants doing credit checks, riverboat captains finding out when the ice jams were coming down the river, railroads controlling trains. On the personal side, a Boston man married a New York woman via telegraph. The telegraph imparted a feeling of nationhood to the new America.

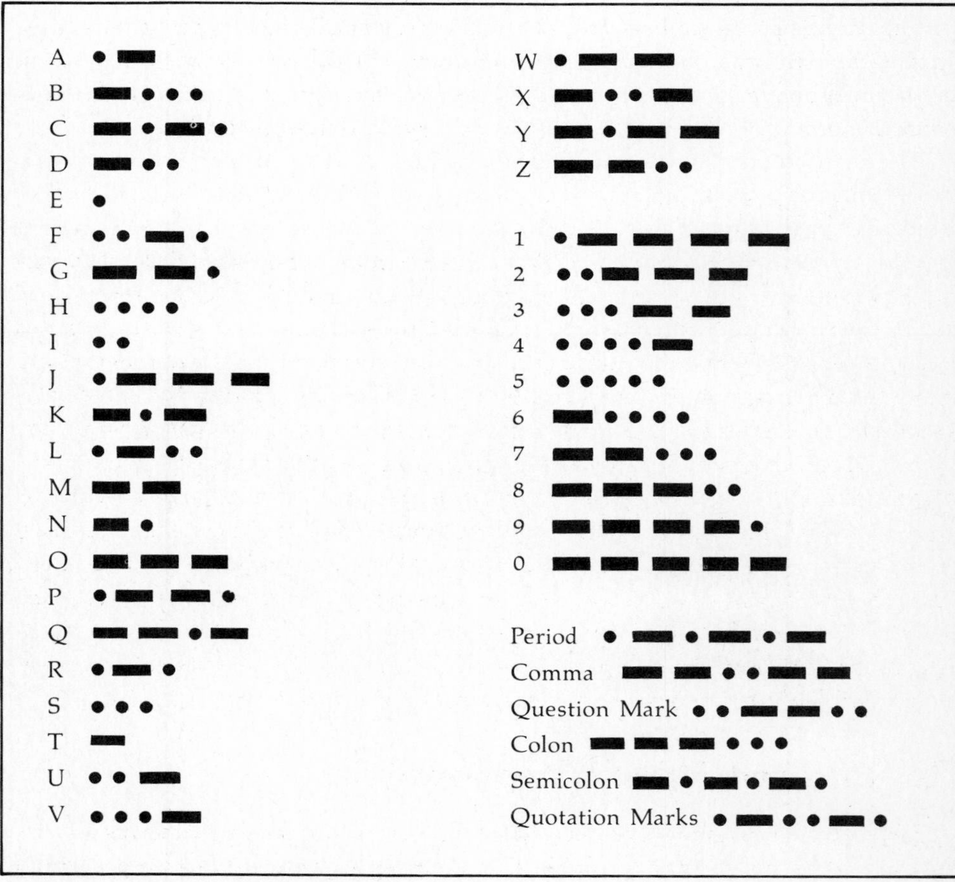

Figure 2-6. The Morse code

Western Union was formed in 1856 from its predecessor, the New York and Mississippi Valley Printing Telegraph Co. In 1861 Western Union strung a telegraph line across the West to California and made a fortune. It built the line in three months for less than $500,000 and then sold $6 million in stock. The going message rate was about $1 per word and the company received government subsidies. This aid put Western Union in a strong position with respect to its chief competitor, the American Telegraph Company (no relation to AT&T), which controlled the transatlantic cable. In 1866 Western Union bought control of American for $40 million.

Western Union held the licenses to the Morse technology, but there were other competing systems. Royal E. House's unreliable printing telegraph and Alexander Bain's chemical telegraph were useful in keeping the rates down, but the Morse system prevailed because of its ease and simplicity of operation, the nominal cost for keys and sounders, and its ready adaptation to primitive conditions. D.E. Hughes invented a better printing telegraph, similar to a modern daisy-wheel printer, but in 1855 the Morse interests bought it for $100,000 and buried it. However, the Hughes system was widely used in Europe.

The Associated Press

The Associated Press was the first **network** using the medium of electrical communication. It was started in the 1840s by a group of New York newspapers because they felt it was wasteful for four different reporters covering a news event to send four identical telegrams to their respective offices. When there was only one telegraph line between New York and Washington, D.C., the telegraph company charged premium rates because it knew that the *Tribune,* the *Sun,* the *Herald,* and the *Express* were all going to print the news. After the competing Bain and House lines did away with the Morse monopoly, a deal was struck between the Associated Press and several telegraph companies to relay messages over the network at special rates. There was considerable argument over what those rates would be, and because telegraph companies charged by the word, clever coding schemes were devised, using a word like "Caserovingedsable" to represent a whole paragraph. This early **data compression** scheme worked well except when an operator missed a letter.

The Relay and Digital Communication

Early Morse systems were very simple; the dots and dashes, or **marks**, were represented by no current on the line, and the **space** between was represented by current. The graphic representation of the letter "B", as it would have been

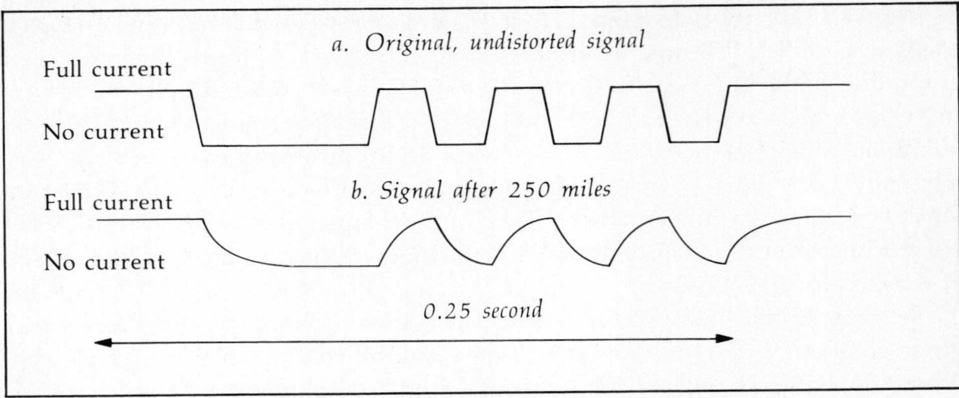

Figure 2-7. Graphic representation of "B" in Morse code

traced by Morse's original receiver, is shown in Figure 2-7. When this digital binary signal travels through, say, 250 miles of wire, it emerges in distorted form, as also shown in Figure 2-7. Because of the electrical characteristics of the line, the signal is still readable after 250 miles, but not after 500 miles. The **relay** shown in Figure 2-8 regenerates in pure digital form the signal to be sent to the destination or the next relay. The relay is merely an electromagnet activating mercury contacts in a new circuit. Through relays, as developed by Morse, telegraph signals could be sent across the country in undistorted form.

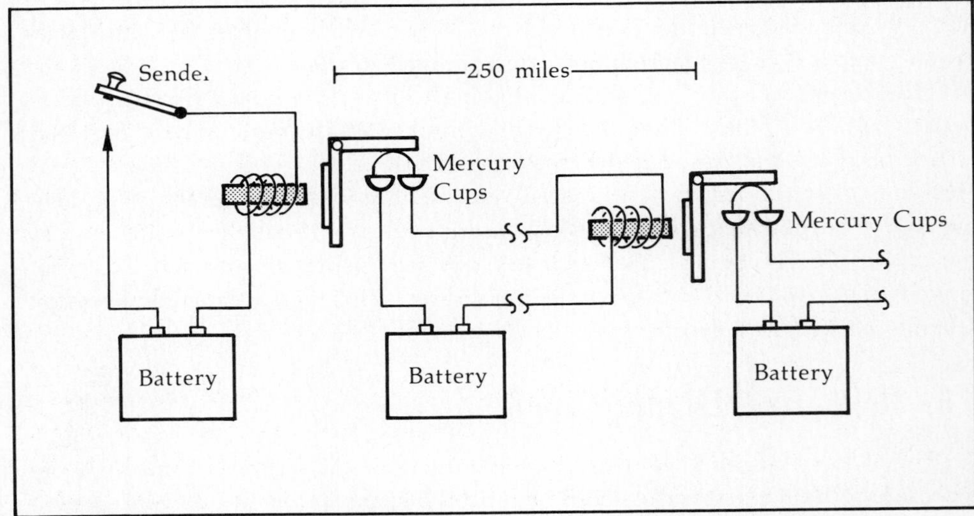

Figure 2-8. Telegraph Relay System

Modern digital data communications also depends on relays, but the relays are electronic and operate at high speed.

It was soon discovered that sounders worked more efficiently when current both pushed and pulled the armature, eliminating the need for a spring. Thus **double current** telegraphy used a forward current for a mark and a reverse current for a space. The PC uses the same technique for serial communication, using a negative voltage for a mark and a positive voltage for a space.

The first telegraph lines were either **simplex**, meaning they could transmit messages in one direction only, or **half-duplex**, meaning they could be manually reversed to allow messages to be sent in one direction at a time.The 1850s saw the development of several **full-duplex** techniques that allowed the simultaneous transmission of messages in both directions.

The first telegraphs used a return wire to complete the circuit, requiring at least two conductors for any line. It was soon discovered that the earth made an adequate return path, and subsequent circuits were single wire.

Other Technical Developments

Telegraph development in the late 1800s followed its own course in England and France. Wheatstone developed a **perforator** for Morse code that produced paper tape, as shown in Figure 2-9. The perforator allowed operators to prepare messages off-line. A high-speed reader would translate the tape into Morse code, and a pen would print the dots and dashes on paper tape at the receiving end. This tape format, devised in 1855, was used into the 1920s and is similar to the format used in telex machines today. Even early microcomputer operating systems provided for a paper tape reader (RDR:) and punch (PUN:).

Another of Wheatstone's developments was the **A.B.C. Telegraph**, which looked like a telephone dial except it had 26 letters instead of 10 numbers. When the sending operator dialed a letter, a sequence of electrical pulses was sent down the line, 1 pulse for "A", 2 for "B", 3 for "C", and so on. A similar dial at the receiving end would rotate to the same position as the sending dial, indicating the proper letter. The A.B.C. instrument dated from 1839, and a printing option was added in 1841. The competing needle telegraph, used by skilled operators, was still faster than the A.B.C. system.

The early telegraph lines could transmit code faster than any human could key it. Paper tape was one way to maximize the use of an expensive resource, but the delays in processing the tape at both ends diminished the instantaneous effect of the medium. Another approach was to let a group of operators **time-share** the same line. In 1874 Emile Baudot invented a **multiplex** telegraph in

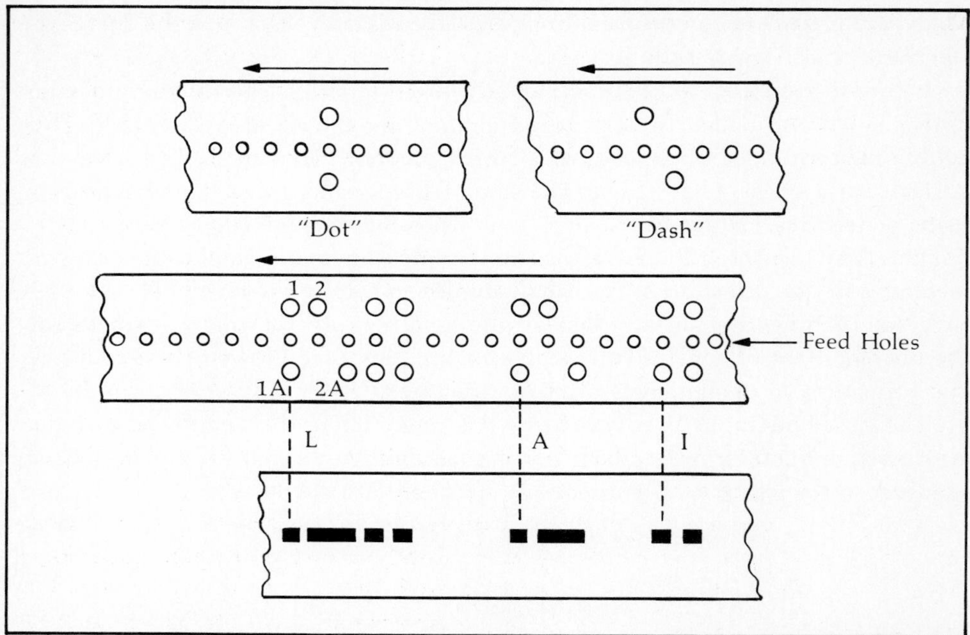

Figure 2-9. Perforated tape showing Morse code

Figure 2-10. Baudot's multiplex telegraph

France that allowed six operators to send messages over the same line. Each operator had a five-key device called a **manipulator**, shown in Figure 2-10. The six manipulators were attached to a **distributor** similar to the one in a car. An identical distributor on the receiving end, synchronized to the sending distributor, fed the received codes to six different printers. Each of the six operators had to key a character at exactly the right time, determined by the click of a cadence relay on the manipulator. Baudot's five-level code was used throughout France in the 1880s and in England in the 1890s.

Englishman Donald Murray used Baudot's system for single-channel telegraphy in 1901 but changed the code to suit his own mechanism. Thus what is commonly known as Baudot code is really Murray code. Internationally, it's known as CCITT Alphabet #2.Western Union adopted it for use in 1896. Notice from Figure 2-11 that there are only 32 values of the code and that a shift character is necessary to switch between numbers and symbols. This code is still in use on the telex network and in the deaf community.

The Morse system was not dead, however. F.G. Creed picked up on Wheatstone's Morse tape system and invented a receiver that perforated paper tape. Another machine converted the Morse tape to print because no printer was fast enough to work directly from the wire. These systems were still in use in 1920, but the Baudot systems had almost entirely replaced the Morse systems by 1944, the centenary year of the telegraph.

The Teletype and Asynchronous Communications

Wheatstone's A.B.C. Telegraph was an **asynchronous** device. One character was transmitted, and then both sending and receiving mechanisms reset themselves for the next character. The interval between characters did not matter. Data transmission was slow because as many as 26 data pulses plus a long reset pulse were needed for a single letter.

In contrast, the Baudot and Murray systems used continuously rotating distributors. These distributors had to be kept perfectly **synchronized**, a task requiring great attention by the operators. Characters were transmitted at a steady rate and were usually supplied from paper tape. This type of **synchronous** data communication is used on high-speed digital data lines today. Your PC uses it when communicating directly to IBM mainframes.

An asynchronous system permitting reliable, unattended operation was developed during World War I by E.E. Kleinschmidt and others. That system resulted in the teletypewriter machine in use today. The machines had rotating distributors, but a clutch started and stopped the rotation for each character. A

• Denotes positive current **Code Signals**							Lowercase	Uppercase	
								CCITT standard international telegraph alphabet No. 2 used for telex	**North American teletype commercial keyboard**
Start	1	2	3	4	5	Stop			
	•	•				•	A	—	—
	•			•	•	•	B	?	?
		•	•	•		•	C	:	:
	•			•		•	D	Who are you?	$
	•					•	E	3	3
	•		•	•		•	F	Note 1	!
		•		•	•	•	G	Note 1	&
			•		•	•	H	Note 1	#
		•	•			•	I	8	8
	•	•		•		•	J	Bell	Bell
	•	•	•	•		•	K	(	(
		•			•	•	L	)	)
			•	•	•	•	M	.	.
			•	•		•	N	,	,
				•	•	•	O	9	9
		•	•		•	•	P	0	0
	•	•	•		•	•	Q	1	1
		•		•		•	R	4	4
	•		•			•	S	'	'
					•	•	T	5	5
	•	•	•			•	U	7	7
		•	•	•	•	•	V	=	;
	•	•			•	•	W	2	2
	•		•	•	•	•	X	/	/
	•		•		•	•	Y	6	6
	•				•	•	Z	+	"
						•	Blank		
	•	•	•	•	•	•	Letters shift		
	•	•		•	•	•	Figures shift		
			•			•	Space		
				•		•	Carriage return		
		•				•	Line feed		

Note 1: Not allocated internationally; available to each country for internal use.

Figure 2-11. The Baudot or Murray code

start bit immediately preceded each character and a **stop bit** followed it. Figure 2-12 shows the sending mechanism. Depressing a key such as "Y" allowed a combination of bars called bails to make contact. This combination corresponded to the Baudot code and was serialized by the distributor, which added start and stop bits. On the receiving end another distributor activated a combination of five electromagnets, causing the "Y" to be printed. This is the same scheme used in modern PC asynchronous communications, but now an eight-level code

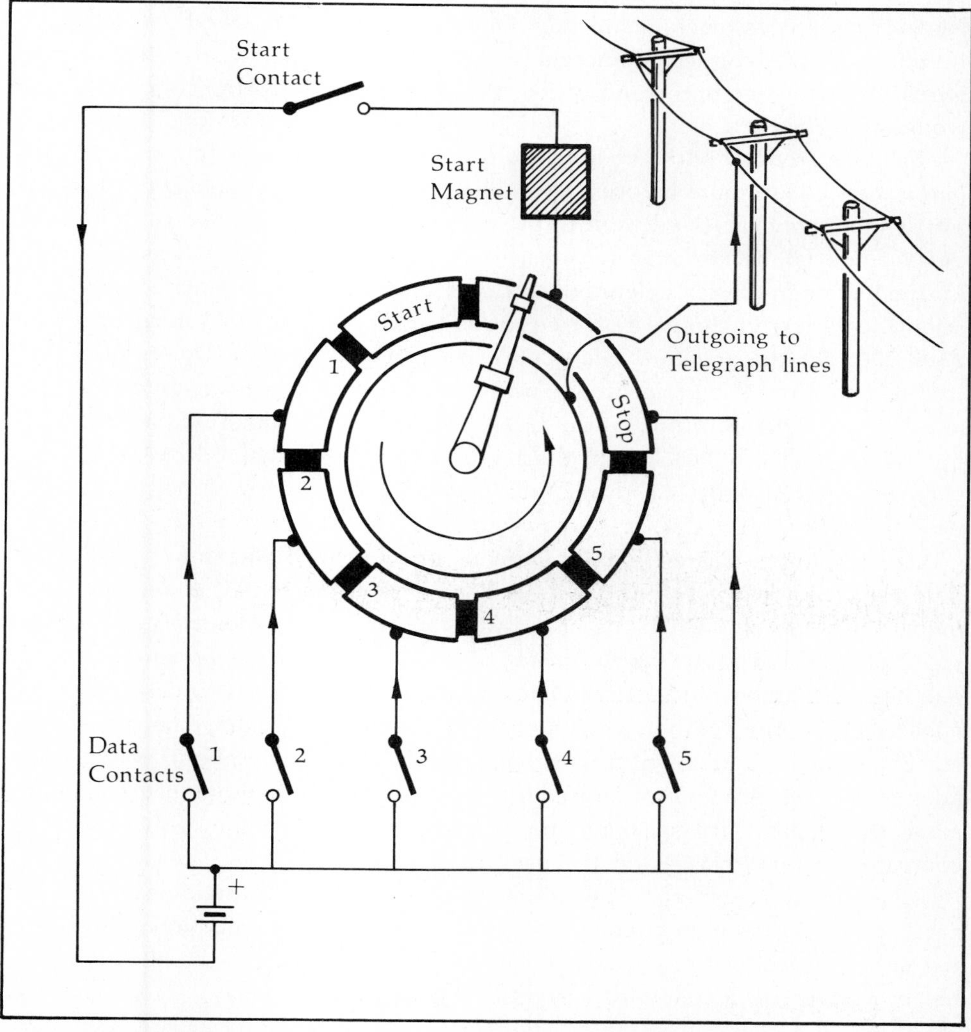

Figure 2-12. Teletype sending mechanism

is used instead of the five-level code, and the distributor has been replaced by a silicon chip.

The Telephone

Telegraph communication took on a secondary role with Alexander Graham Bell's invention of 1877. The telephone displaced the telegraph in the public eye because with it anyone could have a phone at home. There were no codes to learn or expensive machines to buy. One simply gave the operator the desired number and was connected. Acceptance of the telephone resulted in a web of wires linking every home and office. Without those wires PC communication would be difficult.

Bell was credited with the invention of the telephone, but he arrived at the patent office just hours before a rival, Elisha Gray, filed his application. Bell had a true monopoly for 17 years until the patent ran out, but he had to fight hard. Bell's financial backer and father-in-law, Gardiner Hubbard, was originally interested in multiplex telegraph systems and dismissed the telephone as a scientific curiosity. Hubbard offered to sell the whole deal to Western Union for $100,000, but the arrogant telegraph giant refused. Western Union later realized its error and tried to compete, using telephone apparatus invented by Gray and Thomas Edison. Actually, the Gray and Edison telephone was an improvement over Bell's, but Bell held the key patents and withstood over 100 legal challenges. Eventually, Western Union yielded, turning over all its phone business to Bell.

Bell and his associate, Thomas Watson, promoted the telephone by staging a demonstration with musicians playing at a remote site. The audience was impressed, but complained the effect was "supernatural." However, businesses soon saw the telephone's value, using point-to-point lines between companies and between homes and offices. The **exchange** was invented, which connected subscribers to one another with the help of an operator. Phone companies were started in cities and towns throughout the East, and the phone was quickly adopted by America and integrated into its social life. Telephone users did have some initial difficulty speaking into the microphone, so the early telephone companies offered classes on the use of the new devices.

Like the telegraph, early telephone lines consisted of a single wire with the earth acting as a return circuit. This worked until the introduction of the electric light and trolleys. Eventually there was so much static on the lines that Bell had to convert to a two-wire system that is still in use today.

At the end of the century Boston business interests took over the company from Bell and Watson, making it strong enough to compete after the patents ran out. When the patents did expire, it was war, with at least two phone companies in each city, one Bell and the other independent. There was, of course, no government control. AT&T (that name appeared in 1885) steadfastly refused to allow the independents to interconnect with the Bell long-distance lines, thus putting the independents at a great disadvantage. The independents, usually catering to a different class of people than the Bell subscribers, survived by offering cheaper rates. All of this meant that each business needed several phones, one from each phone company.

AT&T resisted the independents for quite a while under the direction of Theodore Vail, the builder of the modern Bell System. Vail was a nice guy with the public interest at heart, but the purse strings were controlled by J.P. Morgan, who wanted maximum profits. AT&T even took over a controlling interest in Western Union, but after Morgan's death in 1913, Vail yielded to public and government pressure, getting rid of Western Union and allowing the independents to interconnect (an agreement known as the Kingsbury Commitment). It wasn't until 1945, though, that the last "two-phone" city, Philadelphia, went completely over to Bell.

Early long distance was crude because there were no electronics for amplifying the signal; telegraph-style relays could not be used. A line was set up between New York and Chicago using expensive heavy-gauge copper wire and a new invention called the loading coil. Coast-to-coast service only began in 1915 with Lee De Forest's invention of the Audion vacuum tube. And even though telegraph messages were sent under the Atlantic in 1858, transatlantic phone service was delayed until 1956, when Bell Labs developed torpedo-shaped underwater amplifiers called **repeaters**.

AT&T entered the radio business with New York radio station WEAF in 1923. No one yet knew what to expect from radio. One AT&T executive speculated that people would call up radio stations to give "radio talks." Early programming consisted of AT&T employees singing and playing musical instruments. Time was rented haphazardly to anyone for $200 per hour.The first taker was a real estate company that bought 15 minutes of time to announce a development, thereby creating the first commercial.Things quickly became more organized, with radio taking the country by storm. AT&T formed a radio network, at first refusing to let non-Bell stations hook up to its lines. In 1926 AT&T sold its radio interest to RCA, but retained its lucrative business of renting lines to radio networks. It wasn't until the 1970s that the talk-show format once again allowed listeners to phone up radio stations for "radio talks."

The Telegraph System At Mid-Century—Message Switching

In 1944 Western Union had almost 19,000 offices and 14,000 agencies in the U.S. Only 50 percent of all homes were served by telephone, so the telegraph was still an important means of communication.When a customer sent a telegram, the following events took place:

1. The customer presented a written message to a branch office.
2. The branch office keyed in the message, transmitting it directly to its main office.
3. The main office printer printed it.
4. A conveyor belt delivered the printed message to a trunkline operator.
5. The trunk operator keyed the message to a distant main office.
6. The distant main office printed the message.
7. A conveyor belt delivered the printed message to a local operator.
8. The operator keyed the message to a destination local office.
9. The destination local office printed the message.
10. A messenger delivered the message to the addressee.

In some cases pneumatic tubes as long as three miles replaced the local loops, but the process was unwieldy, to say the least. A reperforator system was later devised whereby incoming messages were punched and printed on the same tape. An operator had to read the address on the message and set up the switchboard for the destination office. The tape was then read into the next link. A variation used by the Postal Telegraph Company had the incoming tapes manually distributed to readers permanently attached to outgoing lines.

Printing on paper tape was done instead of printing on paper because carriage return and line feed characters weren't necessary and mistakes could be easily cut out. Operators stuck the gummed tape onto message blanks.

An automatic telephone switchboard was not practical for telegram traffic because the messages were very short; setting up an entire circuit from one local office to another wasn't worthwhile. Large dispersed companies with their own private systems had **message centers** where messages were automatically switched. There were still banks of reperforators, however, since no better way to store data was available in the 1940s.

Teletypewriter Exchange Service

Western Union and the Teletype Corporation both provided leased lines for point-to-point teletypewriter service. In 1931 AT&T bought Teletype and proceeded to set up a national teletypewriter exchange called TWX. The machines used five-level Baudot code at a speed of 60 words per minute (or 45.5 bits per second) with the digital signal converted to audio tones for use on the telephone circuits. As many as 16 teletypewriter circuits could be accommodated on a single telephone circuit with the use of 16 different tones. Telephone operators handled the switching as they did for phone calls.

After World War II, a new service using eight-level code was started, running at 100 words per minute (or 110 bits per second [bps]). A separate automatic switching system enabled nationwide dialing of similar teletypewriters. This transmission method was very close to that used in today's asynchronous PC communication.

After World War II, Western Union set up its own service called Telex. It was compatible with telex services worldwide, allowing subscribers to reserve hotel rooms in Monrovia or order merchandise from Hong Kong. Five-level Baudot code was sent at 66 words per minute (50 bps). AT&T eventually sold the TWX business to Western Union and the 45.5 bps system was phased out, though the equipment is still in use in the deaf community. Today Western Union operates two side-by-side systems called Telex I (the old telex) and Telex II (the old TWX). Intersystem communication is via computer, and ITT and RCA offer competing services. There are 1.5 million subscribers in the worldwide network, all reachable from your PC.

Telex users generally have a Teletype Model 33, as shown in Figure 2-13. This is an electro-mechanical machine that is left in auto-answer mode and prints any message that comes in. Outgoing messages are prepared on paper tape and then transmitted after the destination number is dialed. There are both eight-level and five-level versions of the Model 33.

Nationwide Communications Networks

As soon as long-distance telegraph and telephone lines were established, engineers attempted to use them more efficiently. Telegraph people first concentrated on Baudot-style **time-division multiplex** schemes in which five-level characters from different messages were interleaved, as shown in Figure 2-14. This system worked with and without paper tape, and the usual scheme multiplexed four "virtual" messages on each digital line. A later method called Varioplex allowed a variable number of messages to be interleaved.

Photo by George Vrana

Figure 2-13. Photo of Teletype Model 33

Telegraph companies developed **carrier-current** systems starting in 1927. The first systems used an **amplitude modulation** of tones generated by rotating wheels as used in Hammond organs. A mark was silence, and a space was a 1000 Hz tone. If the character transmission rate were slow enough, the signal would sound like a series of "pips." Later, **frequency modulation**, a technique by which the carrier frequency was shifted rather than turned on and off was developed. Every time your PC communicates over the phone lines, a device called a **modem** utilizes frequency modulation to convert digital signals to analog signals suitable for transmission. Chapter 9 explains this in more detail.

A typical cable TV system delivers a dozen TV channels over a single coaxial cable. Telephone engineers originally used frequency modulation to multiplex hundreds of telephone conversations on one cable. Today most telephone traffic is handled by **frequency-division multiplexing** using coaxial cables and microwave links. This is a complicated multi-tiered system whereby groups of channels are shifted to occupy specific portions of the frequency spectrum (Figure 2-15). A single channel could contain your voice or tones from your PC's modem.

With the arrival of computers and high-speed digital circuitry, the telephone networks began to go digital. In a digital communication system, voice signals

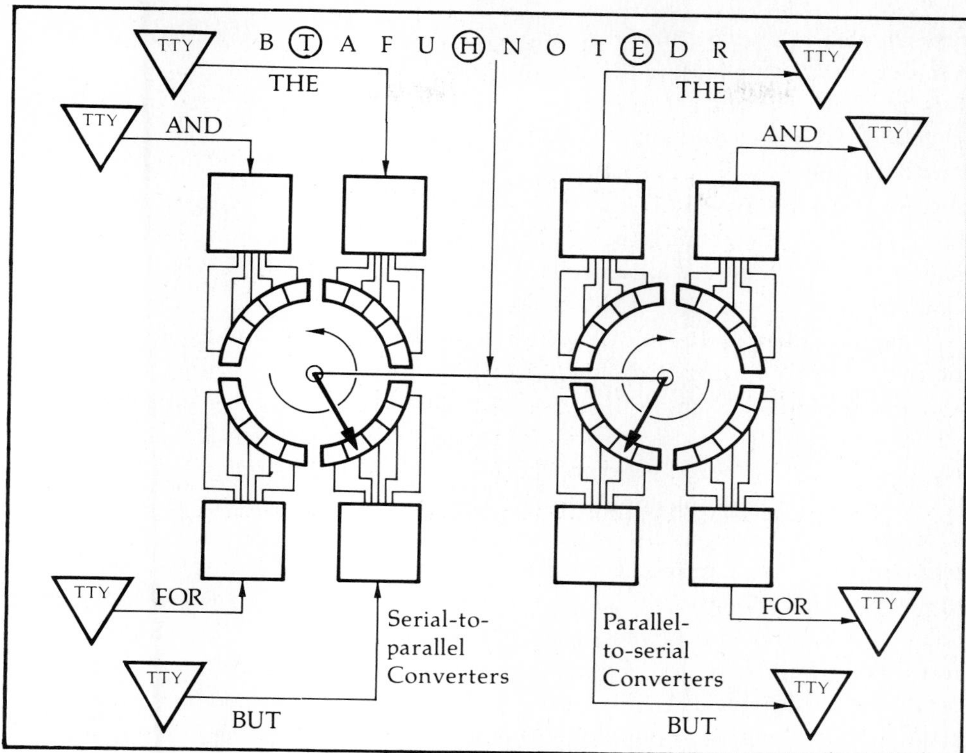

Figure 2-14. Time-division multiplexing

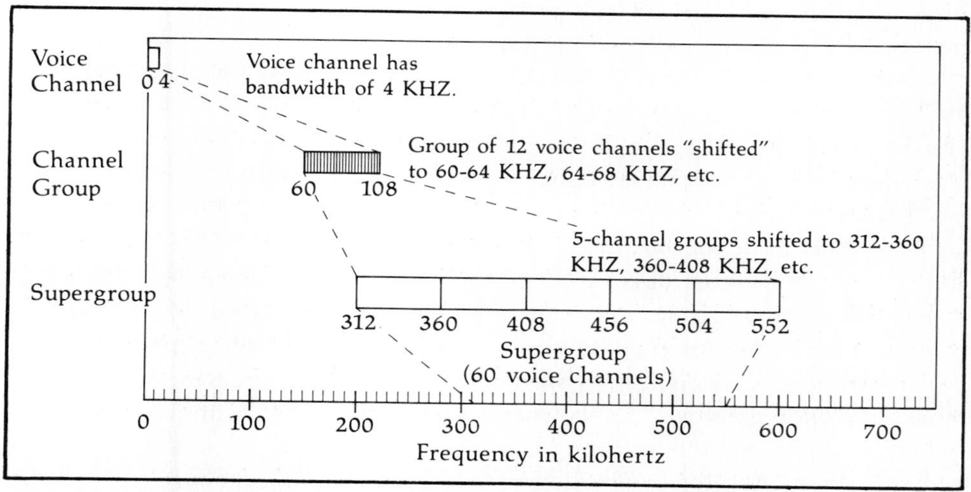

Figure 2-15. Frequency-division multiplexing

are sampled at regular intervals, and the instantaneous voltages are converted to 7-bit binary numbers, which are transmitted serially just as telegraph characters are. This system, called **pulse code modulation** (PCM), is used in the newly developed compact-disk digital audio system. AT&T's **T1** carrier system can carry 24 one-way speech channels, each with a data rate of 64,000 bits per second, through a pair of wires with **repeaters** (electronic relays) every 6000 feet. T1 is the electronic equivalent of the time-division multiplexing scheme shown in Figure 2-14. Numerically coded voice samples replace the individual characters, and operation is thousands of times faster.

The new fiber optic cables are capable of handling much more message traffic than are standard wire cables. A signal is detected by the presence of light in a glass fiber rather than by the presence of an electrical voltage on a conductor. There is very little distortion of the signal and the system is immune to all electrical noise. Repeaters are still necessary though, because the optical fibers eventually attenuate, or diminish, the light after a few miles.

Digital carrier systems are a natural for data communications because modems are not required. Unfortunately, there's no easy way to extend the digital channel directly to your house. If you send data to a friend across the country, your modem converts the digital codes from the PC into tones. Those tones may then be redigitized to pass through a T1 line and converted back to tones for the final leg. At the receiving end, your friend's modem recreates the original digital signal—at least you hope it's the original signal. Meanwhile, you've paid for a regular long-distance call.

Large businesses can **lease** digital lines to interconnect their mainframes, but it's expensive. How can you as a PC owner take advantage of this digital network? The **packet-switched networks** are the answer. Remember the telegraph message switching centers with the paper tape reperforators? That idea was originally adapted to computers by the airlines. Entire messages were stored on disk instead of paper tape at the switching center, and all switching was automatic. The addressee didn't see the message until the sender had finished transmitting all of it.

In the late 1960s the Advanced Research Projects Agency (ARPA) of the U.S. Department of Defense developed a new kind of network that linked dissimilar computers at participating universities throughout the country. Messages were broken down into small chunks of 1000 characters called **packets**. The packets were sent through high-speed digital channels from computer to computer, like "hot potatoes." Every packet contained a destination address, and each computer along the way would do its best to quickly unload the hot potato and send it in the proper direction. If any computer failed, there was a path around it.

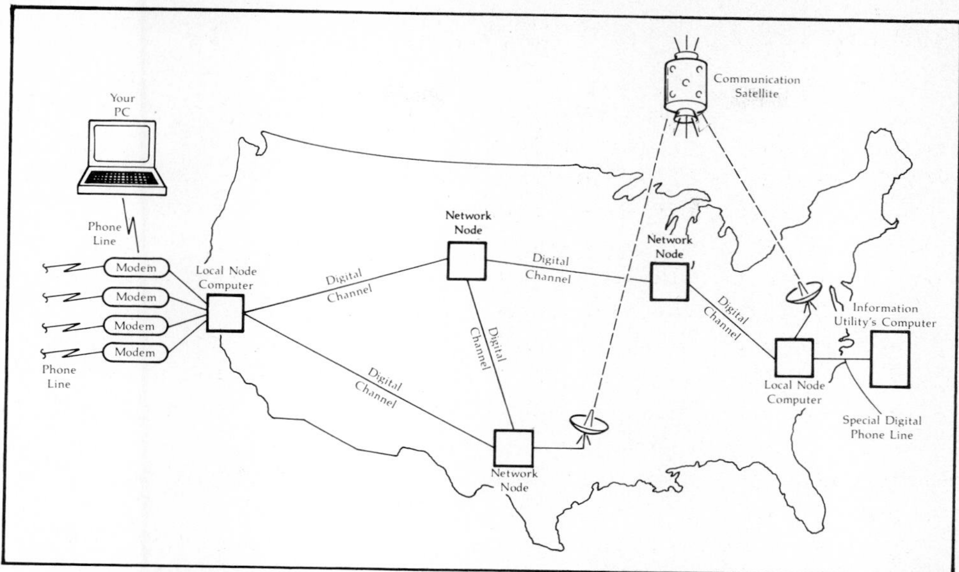

Figure 2-16. Packet-switched network

ARPANET worked well, and soon there were two public packet switching networks, Tymnet and Telenet. Tymnet was built to support Tymshare, a national computer timesharing system. Telenet was later bought by GTE. Packet switching is now big business, and there are always new competitors. AT&T has been conspicuous by its absence.

Your PC uses packet switching every time you connect up to one of the national information utilities such as The Source or the Dow Jones News/Retrieval Service. As shown in Figure 2-16, you dial a local number to connect to the neighborhood **node** of the network. You have a conventional link to the node, using over-the-phone-line modem tones. A computer at the node accumulates a complete line of your input, builds one or more packets, and then sends them off through the digital network. A dedicated digital phone line brings the packets into the computer room in Virginia (in the case of The Source). The computer sends its response back in packets, and your local node converts the packets into the asynchronous format your PC understands.

Because the packets are sent at a high data rate, your message occupies the line for only a small percentage of the time. The end result is that you save money. Daytime connect charges are only about $6 per hour as compared to long distance rates of $30 per hour. To make a long story short, we've come full circle from Morse's telegraph—digital communication to digital communication.

THREE

AN INTRODUCTION TO ASYNCHRONOUS COMMUNICATION

If your only goal were to connect your PC to a particular information utility, you could present your computer dealer with a blank check and a list of your wishes. Your PC would be delivered with a telephone cord dangling from the rear, allowing you to plug into any standard phone jack. Your dealer could even give you a diskette to make the PC dial and log on automatically when you turned on the power. Since you're reading this book, however, you're more than likely a person who evaluates the evidence in order to make your own decisions. This chapter is an overview of the communications hardware and software you need to log on to an information utility like The Source. In Chapters 6 through 9 you can look at the details of ports, cables, modems, and communications programs.

Fundamentals of Asynchronous Communication

Asynchronous communication is the primary link with the world outside your PC. In Chapter 2 you saw that asynchronous communication was a direct descendant of the telegraph. As a matter of fact, you can still connect your PC directly to the Teletype Model 33 used in the modern telegraph system. Conceptually, the asynchronous link is one wire in each direction over which characters are sent serially, one at a time, in a kind of high-speed Morse code. Figure 3-1 shows a direct serial connection between two computers.

Think of the serial link as a two-way telegraph line, and recall Morse's original telegraph receiver. Attached to a swinging pendulum on that device was a pencil that wrote on a slowly moving paper tape. A Morse code "B" caused the pencil to draw the waveform illustrated in Figure 2-7. A laboratory instrument called an **oscilloscope** also draws waveforms, but it uses an electron beam instead of a pencil. The beam paints the waveform on the screen the same way your PC's monitor displays text. The Morse receiver might have drawn the waveform for a "B" in a second, but the oscilloscope can draw the same character representation in as little as a millionth of a second (a microsecond). The PC's character-processing times are measured in thousandths of a second (milliseconds).

Figure 3-2 shows the modern representation of a "B" as it would appear on an oscilloscope. The code is now **ASCII** (American Standard Code for Information Interchange), and the voltage levels used are plus and minus 12 volts. The

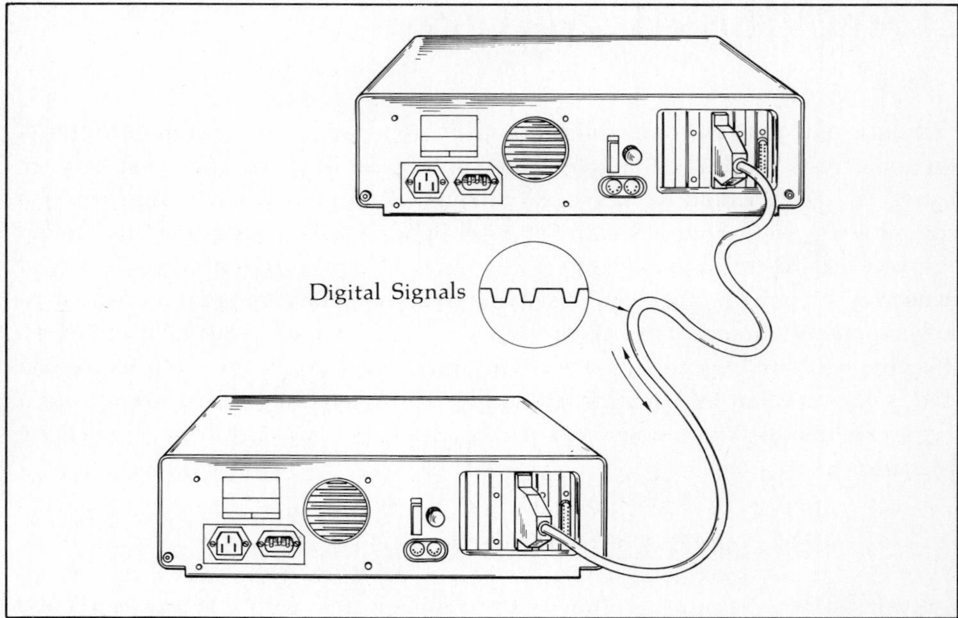

Figure 3-1. Direct serial connection between two computers

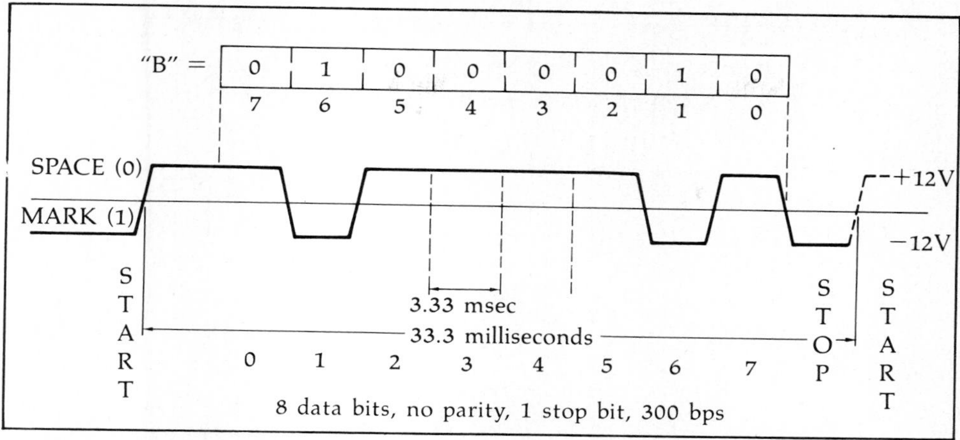

Figure 3-2. Digital signal for an ASCII "B"

signal is a **digital** signal because the voltage can have only two values: +12 volts is a logic "0", or **space**, and −12 volts is a logic "1", or **mark**. Logic 1s and 0s are what digital electronics is made up of, and there are many reference books on the subject.

Electrical communication is instantaneous except for the minor delays caused by the non-infinite speed of light and by the limitations of microelectronics. If the sending end of the line is at +12 volts, so is the receiving end. The oscilloscope picture in Figure 3-2 is really not a snapshot, but rather a time exposure requiring 33 milliseconds.

PC-to-PC communication requires a digital data link, but telephone circuits were designed for voice. The mouthpiece, or transmitter, in the telephone handset converts sound waves into their electrical equivalent. Instantaneous sound pressure values are translated into voltages and transmitted through the phone system. This **analog signal** is converted back to sound pressure at the earpiece of the receiver. Voice signals have components at different frequencies, and the phone system accommodates a frequency **bandwidth** (range) of 300-3100 Hz. Contrast this with your stereo's 20-20,000 Hz bandwidth.

If you fed the PC's plus and minus 12 volt digital signal directly into the phone line, there would be an unintelligible mess on the other end because the digital signal is outside of the frequency range of the telephone system. You must buy a device to convert the digital signal to an analog signal that is compatible with the phone system. A **modem**, short for modulator-demodulator, converts +12 volts into a 1270 Hz tone and −12 volts into a 1070 Hz tone, as shown in Figure 3-3. If you connected a modem to Morse's transmitter and listened in on the phone line, the dots and dashes would come so slowly that

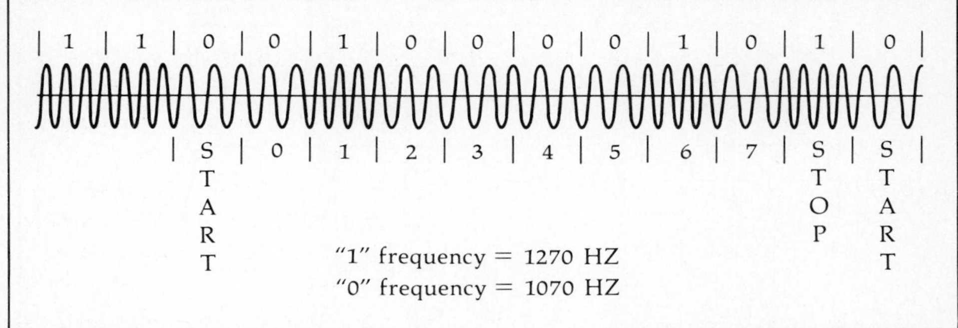

Figure 3-3. Analog signal for "B" as transmitted by phone line

you could hear the frequency shifts—a sort of warble. The PC sends data so quickly that the sound is more like a gurgle.

If you connect two PCs via phone line, you need two modems, one at each end, as shown in Figure 3-4.

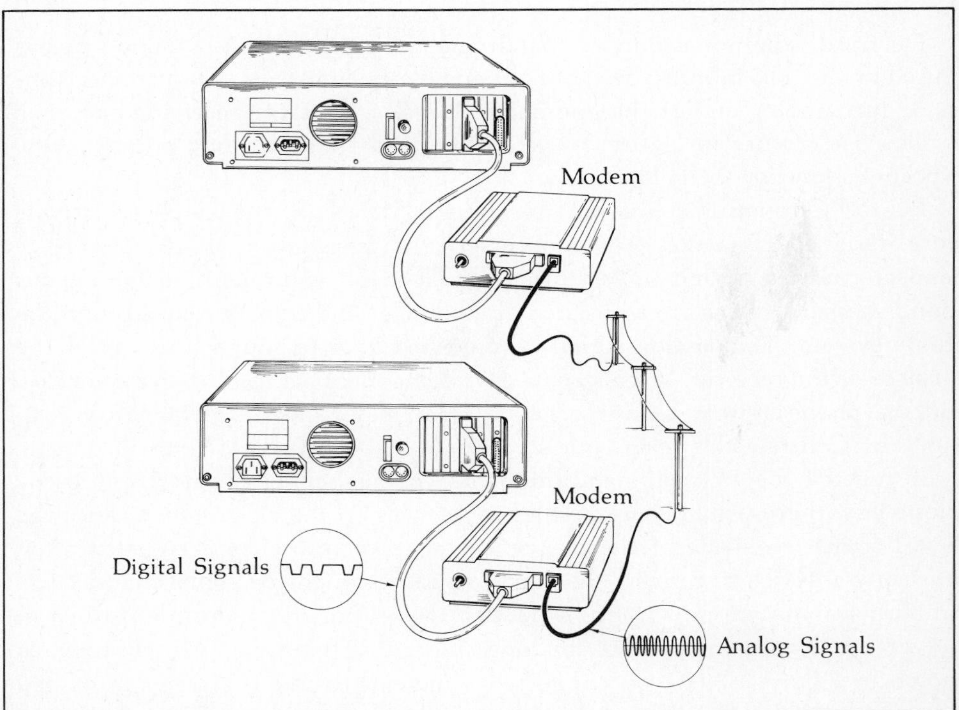

Figure 3-4. PC-to-PC connection via phone line

Speed

An asynchronous serial interface operates at a fixed speed, and both ends of the link must operate at the same speed. Data transmission speed is measured in **bits per second** (bps). Each eight-bit character, or byte, must have a **start bit** preceding it and a **stop bit** following it. These start and stop bits will be explained in more detail in Chapter 9, but for now all you need to know is that each character requires ten bits, not eight. Figure 3-2 shows a 300 bps signal; the time required to send each bit is 3.33 milliseconds (1/300 second). If a stream of eight-bit characters were sent back-to-back with a start bit immediately following the previous character's stop bit, 30 characters per second (cps) would be sent. In general, you can divide the speed in bits per second by 10 to get characters per second. The PC supports a wide range of speeds, but the important speeds are 300, 1200, and 9600 bps.

Sometimes the word **baud** is used instead of bps. Technically, baud is not the same as bits per second, but the terms are used interchangeably in the industry. If someone claims to have a 1200 baud modem, you can assume a 1200 bps modem. Chapter 8 explains more about baud rates.

Even though PCs and other computers can communicate at speeds up to 9600 bps, affordable modems have a limit of 1200 bps. There are other alternatives but no real standards. You could communicate point-to-point with identical high-priced 4800 bps modems at each end, but that kind of modem wouldn't get you data from the Dow Jones Information Service any faster. High-speed communications are possible locally over **leased** telephone lines at 9600 bps using special **digital modems**. Digital signals are sent directly onto the line and **conditioned** on the other end in the same way that Morse's telegraph signals were processed by his relays. You can minimize problems by renting these modems from your local phone company.

Serial Ports

Figures 3-1 and 3-4 are simplifications of real PC activities. You can't just attach two wires to your PC as you would attach speaker wires to your stereo receiver. Unless you have an IBM XT with built-in communications hardware, you must buy an **Asynchronous Communications Adapter** card or a multi-function card containing the circuitry for a **serial port**. The card goes into a PC expansion slot, and a connector on the back allows you to plug in a cable to a modem or to another computer. Figure 3-5 shows the serial port connector on a popular multi-function board. Multi-function boards are a good value because they often provide, in addition to a serial port, a battery-operated clock/calendar, a parallel port, and space for 256K or more memory.

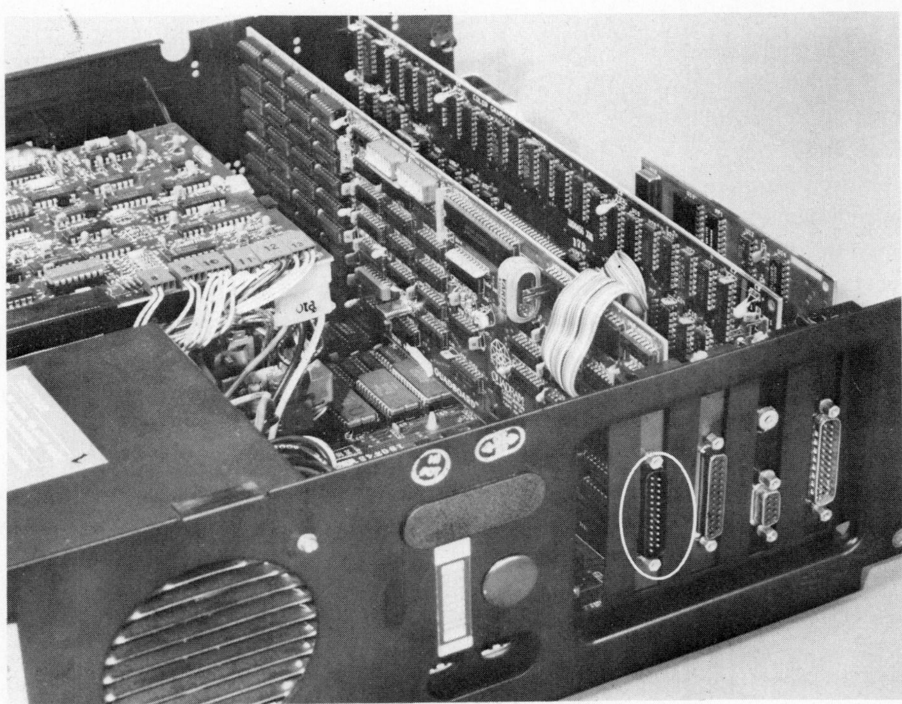

Figure 3-5. Multi-function board serial port connector

Modems

The modem shown in Figure 3-6 is an external or stand-alone unit attached to the PC with a cable. Another type of modem is built onto a plug-in card along with the necessary serial port. You don't need the box or the cable as you do with the stand-alone modem; the phone wire leads directly to the modem card, which is plugged into an expansion slot inside the PC, as shown in Figure 3-7.

Most modems for the PC are capable of operating at either 300 bps or 1200/300 bps, and most are so automated that they can automatically dial outgoing calls and answer incoming calls, eliminating the need for a telephone. The more you pay, the more bells and whistles you get. A manual 300 bps modem is at the bottom of the scale, and the fully automatic 1200/300 bps model is at the top. Fortunately, new integrated circuit chips and mass production techniques are quickly lowering the price of all modems.

Figure 3-6. External modem

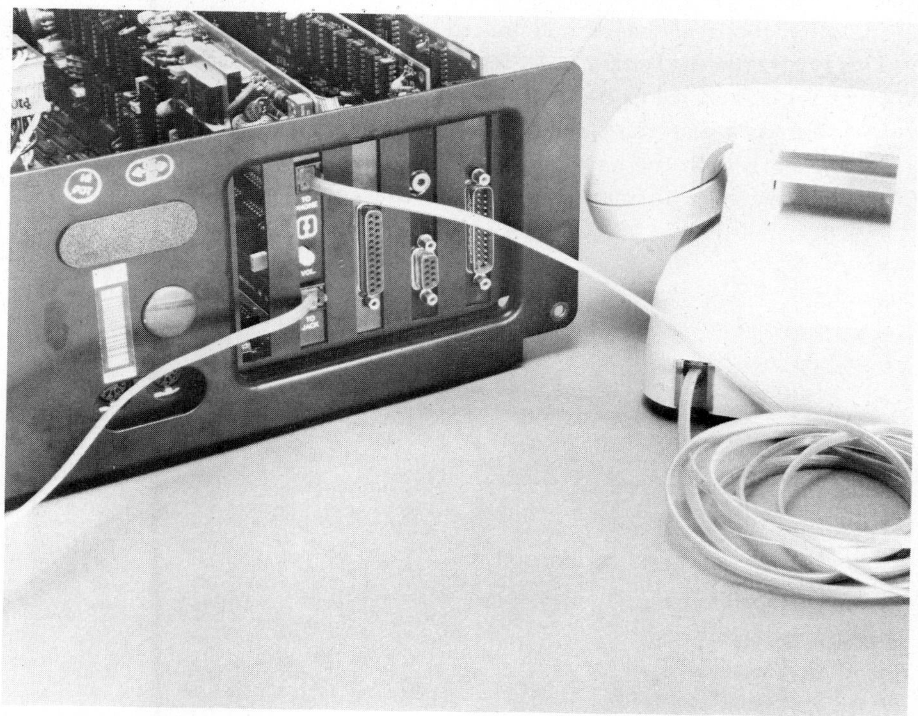

Figure 3-7. Modem card installed in the PC

Cables

You don't need a cable if you're using an internal circuit-card modem. If you're using a stand-alone modem or if you're connecting two computers in the same building, you must select the right cable. A typical cable is shown in Figure 3-8, but cables can have different connectors. And cables that look alike may be wired differently. There's an easy way out of this—just ask your dealer for the right cable. If you have an IBM PC, there are only two types of cables to consider: the modem cable and the **null modem** cable. These cables have 25-pin connectors called **DB-25**s on each end, but only from 3 to 9 pins are actually connected. Chapter 9 explains cables in more detail and also gives details about the **RS-232C** electrical standard, which defines the voltage levels and the purpose of each pin.

Communications Programs

Ports, modems, and cables are tangible. Ports and cables are generic, and there are only about a dozen modems to choose from. Software is another story. The 1983/1984 *PC World Annual Software Review* lists 65 different communications programs, and that's certainly not all of them.

Your program must match your communications task. Not only must the program work with the hardware you have, but it also must work with the remote computer or information utility at the other end of the link. The

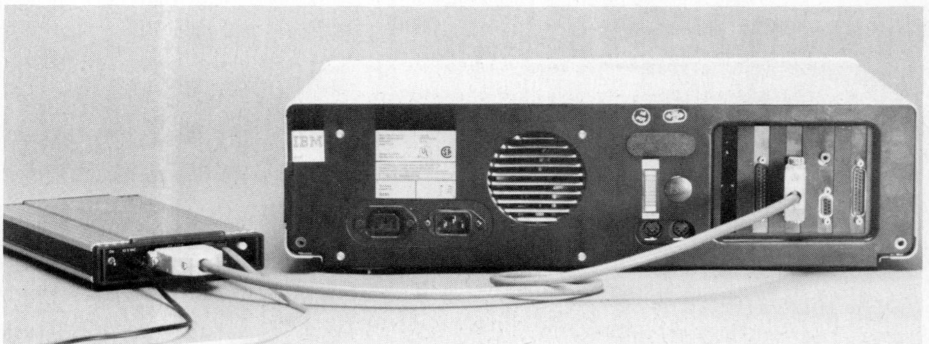

Figure 3-8. Serial cable to connect PC with external modem

program should also be easy to use and should fit your way of thinking. A communications program is about as personal as a word processor program.

Some communications programs are free with the purchase of a modem, but most must be purchased separately. Some programs will only work with certain types of modems.

General-purpose programs work with most information utilities and remote computers. They turn your PC into a smart terminal. Getting the PC to act as though it were one of a number of popular smart terminals is a feature known as terminal emulation. Many of the general-purpose communications programs also allow you to do things like maintain directories of often-used phone numbers, automatically log on to services like The Source or CompuServe, and save copies of your transactions in disk files. One of the more advanced features found on some communications programs is the ability to transfer files to and from a remote computer, a function known as **uploading** and **downloading**. In addition, some programs are able to transfer files by using what is known as an **error-checking protocol** to guarantee error-free transmissions. In cases where you need to operate one PC from another PC at a remote site, you need to look for programs that allow for **remote control**. The features of some of the more common general-purpose programs are covered in detail in Chapter 7.

Special-purpose programs interact with a particular host program or information utility. An example is the Dow Jones Market Manager, which automatically dials the Dow Jones News/Retrieval Service for an up-to-date evaluation of your stock portfolio. CompuServe supplies a program that interacts specifically with its service, making extensive use of graphics in controlling the display. Special-purpose programs will be covered in detail in Chapter 6.

The very latest communications programs provide color graphics according to **NAPLPS** (North American Presentation Level Protocol Standard), a standard postdating IBM's original Color/Graphics Monitor Adapter. NAPLPS requires a minimum of 16 colors on a high-resolution graphics screen, but the IBM adapter provides only 4. If you communicate with an NAPLPS videotex service, you must have an improved graphics card and you must be sure your program supports the host's communications standard.

A Feast at a Chinese Restaurant

When you order a meal at a Chinese restaurant, you select dishes from menu group A, group B, and so on. When you configure your PC for communications you do the same thing. Here is a communications "menu," followed by some typical "dinners" for different budgets and appetites.

Menu

Group A

Asynchronous Serial Ports

1. Built-in port standard with IBM PC XT	*no charge*
2. Built-in port standard with IBM-compatibles	*no charge*
3. IBM Asynchronous Communications Adapter	$120.00
4. Multifunction board with serial port included	$300.00+

Group B

Modems

1. 300 bps, manual dial, external to PC	$80-100
2. 300 bps, auto dial, auto answer, external	$160-290
3. 1200 bps auto dial, auto answer, external	$400-700
4. 1200 bps auto dial, auto answer, PC card	$300-600

Group C

Cables

1. Straight-through, 9 pins connected	$25
2. Null modem, simple configuration	$25
3. Special cable for IBM-compatible computers	$25

Group D

Communications Programs

1. 300-9600 bps, terminal emulation, upload/download	$100
2. 300-9600 bps, error-free micro-to-micro file transfer, remote control	$150

3.	300-1200 bps, autodial, error-free micro-to-micro file transfer, upload/download	$35
4.	300-1200 bps, full-featured except terminal emulation	$80-$120
5.	300-9600 bps, full-featured	$200
6.	1200 bps NAPLPS videotex with color graphics	$100

Dinner Suggestions

	Choose one from each group			
	A	*B*	*C*	*D*
PC to local microcomputer—PC or Apple running MS-DOS OR CP/M *You are transferring files back and forth between your PC and another microcomputer. You can have complete control at either end.*	3,4		1,2	2,5
PC XT to local minicomputer—HP, DEC, and so forth *You are emulating a popular terminal such as a DEC VT-100 or IBM 3101.*	1		1,2	1,5
PC to remote PC or information utility, low budget *You can transfer files from PC to PC with error checking, and you can save information on disk. A dialing directory stores commonly used telephone numbers.*	4	1	1	3
PC to remote PC, external modem *1200 bps is the maximum speed, and you need remote control and error checking file transfer protocol.*	3,4	3	1	2,4,5
PC to information utility, modem card *You can choose the $200 full-featured program, but you can get by with the free program that comes with the modem.*		4	4,5	
PC to NAPLPS videotex, modem card *You will also need the improved color/graphics adapter.*		4	6	

NOTE: Commas mean or; 3,5 under A means the IBM async card or a multifunction card.

Getting Started

Computer consultants used to advise buyers to "choose the software, then buy the hardware it runs on." Recently that advice has become "Choose the software, then configure the IBM PC to run it." You choose software to meet certain objectives, and then you get the communications hardware the software requires. Perhaps you want to transfer information between a PC and another micro in the office, or possibly you need your PC to double as a terminal for your VAX. That limits your choice of communications programs and eliminates the need for a modem.

If you need to connect to an information utility, there's another layer of decision-making; you must decide which utility you want to use. If you need telex service through your PC, you can choose from several utilities with varying grades of service and pricing schemes. One service may require you to have a special communications program just for telex messages; others may allow you to use a general-purpose program. Furthermore, some communications programs may only work with a particular modem, a Hayes Smartmodem for example.

To finish the analogy, once your meal is on the table, there's a surprise. The restaurant doesn't have knives and forks. You must use chopsticks. Learning to use your new hardware and software is equivalent to learning to eat with new utensils. If you're already familiar with your PC, you have a head start, but you will make some mistakes. If you're without any computer experience, you may not want to start off with data communications. Learn to use a word processor program or a spreadsheet just to get comfortable with the machine.

The more you understand about information utilities, communications programs, hardware, and theory, the better equipped you will be. You will be able to make informed choices about the complex maze of products.

FOUR

INFORMATION UTILITIES AND ELECTRONIC MAIL

Have you ever played the computer game Adventure? To play this game, you use commands like GO NORTH to navigate through a large, multi-chambered cave. The computer might respond, "THERE IS AN AX LYING NEXT TO YOU." If you reply, "PICK UP AX," you can defend yourself when an evil dwarf attacks you in the next chamber. The object of the game is to find all of the treasures and exit alive from the cave.

Navigating through information utilities like The Source, CompuServe, or the Dow Jones News/Retrieval Service is just like wandering through a cave. No, a dwarf won't attack you; your VISA credit line disappears instead. The "treasure" is information, pure and simple. Your job is to make a mental map of the cave, marking the spots where you found the good stuff. In a short time, you'll be as skilled with your information service as the hard-core Adventure players are with their game.

You learn to play Adventure by playing Adventure; you learn about information utilities by subscribing and logging in. This chapter is not a user's manual, but rather a guide to what is currently available on these services. Don't worry about passwords, phone numbers, and log-in procedures. They will be obvious once you subscribe to a service. If you've ever successfully used an automatic teller machine, you can use an information utility.

Another point is that the on-line information industry is changing rapidly. Use this chapter to select the services that interest you; then use Appendix G to write or phone the selected firms for current information. Many have toll-free phone numbers, and all are willing to mail you an information packet listing current services and rates.

The Electronic Publishing Industry

When you log in to an information utility, you (with the help of your communications program) dial a number, enter some codes, and watch as your PC is connected to a **host** computer. In the process, a large cross section of American business gets involved. Here is an example. Your local phone company, owned by one of the new Bell holding companies, connects you to a packet-switched network like GTE's Telenet that, in turn, connects you to an information utility like CompuServe (owned by H & R Block), whose computers are in Ohio. Once on CompuServe, if you ask for the Offical Airline Guide (OAG), you are then transferred to Dun & Bradstreet's OAG computer in Chicago, which uses a data line leased from AT&T.

An information utility like CompuServe is, in industry jargon, a **system operator** whose information comes from **information providers** such as OAG and UPI (United Press International). You subscribe to CompuServe, and CompuServe bills you. You pay CompuServe's standard rate, a fixed hourly charge for the packet-switched network, plus another charge for your time on a service like OAG. The CompuServe-OAG connection is called a **gateway** because it allows you to go from the computer of one service to the computer of another.

Most services include the network charges in their hourly rate. Sometimes the information provider bills you directly, passing on a percentage to an invisible system operator. Information providers can and do change system operators, and others provide identical services through several system operators. Find out what services are available before you subscribe.

The Source

The Source is a system operator and information provider owned by *Reader's Digest* and Control Data Corporation. It contains a healthy mix of business and consumer services and has over 50,000 subscribers. The following paragraphs describe what The Source has to offer.

Communications

SourceMail This is an electronic mail service that allows you to send messages to other Source subscribers. Letters sent to you are placed in your electronic mailbox, and each time you log in to The Source you can check your box for any new mail. Once you read a letter in your box, you can send an immediate reply or save the letter in a file. The features of SourceMail are covered in more detail in the "Electronic Mail" section of this chapter.

Chat This service allows you to carry on an on-line conversation with other Source subscribers. To use Chat, you first list the account numbers of all subscribers currently on-line. If you see the number of someone you know or would like to talk with, you can type a message to interrupt the other party. You can turn off the Chat facility to prevent others from interrupting you if you wish.

Teleconferencing Participate, The Source's teleconferencing system, allows you to join any number of ongoing conferences on a wide variety of subjects. One of the most popular Source features, teleconferencing allows any number of users to participate in an on-line discussion in which the proceedings of the conference are stored as notes in a central computer. Once you join a conference, you have access to all the notes that make up the proceedings, and each time you log on, you receive all the notes since you last logged on. Here's one day's list of active conferences:

```
PARTICIPATE ON THE SOURCE
-------------------------

"THE MACINTOSH APPLE" (10160) APPLE'S 32-BIT MICRO ON THE HORIZON.

"IBM PEANUT" (6195) NOW THAT IT'S HERE, WHAT'S IT GOT? ANSWER 47
OF THIS CONFERENCE LISTS ALL THE SPECS.

"CHIMO" (12528) THE INTERACTIVE NEWSLETTER OF PARTICIPATION
SYSTEMS, INC., CREATORS OF PARTI.

"NETWORKING" (13271) PARTICIPATE IN THIS ELECTRONIC LECTURE ABOUT
THE WORLD VILLAGE WHICH YOU'RE HELPING TO BUILD HERE IN PARTI.

"POLITICS" (7860) MARINES, BEIRUT, SOVIETS, ET AL, IN ONE OF THE
LIVELIEST OF CONFERENCES.

"RELATING - FOR YOU" (9576) HOW THIS NEW MEDIUM IS AFFECTING US
ALL.

"FAMILY & COMPUTERS" (5665) TELECOMPUTING FAMILIES TALK ABOUT
THEIR EXPERIENCES ONLINE.

"CHATTER" (4361) THE HIGH DRAMA OF CADOISM LIVES ON PARTI!

"CDC PLATO" (9253) CONTROL DATA'S HIGHLY REGARDED CAI SYSTEM
NEARS THE MICRO WORLD.
```

```
"HALLOWEEN" (10665) RESIDUAL GOBLINESQUERIE (!)

"COMPUTER KIDS" (8640) THE 414'S AND 'WARGAMES': THE ISSUE IS
SECURITY AND/OR INNOCENT ADOLESCENT BOYISH CURIOSITY.

"IP" (8218) OR 'INDUSTRIAL POLICY', THE DEBATE RAGES OVER WHAT IT
SHOULD BE.

"PITS" (8767) STUMPED OVER THE NEW RELEASE OF AN OLD FAVORITE?
TRADE SECRETS WITH OTHER STUMPEES.

"COMPUTER TEACHER" (11999) TELECOMPUTING IN THE CLASSROOM.

"APPLE STOCK" (10083) BATTERED OR BOLSTERED?  MARKET ANALYSIS OF
THE COMPUTER MAKER'S FORTUNES.

"TELECONSULTANTS" (452) SHARE EXPERTISE AMONG PROFESSIONAL
CONSULTANTS.

"ADS" (8210) LISTING OF NAMES AND PHONE NUMBERS OF POPULAR CBBS
AROUND THE COUNTRY.

"MCI MAIL" (10125) DISCUSS MCI'S VENTURE INTO ELECTRONICA.
```

These are formal conferences with a moderator who keeps order. There are hundreds of informal conferences branching off of these. You can organize your own conferences, but you have to pay for the disk space. You can have private conferences (ideal for business use), and you can create a ballot for voting by conference readers. Participate is one of the more difficult Source features to learn, but there's a practice conference for you to learn on.

Bulletin boards Source subscribers can electronically post classified ads and general notices. Most classifications are computer-oriented, but you can find autos for sale and houses to swap. Here's a sample:

```
<R>ead,<PO>st,<PU>rge,<S>can, or <H>elp:s
<C>ategory,<U>ser ID,<D>ate,<K>eyword:c

Categories, or <H>elp:ibm
Searching...
84 notices valid.

<N>arrow, <E>xpand or Return for all :n
<C>ategory,<U>ser ID,<D>ate,<K>eyword:k

Keyword(s) or <H>elp:program
Searching...
5 notices valid.

<N>arrow, <E>xpand or Return for all :
Wait...
1     10 DEC TCS091 NEW TERMINAL PROGRAM TUTORIAL(IBM)
2     09 DEC ST3899 DOWNLOAD FREE PROGRAM - IBM(IBM)
3     06 DEC TCZ561 NEED A GOOD IBM BBS PROGRAM(IBM)
4     06 DEC ST5468 FORT MILL PROGRAM UPDATE(IBM)
5     03 DEC TCF070 FINANCE PROGRAMS(IBM)

Enter item(s),<H>elp,or Return for all :5

IF ANYONE CAN GIVE ME A GOOD REVIEW OF PERSONAL FINANCE PROGRAMS
```

```
I WOULD APPRECIATE IT.  A FRIEND AND I ARE INTERESTED IN
ACQUIRING PERSONAL FINANCE PROGRAMS SEPARATELY. BECAUSE OF OUR
DIVERGENT INTERESTS WE MAY NEED DIFFERENT PROGRAMS THAT FOCUS ON
DIFFERENT AREAS SUCH AS STOCKS VS. CHECKING.

THANKS

LOUIE/TCF070
```

Messages are automatically purged from the system after seven days, but they're free.

User directory With this directory you can voluntarily list your name and your interests so that others with similar interests can get in touch with you. You can scan the list by state or by interest. Here are some examples:

```
5 notices valid.

On which keyword(s) do you wish to search:
Account name (A), First name (F), state (S), or
Interests (I).  (other options are "STOP", "ALL", or "SI")? i

Keyword(s): parrot

TCT856/ALAN/MA/PARROTS SYSOPS(SABRE,ADS,APOLLO,PARS)DEREK AND CLIVE CHAT
TCY157/PEGGY/CA/TVNEWS/PARROTS/SCOTTISH TERRIERS/LOS ANGELES.

State: WA

CL0020/COMPUTERLAND OF BELLEVUE/WA/IBM,APPLE,XEROX,ALTOS,VECTOR,WANG,ETC...
CL0026/MIKE/WA/VIDEOTEX/OFFICE OF FUTURE/TELECOM/PABX/APPLE/BUSINESS/MERCEDES
CL0649/RUSTY/WA/CHESS,PENTE,PET,SWTP,DEC-PDP11/23,CHAT,APPLE PROCESSING
CL1119/JEFF/WA/COMPUTERS,WARGAMING,D&D,ADVENTURE
CL1451/JOHN/WA/APPLE/SPACE/L-5/ROBOTS/LASERS
```

Mailgrams This is the same as a Western Union message. The message is electronically sent to the city nearest the recipient, printed, and mailed. This service is expensive at $5.15 for 100 words, but you do get a confirmation copy. E-COM and MCI mail are cheaper.

E-COM This service is the U.S. Postal Service equivalent of Mailgrams. The cost is $1.35 for one page and $0.25 for the second, including postage. Without the services of The Source, you would need special software to send a message via E-COM (see Chapter 6 for more details.)

News and Information

UPI You can search United Press International's stories by date and keyword, selecting national, regional, or state news and features. **Sports** news includes up-to-the-minute UPI scores and stories you access by state and keyword. It's convenient, but scanning through the newspaper is easier and cheaper. The Source is more up-to-date than the newspaper, but a radio also gives you the latest news.

Business, political and economic news These features, also available from several other services, include The Source's BIZDATE business news update and U.S. News Washington Letter, published by *U.S. News and World Report*.

Business Services

Many business services are **Source*Plus** services, meaning you pay an additional premium over the regular rates each time you use the service.

Stock and company information Current stock prices and stock performance reports are available to help you monitor and analyze your stock portfolio. Appendix C contains a comprehensive comparison of the stock and company information available from The Source, CompuServe, and the Dow Jones News/Retrieval Service.

Employment services Selected employment agencies post jobs and resumes, indexed by job class, location, and salary. For example, you can search for all communications jobs in California with salaries over $40,000, or all the applicants who qualify for them. You don't see the name of the company or applicant, but you can use a reference number to contact the employment agency.

Information management The programs *Compudex* and *INFOX* let you create financial models and databases. However, you could do it more cheaply with your own copy of *Multiplan* or *dBASE II*.

Reference Management Contents, Ltd., provides 200–250-word abstracts of all articles from leading business and financial publications. You request an abstract by author, journal name, and keyword, and you can order a complete copy for $10. Another firm, Information On Demand (IOD), does library research for a fee.

Consumer Services

Comp-U-Store You can browse through over 50,000 products listed in Comp-U-Card International's computer. If you sign up with Comp-U-Store, you can order merchandise and charge it on your credit card. The next page shows a sample browse session.

```
 #           Categories
---     -------------------------
  1     Appliances
  2     Cameras & optical equipt.
  3     Cars & car stereo
  4     Tableware
  5     Luggage
  6     Sporting goods
  7     Stereo & audio equipment
  8     TV & video equipment
  9     Other electronics
 10     Computers & accessories
 11     Miscellaneous
Enter A Category # :7

Code        Product
---- ------------------------
PTCS Portable cassette players
RADO Radios
STAC Stereo accessories
STBC Stereo blank cassettes
STBR Stereo blank tape (reel)
STCS Stereo cassette decks
STCT Stereo cartridges
STDA Digital audio players
STEQ Stereo equalizers
STHP Stereo headphones
STIA Stereo integrated amplifs
STMP Stereo microphones

enter selection:stda

Code   Manufacturer
---- -------------------------
HTCH  HITACHI
AKAI  AKAI
FSHR  FISHER
MRNZ  MARANTZ
SNSU  SANSUI
Type of equipment?
(NP) No preference
(1) Disc player
(2) Tape player/recorder
(3) Audio processor
>1
Type of loading?
(NP) No preference
(1) Front-load
(2) Top-load
>np
Remote capability?
(NP) No preference
(1) Yes
(2) No
>np
Ship-to State
(necessary for quote)
>wa
WASHINGTON (Y or N):y
What's the most you will spend?
>$2000
Digital audio play Page  1 Of  1
 #  Mfg    Model       FDC
 1 FSHR  AD850ADP11  639.51
 2 HTCH  DA1000      611.55
 3 AKAI  CDD1        649.75
 4 MRNZ  CD73        665.68
 5 SNSU  PCV1000     618.69
 6 HTCH  DA800       611.55
```

If you've shopped for these products in local hi-fi stores, you'll realize that Compu-U-Store saves you about 40 percent. Comp-U-Store is more convenient than mail-order shopping, but it's no substitute for going to the store and bringing home the goods. You may have to wait several weeks for delivery, and you can't tell if your selection is in stock.

Professional Book Center This service enables you to order books, but ordering is "blind." You describe your book as well as you can on an order form and send it. If the Book Center has the book, it is sent to you; otherwise a cancellation is sent by regular mail.

Records and tapes MusicSource lets you search for and order records; RadioSource lets you order tapes of classic radio programs.

Restaurant guides Mobil Oil's National Restaurant Guide allows you to search for restaurants throughout the United States and Canada. You can search by city, types of foods, and so forth.

Entertainment

Games This service sets you against the computer. Play games like Adventure, Castlequest, or Trek, or plot your biorhythms. You can save on connect charges by downloading some programs to run on your PC.

Movie reviews Short reviews by Cineman are presented. Here's an example:

```
MINI MOVIE REVIEWS BY CINEMAN SYNDICATE.  ALL RIGHTS RESERVED.
FIRST LOVE - BORING
AN ADOLESCENT SOAP OPERA ABOUT A COLLEGE STUDENT'S SEARCH FOR
TRUE LOVE. THE STORY, WHICH TAKES PLACE ON A FICTITIOUS COLLEGE
CAMPUS, IS BLAND AND GLOOMY MUCH OF THE TIME. THERE'S A LOT
OF SEXUAL ACTIVITY GOING ON, BUT IT'S OVERLAID WITH SILLY
DIALOGUE AND SQUEAKY-CLEAN ROMANTIC SENTIMENT. STARS WILLIAM
KATT AND SUSAN DEY AS THE YOUNG LOVERS. DIRECTED BY JOAN
DARLING.
*R
```

The system includes over 1000 reviews of old movies that appear on TV as well as current releases.

Travel

Air schedules Domestic and international air schedules are available. A sample is shown on the following page.

```
-> travel

 Enter Departure City / Destination City in the format
 CITY, STate / CITY, STate  TIME(s)   (Times Optional)
 EXAMPLE:   Chicago, Il / New york, Ny      0900A-0200P

 seattle, wa/philadelphia, pa

 FROM: SEATTLE, WA
   TO: PHILADELPHIA, PA


 DEPART  APT  ARRIVE  APT   FLIGHT   CLASS  DAYS      MEALS  PLANE STOPS
 07:35A       04:39P        EA 0322  FYBML  1234567    BLB    727     1
      EFFECTIVE 12/15/83
 10:26A       07:55P        UA 0144  FYBQM  1234567    LDL    D10     1
                           DISCONTINUE 12/14/83
 10:35A       07:55P        UA 0144  FYBQM  1234567    LDL    D10     1
      EFFECTIVE 12/15/83
 11:15A       08:15P        NW 0008  Y      1234567    LD     747     1
 12:33P       09:54P        UA 0494  FYBQM  1234567    LDL    DC8     1
                           DISCONTINUE 12/14/83
 12:33P       09:54P        UA 0494  FYBQM  1 34567    LDL    DC8     1
      EFFECTIVE 12/15/83
```

You get schedules just the way they're printed by the airlines. Fares are not listed.

Hotels The Mobil National Travel Guide can help you search for a hotel. Vacancies are not listed.

Firstworld Travel Club This is really a travel agency accessible by SourceMail. You use The Source to find a flight and a hotel, and then you make your reservations using the travel club, charging your tickets to your credit card. This is okay, but a travel agent can provide the same service for the same price.

Other Source Services

Programming The Source's Prime computers can be programmed in BASIC/VM, FORTRAN 66, and Pascal. A line editor lets you write programs. However, it's not clear why you would program on The Source's computers instead of on your own.

Disk files The Source contains a powerful file system that lets you organize your personal disk files in a hierarchical structure. Some of those files, called **sharefiles**, can be accessed by other subscribers. It's easy to transfer a file to another subscriber, either by copying it to that person's sharefile area or by including it in a SourceMail letter. Any Source information can be routed to a **COMO** file instead of to your screen. The COMO file can then be saved and edited or sent to another subscriber. A researcher could use a COMO file to collect business information and then mail that file to the client.

Personal publishing You can publish information by making it available in your sharefiles area and by advertising it through The Source's bulletin board system, POST. If the response is favorable, you can ask The Source to include it in the more accessible public file area. Once your information is placed in the public file area, you receive a royalty based on subscriber access. One example is an on-line personal computing magazine that reports late-breaking microcomputer developments. Unfortunately, it does not have much depth.

What's new The Source has a special menu of new items. For example:

```
          ***************
     ******   WEEKEND   ******
          ***************

        DECEMBER 10-11, 1983

1  A WEEKEND TO REMEMBER, BECAUSE...
2  A GLIMPSE AT THE WEEKEND'S BEST TV SHOWS
3  How to Choose Your Christmas Tree - The Business Thrives
4  WRITE-AWAYS: Attention Art & Coin Collectors
5  THE OPINION FORUM: Does the U.S. Have Adequate Civil Defense?
6  What You Should Know in Buying a Home Computer
7  YOUR WEEKEND HOROSCOPE
8  PERSONALITY PROFILE: Comedian Eddie Murphy
```

Using The Source

You can navigate in The Source entirely by **menus** if you want to. Here's The Source's main menu:

```
THE SOURCE MAIN MENU

1  NEWS AND REFERENCE RESOURCES
2  BUSINESS/FINANCIAL MARKETS
3  CATALOGUE SHOPPING
4  HOME AND LEISURE
5  EDUCATION AND CAREER
6  MAIL AND COMMUNICATIONS
7  CREATING AND COMPUTING
8  SOURCE*PLUS
```

Once you're used to the system, you can switch to the **command mode**. For instance, if you type EMPLOY JOB COMP in command mode, you will start a search for computer jobs. Actually the search won't start immediately. You'll be asked for more information.

Some features use the **Genindex** format, which stores information in numbered pages. You can search an index to find page numbers and then display those pages. Consider this example:

```
ENTER A SUBJECT, A PARAGRAPH NAME, "STOP", OR "HELP"   FOR INSTRUCTIONS:
california

WINES IN THE UNITED STATES.........P011
CALIFORNIA CHARDONNAYS.............P048
CALIFORNIA SAUVIGNON BLANC.........P049
CALIFORNIA CABERNET SAUVIGNON......P050


ENTER A SUBJECT, A PARAGRAPH NAME, "STOP", OR "HELP"   FOR INSTRUCTIONS:
p048

                     CALIFORNIA CHARDONNAYS

    MANY OF THE SOUTHERN CALIFORNIA CHAPTER DIRECTORS GATHERED
RECENTLY........
```

Plan on spending a few hours learning your way around The Source. Don't get frustrated. You'll feel at home very quickly.

Costs

There is a $100 registration fee that includes account setup, ID and password assignment, and the *User's Manual and Command Guide.* Some dealers may include a free Source subscription when you purchase communications hardware, so take the time to look for a good deal.

The hourly rates as of October 1, 1983, are shown in Table 4-1.

Table 4-1. The Source's Hourly Rates

	Monday—Friday 7:00 A.M.—6:00 P.M.	Monday—Friday 6:00 P.M.—7:00 A.M. weekends and holidays
300 bps	$20.75	$7.75
1200 bps	$25.75	$10.75
SOURCE*PLUS value—added service		
300 bps	$39.75	$34.75
1200 bps	$44.75	$37.75

Your subscription includes two disk storage records of 2048 characters each. Additional records cost between $0.05 per month and $0.50 per month depending on the quantity.

There is a $1 monthly account maintenance fee, a $9 minimum usage fee, and a $0.25 minimum connect charge. Thus it costs $10 per month just to keep your account, even if you never use the service.

CompuServe

CompuServe is a information utility divided into the business-oriented Executive Information Service (EIS) and the hobbyist-oriented Consumer Information Service (CIS). You subscribe to one or the other, but they have many services in common.

What's Available

Figure 4-1 is an index of what's available on CIS, and Figure 4-2 is the index for EIS. Ignore the codes for the time being, but marvel at the sheer amount of information. Even though cross-indexing inflates the number of entries, there's still a lot to choose from. If you are an EIS subscriber, you can type CIS and access the consumer service, but you can't go from CIS to EIS.

```
********************************
             INDEX
--------------------------------
COMPUSERVE INFORMATION SERVICE
--------------------------------
AAMSI Medical Forum:...Go SFP-5
AID calculations:.....Go PCS-72
AMEX prices (MQUOTE):.Go FIN-20
ASCMD (SIG):...........Go SFP-7
A.S.I. Monitor:.......Go ASI-10
AVSIG:.................Go SFP-6
Academic American Encyc:.Go AAE
Access:...............Go PCS-46
Access phone numbers:Go CIS-177
Adult education:......Go TCB-13
Adventure game:.......Go GAM-11
Advertisers, TODAY:......Go EBB
Advertising:
 For sale.............Go HOM-24
 Notices..............Go HOM-24
 Today Magazine..........Go EBB
 Want ads.............Go HOM-24
Advertising, classified:
 StL Post-Dispatch..Go SPD-1002
Advice:
 Aunt Nettie.............Go NET
African weather:......Go CNS-17
Agribusiness:.........Go SFP-10
Agricultural news:....Go CNS-14
Air travel:
 Firstworld Travel Club..Go TVL
 Official Airline Guide..Go OAG
 Pan Am..................Go PAN
 Travel Fax..............Go ESC
Air travel delays:.......Go PDG
Aircraft:................Go ASI
Aircraft insurance:......Go AVL
Airline guide:...........Go OAG
Airport delay guide:.....Go PDG
Alternative Education:...Go AES
Altertext reports:.......Go ALT
Amateur Radio:........Go HOM-11
Analogies test:.......Go TMC-15
Annual reports:.......Go FIN-18
Apple, programs for:..Go PCS-45
Apple User's Group:...Go PCS-51
Appliances for sale:.....Go CUS
Arcade (SIG):........Go HOM-138
Art gallery:.........Go HOM-101
Articles, computer:......Go PER
Asian weather:........Go CNS-17
Assoc. Press Access:..Go IND-52
```

Figure 4-1. CompuServe Consumer Information Service index

```
Assoc. Videotex Wire:....Go APV
Astrology Game:.......Go GAM-45
Astronautics:........Go HOM-127
Atari Forum:.........Go PCS-132
Athlete's Outfitter:.....Go HAN
Athletic equipment:.Go CUS, HAN
Atlas, shopping service:.Go TRV
Attorneys:............Go SFP-40
Author's (SIG):......Go PCS-117
Auto information:
 Gov't publication.....Go GPO-6
 Popular Science.........Go PSC
AutoNet:.................Go ATO
Autos, buying:
 AutoNet.................Go ATO
 StL Post-Dispatch..Go SPD-1002
Aviation:
 ASI Monitor..........Go ASI-10
 EMI Flight Planning.....Go EMI
 NWS Aviation Weather....Go AWX
 Official Airline Guide..Go OAG
 Peak Delay Guide........Go PDG
Aviation Rules & Reg:....Go AVR
Aviation Safety Inst:....Go ASI
Aviation (SIG):........Go SFP-6
Aviation weather:........Go AWX
Bacchus Data Services:...Go VIN
Banking, electronic:..Go HOM-45
Banks:
 Huntington Nat'l Bank...Go HNB
 Shawmut Bank of Boston..Go SHW
 United American Bank.G HOM-152
Banshi game:..........Go GAM-30
Basic CompuServe:.....Go PCS-73
Beef prices:..........Go CNS-12
Belmont Golf Association:Go BEL
Belmont's golf (SIG):Go HOM-129
Billing, general:......Go CIS-4
Billing, reviewing:..Go CIS-176
Biorhythms:...........Go GAM-29
Blackjack game:.......Go GAM-13
Bliss language:.......Go PCS-74
Book, reviews:
 AAMSI, medical journals.Go AAM
 Hollywood Hotline.......Go HHL
 Rainbo's Reviews........Go WIT
Books, ordering:
 Fifth Avenue Shopper....Go FTH
 Howard Sams' Books......Go SAM
Boston, Shawmut Bank:....Go SHW
Bridge game:..........Go GAM-18
Brokerage:.......Go UMC, Go TKR
Brokerage, diamond:......Go RDC
Budgeting, home:
 Gov't publications....Go GPO-4
 Investors Diversified.Go IDS-6
 CompuServe...........Go HOM-80
Bulletin board:.......Go HOM-23
Business, farming:....Go SFP-10
Business Information Wire:G BIW
Business news:
 AP Videotex Wire........Go APV
 Business wire...........Go TBW
 Canadian, U.S., Int'l...Go BIW
 CompuServe...........Go FIN-10
 StL Post-Dispatch..Go SPD-1005
 Washington Post......Go TWP-12
CB Interest Group:......Go HOM-9
CB Radio simulation:
 CB Etiquette..........Go CB-40
 Direct access to.......Go CB-1
 Instructions..........Go CB-15
 Introduction..........Go CB-10
CB Society:..............Go CUP
CEMSIG:..............Go CEM-450
CP/M user's group:....Go PCS-47
Cameras for sale:........Go CUS
Canadian:
Child care:............Go GPO-8
Children, education:.....Go AAE
Children's games:.....Go TMC-27
Cinema news:.............Go HHL
Clarke School for Deaf:..Go CSD
Classified ads:
 StL Post-Dispatch..Go SPD-1002
Clinical advice:.........Go HSX
Clothing, fashion:.......Go GAN
Clothing, sport:.........Go HAN
Cocoa news:...........Go CNS-15
Coffee news:..........Go CNS-15
College cost program:..Go TCB-6
Color computer (SIG):Go PCS-126
Color graphics:.......Go CIS-91
Columbus area:
 Banks................Go HOM-45
 Chamber of Commerce.....Go CCC
 Education...............Go CCC
 SIG.................Go CCC-150
Command level:........Go PCS-71
Commentaries:
 Video...................Go VIF
Commodities calendar:..Go HCI-7
Commodities future:...Go CNS-12
Commodities glossary:Go HCI-230
Commodity News Service:
 Agricultural news....Go CNS-14
 Commodity prices.....Go CNS-12
 Economic news...........Go CNS
 Futures indus news...Go FIN-10
 Futures mkt prices...Go CNS-12
 General news.........Go CNS-15
 Metals news..........Go CNS-15
 Weather..............Go CNS-17
Commodore newsletter:....Go CBM
Commodore VIC (SIG):.Go PCS-160
Comm. Industry Forum:.Go SFP-35
Company forecasts:....Go FIN-18
CompuServe commands:..Go CIS-11
Comp-U-Store:............Go CUS
Computer, books:.........Go SAM
Computer aided learning:
 CompuServe..........Go PCS-121
 Edutech.................Go CAI
Computer Art (SIG):..Go PCS-157
Computer club news:
 Computers & Electronics.Go CEM
Computer Magazine Index:.Go PER
Computers & Electronics:.Go CEM
Concentration game:...Go GAM-32
Consumer items for sale:.Go CUS
Consumer news:
 Software............Go PSP-101
Continuing education:.Go TCB-13
Cooking (SIG):.......Go HOM-109
```

Figure 4-1. CompuServe Consumer Information Service index (continued)

```
Corporate news release:..Go TBW
Corporations:............Go INC
Copper futures prices:Go CNS-12
Copper news:..........Go CNS-15
Cotton futures prices:Go CNS-12
Cotton news:..........Go CNS-14
Court cases, aircraft:...Go AVL
Cross Assemblers:.....Go PCS-75
Current rates:........Go CIS-53
Database, how to use:.Go CIS-11
Database searches:.......Go IFT
dataFAMILIAE:............Go PFL
Decwars game:.........Go GAM-19
DEFALTS, setting:......Go CIS-6
Department of State:.....Go DOS
Diamond System:..........Go RDC
Discounted goods:........Go SAV
Disk area:............Go PCS-71
Document delivery:.......Go IOD
Document retrieval:......Go IFT
Documentation ordering:Go CIS-8
Dress:...................Go GAN
Drugs, medicine:.....Go GPO-399
EMI Flight Plans:........Go EMI
Earnings forecasts:....Go FIN-4
Economic news:.........Go FIN-10
Economy:
 Forecasts...............Go MMS
Editorials:
 Washington Post......Go TWP-17
Education:
 Academic Encyclopedia...Go AAE
 Clarke School for Deaf..Go CSD
 Edutech (PILOT).........Go CAI
 The College Board.......Go TCB
 The Multiple Choice.....Go TMC
Education, family:.......Go PFL
Educational games:
 Super Brain Challenge.G TMC-19
 Witty Write-Ins......Go TMC-18
GameSIG Archives:........Go GSA
Gandolf's Reports:.......Go GAN
Gardening:...............Go VIC
Gasoline, saving:...Go GPO-1131
General banking:......Go HOM-45
Godiva Chocolate:........Go FTH
Gold:
 Future prices..Go FIN-4,CNS-12
 News.........Go FIN-4, CNS-15
Golf, Belmont Golf Asso:.Go BEL
Golf, Official PGA Tour:
 Biographies.............Go PGA
 Players.................Go PGA
 Statistics..............Go PGA
Golf (SIG):..........Go HOM-129
Gomoku game:..........Go GAM-22
Good Earth (SIG):....Go HOM-145
Grain prices:.........Go HCI-10
Grains futures:.......Go CNS-12
Grolier's Encyclopedia:..Go AAE
Ground water:............Go WWA
Hammurabi game:.......Go GAM-37
HamNet (SIG):.........Go HOM-11
Handicapped, deaf:.......Go CSD
Health and fitness:....Go GPO-5
Heath User's Group:...Go PCS-48
Heathkit Catalog:........Go HTH
Heinold Commodities:.....Go HCI
Help:................Go CIS-162
Help (documentation):..Go CIS-8
Hi-Tech Forum:.......Go CCC-150
High tech news:..........Go ALT
Hollywood Hotline:.......Go HHL
Home banking:.........Go HOM-45
Home finance:.........Go HOM-80
Home services:...........Go HOM
Home management programs:
 Amortize a loan......Go HOM-17
 Calculate a raise....Go HOM-15
 Checkbook balancer...Go HOM-14
 Net worth............Go HOM-16
Horticulture:....Go SFP-10, VIC
House plants:............Go VIC
Howard Sams' Books:......Go SAM
Human Sexuality:.........Go HSX
Humor, satire:...........Go KCS
Huntington, bank:........Go HNB
Husbandry:............Go SFP-10
IBM-PC (SIG):........Go PCS-131
IDS:.....................Go IDS
IRA:.................Go IDS-567
Immigration:........Go Pan, ESC
Incorporating Guide:.....Go INC
Index:
 AAMSI journals..........Go AAM
 CompuServe..............Go IND
 Computer Periodical.....Go PER
 Stock Market..........Go FIN-4
Industries, farming:..Go SFP-10
Information, music:......Go MUS
Information on Demand:...Go IOD
Information Retrieval Ser:G IFT
Insurance:
 Dental..............Go IDS-283
 Disability..........Go IDS-277
 Employee Benefits...Go IDS-257
 Health..............Go IDS-269
 Life......Go IDS-587, 192, 260
 Miscellaneous.......Go IDS-286
Insurance, aircraft:.....Go AVL
Intelligence test:....Go TMC-28
Interest rate:...........Go MMS
Investment news:......Go FIN-10
Investments:
 Diamond.................Go RDC
 MicroQuote...........Go FIN-20
 Quick Quote..........Go FIN-20
 Tickerscreen............Go TKR
Investors Diversified:...Go IDS
Job, in the home:....Go HOM-146
Jobs:
 StL Post-Dispatch..Go SPD-1002
Jumbled words test:...Go TMC-43
Kesmai:...............Go GAM-46
Kitbuilding:.............Go HTH
LSI (SIG):............Go PCS-49
Languages on CompuServe:
 Bliss................Go PCS-74
 Cross Assemblers.....Go PCS-75
 Fortran..............Go PCS-80
 Macro................Go PCS-76
 Pascal...............Go PCS-77
 Snobol...............Go PCS-79
```

Figure 4-1. CompuServe Consumer Information Service index (continued)

```
Legal:
  Forum................Go SFP-40
  Incorporating Services..Go INC
Library, electronic:.....Go AAE
Lineprinter art:.....Go HOM-101
Liquid Green:............Go UMC
Literary (SIG):......Go HOM-136
Livestock futures:....Go CNS-12
Livestock prices:.....Go HCI-10
MMS Financial Analysis:..Go MMS
MNET-11 (SIG):.........Go PCS-53
Macro:.................Go PCS-76
Macroeconomics:..........Go MMS
Magazine, advertisers:...Go EBB
Magic Cube solution:..Go GAM-35
Mainstreaming:...........Go CSD
Maintenance equip:...Go MIN-100
Manuals, documentation:Go CIS-8
Manufacturer's newsletters:
  Commodore...............Go CBM
  RCA.....................Go RCA
  Tandy...................Go TRS
Maps, road travel:.......Go TRV
Marine weather:..........Go WEA
Market prices:........Go FIN-20
Market research:.........Go IOD
Massachusetts, banking:..Go SHW
Max Ule's Tickerscreen:..Go TKR
Medical:
  AAMSI Forum...........Go SFP-5
  ASCMD Forum...........Go SFP-7
  FOI Newsline............Go FOI
Medical newsletter:......Go AAM
Metal futures prices:.Go CNS-12
Metal prices:.........Go HCI-10
Microcomputers:
  General..............Go PCS-10
  RCA.....................Go RCA
  Tandy...................Go TRS
MicroQuote:...........Go FIN-20
Microsoft (SIG):.....Go PCS-145
Mine-Equip:..........Go MIN-100
Money market:............Go UMC
Monthly charges:.....Go CIS-176
Mortgage budgeting:....Go GPO-4
Movie reviews:
  CompuServe............Go NMM-1
  Hollywood Hotline.......Go HHL
  SHO-TIME Catalog........Go MOV
Multiple Choice, the:....Go TMC
Multi-Player Game SIG:G GAM-300
Music:...................Go MUS
Music Forum:.........Go HOM-150
Music Info. Service:.....Go MUS
Musus-Pascal (SIG):...Go PCS-55
Mutual Funds:Go IDS-245, PCS-55
NASA:................Go HOM-127
NIPSIG:..............Go HOM-132
NOAA weather:....Go WEA, Go AWX
NTSB cases (aviation):...Go AVR
NWS aviation weather:....Go AWX
NYSE prices (MQUOTE):.Go FIN-20
Names of users:........Go HOM-4
Nat'l Issues (SIG):..Go HOM-132
National Water Well Ass:.Go WWA
National Weather Service:Go AWX
Netwits:.................Go WIT
Netwits (SIG):.......Go WIT-100
New Issues(securities):G TKR-40
New product news:
  Popular Science.........Go PSP
New services:............Go NEW
New York Fashion Report:.Go GAN
News, CB:................Go CUP
Newsletters:
  AAMSI Communications....Go AAM
  Altertext...............Go ALT
  Commodore...............Go CBM
  RCA.....................Go RCA
  Tandy...................Go TRS
Newspapers:...........Go HOM-10
Node locations:.......Go CVP-66
No. American weather:.Go CNS-17
Notices (Bullet):.....Go HOM-23
Nutritional analysis:Go GPO-401
OK level:.............Go PCS-71
OTC prices (MQUOTE):..Go FIN-20
Office supplies:.........Go SAV
Official Airline Guide:..Go OAG
Ohio, banking:...........Go HNB
Ohio Scientific(SIG):Go PCS-125
Options, stock:........Go FIN-4
Orch-90 archives:........Go ORC
Orch-90 music (SIG):..Go HOM-13
PGA Official Tour Guide:.Go PGA
PUG (Panasonic SIG):.Go PCS-114
Pan Am:..................Go PAN
Panasonic (SIG):.....Go PCS-114
Parenting & Family Life:.Go PFL
Pascal (SIG):.........Go PCS-55
Password, changes:...Go CIS-175
Peak Delay Guide:........Go PDG
Pensions:................Go INC
Periodical Guide:........Go PER
Personal computing:......Go PCS
Personal development:....Go AES
Personal finance:
  Alternative Education...Go AES
  Gov't publications....Go GPO-4
  Home Management.......Go HOM-80
  Investors Diversified.Go IDS-6
Personality profile:..Go TMC-17
Pets:.................Go SFP-37
Pilot weather:...........Go AWX
Plants:..................Go VIC
Politics:
  AP Videotex Wire........Go APV
  Washington Post......Go TWP-15
Popular Science Magazine:
  Automotive News.........Go PSC
  New products............Go PSP
  Science & Technology....Go PSE
  Software reviews........Go PSP
Pork prices:..........Go CNS-12
Portfolio valuation:...Go FIN-4
PowerSoft's XTRA-80:..Go PCS-56
Precious metals:......Go CNS-12
Precious metals news:.Go CNS-15
Prescriptions:.......Go GPO-399
Prime interest rate:.....Go HNB
Primetime Radio Classics:Go PRC
Professional:
  Agribusiness database...Go IFT
  Eng/Technical database..Go IFT
```

Figure 4-1. CompuServe Consumer Information Service index (continued)

```
 Environmental database..Go IFT
Programmer's (SIG):..Go PCS-158
Programming area:.....Go PCS-71
Programming languages:Go PCS-72
Programs from users:..Go PCS-46
Programs for sale:....Go PCS-45
Programs, medical:.......Go AAM
Public access:........Go PCS-46
Quick Quote:..........Go FIN-20
RCA Newsletter:..........Go RCA
RCA (SIG):............Go PCS-57
Radio:
 Amateur..............Go HOM-11
 Old radio shows.........Go PRC
Radio Shack computers:...Go TRS
Rainbo's Reviews:........Go WIT
Rates, CompuServe:....Go CIS-53
Real estate, ads:
 StL Post-Dispatch..Go SPD-1002
Recipes (SIG):.......Go HOM-109
Recordkeeping, home:.Go GPO-228
Reference guide:.........Go AAE
Referral Service, law:Go SFP-40
Regulatory Affairs Prof:.Go FOI
Reservations, airline:
 Firstworld Travel.......Go TVL
Resource, water:.........Go WWA
Retirement:..............Go INC
Reviews, games:..........Go GSA
Reviews, software:
 Popular Science.....Go PSP-101
SAT test information:.Go TCB-18
SIGS:
 AAMSI.................Go SFP-5
 Arcade..............Go HOM-138
 ASCMD.................Go SFP-7
 Ask Mr. Fed..........Go MMS-20
 Atari...............Go PCS-132
 Author's............Go PCS-117
 AVSIG.................Go SFP-6
 CBIG..................Go HOM-9
 CEMSIG..............Go CEM-450
 Commodore...........Go PCS-160
 Commodore Pet.......Go PCS-116
 Commodore 64........Go PCS-156
 Commodore VIC 20....Go PCS-155
 Communications.......Go SFP-35
 Computer Art........Go PCS-157
 Cooks' Underground..Go HOM-109
 CP/M Group...........Go PCS-47
 Educational Research.Go HOM-28
 Educators'..........Go HOM-137
 Entertainment........Go HOM-29
 Environmental........Go SFP-38
 Family Matters......Go HOM-144
 FireNet..............Go SFP-36
 Food Buyline........Go HOM-151
 Games (Scorpia).....Go GAM-310
 Golf................Go HOM-129
 Good Earth..........Go HOM-145
 HamNet...............Go HOM-11
 Hi-Tech.............Go CCC-150
 HUG (Heath)..........Go PCS-48
 IBM-PC..............Go PCS-131
 Legal................Go SFP-40
 Literary............Go HOM-136
 LSI Users............Go PCS-49
 MAUG (Apple).........Go PCS-51
 Microsoft...........Go PCS-145
 MNET-11..............Go PCS-53
 MNET80 TRS-80........Go PCS-54
 Multi-Player Games..Go GAM-300
 Music...............Go HOM-150
 MUSUS=Pascal.........Go PCS-55
 Netwits.............Go WIT-100
 NIPSIG..............Go HOM-132
 ORCH-90..............Go HOM-13
 OSI.................Go PCS-125
 PowerSoft's XTRA-80..Go PCS-56
 Programmer's........Go PCS-158
 PUG (Panasonic).....Go PCS-114
 RCA Group............Go PCS-57
 Space...............Go HOM-127
 Sports..............Go HOM-110
 TeleComm.............Go PCS-52
 Travel..............Go HOM-157
 TRS-80 color........Go PCS-126
 TRS-80 Model 100....Go PCS-154
 Veterinarians........Go SFP-37
 Work-at-Home........Go HOM-146
St. Louis Post-Dispatch:.Go SPD
Sams, Howard Books:......Go SAM
Satire:..................Go KCS
Saving Accounts:......Go HOM-45
Saving-Scan:.............Go SAV
Scott Adams' games:...Go GAM-28
Scramble game:........Go GAM-43
Self-employment:.........Go SBR
Services for the Deaf:...Go CSD
Shawmut, bank:...........Go SHW
Shop-at-home:.........Go HOM-40
Shopping:
 Cars....................Go ATO
 Fifth Avenue Shopper....Go FTH
 Musical.................Go MUS
 Radio shows.............Go PRC
 Saving-Scan.............Go SAV
SHO-TIME Movie Catalog:..Go MOV
Shuttle, space:......Go HOM-127
Silly Fill-Ins:.......Go TMC-41
Silver futures prices:Go CNS-12
Silver news:..........Go CNS-15
Ski conditions:..........Go WEA
Small business reports:..Go SBR
Smoking and health:..Go GPO-398
Snobol:...............Go PCS-79
Soaps, television:.......Go HHL
SOFTEX:...............Go PCS-45
Software Authors' SIG:Go PCS117
Software Exchange:....Go PCS-40
Software reviews:
 Popular Science.....Go PSP-101
So. American weather:.Go CNS-17
Space (SIG):.........Go HOM-127
Special Interest Groups:
 Access to.Go HOM-50, Go PCS-50
 Commercial...........Go PCS-50
 Descriptions.Go HOM-50, PCS-50
 General..............Go HOM-50
 Hardware related.....Go PCS-50
 Instructions.Go HOM-51, PCS-58
 Software related.....Go PCS-50
Sport, clothes:..........Go HAN
```

Figure 4-1. CompuServe Consumer Information Service index (continued)

```
Sports news:
 Golf....................Go PGA
 StL Post-Dispatch..Go SPD-1005
Sports (SIG):........Go HOM-110
Sports quiz:..........Go TMC-42
Spotlight, CBers:........Go CUP
Standard & Poors:.....Go FIN-20
Star Trek game:.......Go GAM-26
State capital games:..Go TMC-44
Stereos for sale:........Go CUS
Stevens Business Reports:Go SBR
Stocks, bonds:
 MicroQuote...........Go FIN-20
 Quick Quote..........Go FIN-20
 Tickerscreen.........Go TKR-10
Sugar futures prices:.Go CNS-12
Supplier, athlete's:.....Go HAN
TMC for kids!:........Go TMC-27
TRS-80 color (SIG):..Go PCS-126
TRS-80 computers:........Go TRS
TRS-80 MNET80 (SIG):..Go PCS-54
TRS-80 Model 100(SIG):G PCS-154
TRS-80, programs for:.Go PCS-45
TV soap opera summaries:.Go HHL
Tandy Corp. news:........Go TRS
Technical books:.........Go SAM
Technical research:......Go IOD
TeleComm (SIG):.......Go PCS-52
Telephone access:....Go CIS-177
Tennessee, banking:..Go HOM-141
Terminal parameters:...Go CIS-6
Terminal software:...Go PCS-103
Terminal types:........Go CIS-6
Tests, children:......Go TMC-27
Tests, interactive:....Go TMC-4
Tests, SAT:...........Go TCB-18
Text editors:.........Go PCS-82
The College Board:
 Adult education......Go TCB-13
 Choosing a college...Go TCB-17
 Financial aid........Go TCB-12
 Publications of......Go TCB-15
 SAT test information.Go TCB-18
The National Satirist:...Go KCS
Tickerscreen:............Go TKR
Time used:..........Go CIS-176
TODAY, advertisers:......Go EBB
Trading, commodities:.Go FIN-10
Travel:
 Department of State.....Go DOS
 Firstworld Travel Club..Go TVL
 Official Airline Guide..Go OAG
 Pan Am..................Go PAN
 Travel Fax..............Go ESC
 TravelVision............Go TRV
 Worldwide Exchanges.....Go WWX
Travel, abroad:
 Department of State.....Go DOS
 Firstworld Travel Club..Go TVL
 Official Airline Guide..Go OAG
 Pan Am..................Go PAN
 Travel Fax..............Go ESC
Travel, advisories:......Go DOS
Travel, airline guide:...Go OAG
Travel Fax:..............Go ESC
Travel (SIG):........Go HOM-157
Traveler, airport guide:.Go PDG
TravelVision:............Go TRV
Treasury bills,yields:.Go FIN-4
Trivia:
 Kids.................Go TMC-45
 Movie...................Go HHL
 Radio...................Go PRC
 Unlimited test.......Go TMC-16
Tutorials:
 Edutech.................Go CAI
 Personal Computing..Go PCS-121
UCSD Pascal Group:....Go PCS-55
USDA Grades:..........Go GPO-10
USDA standards:
 Meat...............Go GPO-1340
 Poultry............Go GPO-1405
U.S. Depart. of State:...Go DOS
U.S. News:
 StL Post-Dispatch..Go SPD-1005
 Washington Post.........Go TWP
United American Bank:Go HOM-152
Used cars, buying:..Go GPO-1199
User directory:........Go HOM-4
User information:......Go CIS-4
User's programs:......Go PCS-30
VIC-20 (SIG):........Go PCS-116
Vacationing:.............Go WWX
Value Line Database:..Go FIN-20
Vegetables:..............Go VIC
Veterinarians Forum:..Go SFP-37
Victory Garden:..........Go VIC
Video information:.......Go VIF
Videotex, views on:..Go CVP-154
VIDTEX executive:....Go PCS-103
Viewpoint, CompuServe:.Go CVP-5
Want ads (Bullet):....Go HOM-23
War games:
 Decwars..............Go GAM-19
 Megawars.............Go GAM-20
 Space War............Go GAM-25
Washington, D.C. area:
 StL Post-Dispatch..Go SPD-1005
 Washington Post......Go TWP-12
Washington Post:.........Go TWP
Water, ground:...........Go WWA
WaterLine:...............Go WWA
Weather:
 AP Videotex Wire........Go APV
 African weather......Go CNS-17
 Asian weather........Go CNS-17
 Aviation weather........Go AWX
 European weather.....Go CNS-17
 Extended forecasts......Go WEA
 N. American weather..Go CNS-17
 S. American weather..Go CNS-17
 Sports forecasts........Go WEA
 State forecasts.........Go WEA
What's New:..............Go NEW
Wheat prices:.........Go CNS-12
Wine guide:..............Go VIN
Wire service news:
 (see Associated Press access)
Word processors:......Go PCS-86
Work-at-Home (SIG):..Go HOM-146
World news:
 AP Videotex Wire........Go APV
 Associated Press.....Go IND-52
 Washington Post......Go TWP-16
```

Figure 4-1. CompuServe Consumer Information Service index (continued)

```
Worldwide Exchanges:.....Go WWX
Yachts:..................Go WWX
-------------------------------
 ASSOCIATED PRESS NEWS ACCESS
-------------------------------
Financial wire:
 St. Louis Post..........Go SPD
 Washington Post.........Go TWP
Sports:
 St. Louis Post..........Go SPD
 Washington Post.........Go TWP
U.S. News:
 St. Louis Post..........Go SPD
 Washington Post.........Go TWP
Washington News:
 St. Louis Post..........Go SPD
 Washington Post.........Go TWP
World News:
 St. Louis Post..........Go SPD
 Washington Post.........Go TWP
-------------------------------
 Quick Access to Page Numbers
A......Page  4  M......Page  42
B......Page 10  N......Page  46
C......Page 14  O......Page  48
D......Page 21  P......Page  49
E......Page 22  R......Page  56
F......Page 26  S......Page  58
G......Page 30  T......Page  68
H......Page 35  U......Page  73
I......Page 38  V......Page  74
L......Page 41  W......Page  75
```

Figure 4-1. CompuServe Consumer Information Service index (continued)

```
******************************
            INDEX
------------------------------
 EXECUTIVE INFORMATION SERVICE
------------------------------
AAMSI
  SIGS                       PF-30
AAMSI Communications
  Newsletters                AAM
AAMSI Forum
  Medical                    PF-30
AAMSI, medical journals
  Book, reviews              AAM
AP Viewdata Wire
  Business Information       APV
AP Viewdata Wire
  Entertainment              APV
AP Viewdata Wire
  Weather                    APV
AP Viewdata Wire
  Politics                   APV
AP Viewdata Wire
  World news                 APV
ASCMD
  SIGS                       PF-30
ASCMD Forum
  Medical                    PF-30
ASI Monitor
  Aviation                   ASI-10
AVSIG
  SIGS                       PF-10
Air travel delays            PDG
Aircraft                     ASI
Aircraft insurance           AVL
Airline guide                OAG
Airport delay guide          PDG
Annual reports               IQ
Apple, programs for          SHO
Appliances for sale          CUS
Assoc. Viewdata Wire         APV
Associated Press
  World news                 IND-52
Associated Press News
  Federal gov't news         APN-5
Attorneys                    PF-20
Aviation (SIG)               PF-10
Aviation Rules & Reg         AVR
Aviation Safety Inst         ASI
Aviation weather             AWX
Aviation weather
  Weather                    AWX
Banking, electronic          BAN
Baseball (AP wire)           APN-16
Billing, general             GUI
Billing, reviewing           GUI
Boston, Shawmut Bank         SHW
Brokerage                    BRO
Bulletin board               NBB
Business news
  Canadian                   BIW
Business wire
  Business Information       TBW
CP/M Group
  SIGS                       PF
CP/M user's group            PF
Cameras for sale             CUS
Canadian, U.S., Int'l
  Business Information       BIW
Central Trade Bank           BAN
Central Trade Bank
  Banks                      BAN
Changing password            GUI
Changing terminal type       GUI
Charges, monthly             GUI
```

Figure 4-2. Executive Information Service index

Topic	Code
Checking, banking	BAN
Commodities glossary	HCI-230
Comp-U-Store	CUS
CompuServe	
Index	IND
CompuServe	
Business Information	NWS
Consumer items for sale	CUS
Corporate news release	TBW
Currency exchange	
Canadian	BIW
Current rates	GUI
DEFALTS, setting	GUI
Database searches	IFT
Database, how to use	GUI
Document delivery	IOD
Document retrieval	IFT
Documentation ordering	GUI
Drugs, medicine	GPO-399
EMI Flight Planning	
Aviation	EMI
EMI Flight Plans	EMI
Earnings forecasts	IQ-600
Economic news	NWS
Electronic banking	BAN
Electronic mail	IPX
Electronic shopping	CUS
Expert Investor	
Stocks, bonds	IQ-200
Extended forecasts	
Weather	WEA
FAA reports	ASI-12
FAA rule changes	AVR
FDA	
Food information	FOI
FILGE instructions	CVP-23
FIRSTWORLD Travel Club	TVL
FOI Newsline	FOI
FOI Newsline	
Medical	FOI
Fedwatch newsletter	MMS
Feedback, CompuServe	COM
Financial advice	TWP-12
Financial forecasts	IQ-600
Financial information	IQ
Financial insurance	IDS-5
Financial news (AP)	IND-52
Financial services	IQ
First Tennessee Bank	BAN
First Tennessee Bk	
Banks	BAN
Firstworld Travel	
Reservations, airlin	TVL
Firstworld Travel Club	
Travel	TVL
Firstworld Travel Club	
Air travel	TVL
Food & Drug Admin	FOI
Funds Management	UMC
General banking	BAN
Grain prices	HCI-10
Heinold Commodities	HCI
Help (documentation)	GUI
Hockey (AP wire)	APN-16
Home banking	BAN
Huntington Nat'l Bank	
Banks	HNB
Huntington, bank	HNB
IBM-PC	
SIGS	PF
IBM-PC (SIG)	PF-40
IDS	IDS
Information	
Securities	MMS
Information Retrieval SerG	MMS
Information on Demand	IOD
Investment	
Commentaries	INV
Investment News & Views	INV
Investment news	NWS
Investors Diversified	IDS
Investors Diversified	
Personal finance	IDS-6
Legal	
SIGS	PF
Legal Forum	PF-20
Legal issues	PF-20
Liquid Green	UMC
MMS Financial Analysis	MMS
Manuals, documentation	GUI
Marine weather	WEA
Market prices	IQ
Market research	IOD
Massachusetts, banking	SHW
Medical Records	HRC
Medical newsletter	AAM
Medicine, consumer	HRC
Metal prices	HCI-10
Microsoft	
SIGS	PF
Microsoft (SIG)	PF
Money market	UMC
Money supply	MMS
Monthly charges	GUI
Mutual Funds	IQ
NOAA weather	WEA, AWX
NTSB cases (aviation)	AVR
NWS Aviation Weather	
Aviation	AWX
NWS aviation weather	AWX
NYSE prices	IQ-300
Names of users	COM
National Weather Service	AWX
New services	NEW
Newspapers	NWS
Node locations	CVP-66
Notices	NBB
Notices (Bullet)	NBB
OTC drugs	HRC
OTC prices	IQ-300
Official Airline Guide	
Air travel	OAG
Official Airline Guide	
Travel, abroad	OAG
Official Airline Guide	OAG
Official Airline Guide	
Travel	OAG
Official Airline Guide	
Aviation	OAG
Ohio regional news	APN-5
Ohio, banking	HNB
Options, stock	IQ
Peak Delay Guide	
Aviation	PDG

Figure 4-2. Executive Information Service index (continued)

Peak Delay Guide	PDG
Pilot weather	AWX
Portfolio valuation	IQ
Prime interest rate	HNB
Programs for sale	SHO-20
Programs, medical	AAM
Quick Quote	
Stocks, bonds	IQ-300
Rates, CompuServe	GUI
Reference guide	AAE
Referral Service, law	PF-20
SOFTEX	SHO
Saving Accounts	BAN
Scores (AP)	
Sports news	APN-16
Shawmut Bank of Boston	
Banks	SHW
Shawmut, bank	SHW
Shop-at-home	SHO
Small business reports	SBR
Software Exchange	SHO
Sports forecasts	
Weather	WEA
Standard & Poors	IQ-500
State forecasts	
Weather	WEA
Stereos for sale	CUS
Stevens Business Reports	SBR
Stock Market	
Index	IQ
Stocks	
Canadian	IQ
Technical research	IOD
Telephone access	GUI
Tennessee, banking	BAN
Time used	GUI
Trading, commodities	BRO
Travel, airline guide	OAG
Traveler, airport guide	PDG
Treasury bills,yields	IQ
User directory	COM
User information	GUI
Value Line Database	IQ-500
Want ads	NBB
Want ads (Bullet)	NBB
Washington Post	TWP
Washington Post	
Business Information	TWP-12
Washington Post	
U.S. News	TWP
Washington Post	
Editorials	TWP-17
Washington Post	
Federal gov't news	TWP
Washington Post	
World news	TWP-16
Washington Post	
Politics	TWP-15
Washington Post	
Washington, D.C. are	TWP-12
What's New	NEW

Figure 4-2. Executive Information Service index (continued)

CIS has many more features than EIS, but EIS does have a few communications and financial decision-making features not included in CIS. All of the investment and stock quote services are the same, even though the codes used to access the information are different. This section highlights a few of CompuServe's services, indicating whether a particular service is unique to EIS. Look ahead to the "Stock and Company Information" section and the "Electronic Mail" section for CompuServe's offerings in those areas.

News CompuServe offers Associated Press (AP) news. It's almost like having an AP teletype on your desk; you get just what comes over the wire. You select stories from the menu, as in the following example:

```
Associated Press News Highlights

1 Latest News-     7 Entertainment
  Update Hourly
2 Weather          8 Business News
3 National         9 Wall Street
4 Washington      10 Dow Jones Avg
5 World           11 Feature News
6 Political       12 History
Key <ENTER> for Sports
!5
```

```
1 Walesa Urges Polish Dialogue
2 Pope Asks Lutherans for Unity
3 Beirut Refugees: Daily Terror
4 Protests Continue in Germany
5 Pope to Visit Lutheran Church
6 Poles 'Will Not Be Crushed'
7 Egypt Criticizes Aid Program
8 Islamic Ministers End Meeting
9 New President for Bangladesh
0 Salvador Fighting Said Heavy
Input a number or key
```

The actual stories are the same ones that you'd see in the newspaper. Newspapers, however, exclude some stories and shorten others. The *Washington Post* and the *St. Louis Dispatch* are included on CompuServe. Here are a few menus from the *Post*:

```
Washington Post          Page TWP-1

1 News Summary & Calendars
2 The Administration
3 Congress
4 Business & Economy
5 Science & Technology
6 The Courts & The Law
7 Politics
8 World & Nation
9 Editorials & Commentaries
10 Associated Press News

!9

1 Editorial News Digest
2 Happy New Year From OPEC
3 Remembering KAL 007
4 Insanity: Opinions
5 Mann on Shopping Days
6 Geyelin on Hussein
7 Rosenfeld on Reagan's Way

!7

By Stephen S. Rosenfeld
   There is a paradox in Ronald
Reagan's approach to national
security..........
```

Stock and company information Comprehensive stock and company reports are available on both EIS and CIS. Appendix C contains a comparison of the financial services available on CompuServe, The Source, and the Dow Jones News/Retrieval Service.

Weather Up-to-date forecasts are available from the U.S. Weather Service.

You can also get state forecasts and specialized forecasts. For example:

```
WEATHER              Page WX-3
 1 State Forecasts
 2 Extended Forecasts
 3 Forecast Explanation
 4 Probability of Precip.
 5 Marine Forecasts
 6 Sports Forecasts
 8 Weather Warnings
12 Aviation Weather Menu

Selection: 1

STATE FCSTS

ID: wa

SEA 111000
 STATE FORECAST FOR WASHINGTON
 NATIONAL WEATHER SERVICE SEATTLE WA
 210 AM PST SUN DEC 11 1983

 WESTERN WASHINGTON
 PERIODS OF SHOWERS AND PARTIAL CLEARING TODAY AND TONIGHT.  DECREASING
 SHOWERS AND LOCAL FOG EARLY MONDAY.  SHOWERS INCREASING AGAIN MONDAY
 AFTERNOON. HIGHS 45 TO 50.  LOWS 35 TO 40.
```

Here's a part of the ski report for Salt Lake City:

```
SNOW DEPTHS AND NEW SNOW AT UTAH SKI AREAS AS OF 6 AM SUN DEC 11 1983
      AREA        SNOW DEPTH   NEW SNOW    REMARKS
ALTA                  95           4
BEAVER MOUNTAIN       89           3
BRIAN HEAD            45           0
BRIGHTON              90           1
MT. HOLLY             MM          MM
NORDIC VALLEY         54           0
PARK CITY             90           8
PARK WEST             76           3
POWDER MOUNTAIN      120           0
SNOW BASIN            94           2
SNOWBIRD              81           5
SOLITUDE              83           7
SUNDANCE              87           0
```

American Academic Encyclopedia You can access the entire *American Academic Encyclopedia* for an extra $5 per hour. You enter a keyword, and Grolier takes it from there. For example:

```
            Welcome to
   GROLIER'S ACADEMIC AMERICAN
          Encyclopedia

Search term: africa
Grolier                     Search
```

```
AFRICA
11 articles selected
1 Africa
2 Africa, history of
3 African archaeology:
4 African art
5 African hunting dog
6 African languages
7 African literature
8 African music
!5

African hunting dog
--------------------------------
The African hunting dog, Lycaon
pictus, is a wild CARNIVORE in
the DOG family, Canidae, order
Carnivora. It may be 104 cm (41
in) long and weigh 23 kg (50
lb). Sparse, mottled hair.......
```

The information is just what you'd expect from an encyclopedia, except that it doesn't include pictures. However, don't expect the information to be any more up-to-date than it is in the printed edition.

Special interest groups (SIGs) The CompuServe special-interest groups (SIGs) serve as high-capacity national computer bulletin boards (CBBs). IBM PC owners will be particularly interested in the IBM PC SIG. Here are the sections of the IBM PC SIG and a scan of a few messages:

```
0 - General Information
1 - User Updates/Fixes
2 - Product Reviews
3 - Standards
4 - Programming
5 - Communications
6 - Software Library
7 - Fun & Games
8 - Ask the SysOps

22270:  HAYES 1200B                  Sec. 5 - Communications
22272:  vertical placement of pc     Sec. 0 - General Information
22273:  #22140-applic.gen.           Sec. 2 - Product Reviews
22275:  Rbase / Kman                 Sec. 2 - Product Reviews
```

You can scan, read, and leave messages in the various sections of the SIG. Other SIG members can reply publicly to your message. Usually there is a long thread of notes on a particular subject. Reading through that thread will inform you of everyone's opinion on a new product or service. If you have a problem with your PC, a program, or CompuServe, leave a message. Someone is sure to get back with an answer, usually within minutes. If anyone leaves you a message, you will get it the next time you enter the SIG.

Demographic information (EIS only) You can get the latest census information (number of households, income, number of families, growth rate, racial and age breakdowns, and so forth) in any geographical area you specify. Area is specified by ZIP code, county, state, or the United States as a whole. This service is expensive, but you can get an estimate before you begin.

Official Airline Guide This is the same service the travel agents use. There is a $21-$32 hourly premium charge, but look at what you get:

```
ENTER DEPARTURE CITY NAME OR CODE
   SEA

ENTER DESTINATION CITY NAME OR CODE
   PHILADELPHIA

ENTER DEPARTURE DATE
OR PRESS RETURN KEY TO USE 27 NOV
   28NOV

ENTER DEPARTURE TIME
OR PRESS RETURN TO USE 600AM


          DIRECT FLIGHTS      MON-28 NOV
FROM-SEATTLE;TACOMA,WA,USA
# TO-PHILADELPHIA,PA;WILMINGTON,DE,USA
 NO EARLIER DIRECT FLIGHT SERVICE
1 1026A  SEA  755P  PHL UA 144 D10 L 1
2 1115A  SEA  815P  PHL NW   8  *  L 1
NW   8 747-MSP-D10
3 1233P  SEA  954P  PHL UA 494 D8S L 1
 NO LATER DIRECT FLIGHT SERVICE
PRESS RETURN KEY FOR CONNECTIONS
ENTER CX,X#,F#,RS       (#=LINE NUMBER)


           CONNECTIONS        MON-28 NOV
FROM-SEATTLE;TACOMA,WA,USA
# TO-PHILADELPHIA,PA;WILMINGTON,DE,USA
1   700A  SEA 1025A  DEN UA 160 D10 B 0
  1123A  DEN  443P  PHL UA 694 767 L 0
2   710A  SEA 1245P  STL TW 560 L10 B 0
   137P  STL  437P  PHL TW 756 72S S 0
3   745A  SEA  125P  ORD UA 140 D10 B 0
   240P  ORD  532P  PHL UA 100 D10 S 0
ENTER +,-,DF,X#,F#,RS   (#=LINE NUMBER)
   ?ORD


    *RESPONSE TO YOUR HELP REQUEST*
ORD=     CHICAGO,IL,USA/OHARE

   X1

  EXPANDED CONNECTION DISPLAY (1 OF 2)
LEAVE-  7:00A    ON-28 NOV
FROM-SEATTLE;TACOMA,WA,USA
UNITED AIRLINES FLIGHT 160
AIRCRAFT-MCDONNELL DOUGLAS DC10-ALL SER
CLASS-FIRST/COACH/ECONOMY
MEAL-BREAKFAST
```

```
ARRIVE-10:25A
AT-DENVER,CO,USA

ENTER + FOR SECOND FLIGHT INFORMATION
  F1

FARES IN US DOLLARS              MON-28 NOV
SELECTED FOR SEA-UA 160 DEN-UA 694-PHL

#   ONE-WAY  RND-TRP ARLN/CLASS FARECODE
 NO LOWER FARES IN CATEGORY
1*             349.00 UA/B-UA/B  BXE730
2*             399.00 UA/B-UA/B  BWE730
3*             460.00 UA/B-UA/B  BE70
4   345.00            UA/Y-UA/Y  Y
5   414.00            UA/F-UA/F  F
 NO HIGHER FARES IN CATEGORY
 * ENTER L# TO VIEW LIMITATIONS
ENTER L#,X#,S,RS          (#=LINE NUMBER)
  L1

LIMITATIONS DISPLAY              MON-28 NOV
SEA-PHL    UA/B-UA/B  FARECODE:BXE730
UNITED AIRLINES
FARE DESCRIPTION: ADVANCE PURCHASE
 EXCURSION FARES
BOOKING CODE: B.

FARE IS ONLY AVAILABLE FOR TRAVEL FROM
 TUE THRU WED.

MINIMUM STAY REQUIRED IS 7 DAYS.
PRESS RETURN TO VIEW MORE LIMITATIONS
ENTER F TO RETURN TO FARE DISPLAY
ENTER S TO RETURN TO SCHEDULE DISPLAY


LIMITATIONS CONTINUED            MON-28 NOV
SEA-PHL    UA/B-UA/B  FARECODE:BXE730
UNITED AIRLINES
MAXIMUM STAY ALLOWED IS 30 DAYS.

PURCHASE TICKET FOR TRAVEL NO LATER
 THAN 14 DAYS BEFORE DEPARTURE.
 * END OF LIMITATIONS DISPLAY *
```

Notice that it lists the flights for a particular day and time range and all the fares. This service will be cost-effective once airlines and travel agents give discounts to travelers booking their own flights by computer. This is bound to happen, but until then, you are better off letting a travel agent pay for the computer time.

Using CompuServe

EIS provides a typeset and index-tabbed manual for the EIS business services. If you subscribe to CIS, you get a looseleaf manual that you can supplement with on-line instructions you download from the service. Make sure you download an up-to-date copy of the index.

You can access CompuServe with menus, but with so many features, that

Table 4-2. *CompuServe EIS and CIS Hourly Rates*

	Monday—Friday 8:00 A.M.-6:00 P.M.	Monday—Friday 6:00 P.M. to 5:00 A.M. Weekends and holidays
Direct access through CompuServe's network (large cities)		
300 bps	$12.50	$6.00
1200 bps	$15.00	$12.50
Tymnet/Telenet access		
300 bps	$22.50	$8.00
1200 bps	$25.00	$14.50

becomes tedious quickly. Each time you see an exclamation point (!) at the bottom of the screen, you can type one of the menu choices or GO XXX, where XXX is the code in the index (see Figures 4-1 and 4-2). Sometimes there are delays as you're shunted to the right computer.

Costs

The CompuServe CIS sign-up kit costs $39.95 and includes a looseleaf manual and five hours of connect time. You may be able to get this free with a modem purchase. An EIS subscription costs $139.95 and includes CIS access, a typeset manual, two hours of connect time, and the *VIDTEX* program described in Chapter 6.

Connect charges for both EIS and CIS are shown in Table 4-2.

Dow Jones News/Retrieval Service

The Dow Jones News/Retrieval Service started in 1974 as a stockbrokers' information service, but now it has over 100,000 subscribers and predicts 250,000 by the end of 1984. By far the largest of the information utilities, it's growing fast because of gateways from other services. MCI Mail subscribers can access Dow Jones information as though they were Dow Jones subscribers.

Here's what the Dow Jones News/Retrieval Service contains:

```
        Dow Jones Business
    and Economic News Services

//DJNEWS   Dow Jones News
//FTS      Free-Text Search
             of Dow Jones News
//UPDATE   Weekly Economic
             Update
//WSJ      Wall Street Journal
             Highlights Online

        Dow Jones Quotes

//CQ       Current Quotes
//DJA      Historical Dow Jones
             Averages
//HQ       Historical Quotes

          Financial and
       Investment Services

//DSCLO    Disclosure II
//EARN     Corporate Earnings
             Estimator
//FORBES   Forbes Directory
//KYODO    Japan Economic Daily
//MEDGEN   Media General
//MMS      Money Market Services
//OAG      Official Airline
             Guide

         General News and
       Information Services

//INTRO    Free Information about
             News/Retrieval
//ENCYC    American Academic Encyclopedia
             from Grolier
//MOVIES   Movie Reviews
//NEWS     World Report
//SPORTS   Sports
//STORE    Comp-U-Store
//SYMBOL   Symbols Directory
//WTHR     Weather
//WSW      Wall Street Week
```

The stock quotes and company-specific investment services are explained in Appendix C. What follows are a few highlights from the remaining services.

Dow Jones News *Barron's* and the *Wall Street Journal* print hundreds of articles relating to specific companies and industries. You could clip articles about your favorite companies and save them in a scrapbook, but that assumes you know in advance which companies to watch. If you have a sudden need for information about a particular company, that foot-high stack of *Wall Street Journal*s in the corner isn't going to be much help. Dow Jones News can help you by retrieving articles from as far back as 90 days. You merely specify the company by stock symbol, or you choose from one of 100-plus categories such as accounting, food and beverages, mining and metals, truck lines, the Federal Reserve Board, bond market news, and bankruptcies.

Free-Text Search This is an extremely powerful method of searching all the Dow Jones publications based on any words, names, dates, or numbers. You can go back as far as June 1979. A 30-page manual teaches you how to use the service; you will need several sessions of practice. Here is a sample session:

```
DJ/NRS   - SEARCH MODE - ENTER QUERY
    1_:       VIDEOTEX                    ← Search for all documents containing the word "videotex"

RESULT         51 DOCUMENTS               ← "1" is the reference number for this query

    2_:       VIDEOTEX AND IBM            ← Now search for all documents containing "videotex" and "ibm"

RESULT         10 DOCUMENTS               ← "2" is the reference number; 10 documents are available

    3_:       ..LIMIT/1 DD WL 831101,831231
                                          ← Search all documents found in "1",
1 DD WL 831101,831231                       choosing those from Nov, Dec, 1983
RESULT           3 DOCUMENTS
                                          ← Print all parts of all documents found
    4_:       ..P 3 ALL/DOC=ALL             in query "3"

              DOCUMENT=       1           ← First document

AN         111205-0229.                                            ← Document ID
HL         BANK OF AMERICA STARTS UP HOME BANKING BY COMPUTER      ← Headline
DD         12/02/83                                                ← Date
SO         WALL STREET JOURNAL (J)                                 ← Source
CO         BAC    ADP    CHL    FNC                                ← Companies
IN         BANKS, THRIFT INSTITUTIONS (BNK)                        ← Industry
           COMPUTERS (EDP)
TX            N.Y. -DJ- BANK OF AMERICA, THE COUNTRY'S BIGGEST     ← Text of article
           COMMERCIAL BANK, ROLLED OUT A HOME-BANKING PROGRAM FOR
           PERSONAL-COMPUTER OWNERS THIS WEEK AND ONE BANK EXECUTIVE
           PREDICTED THE SERVICE WILL HAVE 25,000 SUBSCRIBERS IN
           CALIFORNIA BY THE END OF 1984.........

    4_:       ..P 2 HL,DD/DOC=ALL         ← Print headlines and dates from all
                                            documents in query "2"
              DOCUMENT=       1
HL         BANK OF AMERICA STARTS UP HOME BANKING BY COMPUTER
DD         12/02/83
              DOCUMENT=       2
HL         IBM - VIDEOTEX SYSTEM -2-
DD         06/23/83
              DOCUMENT=       3
HL         IBM ANNOUNCES GRAPHICS, NEW FUNCTIONS FOR VIDEOTEX SYSTEM
DD         06/23/83
              DOCUMENT=       4
HL         GROWTH IN AUTOMATIC TELLER MACHINES MAY BE COMING TO END
DD         06/20/83
              DOCUMENT=       5
HL         AMER EXPRESS UNIT IN VIDEOTEX DATA PACT WITH VIDEODIAL INC
DD         05/04/83

    5_:       JAPAN AND VIDEO$            ← Select all articles about Japan and
                                            with root word video
```

```
RESULT          219 DOCUMENTS           ← Too many
    6_:         ..SET DETAIL=ON         ← Ask to see search details
R4661 * SET-COMMAND HAS BEEN EXECUTED. RETURN TO CONTINUE.
    6_:         JAPAN AND VIDEOD$       ← Narrow the search to root videod
R1    JAPAN                                  6027 DOCUMENTS
R2    VIDEOD$
R3    VIDEODIAL                                 1 DOCUMENT
R4    VIDEODIAL'S                               1 DOCUMENT
R5    VIDEODISC                                70 DOCUMENTS
R6    VIDEODISCS                               27 DOCUMENTS
R7    VIDEODISK                                47 DOCUMENTS
R8    VIDEODISK-PLAYER                          1 DOCUMENT
R9    VIDEODISKS                               20 DOCUMENTS
DJ/NRS    - SEARCH MODE
00009 JAPAN AND VIDEOD$
RESULT          24 DOCUMENTS
```

There are other options in Free-Text Search. You can make a query with adjacent words, word combinations specified in the same sentence or paragraph, and complex logic. Free-Text Search is available weekdays only from 6:00 A.M. to midnight Eastern time. You are transferred through a gateway to the computers of the Bibliographic Retrieval Service (BRS) for this service.

***Wall Street Journal* highlights** You can read headlines and summaries from the *Wall Street Journal's* five most recent editions. Front-page news items, back-page features, market pages, and editorial columns are available in full text form.

Weekly Economic Survey Here are forecasts by economic analysts at 50 leading financial institutions as prepared by Money Market Services, Inc. Figure 4-3

```
              (1) FORECASTS OF THE DOLLAR/STERLING EXCHANGE RATE
PCT.OF            IN TWO WEEKS (XXX) AND THREE MONTHS (:::)
TOT.RESP.         ("X:X" REPRESENTS OVERLAPPING DATA)
  I                                                         MEDIANS:
  I                                                         2 WEEKS = $1.4425
20+                    XXX         XXX                      3 MONTHS =$1.4725
  I                    XXX   XXX   XXX             :::
  I              XXX   XXX   XXX   XXX             :::
  I              XXX   XXX   XXX   XXX   :::       :::
  I        :::   XXX   XXX   XXX   XXX   X:X   :::   :::         :::
10+        :::   XXX   XXX   XXX   XXX   X:X   :::   :::         :::
  I        X:X   XXX   XXX   X:X   XXX   X:X   :::   :::   :::   :::
  I  :::   X:X   XXX   XXX   X:X   X:X   X:X   :::   :::   :::   :::
  I  :::   X:X   XXX   XXX   X:X   X:X   X:X   X:X   :::   :::   :::
  I  :::   X:X   X:X   X:X   X:X   X:X   X:X   X:X   :::   :::   :::
 0+-----+-----+-----+-----+-----+-----+-----+-----+-----+-----+-----+-->
  LESS  1.41  1.42  1.43  1.44  1.45  1.46  1.47  1.48  1.49  1.50  MORE
```

Figure 4-3. Economic forecast from Money Market Services, Inc.

is a sample forecast. As discussed in Chapter 7, you can use a communications program to save forecasts on disk for inclusion in your word-processed memos or reports.

Forbes directory The top 500 U.S. corporations are ranked by sales, profits, assets, and market value. Find out where your company fits in.

General news and sports You select stories from menus as you do with other information utilities. There's no keyword searching. Here's a sports example:

```
 DOW JONES NEWS/RETRIEVAL SPORTS REPORT
    FRONT PAGE AT 1:05 A.M. MONDAY
               FROM UPI

1  Redskins Overpower Cowboys 31-10
     *** NFL Special Report ***
2  Larry Holmes Resigns WBC Title
     Rather Than Fight Greg Page
3  U.S. Earns Golf's World Cup;
     Canada, Australia Take Second
4  Andreychuk Keys Sabres' NHL Win;
     Soviets Even Series With U.S.
5  Sunday's National Scoreboard
---------------------------------------

12/12/83                   PAGE 1 OF 4
          STATS AND STANDINGS

 1    College Football Bowl Matchups:
        Dates, Rankings, Records
 2    Bowl Team Comparisons:
        Opponents In Dec. 10-23 Games
 3    NCAA Playoffs: Schedules
        For Divisions I-AA, II And III
 4    NAIA Playoffs: Schedules
        For Divisions I, II
 5    UPI College Football Top 20
        At End Of Regular Season

SPORTS 12/12/83            PAGE  1 OF  3

   Sunday's National Scoreboard

                 ---
         National Football League
     Seattle 17, New York Giants 12
     Chicago 19, Minnesota 13
     Houston 34, Cleveland 27
     San Francisco 23, Buffalo 10
     Cincinnati 17, Detroit 9
     Washington 31, Dallas 10
        ........
```

Using Dow Jones News/Retrieval Service

The Dow Jones News/Retrieval Service doesn't pretend to be menu-driven. When you type the // commands to begin using the service, the computer asks you for further information. If you want a stock quote, just enter the Current

Quotes service by typing //CQ. You can then start entering stock symbols. Generally, Dow Jones tries to interpret your input as a stock symbol, so you can type IBM as soon as you log on. If IBM doesn't work, try /IBM.

There are a few annoyances. Dow Jones doesn't interpret backspaces; if you make a mistake, you must leave the current line as is and retype your entry on a new line. There are no prompts at the end of each page; you must press the ENTER key when the screen stops scrolling. If you need to interrupt the flow of text to your screen, you can type CTRL S—unless you are using Tymnet. With Tymnet you must first log in in a special way, typing a CTRL R just before specifying Dow Jones. This can be automated in your communications program, but it's tricky.

To use this service, you will need a $10 book called *The Dow Jones News/Retrieval Fact Finder*. It lists all the symbols for stocks, bonds, mutual funds, and treasury issues, and it also serves as a user's guide. Tymnet and Telenet phone numbers plus log-in procedures are included.

Costs

If you subscribe on your own, there's a $49.95 sign-up fee that includes a manual. However, the service is included with any Dow Jones software package you buy. MCI offers the service with no sign-up fee and no manual. Some modem manufacturers offer free subscriptions. Lower rates are available by paying monthly or annual fees. Otherwise, there is no minimum charge.

The connect charges are shown in Table 4-3. At 1200 bps, all rates are double.

Table 4-3. Dow Jones News/Retrieval Service Hourly Rates

300 bps service	*Prime Time*	*Non-prime Time*
Dow Jones Business and Economic News	$72	$12
Dow Jones Quotes	$54	$9
Financial and Investment Services	$72	$54
General News and Information	$36	$18
Free-Text Search	$72	$36

Prime time starts at 6:00 A.M. Eastern time and ends at 6:00 P.M. local time. The service is unavailable from 4:00 A.M. to 6:00 A.M. Eastern time.

Research-Oriented Information Utilities

The Source, CompuServe, and Dow Jones News/Retrieval Service are oriented toward the general public. Another group of information utilities caters to researchers and librarians.Their goal is to make available on a computer as much published material as possible.These utilities, sometimes known as **on-line databases**, have the following features in common:

Billions of characters of data on-line

Full texts of publications as well as abstracts

Academic, technical, and business orientation

A high cost per hour

Fortunately, several system operators have seen fit to offer a subset of their information at discount prices on evenings and weekends. This subset often contains such interesting things as a listing of American books in print, a database of microcomputer software, and an index to microcomputer magazine articles. There's lots of industry-specific information too.

Dialog Information Services

Dialog is owned by Lockheed and can thus take advantage of Lockheed's surplus computing power. As of October 1983, there were 518 separate databases covering science, engineering, social sciences, business, and economics. The selection is so rich that any partial list would do it a disservice. If you're serious about spending money for real information, send away for the free 47-page catalog.

If you refer back to the description of Dow Jones' Free-Text Search, you'll get an idea of how a Dialog search works. Most of the data available through Dialog consists of abstracts and citations, referred to as "records." Dialog will deliver a photocopy of the full text for a fee. Another service called SDI (Selective Dissemination of Information) causes a search to be run every time a database is updated.

The average cost of using Dialog is $45-$95 per hour with an additional charge, typically $0.25, for each record retrieved. Some services such as patent searches cost $300 per hour. Tymnet and Telenet charges are extra at $8 per hour. Think carefully before using this service; it might pay to have a professional do the searching for you.

The Knowledge Index

Dialog operates an after-hours service called The Knowledge Index. This is a subset of the Dialog databases. It costs a flat $24 per hour, communication charges included, and is available from 7:00 P.M. to 11:00 P.M. Eastern time, weekdays only. The $35 subscription fee entitles you to two free hours and a user's workbook. Dialog and The Knowledge Index are separate services with separate billing and contract forms.

NEXIS

NEXIS is an information utility specializing in full text databases. Mead Data Central, the system operator, once required subscribers to use a special terminal. Now Mead allows you to use PCs either with a proprietary communications program ($250) or with a general-purpose program emulating an IBM 3101 terminal. Document printing can't be done with the PC, however. You must lease Mead's special printer, connected to a separate phone line, and pay a print fee of a penny a line. You are forbidden to download the text that you read at your terminal.

NEXIS contains the full text of 15 newspapers, including the *New York Times*, and 31 magazines including *Byte*, *Business Week*, and *Newsweek*. Wire services are on-line too, including Reuters and Xinhua. The news goes back as far as 1977. There are also over 50 industry newsletters on-line. The Information Bank is another NEXIS service, providing abstracts from 60 newspapers, magazines, and periodicals.

What does it cost? Peak time is $90 per hour, going down to $30 per hour for organizations buying more than 100 hours per month. Off-peak time (after 7:30 P.M. local time) is $45 per hour. There's also an extra charge for "search units," which is related to the number of keywords ocurring during a search. Mead operates its own communications network, so there are no Tymnet/Telenet surcharges. Service is only offered at 1200 bps.

Mead also operates a legal service called LEXIS and a patent search service called LEXPAT, both available through PCs.

BRS/After Dark

Bibliographic Retrieval Service (BRS) operates a professional-oriented service similar to Dialog's information retrieval service. BRS/After Dark is a low-cost subset available from 6:00 P.M. to midnight local time. Prices range from $6 to $20 per hour, with a $50 sign-up fee and a $12-per-month minimum. The hourly rates include all communications charges and there's no extra charge for 1200 bps. There are 28 BRS/After Dark databases in the following categories:

Sciences and medicine

Business and finance

Reference

Education

Social sciences and humanities

One service available through BRS/After Dark that is of interest to microcomputer owners is Online, Inc.'s Micro-Software Directory. You can order an information packet from BRS to see if any other service interests you.

NewsNet

NewsNet is a collection of about 200 on-line industry newsletters. Each of the newsletter publishers has a specific access charge and a special policy for printed-edition subscribers. NewsNet's charges are shown in Table 4-4.

Table 4-4. NewsNet's Hourly Rates

Prime Time	*Validated Newsletter Subscribers*	*Non-Subscribers*
300 bps	$24 (basic rate)	$48
1200 bps	$48	$96

A few newsletters are more expensive, and some newsletters are available only to subscribers of the printed edition. A discounted basic rate of $18 per hour applies from 8:00 P.M. to 8:00 A.M. Eastern time.

The following are a few newsletters from the list:

Computer Market Observer
International Petroleum Finance
Hollywood Hotline
Nuclear Waste News
Computer Farming Newsletter
Bank Network News
Worldwide Videotex Update
Charitable Giving
Fiber/Laser News
Washington Credit Letter
Online Database Report
Television Digest
Telephone News

NewsNet also provides electronic mail, a personalized news clipping service, and sample newsletters available at the basic rate.

Information for Specific Industries and Professions

There are dozens of information utilities specializing in particular industry groups, professions, and companies. One example is **Westlaw** from West Publishing Co., which allows lawyers to search court cases and federal regulations according to keywords in a manner similar to Free-Text Search on the Dow Jones News/Retrieval Service. When a keyword has been found, the relevant document appears immediately on the screen with the keywords **highlighted**. All the details are there on the screen for any lawyer to see. Westlaw includes a case cross-referencing system called Shepard's Citations. If you enter a case number, the system shows you all other cases that reference that case. Gateways to BRS, DIALOG, and other services are included. The cost is about $100 per hour.

Many smaller information utilities turn to one of the large system operators to run their services. Dialcom, a division of ITT, is a leader in this field. The information utility bills its subscribers directly, paying Dialcom disk storage charges and $9 per hour of subscriber connect time. Tymshare and Tymnet offer similar services. One Dialcom customer, Impact 1040 of Bellevue, Washington, operates a limited partnership database. Brokers can choose limited partnerships for their clients, and then "cut and send" information to those clients by electronic mail.

Electronic Mail

Both The Source and CompuServe have had electronic mail for several years, and large corporations have been using their own systems, often operated by the packet-switched networks. Now the U.S. Postal Service has started the same type of service, as has MCI, the telecommunications giant. The telex system was there all along — a worldwide electronic mail system serving 1.5 million subscribers. Now the telex network is blossoming with new features and access methods.

Your PC can connect to all these electronic mail systems, but only to one at a time. This is reminiscent of the days when there were several telephone companies in each city, and business customers needed one telephone wired to each telephone company's network.There is a difference, though. Independent telephone companies were deliberately excluded from the Bell System as part of Theodore Vail's effort to build a monopoly. Electronic mail systems are not interconnected because nobody bothered to set standards.

If you were serious about electronic mail, you'd begin your business day by checking eight electronic mailboxes. How else would you communicate with your friends on The Source, CompuServe, MCI, Telemail, On-Tyme, Dialcom, Graphnet, and ITT Timetran? Fortunately, something is being done about this. An international conference scheduled for the beginning of 1984 is supposed to establish standards. Once those standards are implemented, you will have one mailbox with the service of your choice. That service will have a prefix code that your correspondents will use when sending you mail. You'll be able to send outgoing mail to any other electronic mail subscriber.

When you select an electronic mail service today, you must first make a list of the people with whom you correspond. If they all have telex numbers, then you choose one of three (or more) telex carriers. If they're all Source subscribers, then you join The Source. If you're just getting started, you can evaluate the features, ease of use, and cost of the electronic mail systems available. The information in this section will help you make that choice.

SourceMail

With any electronic mail service, you should use a word processing program or text editor to write all but the shortest letters off-line. This saves connect charges and lets you compose your letter just the way you want it. Be sure that your word processor outputs carriage returns after each line of text, and that the lines aren't longer than the limit set by the electronic mail service.

SourceMail works very well with communications programs, sending and receiving mail smoothly to and from PC disk files. The procedure for sending a letter to a hypothetical subscriber TCA123 is as follows:

1. From the command prompt, type MAIL TCA123.
2. Enter a subject as prompted.
3. After the prompt ENTER TEXT:, have your communications program transmit the disk file.
4. Type .S on a line by itself.

The procedure for receiving a letter is

1. From the command prompt type MAILCK to see if you have any mail.
2. Set up your communications program to save (capture) all incoming characters in a disk file.
3. Type MAIL R.
4. Watch as mail is received.
5. Turn off the disk capture feature.
6. Answer D for delete or S for save when prompted for DISPOSITION.

There are all sorts of options with SourceMail:

- You can selectively read mail, choosing unread or express mail.
- Incoming mail may be filed by category (on the Source's disk) for later reading or processing.
- You can send mail to multiple addressees. This feature is sometimes used for "electronic junk mail."
- You can request carbon copies, acknowledgements, and delayed delivery.
- Outgoing mail can originate from a Source disk file that you created using The Source's editor or that you received from another subscriber.
- You can send a message to a non-subscriber with the E-COM option for $1.35. The details of E-COM are explained in Chapter 6.

There's no extra charge for SourceMail; you're charged only for the connect time and there's no limit on the length of a letter. Don't forget it costs money to log in and read your incoming mail. During business hours, it could easily cost $1 to check your mailbox and send or receive a letter.

CompuServe CIS EMail

CompuServe's CIS electronic mail service is distinct from the EIS service, which is described separately. Functionally, EMail works the same as SourceMail with one difference. EMail requires you to first load your message into a temporary file called a **workspace** using a line editor called *FILGE*. This editor is similar to the PC DOS EDLIN program. Fortunately, *FILGE* accepts data uploaded from your PC's disk files, so you can compose messages off-line with your word processor.

After your message is in the workspace, you can edit it and then send it to a CompuServe subscriber. EMail doesn't offer sophisticated features such as multiple addressees and carbon copies, but you can send the same message several times. If you have any mail waiting, EMail alerts you when you log in.

CompuServe EIS InfoPlex

With CompuServe's EIS InfoPlex electronic mail system you enter your message directly, either from the keyboard or by uploading a PC disk file. You can edit the message and send it to one or several addressees. There's a way to scan incoming messages and to save them in a CompuServe disk file. Needless to say, you can download any message to your PC's disk. An E-COM hookup allows any message to be sent via mail for $0.79 plus the $0.26 E-COM charge. Soon you'll be able to send E-COM form letters from a stored list of addresses.

MCI Mail

MCI Mail, "the nation's new postal system," is a new service introduced with great fanfare in mid-1983. Here are the highlights of the basic service:

- You can send a 3,500-character electronic letter to any other MCI subscriber for $1.
- A letter will be printed on a laser printer in a city near the addressee, stuffed into a distinctive orange envelope, and then delivered by the U.S. Postal Service—all for $2.
- Next-day courier delivery costs $6.
- Four-hour courier delivery to addresses in major cities costs $25.
- There are no connect charges, communications charges, or monthly minimums. You can log in via local numbers in large cities and toll-free numbers elsewhere.

- Access to the Dow Jones News/Retrieval Service is included, but you must pay MCI for the time you use.

MCI Mail is extremely easy to use; you're guided by clear menus every step of the way. Addresses consist of subscribers' names. You type the addressee's name, and the system searches its subscriber list for a match. If there are duplicate names, you're prompted to choose one from a list. If the name isn't found, the letter will be sent by mail. To enter a message, you type in one line at a time or upload it from a PC disk file. You get a chance to edit the message before you send it. If you don't send the message, it remains in your workspace until you log in again. The same letter may be sent to multiple addresses, and carbon copies are allowed.

MCI Mail is a useful and cost-effective service targeted to home users as well as businesses. How does MCI's cost per letter compare to The Source's and CompuServe's? Assume it takes four minutes to transmit or receive a letter at 300 bps, counting the time it takes to access the electronic mail function. Don't forget that electronic transmission requires four minutes on each end for a total of eight minutes. The comparison is shown in Table 4-5.

MCI uses laser printers and allows three pages, but E-COM uses dot-matrix printers and allows only two pages.

For a subscription charge of $10 per month, you get an advanced service that permits you to store form-letter address lists. You can also store a letterhead and signature that the laser printer reproduces on the message.

The Telex System

The telex system is a hopelessly old-fashioned communications network, but it does have 1.5 million subscribers and extends to the remotest parts of the world. If you look closely at business cards and stationery, you'll notice that a surprising number of companies have telex numbers. Most telex users have a teletype machine connected to a leased line with a combined fixed cost of over a

Table 4-5. Cost Comparison of Electronic Mail Services

	Electronic Mail	*Postal Delivery*	
SourceMail, business hours	$2.77	$2.73	(E-COM)
CompuServe, business hours	$1.67	$1.88	"
SourceMail, evenings and weekends	$1.03	$1.87	"
CompuServe, evenings and weekends	$0.80	$1.45	"
MCI Mail	$1.00	$2.00	

hundred dollars a month. Incoming messages are printed as they come in, and outgoing messages are prepared on paper tape and then transmitted.

The AT&T breakup is raising the cost of leased lines, and users are realizing that their teletypewriters are outdated. There's a rush to provide replacement services to telex subscribers. Telex carriers Western Union, RCA, and ITT are taking the lead, setting up **store-and-forward** message systems accessible from PCs. These store-and-forward message systems consist of computers that receive messages over phone lines and then store them on disk to be ultimately forwarded to your PC when you call in for your messages. The telex subscriber can thus eliminate the teletype and the leased line and use the PC to communicate with the carrier's computer. It works the same way as electronic mail.

There is a difference, however, between using an ordinary telex terminal and using a store-and-forward service with a PC. The way messages are sent is similar, but messages are not received automatically with a store-and-forward service. Incoming messages accumulate in an electronic mailbox in the carrier's computer, and the recipient must dial in to check for new messages. The dialing can be automated, of course, but there's no longer a direct communication link with the recipient. The sender of a message may think a message has been received, but that message could be languishing in the recipient's mailbox. Telex carriers can configure their computers to dial the recipient when a message comes in, but the recipient's PC and modem must be on and ready to receive a call in order for the message to be received.

The **answerback** is a standard feature on the telex network. Both teletypewriters and PCs are supposed to send back a predetermined message when interrogated. If you know your respondent's answerback, you can verify that you have made the right connection. The next time you see a telex number—it's five to seven digits long—look for the answerback immediately following. It's usually one or two words or abbreviations derived from the company's name and city.

Telex messages are are charged by the minute. The assumed transmission rate is 66 words per minute (50 bps, Baudot code); a word consists of six characters including spaces. The domestic telex rate is about $0.50 per minute, which means a 66-word message costs $0.50. A telex to Japan costs $1.80 per minute plus the domestic charge of $0.50.

ITT Timetran

ITT Worldcom's Timetran telex service is the first choice of casual telex users because there's no set-up fee or minimum monthly charge. You apply for a telex number, and in about a month you receive it. In the interim you can immediately start sending and receiving telex messages through a local ITT number. Timetran is a **half-duplex**, store-and-forward service, which means it is very difficult to use with general-purpose communications programs. The *TLX-A-SYST* program, described in Chapter 6, is highly recommended.

Timetran has both good and bad points:

- Your ITT representative is alerted if your messages aren't picked up within five days. He or she then mails printed copies to you (not without some scolding). If you persistently ignore your messages, your subscription will be dropped.
- If an incoming message is garbled while it is being received by your PC, you can't recover it without having ITT reload the message from a backup tape. That takes time and effort.
- You can send the same message to multiple addressees, and you can enter a department code for itemized billing.
- Timetran provides other telex-related services such as overseas cablegrams.
- You can reach Western Union and ITT telex numbers directly, but the prefix 23 must be appended to RCA numbers. You must know how to recognize an RCA number.
- While you must enter a password to get messages from your mailbox, no password is necessary to transmit a telex. Thus any hacker can send messages on your account, knowing only your telex number and your answerback.
- Experiments show that the system adds about 30 seconds of overhead to a message.

RCA Global Communications

RCA's service costs $15 per month, but it offers some improvements over ITT's Timetran. Each message that you retrieve from your mailbox is followed by an ID number. You (or your computer) must repeat that number back to RCA as an acknowledgment. Your message stays in the mailbox until successful acknowledgment is received, thereby preventing lost messages. If you don't claim messages after a certain interval, a member of the RCA staff will advise you by voice telephone. The RCA service does have a real-time mode where you can communicate directly with any telex machine. A dedicated line is not required.

Western Union EasyLink

If you are converting from a Western Union telex system that uses a teletype, EasyLink is for you because you don't have to change your telex number. There's also a full-duplex mode, allowing easy operation with a general-purpose communications program. If you get the full service, including international access, your monthly fixed charge is about $50. All store-and-forward services, EasyLink included, offer lower rates when you communicate with other subscribers on the same service. An EasyLink message to a telex machine costs about three times as much as an EasyLink-to-EasyLink message.

FIVE

VIDEOTEX

How would you like to have all the services described in Chapter 4 for $12 per month instead of $6 to $25 per hour? How would you like high-quality, 16-color graphics instead of ordinary text? All this is yours if you're willing to move to southern Florida, and it's warm in the winter too. **Viewtron** videotex is the consumer version of The Source, CompuServe, and Dow Jones News/Retrieval. Once an experiment, it is now a real, commercial service. The first videotex subscribers had to buy or rent a special terminal that attached to the phone line and a TV set, but it's now possible to use properly outfitted PCs and PCjrs as videotex terminals. Residents of Orange County, California, and Chicago are getting videotex services, and the rest of America won't be far behind. If you're excited, keep reading.

The Nature of Videotex

As you may recall from Chapter 1, the word **videotex** is used to describe a number of different types of services. In this chapter videotex refers only to local services using color/graphics terminals and phone-line communications.

Videotex is a new service in the U.S., and it is aimed at the general population instead of an elite group such as businesspeople or computer enthusiasts. No one is really sure that the general public will accept videotex, but some large companies are hoping that it will.

Videotex may be new to the U.S., but England and France have had videotex services since the late 1970s. The British **Prestel** service is run by British Telecom, the government post office and telecommunications monopoly. Prestel was originally intended for the mass market, but it has found a niche in the business world. It offers news, weather, sports, features, and stock market reports. The French **Teletel** system was started as a replacement for telephone directories. All telephone subscribers will eventually be issued a low-cost terminal for looking up phone numbers. The resulting large user base is supposed to support other videotex services. Canada's **Telidon** system is oriented to specific industries such as agriculture.

All videotex services depend on the two-way nature of the telephone connection. **Teletext**, a competing technology, works through one-way cable TV. This service is very limited because the same information is broadcast to all terminals. There are usually about a hundred screen-size pages, each selectable by the viewer, transmitted between the TV frames. In contrast, videotex can offer as many pages as can be stored on the host computer's disk. But comparing teletext to videotex is like comparing *Reader's Digest* to the Library of Congress. Fortunately, it appears that teletext won't get off the ground in the U.S. *Time* magazine has already abandoned plans for a system.

As you might expect, there are varying standards for transmitting videotex. The Prestel and Teletel systems use the **alphamosaic** technique, which means the screen is viewed as an array of 40 × 24 characters or an 80 × 72 matrix of **pixels**, or picture elements. This system supports crude graphics of the type shown in Chapter 6. Transmitting a full screen at 1200 bps takes eight seconds. It's possible to use the PC as a Prestel terminal, but you need a Plantronics Colorplus board and special software from Wolf Data. Then you must pay transatlantic communication charges and be satisfied with quotes from the London stock market. There's supposed to be an American version of Prestel soon.

Telidon has developed a sophisticated **alphageometric** videotex standard. Telidon is the basis for NAPLPS (North American Presentation Level Protocol Syntax), a standard adopted for use in the U.S and Canada. With NAPLPS, pictures are broken down into shapes, and the shapes are translated into a series of commands. Figure 5-1 shows a Florida weather map created with the NAPLPS standard. A partial series of commands used to create this screen would go something like this:

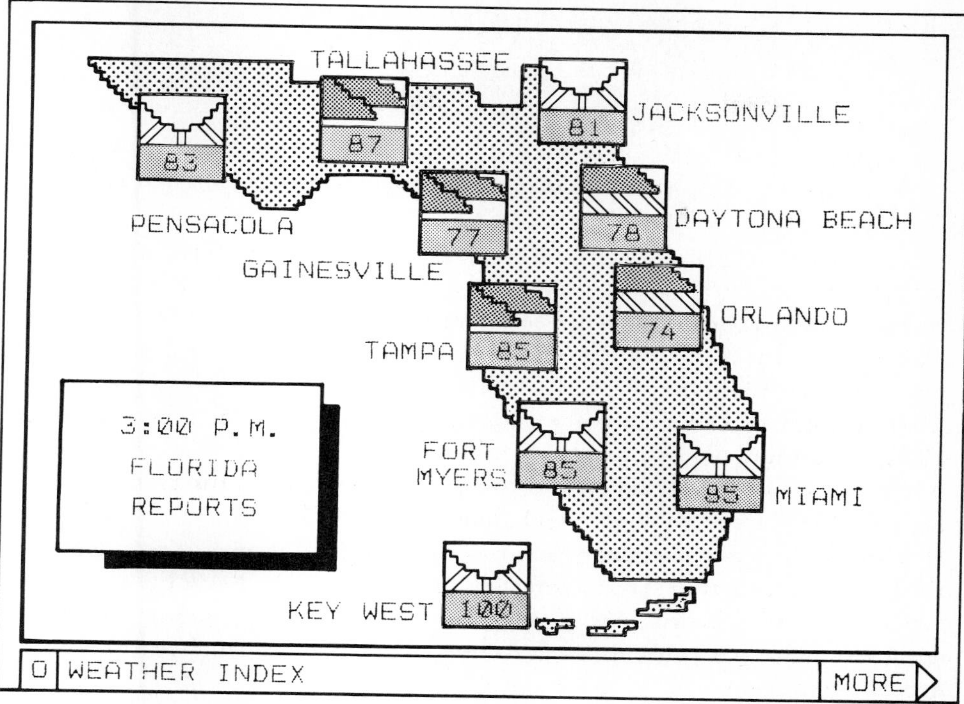

Figure 5-1. Florida weather map created with NAPLPS standard

1. Color the entire screen light blue.
2. Draw a polygon with a black border with the following x,y coordinates:
   1.23, 1.11
   1.23, 3.44
   1.56, 3.44
   (all coordinates for Florida's corners).
3. Color the inside of the polygon green.
4. Define a square box with the following characteristics:
   Border is black
   Horizontal line 2/3 from top
   Top portion colored dark blue.
5. Define the Sun, Partly Cloudy, and Rain symbols.
6. Position the already defined boxes and weather symbols on the map at the following x,y coordinates:
   2, 2

1.77, 4
(all coordinates for the major cities).

7. Fill in the temperatures and city names using black standard-sized type.
8. Draw a rectangle in the lower left corner of the screen and color it orange.
9. Print "3.00 PM FLORIDA REPORTS" in the rectangle in large type.

Note that the boxes and suns are each transmitted just once and then replicated where necessary. Both the city names and the title are transmitted as ASCII text with a prefix code to specify font and size.

NAPLPS makes no assumptions about the resolution of the terminal. A circle appears round on a high-resolution terminal and ragged on a low-resolution terminal. Five hundred and twelve colors are supported, but terminals displaying only 16 colors must choose from among the 16 colors they can display. The NAPLPS standard easily adapts to new display technology, yet it economizes on the number of characters transmitted. Once you see a NAPLPS terminal in operation, you'll realize that finally somebody's done something right. The designers didn't compromise in favor of equipment that in five years would appear primitive.

The videotex technology is in place, but what's required is aggressive promotion. Newspaper publishers are taking the lead because they suspect that videotex will compete with the printed media. In addition, they have the editorial facilities, marketing skills, and capital. Knight-Ridder Newspapers, owner of the *Miami Herald*, has established Viewdata Corporation of America to operate the Viewtron videotex service in south Florida using the NAPLPS standard. The service went on-line on October 31, 1983, the day before IBM announced the PCjr. Viewtron began the service after a 1980-81 trial involving 204 homes in Coral Gables, Florida. So far $26 million has been committed, and the goal is a modest 5000 paid subscribers in the first year. Viewtron will recover its costs if it can establish service in other cities that Knight-Ridder serves. The *Los Angeles Times-Mirror* and the *Chicago Sun Times* have their own ideas about who should establish services. Watch for services in those cities soon.

Viewtron in South Florida

Viewtron is of interest because, at the beginning of 1984, it was the only U.S. commercial videotex service in operation. Viewtron will probably set the standards for other systems to follow, especially for Knight-Ridder services in other cities. It offers a range of services comparable to CompuServe's, but users get local news coverage as well. Here are some examples of what's available:

News Figure 5-2 shows a menu of five news stories. The stories, edited by Viewtron's professional journalists, cover both local and national events. Viewtron usually provides more depth than is found in newspapers as witnessed by the November 1, 1983, PCjr announcement story. There were quotes from IBM experts including Peter Norton.

Banking The national information utilities may let you open an electronic account at a bank in Boston or Columbus, Ohio, but wouldn't you rather use a local bank? Viewtron provides access to 11 south Florida banks. You can query your account balance, transfer funds between accounts, and pay bills to utilities, credit card firms, and department stores. All transactions are **encrypted**, meaning no hacker can tap the line and get your identification code. Figure 5-3 shows a bill payment request.

Business and finance You can connect to selected stock brokerage firms through Viewtron. E. F. Hutton & Co.'s **Huttonline** costs an extra $17 per month. You can use Huttonline to check the status of your portfolio and to

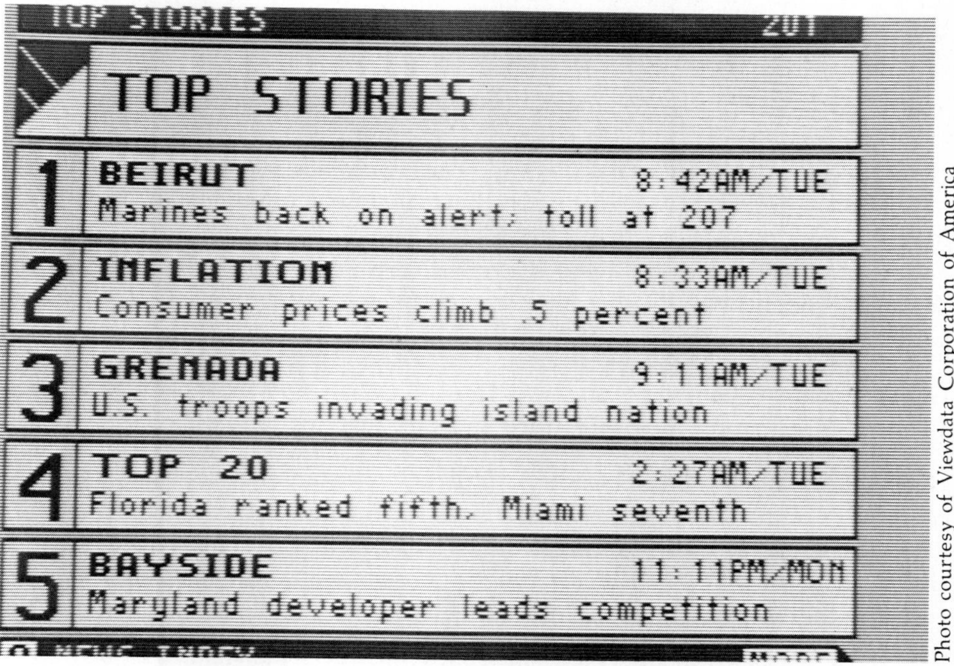

Photo courtesy of Viewdata Corporation of America

Figure 5-2. Viewtron menu of five news stories

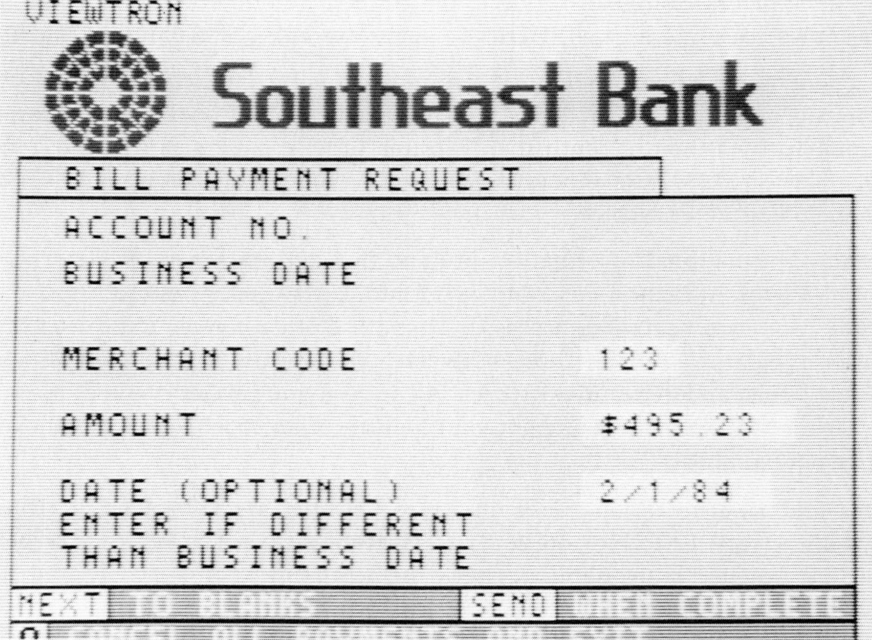

Photo courtesy of Viewdata Corporation of America

Figure 5-3. Electronic banking bill payment request

communicate with your broker, but you can't buy and sell stocks. There's business information from the *Wall Street Journal* and stock quotes from AP that are updated three times a day. With utilities like CompuServe, you can get a current quote by simply entering a stock symbol. With Viewtron you must search through an alphabetical listing of stock quotes, select the appropriate page, and locate the entry yourself.

Official Airline Guide You have free access to OAG's schedules at local airports. Information for other cities and fare information costs $3 per hour.

American Academic Encyclopedia This is the same encyclopedia that often costs extra on national information utilities like CompuServe. It's accessed via a **gateway**, meaning you're automatically transferred to Grolier's computer for this service. Viewtron provides a graphics border around the encyclopedia text. For now there's just text, but before long there will be illustrations too.

Education Viewtron will take you to a Cuban car mechanic's garage for a Spanish lesson. You can also prepare for the SAT (Scholastic Aptitude Test), practice reading and math, take an introductory computer course, or sharpen your management skills. The entire text of the Florida *Driver's License Manual* is available.

Games Sea Battle is a game with amazingly realistic sailing ships firing at one another. With such realism, it's hard to believe you're operating over a 1200 bps line. The usual Lunar Lander, craps, and biorhythms are also included.

Features Viewtron has up-to-date TV listings, a church directory, fashion information, Ask the Experts, household hints, sex counseling, and almost anything else you can think of except ski reports.

Want ads You can buy a one-page classified ad for a week for $1. You can search Viewtron ads or view the ads from the previous Sunday's *Miami Herald*.

Electronic mail Messages are $0.10 each. You can even send electronic greeting cards.

Restaurant and movie reviews Here you'll find write-ups by local journalists. Be careful, though, because there are some restaurant ads as well.

Advertising The $0.25 newsstand price is only a small part of a newspaper's revenue. Like newspapers, Viewtron hopes to make most of its money in advertising. Your advantage with Viewtron is that you can read the ads when you want to. It's like an electronic Yellow Pages. Advertisers include local businesses ranging from major department stores to neighborhood liquor marts. The entire J. C. Penney catalog is on-line through another gateway.

Direct purchase Early videotex trials showed that subscribers actually bought products through the service. This was music to the ears of retailers and was probably the major factor motivating Viewtron investors. Figure 5-4 shows an ad for a doll and a book. How could you resist your child's pleading, "Daddy, please buy that for me"? Decide to buy, and Alice in Wonderland goes on your credit card.

Cost

What does Viewtron cost? The basic charge is $12 per month for unlimited access. You will also pay $1 per hour in communications charges (more on that later). Some services like electronic mail and classified ads are extra, but they're not expensive. Dow Jones offers its complete service to Viewtron subscribers for a fee of $10 per month.

Photo courtesy of Viewdata Corporation of America

Figure 5-4. *Direct buying ad*

The first Viewtron subscribers had to use special Sceptre terminals made by AT&T. Figure 5-5 shows a Sceptre terminal in action. The box containing the electronics is the size of an IBM PCjr and contains a 1200 bps modem. It connects directly to the phone line with a modular plug and to a color TV set through a built-in RF modulator. The keyboard is no better than the PCjr's and is suitable only for tiny fingers. The keys are arranged in vertical columns, but they do follow the typewriter's QWERTY pattern. The Sceptre keyboard is wireless, however, just like the PCjr's.

The Sceptre's list price is $900, but it was being sold for a special introductory price of $600. The cost of the terminal is the biggest hurdle for Viewtron subscribers. Wouldn't it be nice if there were an inexpensive and powerful personal computer that doubled as a Viewtron terminal?

Using Viewtron

How easy is it to use Viewtron? Very easy. Look at the primary screen shown in Figure 5-6. On the actual screen the numbers 1 through 7 stand out

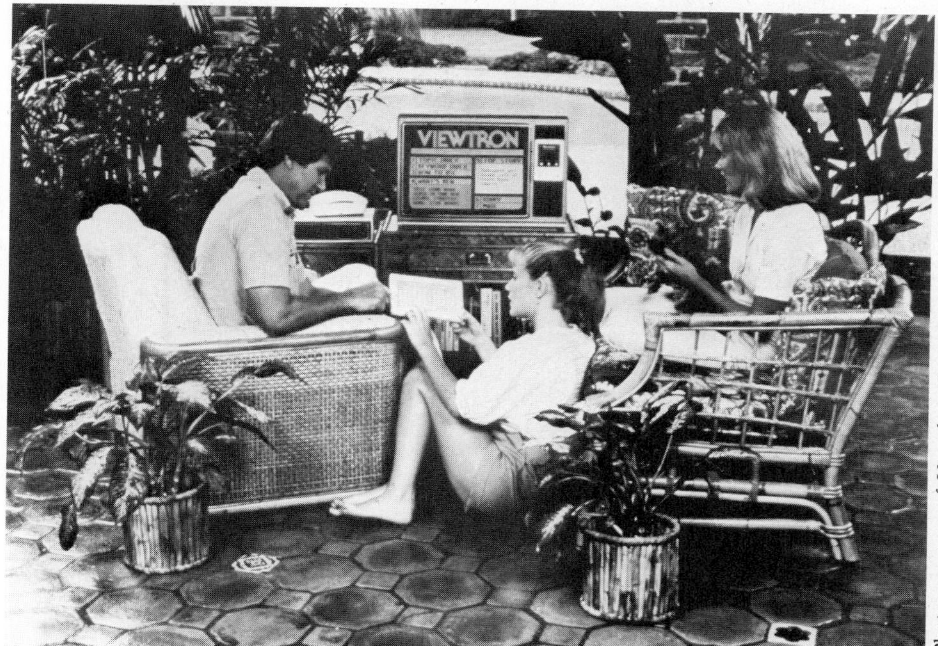

Photo courtesy of Viewdata Corporation of America

Figure 5-5. Sceptre terminal in action

in yellow squares against blue and white text. You can wend your way through the hierarchy of menus or go directly to a particular page by entering a keyword or page number. The keyword list, which you can view, includes some common terms such as TV, MOVIES, and SPORTS. New words are added permanently or temporarily. GRENADA was added during the 1983 invasion of Grenada. Viewtron works a little like CompuServe, but the consistent screen layouts and Sceptre's special keys make Viewtron much easier to learn. You page through stories with the MORE key, and you move to the next story with the BROWSE key. You can also mark and recall pages, a useful feature for price comparisons.

One useful Viewtron feature is the Personal Magazine. You can define 16 pages that can be accessed from your personal table of contents with the letters A through P. You could, for instance, have entries for stock quotes, weather, and sports scores. There's also a personal calendar that causes Viewtron to issue you reminders on specified days.

Photo courtesy of Viewdata Corporation of America

Figure 5-6. Primary Viewtron screen

Connecting to Viewtron

You may have wondered why Viewtron has a separate $1-per-hour communications charge. Since Viewtron is a local service, shouldn't Viewtron time be treated on your monthly phone bill just like any other local call? What's happened is that Southern Bell, the phone company serving the south Florida area, has found a way to make an additional charge for videotex subscriptions. It's only a matter of time before all phone companies charge by the minute for all local calls, so the charge isn't so unreasonable. A subscriber's connection to Viewtron doesn't follow the route of a normal phone call. At sign on, the Sceptre terminal automatically dials a number to connect to a local packet-switched network. From the subscriber's central office (telephone exchange) a packet-switching network takes over. This network is called an **LADT** (Local Area Data Transport).

If it weren't for the LADT, Viewtron would need hundreds of phone lines and modems. Instead, there are just a few high-capacity lines carrying data for many on-line subscribers. This is just a miniature version of Tymnet or Telenet, as described in Appendix E. The only difference is that the network operator, Southern Bell, charges subscribers directly on their phone bills. Tymnet and Telenet charge the system operators who, in turn, pass the charges along to subscribers.

Viewtron subscribers use a **dial-up LADT**. The Sceptre terminal dials the number of the LADT and then sends a code to log in to the Viewtron computer. Communication is synchronous at 1200 bps. A variation, called a **direct access LADT**, allows 4800 bps synchronous communication and simultaneous voice phone calls. This has the obvious benefits of speed, totally error-free transmissions, and a voice channel; but low-cost 4800 bps modems aren't available, and the telephone line to the central office must be specially conditioned and less than 18,000 feet long. So far, direct access LADTs aren't in common use, but they may be soon.

The fact that LADTs require synchronous modems is a combination blessing and curse resulting from government regulations. It's a curse because no existing standard PC communication gear will work, but it's a blessing because it forces the world to accept a very powerful communications standard called **X.25**. Appendix E explains the technical details, but it's the benefits that are important. X.25, in contrast to asynchronous communication, allows more data to be sent at a given transmission speed, allows errors to be detected and corrected, and allows many communications tasks to take place concurrently using the same link. It's packet switching brought right to the terminal. Southern Bell uses X.25 on its LADT because, as a government-regulated telephone monopoly, it is prohibited from converting between different communications protocols. If X.25 is used to connect Viewtron's computers to the network, then X.25 must be used to connect to all subscribers' terminals.

Viewtron does allow certain subscribers to bypass the LADT. Connections can be made directly or via conventional packet-switched networks using standard asynchronous modems. These connections are more expensive than LADT connections and are intended to be temporary.

The PC and Videotex

At the start of 1984 no one claimed to have a PC or PCjr compatible with Viewtron. If you want to get rich, turn on your computer and start programming. Your only worry is that IBM might have a secret room full of clever programmers attacking this very problem. Be advised, though, that the standard IBM PC Color/Graphics Monitor Adapter won't display enough colors to make the NAPLPS standard work. NAPLPS allows 512 colors with a palette of

16 selected for a given screen. The standard IBM PC hardware displays only four colors in the 320 × 200 medium-resolution graphics mode. This is clearly not enough. The Plantronics Colorplus card from Frederick Electronics displays 16 colors in the 320 × 200 mode as does the enhanced model of the PCjr. There is a strong possibility that IBM could introduce an enhanced color/graphics adapter for the PC, bringing that machine up to the PCjr standard.

There is one small problem with the 16-color medium-resolution graphics boards. If a Viewtron screen uses, say, three shades of blue, a 16-color system will assign two different colors to the remaining two blue areas. This might turn out to be red or green, a definitely unaesthetic situation. There are two solutions to this problem. Screen designers could cater to the lowest common denominator, that is, a terminal with only 16 colors. This is as bad as designing software to work on both an Apple and on a PC. The other solution is to use a more sophisticated graphics board that is capable of displaying 256 or 512 colors. The trouble with this solution is that standard RGB monitors display only 16 colors, but most people will be using TV sets anyway.

To use the PC as a Viewtron terminal, you need the enhanced color/graphics capability, a color TV or monitor, a synchronous communications port, a synchronous 1200 bps modem, and special software. Neither the synchronous communications hardware nor the software were available at the beginning of 1984. What's needed is a plug-in circuit card with the synchronous port and synchronous modem. This shouldn't be too expensive to make, considering that AT&T already includes this function inside the $600 Sceptre terminal.

The software is more developed than the hardware. Several companies have said theirs would be ready in the near future. Two Canadian firms, Microstar and Microtaure, have products that worked with Telidon, whose standard is a subset of NAPLPS. Microstar is concentrating on the Canadian business market, but Microtaure claims its product is almost ready for Viewtron. In the U.S., Wolf Data seems about the closest. But when shopping for videotex software, don't be fooled by the ads. Make sure you know a product works with your service before spending money.

It's interesting to compare the Sceptre terminal with the PC. Although the Sceptre claims to be only a terminal, it is built around an 8088 microprocessor chip, the same chip that is in the PC. There are 128K of ROM (read-only memory) and 48K of RAM (random-access memory). The Sceptre displays 200 rows of 256 pixels compared to the PC's 200 × 320 array. The Sceptre does have the advantage of displaying any 16 of 512 colors, but it's restricted to working with a color TV set. The PC, on the other hand, can connect to a high-resolution RGB monitor and thus can display 80 columns of text. Viewtron displays a maximum of 40 columns, but there's nothing in the NAPLPS standard that limits the number of text columns. If properly equipped, the PC can operate with Viewtron-style videotex as well as 80-column text services such as Dialog and BRS. If properly programmed, the PC can save NAPLPS screens to disk, print them, and allow you to create your own pictures.

The PCjr with the Memory and Display Expansion option seems like a natural videotex terminal. The color graphics capability is there, and the software could be stored in a ROM cartridge. All that's necessary is a plug-in synchronous modem to replace the existing 300 bps asynchronous modem. The resulting system would be more expensive than a Sceptre, but it would also function as a full-fledged personal computer. Of course, AT&T could implement MS DOS on the Sceptre.

Many observers think that the PC market and the videotex market will feed on each other. A PC user will subscribe to a videotex service because that's just another thing for the computer to do. A person who wants videotex services will buy a PC because the PC has other uses. Fortunately, it appears Viewtron has enough capital to wait until PCs capable of connecting to the NAPLPS standard become available.

SIX

SPECIAL-PURPOSE COMMUNICATIONS PROGRAMS

Chapter 4 introduced you to information utilities, electronic mail services, and telex carriers. Many of those services offer enhancements like graphics and specially formatted screens that require you to have a **special-purpose communications program** running on your PC. Special-purpose programs are written and distributed by a particular service and are designed to operate with only that service. Contrast this to general-purpose programs, which allow you to communicate with many different services.

What if you do not have the special-purpose program? Some services that require data to be formatted in a unique way, like E-COM for instance, are directly accessible only if you have the proper communications program. Other utilities, like CompuServe, are accessible with a general-purpose communications program, but certain features like graphics displays will not be available.

This chapter lists special-purpose communications programs designed to work with information utilities like The Source and CompuServe, stock market services, on-line learning facilities, and mail and telex services. The chapter also discusses special-purpose software that will allow you to set up your own bulletin board service.

VIDTEX for CompuServe

CompuServe is the most technically advanced, though often the slowest, of the major information utilities. The service already has some corporate subscribers on a videotex system similar to the Teledon system described in Chapter 5. It's not surprising, then, that CompuServe has introduced the *VIDTEX* program, alias The CompuServe Professional Connection, for the IBM PC.

VIDTEX is a program you should have if you're a subscriber to either of CompuServe's Consumer and Executive Information Services (CIS and EIS). At $69.95, *VIDTEX* offers most of the features of a general-purpose communications program and also supports graphics, error-free file transfers, and more. A stock performance chart may be the only graphics on CompuServe now, but there's bound to be more as the PC population increases. Once software becomes readily available on-line, error-free file transfers will be a must.

One of the most difficult tasks in data communications is configuring a communications program to dial and log in to a service automatically. This confounds experienced hackers as well as novices. Each service has its own requirements for entering the user name and password, and each packet-switched network has a different log-in method. *VIDTEX* is specifically designed for CompuServe and four networks. As you set up *VIDTEX*, you are asked for the following:

Local-access phone number
Network (CompuServe direct access, Tymnet, Telenet, DataPac in Canada)
Baud rate (300 or 1200)
Modem/phone type (auto or manual, touch or pulse tone)
User ID
Password

That's all there is to it. You just enter the data once, and you're ready to log in automatically every time.

VIDTEX allows you to use command **scripts** to go directly to certain parts of CompuServe. Figure 6-1 shows the menu supplied with *VIDTEX*. If you select

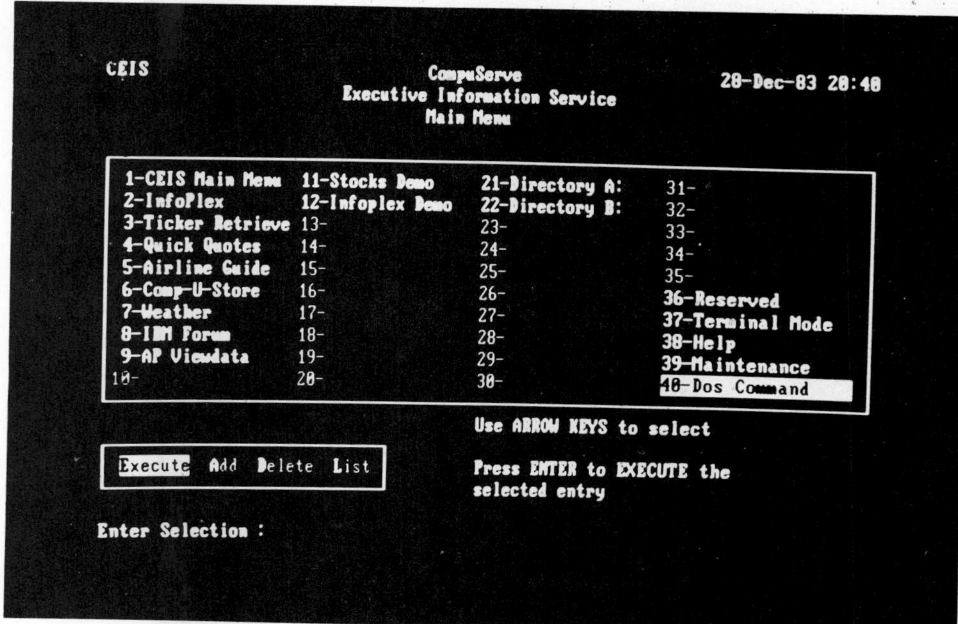

Figure 6-1. VIDTEX *main menu*

item 5, you get the airline guide, 7 gets you the weather, and so on. These scripts are referenced from the menu, and you may create your own. Look ahead to the description of *CROSSTALK* in the next chapter. *VIDTEX*'s scripts are almost the same, and like *CROSSTALK*'s, they are entered via a text editor or word processor program. A line editor called FILGE, similar to the CompuServe version, is supplied with *VIDTEX*. Script writing requires familiarity with CompuServe and programming principles, but the "canned" scripts will comfortably transport you to most CompuServe destinations.

Most information utilities display one line of text at a time. Once the screen fills up, you're prompted to press ENTER for the next screenful. The text **scrolls** up as new lines appear at the bottom. Scrolling text is difficult to read, so CompuServe and *VIDTEX* clear the screen at the start of each page. A heading with a page number always appears at the top of the screen, and new text is written just beneath it. The prompt for a new page always appears in the same place at the bottom of the screen, as shown in Figure 6-2. CIS assumes a 40-column screen, and EIS assumes 80 columns. You always have the option of scrolling if you don't like losing sight of the most recent page.

```
CompuServe                    Page CIS-1

CompuServe Information Service

1 Home Services
2 Business & Financial
3 Personal Computing
4 Services for Professionals

5 User Information
6 Index

Enter your selection number,
or H for more information.
```

Figure 6-2. *Typical CompuServe screen with VIDTEX*

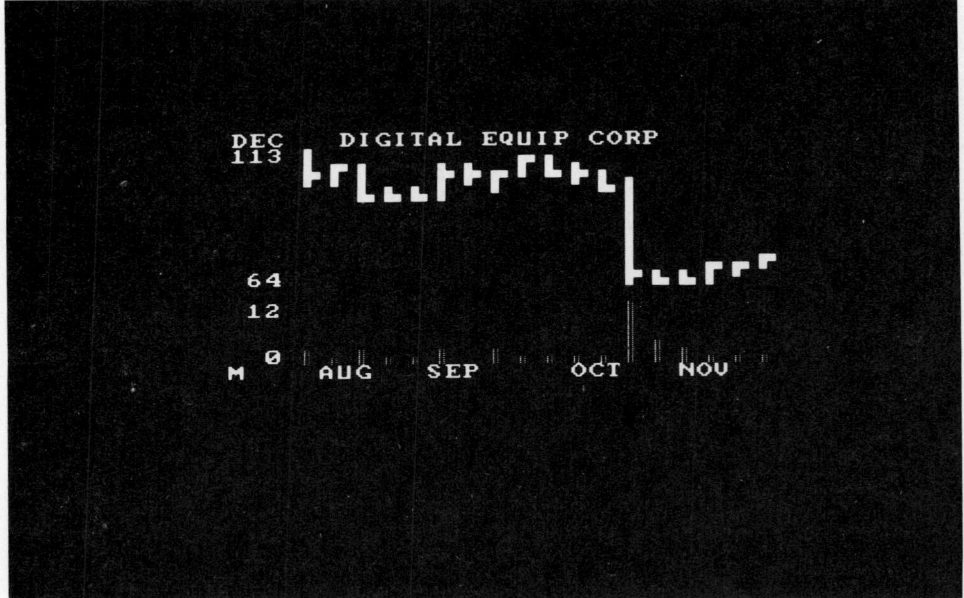

Figure 6-3. *VIDTEX/CompuServe stock chart*

VIDTEX allows you to display CompuServe graphics. For example, Figure 6-3 shows a stock chart as displayed on a monochrome monitor connected to the IBM Color/Graphics Adapter. *VIDTEX* supports a high-resolution graphics mode for use with a color/graphics adapter. If you have the IBM Monochrome Monitor and Monochrome Display Adapter, you can only get rough "semigraphics" as shown in Figure 6-4a. The same screen using the IBM Color/ Graphics Adapter is shown in Figure 6-4b. You don't have to do anything special to see the graphics. CompuServe just tells *VIDTEX* to switch in and out of graphics mode.

VIDTEX can upload and download files from CompuServe using an error-correcting protocol. This is perhaps *VIDTEX*'s greatest advantage; none of the other information utilities guarantees error-free file transfers. You can reliably send an executable program to another CompuServe subscriber, or you can buy software and download it without any danger of losing part of the program. The uploads and downloads work very smoothly. Once you give the command to CompuServe, CompuServe determines you are using *VIDTEX* and the rest is automatic. All you do is specify the CompuServe file name and the corresponding PC file name.

Unfortunately, *VIDTEX* is a new program, and there were a few bugs in the version tested. The Tymnet and Telenet log ins didn't work, and it was impossible to configure a modem using communications port 2 (COM2). It was also necessary to create a new diskette in order to change the log-in parameters. CompuServe is aware of these problems and is working to fix them.

Sourcelink for The Source

The *Sourcelink* communications program is available to Source subscribers for $49.95. *Sourcelink* was designed for The Source, but it also works with other information utilities. On the surface it looks much like *VIDTEX*, but most of its features are just razzle-dazzle. Instead of seeing a menu entry like TRAVEL, you see a color picture of a jet plane. This is great if you can't read, but in that case you won't get much benefit from The Source once you log in. The graphics images don't come from The Source itself, but are generated by the *Sourcelink* program.

Sourcelink does provide the usual automatic dialing and log-in features together with the ability to capture data on disk. *Sourcelink* allows you to transfer files, but those transfers don't use an error-checking protocol. One of the problems with The Source is that it is still geared to ordinary terminals and is not setting itself up to compete with Viewtron-style videotex. There is also a technical problem. *Sourcelink* was the only program tested that required a special setting (switch 3) on the Hayes 1200B modem.

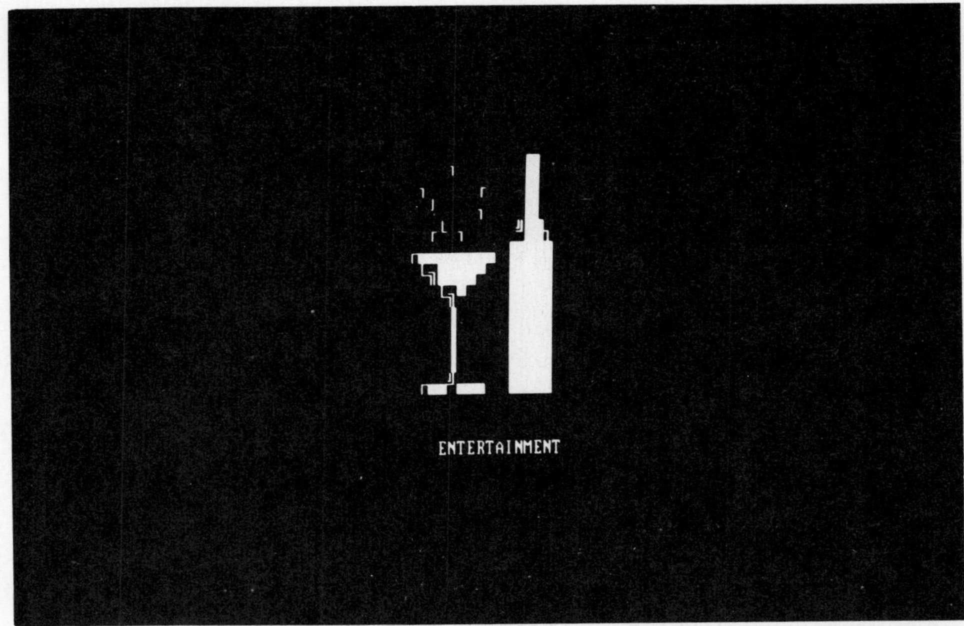

Figure 6-4a. VIDTEX/CompuServe graphics with monochrome monitor and adapter

Figure 6-4b. VIDTEX/CompuServe graphics with color/graphics monitor and adapter

Dow Jones Market Manager

Market Manager, one of a series of programs from Dow Jones, enhances the Dow Jones Current Quote and News/Retrieval services. It manages your stock portfolio, recording all trades and automatically evaluating your stocks from current Dow Jones prices. *Market Manager* minimizes the time you are connected to Dow Jones (**connect time**) and could thus pay for itself in just a few sessions.

Figure 6-5 shows the *Market Manager* main menu. If you select the entry DOW JONES COMMUNICATIONS, you can access the Current Quote and News services. In Current Quotes, you enter as many as five stock symbols. If you had entered IBM, AAPL, and DEC, you would see the screen shown in Figure 6-6. Contrast this to the following "raw" Dow Jones output:

```
STOCK      BID        ASKED
           CLOSE      OPEN       HIGH       LOW        LAST       VOL(100'S)
IBM        120 7/8    121 1/8    121 3/4    120 7/8    121        5488
AAPL       19 3/4     19 2/4
DEC        71 1/4     71 1/8     72 1/4     71         71 1/8     2414
```

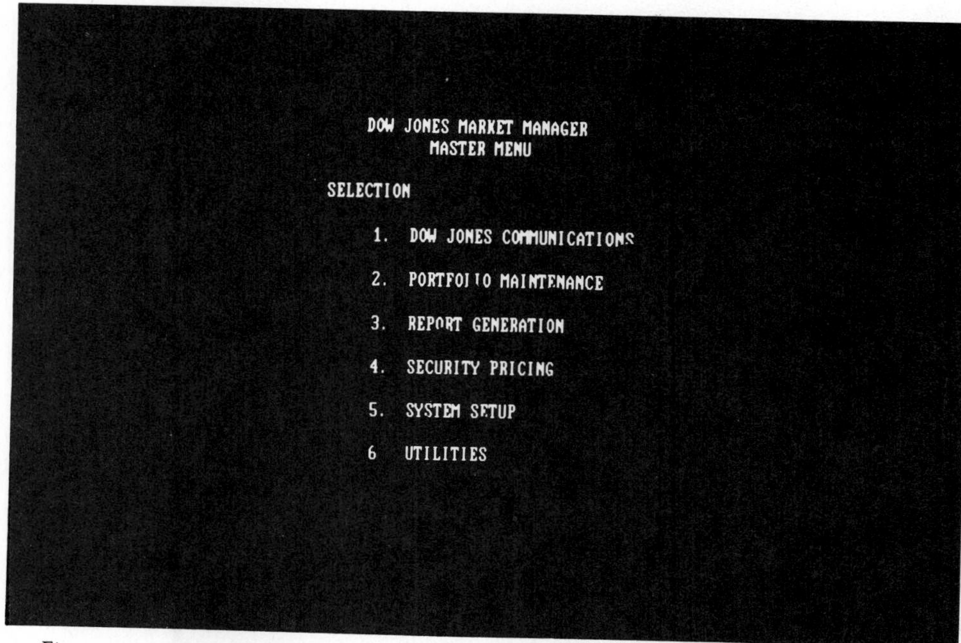

Figure 6-5. Market Manager main menu

CURRENT QUOTES

SECURITY	IBM	AAPL	DEC		
BID/CLOSE	124 5/8	24 7/8	73 7/8		
ASK/OPEN	124 5/8	25	73 3/4		
HIGH	124 5/8		73 3/4		
LOW	123 1/2		73		
LAST	124 1/4		73 1/2		
VOL(100'S)	7692	5739	2806		
CHANGE	-3/8		-3/8		

(QUOTES DELAYED OVER 15 MINUTES)

PRESS <RETURN> TO ENTER MORE SYMBOLS

Figure 6-6. Market Manager current quote

Market Manager's presentation of Dow Jones news is truly amazing. As you may recall from Chapter 4, news is indexed by stock symbols. You are shown an index to a month's stories, and you can retrieve individual stories by code number. However, it's often difficult to remember the codes after the index scrolls off the screen. Figure 6-7 shows *Market Manager*'s solution to the problem. The screen is divided vertically into two windows, the left window for the index and the right for the story. You can use function keys to scroll the index forward and backward, and you can independently scroll the selected story. You can print the index or story, and you can save a complete story to disk for later retrieval once you are off-line.

Market Manager is working hardest when it's managing your personal stock portfolio. The portfolio is a detailed record of all your purchases and sales for the year with dates, share quantities, and amounts. If you tell *Market Manager* about all your trades, it can easily keep track of how many shares of each stock you own at any one time. That's called your **position**. If *Market Manager* knows how many shares of IBM you own, for example, it can dial up Dow Jones to get

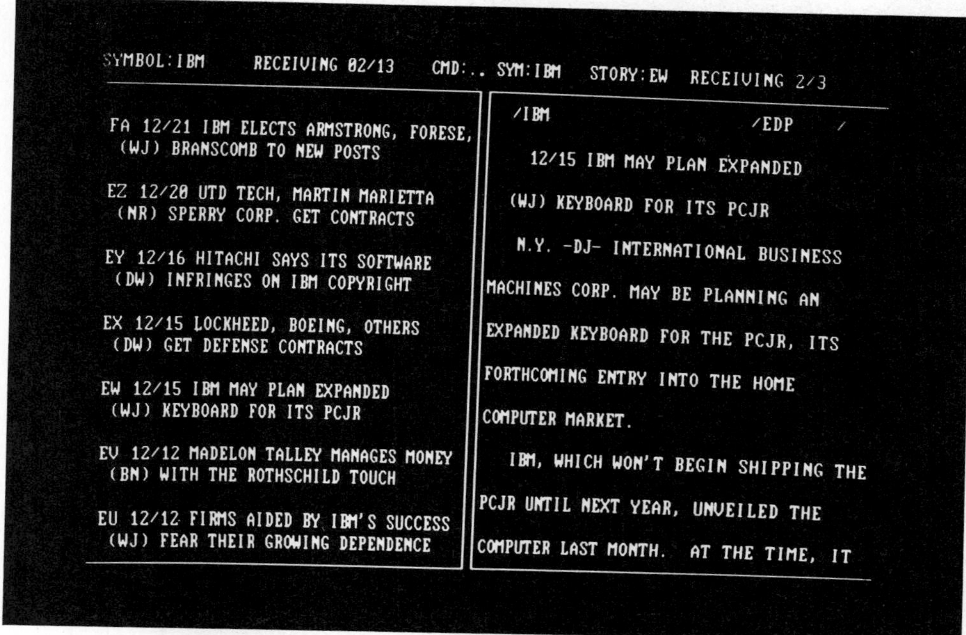

Figure 6-7. Market Manager Dow Jones News screen

the current price per share of IBM and multiply that price by the quantity you own to give you the value of your position. The program can evaluate your entire portfolio, giving you its total value from quotes that are 15 minutes old. You'll probably use this feature most when stock prices are going up.

The Dow Jones service doesn't allow you to trade stocks. It gives you quotes that are 15 minutes old plus news. You buy and sell stock through your broker and manually record the transactions on the PC with the help of *Market Manager.* This is much like entering information into a database management system with fields for stock symbol, quantity, date, and the total amount. Available reports include:

Holdings by portfolio

Holdings by symbol

Realized gains and losses

Year-to-date transactions

Figure 6-8 shows three transactions, reporting that you bought some Apple Computer and IBM stock but later sold half of your Apple stock. Figure 6-9 shows what a bath you took with Apple. Note that the loss is realized: you bought dear and sold cheap. Figure 6-10 shows your current holdings. You have 100 shares of IBM, and you still have 500 shares of Apple. The 12/03/83 PRICE column displays data directly from Dow Jones, and the $VALUE column is simply price times quantity. The unrealized loss is the loss you would take if you sold the stock on 12/03/83. The total value of your portfolio is $21,663.

Market Manager allows for stock splits, a cash balance, options, and selling short, thus satisfying the needs of all but the largest professional investors. One disk holds as many as 500 positions divided among as many as 26 portfolios.

```
                         YEAR-TO-DATE TRANSACTIONS

TODAY'S DATE   12/02/83
==========================================================================

DATE       CODE       TRANSACTION           DESCRIPTION           AMOUNT

--------------------------------------------------------------------------

10/19/83    A         BUY                100 IBM @ 132.00         13200
6/13/83     A         BUY               1000 AAPL @ 65.44         65444
11/15/83    A         SELL               500 AAPL @ 20.00         10000
```

Figure 6-8. Market Manager year-to-date transactions report

```
                              REALIZED GAINS/LOSSES
TODAY'S DATE   12/02/83

==============================================================================
C
O                        PURCHASE                                  SALE          L
D                 -------------------------------------------------------------/
E SYMBOL    QTY   DATE        PRICE      $COST      DATE    PRICE    PRO-    GAIN/
                                                                    CEEDS    LOSS S

-------------------------------------------------------------------------------
  AAPL      500   6/13/83   65.44        32722    11/15/83 20.00   10000  -22722 S

TOTALS:
LONG         0                              0                           0        0
SHORT      500                          32722                       10000   -22722
```

Figure 6-9. Market Manager realized gains/losses report

```
                         HOLDINGS BY PORTFOLIO

TODAY'S DATE  12/03/83

=============================================================================

C       T
O       Y
D       P B                 =========TRANSACTION======  ===12/03/83==== UNREALIZED
E SYMBOL E SS      DATE    QUANT      $COST     PRICE   $VALUE    PRICE  GAIN/LOSS
- ------ - --    ------- --------   --------   ------   ------   ------ ----------

A AAPL   S B    6/13/83    500       32,722     65.44    9,875   19 3/4   -22,847

A IBM    S B   10/19/83    100       13,200    132.00   11,788  117 7/8    -1,412


VALUED SECURITIES LONG     600       45,922             21,663            -24,259
VALUED SECURITIES SHORT      0            0                  0                  0
CASH BALANCE = -68644
```

Figure 6-10. Market Manager holdings by portfolio report

A test of the program went well, although there was an unexplained problem with Tymnet. This illustrates a general rule in PC communications: if one network doesn't work, try another.

There is something important you should know, however. *Market Manager* is written in UCSD Pascal. This means the disks are incompatible with PC DOS; you can't transfer files or use your usual disk format and copy utilities. If you have an IBM PC XT computer, you can't run *Market Manager* because it requires two floppy drives. You must boot from the supplied disk, which contains its own operating system. You're allowed to format and copy data disks but not the program disk. Dow Jones does supply one backup disk, however. One more thing—UCSD disk operations are slow.

Market Manager automatically dials and logs in whenever it determines you're not already on-line. You stay on-line while gathering data, but you are immediately logged out when you proceed to other functions. A small portfolio can be evaluated in 40 seconds of connect time. That's $0.90 in prime time, and $0.15 during off hours. The program costs $299, including a Dow Jones subscription with one hour of free connect time. You must have 128K of memory and a Hayes Smartmodem. Only 300 bps is supported, and your modem must be on communications port 1 (COM1).

Dow Jones has two other programs that accumulate data for off-line analysis. *Market Analyzer* ($349) is for technical analysts. The program collects day-by-day historical quotes for selected stocks and displays and prints elaborate charts. *Market Analyzer* is written in IBM BASIC and thus avoids the problems of UCSD

Pascal. The other program, *Market Microscope* ($699), produces reports using data from Dow Jones Media General Financial Services and the Corporate Earnings Estimator. In theory, this program tells you when to buy and sell stock.

The Desk Top Broker

The Dow Jones *Market Manager* stores your portfolio on the PC's disk, requiring you to enter stock transactions "after the fact." *The Desk Top Broker,* on the other hand, lets you use your PC to buy and sell stock, and it stores your portfolio in a central computer. You're not actually connected directly to the stock exchange, but it's almost as if you were. C. D. Anderson & Co. is your broker, and the company charges standard discount commission rates. You place an order through your PC, and in 60 to 90 seconds the order is executed and confirmed. There is a human in the loop; an operator in the Anderson "wire room" passes your order along to the exchange.

The Desk Top Broker is a combination service and PC communications program. You can use an ordinary terminal, but the $195 sign-up fee includes a copy of the program. In other words, the program is free. Once you're on, you pay $0.40 a minute for prime time (including Telenet charges) plus the usual commission on trades. There are, however, some extras you'll probably want to pay for.

You may have noticed that Dow Jones, CompuServe, and the other information utilities provide stock prices that are 15 minutes old. These outdated prices are more or less public information like the weather forecast and news headlines. Dow Jones gets the quotes from the individual stock exchanges for a flat rate and agrees to delay their broadcast. Current or last-sale prices are the property of the stock exchanges, and they sell the information at a fixed monthly rate per terminal. Brokers have been the primary customers, and the price used to be high. Now, with increased interest in PC communications, the subscriber base is widening and the prices are dropping. The most recent monthly rates for *The Desk Top Broker* customers were

New York Stock Exchange	$62.00
American Stock Exchange	$11.65
NASDAQ over-the-counter	$11.25
Options	$45.00

These quotes are only available as a package for $133.40. There was a rumor that rates would drop sharply, so check with C. D. Anderson for the current ones.

If your orders are confirmed in 90 seconds, it doesn't make sense to work from quotes that are 15 minutes old. Count on paying extra for the current and last-sale prices. Obviously *The Desk Top Broker* is for serious investors who need to follow every price fluctuation as it happens. Amateur investors may be better off phoning orders in to their broker, knowing that the broker's computer is keeping the records.

Figure 6-11 shows a BUY transaction on the PC screen. Available reports include

Currently priced portfolios (personal, IRA, and KEOGH)
Portfolio value summary with itemized yields
Itemized schedule of long- and short-term capital gains and losses
Capital gains tax reports
List of open orders comparing market prices to limit prices.

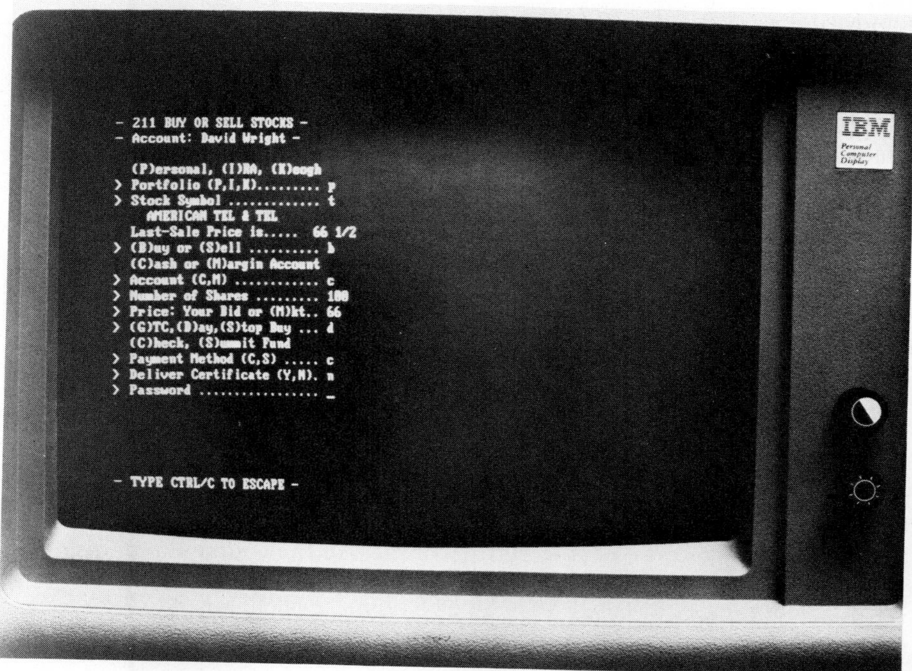

Photo courtesy of C.D. Anderson and Co.

Figure 6-11. Desk Top Broker "BUY" transaction

PLATO Homelink

If you've read any PC magazines lately, you've seen the ads for *PLATO Homelink.* The original name was *Microlink,* but it conflicted with another product. Control Data Publishing has been promoting PLATO educational systems for some time. School systems were the primary customers, but installation was expensive and large multi-terminal minicomputers were required. Now PLATO is available to PC owners, but all the courseware resides in Control Data's central computer system. The PC acts like a terminal with graphics capabilities.

The *Homelink* program is packaged with a PLATO subscription. You pay $50 for the program plus an annual registration fee of $10. Connect time is $5 per hour with no monthly minimum. The system is on-line evenings and weekends only. You can't access PLATO without a PC and *Homelink,* and you must have a Color/Graphics Monitor Adapter and a monochrome or color monitor. Needless to say, you need a serial port and a modem.

PLATO cashes in on kids' love of games and graphics. There are over 150 educational courses available, most of which are oriented to young persons. The games are cleverly mixed in with the courses, but it would still be difficult to get your child to choose "Complex Sentences With Adjective Clauses" over "Skywriting" and "Spider Web." There's even a sprinkling of adult courses such as "Aviation Ground School."

Homelink is slickly packaged with five manuals explaining access, billing, text processing, graphics design, and electronic mail. *Homelink*'s price is right, especially for experimenting. Try it for a while; then judge its features against those in resident PC programs. For example, you could buy a nutrition course on disk for $50, but you could have 10 hours on PLATO for the same amount. Would you and your family ever spend more than 10 hours on one course? If so, buy the disk.

TeleLearning

TeleLearning Systems believes that all students need access to a human instructor. Using this principle, it has built a total educational system around the PC and a mainframe computer operated by Dialcom. You enroll in the Electronic University, receiving a special PC program and a course catalog. You register for selected courses, paying by the course. All the course materials, including textbooks and PC program disks, are mailed to you. The TeleLearning programs include not only your lessons and examinations but also a communications function. Any time you need help, you can access the human instructor via electronic mail. You can also use the communications function to send completed exams to TeleLearning and to register for new courses.

What kind of courses are offered? There's a surprising variety, ranging from adult education to business to young-adult subjects. TeleLearning's courses are much more serious than PLATO's, and there are no games. Here are some samples from about 200 courses:

Getting Started With Your IBM Personal Computer

Designing and Selling a Video Game

Contemporary American Poetry

Bicycle Maintenance and Repair

Intimate Communications Between Men and Women

Assertive Parents—Happy Children

Controlling Your Compulsive Eating

First Aid for the Weekend Athlete

A Career as a Stockbroker

How to Survive as Tenant

Basic Concepts in Astrology

Tax Planning

Wines Around the World

California Cuisine

Construction Cost Estimating

How to Write a Business Plan

How to Play the Opening in Chess

Marine Biology

Personel Math Tutor Program

Space Adventure Series: Let's Orbit the Earth

Solving the SAT

Don't forget that TeleLearning is a new service and that there'll be some rough edges at first. But there's a lot of substance to the catalog, so it's definitely worth a try. Don't forget that you're running the courses from PC diskettes, so you're not using up time at $5 per hour as you would with PLATO. TeleLearning's instructor communications charges are included in the fixed course fees. Each course costs between $50 and $90.

TLX-A-SYST

Chapter 4 explained the telex services offered to PC users by Western Union, ITT, and RCA. You can use a general-purpose program like *CROSSTALK* with these services, but you'll go nuts if you try it. *TLX-A-SYST* is a program for heavy (or even occasional) telex users. By all means, get yourself a telex program like this one from American International Communications; it's well worth $250.

Why do you need a special telex program? Consider the following:

- Most telex carriers don't provide any menus or handholding. You have to type the right commands within 20 seconds or you're disconnected.
- It's worthwhile to keep a log of all messages that you transmit and receive. If the carrier loses your messages, the log information will enable the carrier to restore it from a backup file.
- A directory of telex numbers and answerbacks makes telexing convenient just as a dialing directory makes PC communications convenient.

TLX-A-SYST assumes you are using a particular store-and-forward telex carrier. ITT Timetran is the preferred carrier, but RCA is accommodated. Menu-driven operation is extremely smooth. The *TLX-A-SYST* main menu, shown in Figure 6-12, tells the whole story.

To transmit a message, you prepare the text with a compatible word processing program or with *TLX-A-SYST's* built-in line editor, and then you select the TRANSMIT option. *TLX-A-SYST* automatically dials the carrier, sends your answerback, and sends the message. The carrier responds with a message ID that *TLX-A-SYST* dutifully records in the log along with the date and time. How do you select the recipient? Either by typing in the telex number and typing the answerback, or by typing a two-letter code from the telex directory (Figure 6-13).

To receive messages, you select the RECEIVE option and *TLX-A-SYST* checks your mailbox. If there are any messages there, *TLX-A-SYST* saves them on disk indexed with a receive message ID that *TLX-A-SYST* invents. A record is made in the message log as shown in the following example:

```
                    **** MESSAGE TRAFFIC LOG ****

CODE  T/R MESSAGE ID   TELEX NO    ANSWER BACK     DATE       TIME    USER
A -    T  QFR0513      4990706     XYZZY           12/03/83   11:40   DAVE
B -    T  QFP0712      292932      INTA UR         12/03/83   12:06   DAVE
C -    R  R12032                   TENON SOFTWARE  12/03/83   12:12   DAVE
```

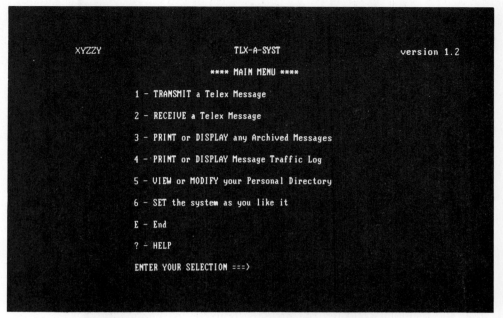

```
XYZZY                         TLX-A-SYST                        version 1.2

                            **** MAIN MENU ****

              1 - TRANSMIT a Telex Message

              2 - RECEIVE a Telex Message

              3 - PRINT or DISPLAY any Archived Messages

              4 - PRINT or DISPLAY Message Traffic Log

              5 - VIEW or MODIFY your Personal Directory

              6 - SET the system as you like it

              E - End

              ? - HELP

              ENTER YOUR SELECTION ===>
```

Figure 6-12. *TLX-A-SYST main menu*

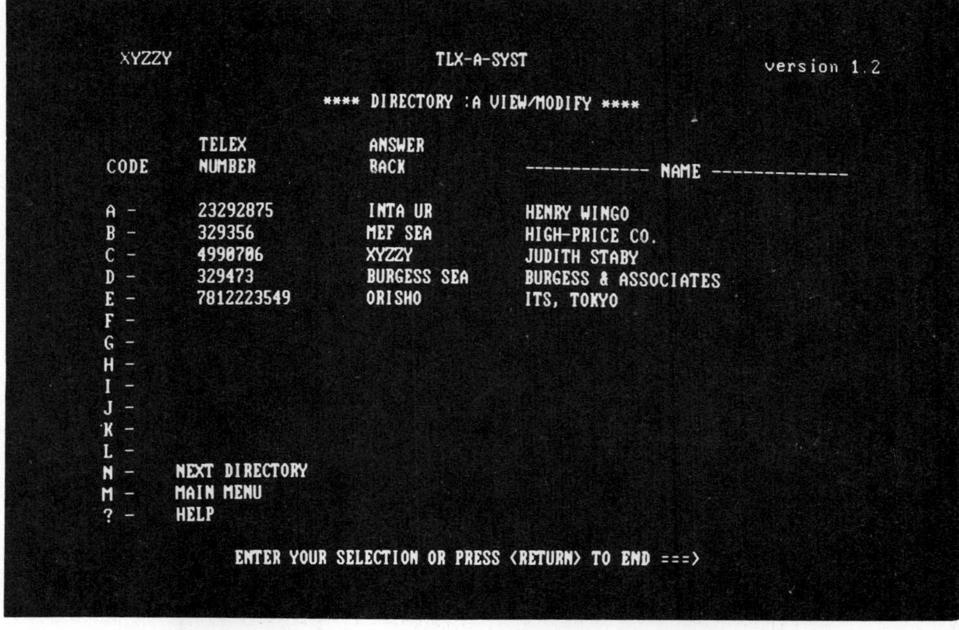

Figure 6-13. *TLX-A-SYST telex directory*

Note that transmitted (T) messages are mixed in with received (R) messages. If there's more than one message in your mailbox, they're all combined into one entry. Many of the received messages will be acknowledgments of messages sent. Here is an example:

```
ZCZC  NDT0006 03/14:44

TIMETRAN
YOUR 12 03 1440 REF QFR0513 TO:
4990706/YZZY           (XYZZY)
SENT 12 03 1444 002.60 MINS

NNNN
```

If you think this message looks cryptic, you're right. It says that message QFR0513 (ITT assigned that number) was received by telex number 4990706 and that the answerback was XYZZY. It often takes several hours to get an acknowledgment. If the recipient is with the same carrier (ITT in this case), you'll get the acknowledgment almost immediately. However, this doesn't mean that the recipient collected the message from his or her mailbox.

TLX-A-SYST's manual is oriented to the first-time computer user. It's ideal for a clerical staff who may be familiar with the old-style telex system. Configuration (access phone number, baud rate, and so forth) is done from a menu and is straightforward. During testing there was a minor problem with logging in with an automatic modem, but the American International Communications staff were helpful and anxious to solve the problem. They're happy to communicate by telex as well as by telephone.

TLX-A-SYST has a few limitations. You can't use it for conversational telexing or for automatic answering of incoming telex calls. You must adjust to mailbox-oriented messaging. If you need to respond quickly, you can have your carrier call your communications line and then immediately phone in to pick up your messages.

Other Telex Programs

Cappcomm Software offers *smarTelex* (version E) to interface with the Western Union EasyLink service. Like ITT Timetran, EasyLink can be set up to call your number when it has a message for you. *smarTelex* answers the phone and accepts the message.

smarTelex (version S) allows the PC to emulate a 50-baud telex machine by supporting on-line conversational mode. Messages may be prepared off-line with *WordStar.* However, since the telex carriers all offer higher-speed dial-up services with conversational capability, there's little need for direct emulation of the 50-baud telex. Both versions of the *smarTelex* program are $449.95 each.

Mailcom and E-COM

E-COM is an electronic mail service provided by the U. S. Postal Service, and *Mailcom* from Digisoft Computers is one of several E-COM-compatible PC programs. It's not practical to use a general-purpose program for E-COM; you must use a program specially designed to format messages in the elaborate E-COM format.

E-COM mail, entered from your PC, is printed by the Postal Service, stuffed in envelopes, and then distributed by U.S Mail—all at a cost of $0.26 per letter. The $0.26 gets you one 41-line page. A second page costs a nickel. It sounds like an unbeatable bargain, but here are some drawbacks:

- You must communicate directly with the E-COM computer at one of 25 Serving Post Offices (SPOs) where the letters are to be printed and mailed. You must use direct-distance dialing, not Tymnet or Telenet.
- You must send a minimum of 200 pieces in a batch. Of course you can send fewer, but you're charged for 200.
- Your mass-mailing name and address files are purged from the Post Office's computers every day at midnight.

E-COM is designed for business mass mailings, but the 200-piece minimum may be reduced in the future. Needless to say, there's political pressure from communications firms to do away with the service altogether. The 25 Serving Post Offices are deliberately not networked, so it appears that the Postal Service is not in the communications business. MCI, Sprint, and AT&T should be happy that E-COM customers must use their lines.

E-COM is used mostly for local mailings. Customers dial a local number, transmit their batches of messages, and the mail is delivered the next day. A small national mailing could be done from one SPO in, say, Chicago. Large national mailings could be speeded up if letters were batched by ZIP code and then sent to the SPO nearest the recipient.

If you've ever used *WordStar* with *MailMerge* or another word processor with form-letter capability, you'll have an easy time with E-COM. E-COM will even draw lines and boxes (for invoices and statements). If you're doing mass business mailings, you're either sending the exact same message to everybody ("Dear Mr./Ms. Computer Buyer"), or you're sending a slightly customized message ("Dear Mr. Schmaltz, I'm sure that you and Mrs. Schmaltz have seen pitches for Florida swampland before..."). E-COM handles both. The first is called a Common Text Message (COT), and the second a Text Insertion Message (TIM). Another type of message, the Single Address Message (SAM), is allowed. This is one letter to one individual.

Here's how COTs are processed through E-COM. The text of the message is prepared as follows:

```
Dear Mr. **:
I'm sure that you and Mrs. ** have seen pitches for Florida swampland....
```

A two-entry address file looks like this:

```
Mr. Victor Schmaltz          ← Entry 1: address line 1
5634 E. 14th St.                        address line 2
Burnt Boot, MT 96332                    address line 3
                                        address line 4
Schmaltz                                insertion text 1
Schmaltz                                insertion text 2
Mr. Stephen Casey            ← Entry 2: address line 1
Apartment 603                           address line 2
8754 Lotus St.                          address line 3
Hohokus, NJ 07639                       address line 4
Casey                                   insertion text 1
Casey                                   insertion text 2
```

Each address is given only four lines. If the address has just three lines, one is left blank. There are two places for text insertion that are indicated by the double asterisks in the message. Thus the address file must have entries for both blanks.

It's necessary to send both the TIM and the address file to the Post Office computer, but you must send it in a strictly defined format. That's where the *Mailcom* program comes in. There are four phases in preparing an E-COM transmission:

1. Prepare the address list using your favorite word processor program or *Mailcom*'s own address list manager. You might even use a database management system.
2. Prepare the TIM message using your word processor or *Mailcom*'s.
3. Use *Mailcom* to format both the address list and the message text according to E-COM specifications. This is called setting up your transmission.

4. Use *Mailcom* to send your transmission to the desired E-COM computer. *Mailcom* error-checks your text and address files prior to sending them to E-COM.

Mailcom handles all tasks through a main menu. After you set up the program with the phone number, dialing prefix, password, baud rate, and so forth, communication is easy and automatic. *Mailcom* knows exactly how to log into E-COM. *Mailcom* costs $195 and comes with a 56-page typeset manual. The E-COM annual fee is $50.

CompuServe EIS allows you to send individual E-COM messages. The charge is $0.79 above the E-COM rate, but the messages are routed to the nearest SPO. So far only SAMs and COTs can be processed; TIMs will come later. You can keep an address list in your CompuServe files, and you don't need to retransmit it with each mailing. The Source has a similar service priced at $1.35 per letter including Postal Service charges.

Computer Bulletin Boards

If you get tired of supporting big businesses by giving money to H & R Block's CompuServe, *Reader's Digest*'s Source, and Dow Jones, read on. Here's your chance to join a grassroots movement—information by and for the people. Computer bulletin boards (CBBs) are information utilities run by public-spirited individuals willing to dedicate a PC and a phone line to the common good. Not only can you dial into these boards, but you can start one yourself. CBB software is absolutely free. You just download it from an existing CBB or from CompuServe's PC special-interest group.

What's a CBB? Picture the bulletin board in your office lunchroom. The board is covered with 3″×5″ cards advertising baby sitting services, vacuum cleaners for sale, and so on. Today's CBBs are almost the same, except there's a different set of things for sale. Consider the following example:

```
Msg #    Date          From                           Subject
-----    ----          ----                           -------

 10    08-03-1983   BOB BRAUNWART             PConnection Modem
 11    08-03-1983   HARRY LOGAN               PC-Talk III
 12    08-07-1983   NELSON STRASHUN           Kind words?
 13    08-08-1983   JIM WRIGHT                MORSE/RTTY PC PGMS
 14    08-10-1983   CHUCK DAVENPORT           PC MODEM GAMES
 15    08-13-1983   BILL FASSETT              Abort/Retry/Ignore
 16    08-15-1983   JAMES SHIELDS             The Midnight PC
 17    08-18-1983   DON EHRLICH               MORSE/TTY DECODING
 18    08-19-1983   JOEY MILLER               WANTED VIC-20 disk
 19    08-21-1983   AMY ROSENBLATT            SORE FOOT?

 - End of Index -
```

```
<S-> Scan Reverse, <S+> Scan Forward, <I-> Index Reverse,
<I+> Index Forward, <R> Read Message, <L> Leave Message
<D> Delete Message, <A>bort to Main menu

Enter your choice:
```

Most CBBs are run by technical types, but there are even a few sexually explicit boards (Kinky Komputer, for example). If enough people had PCs, there could be CBBs devoted to sports, dog breeding, rhododendron hybrids, raising gifted children, political action, and anything else you can think of. But don't wait for someone else to start an interesting board. Start one yourself. That will be an incentive for others who have the same interests to buy personal computers. You can even allow Apple and Commodore owners to dial in.

CBB programs are pretty generic, and they all work the same. Callers dial in and give their name and city. If the program detects a first-time caller, it asks for a password that is stored to validate future access. Once logged in, a caller can list all messages on the board and then read selected messages. Callers can leave messages and delete messages they themselves have left. There's really not much difference between the CBB and the lunchroom board. It's just more convenient and not as geographically limited.

Local CBBs are a good place to practice your PC communications skills. You don't have to worry about the charges for connect time while you scratch your head. You may also get some quick answers to your PC questions. A computer store is a good source of CBB numbers as is the local computer club newsletter. Bulletin boards are usually listed by computer brand and subject matter, so you can ignore the Apple and Radio Shack numbers if you want to. There's an ever-increasing number of PC-oriented boards, so you'll soon find a bulletin board in your area. You can try boards in other cities, but you will ring up a big long-distance bill, and on the more popular boards you will get a constant busy signal.

Busy signals are a fundamental problem with CBBs. The PC can handle only one call at a time. If it could handle more, you'd have to install more phone lines. If the board is popular, you'll never get in except after 3:00 A.M. CompuServe's PC special-interest group (SIG) is almost the same as a CBB, but hundreds of users can connect at the same time. You'll see more messages in an hour on CompuServe than you'll see in a week on some CBBs.

If you do start a CBB, you must first decide if you need a dedicated phone line. If you have that extra line, you must allocate the PC between the bulletin board and your own computing and word processing jobs. You may need a dedicated PC. If you're sharing one line between data and voice, you can get a CBB program with a **ringback** feature. Anyone who wants the computer lets the phone ring once and then immediately redials and is connected. Voice callers can let the phone ring in the normal way.

RBBS-PC

RBBS-PC is a public-domain program that allows you to set up your own bulletin board on an IBM PC. It was originally distributed by the Capital PC Communication Special Interest Group of Washington, D.C. Larry Jordan's name is first on the contributor's list, but Don Withrow, author of *Hostcomm*, claims some credit. *RBBS-PC* can be downloaded for free, and it comes with a 25-page documentation file. You can get it from the CompuServe PC SIG, area XA5. You should download with *VIDTEX*'s error-correcting protocol if you can. Don't forget the instructions. To run *RBBS-PC* you'll need a Hayes or Rixon modem plus 128K of memory, two double-sided floppy disk drives, and DOS 2.00. The program is written in interpretive BASIC, but a compilable version may now be available for 1200 bps use.

You'll need to be thoroughly familiar with your PC to install and run *RBBS-PC*, but you don't have to be an expert. The instructions are clear enough, but plan to spend some time learning them.

RBBS-PC is like one big conference. All messages are public except notes to the system operator (called the SYSOP). Callers can scan the messages, read a message, or leave messages of their own. *RBBS-PC* has provisions for a welcome message, six bulletins (long messages from the SYSOP), and a new user instruction file.

When you call into an *RBBS-PC* system, a log file records your name and the time you logged on and off. A separate log file identifies those callers who stay on a long time. The SYSOP can impose a time limit for each user. A record for each user containing password, equipment, location, time last signed on, and number of times signed on is also maintained.

Here are some features of the program:

- An error-checking protocol called XMODEM is supported for file uploading and downloading. There's a directory of files available for downloading. Callers can download any file listed in the download directory.
- Callers can use menus or drop into "expert" mode once they become familiar with the system.
- Ringback is supported to allow you to use the same phone line for data and voice.

There are a number of functions available to the SYSOP. When there are no callers logged in to the system, the SYSOP can maintain disk files and reconfigure the system. The SYSOP can even log in to the system from a remote computer and check for any messages. On-line conversations can take place between a caller and the SYSOP. It's like conversational typing. There is even a mode called SNOOP that makes the SYSOP's screen an image of the caller's. Next time you log onto a CBB, consider that Big Brother may be watching.

RBBS-PC is an unbeatable program for the price. But if there's something you don't like, there's no one to complain to. You just change the code to suit your needs. It's easier than programming from scratch.

Hostcomm

If you need more than what *RBBS-PC* has to offer, then you'll have to spend some money. *Hostcomm* from Janadon, Inc., is a shell program designed to support electronic mail, conferencing, uploading and downloading using the XMODEM protocol, and custom-written applications. *Hostcomm* by itself costs $170 and is best understood by looking at its main menu:

```
          * * * M A I N   M E N U * * *

Quit (end session)                  Type 1
eXpert user mode (short menu)       Type 2
Enter text message (to sysop)       Type 3
Page the sysop                      Type 4
Upload a file                       Type 5
Download a file                     Type 6
Change download directory #         Type 7
List users log                      Type 8
xModem up/download                  Type 9
conFerence/PC-mail                  Type 10
```

Items 1 through 7 are standard with *Hostcomm,* but items 8, 9, and 10 are special features you buy or write yourself. Notice that the *Hostcomm* shell offers all the features of *RBBS,* except for the actual bulletin board itself and the XMODEM file transfers. Those are extras.

Hostcomm offers several improvements over *RBBS-PC:*

- *Hostcomm* supports 300 or 1200 bps, and the baud rate is set automatically according to the baud rate of the incoming call.
- There may be multiple directories of programs that may be downloaded.
- An elaborate password system restricts certain callers to certain menu options, sets time limits, and determines who has access to certain download directories.
- The mailbox function supports
  Messages from caller to SYSOP
  Messages from SYSOP to individual addressees

Messages from SYSOP to multiple addressees

Bulletins from SYSOP to everyone.

- The configuration screen shown in Figure 6-14 sets up

  The sign-on screen

  Communications parameters

  Disk drives and time limits

  Passwords and access levels

  Special-feature programs.

Hostcomm by itself is useful for businesses with outlying sales offices since it supports the hierarchical organization model. Headquarters can communicate with regional offices, but the offices can't communicate with one another. Sales staff can enter orders, and the main office can send product bulletins and order confirmations. The main office needs *Hostcomm,* but the branches can use a general-purpose communications program, such as those described in Chapter 7.

The *Hostcomm* special-feature programs are supplied by RMS Software but are distributed by Janadon. The Host Utilities module supports XMODEM

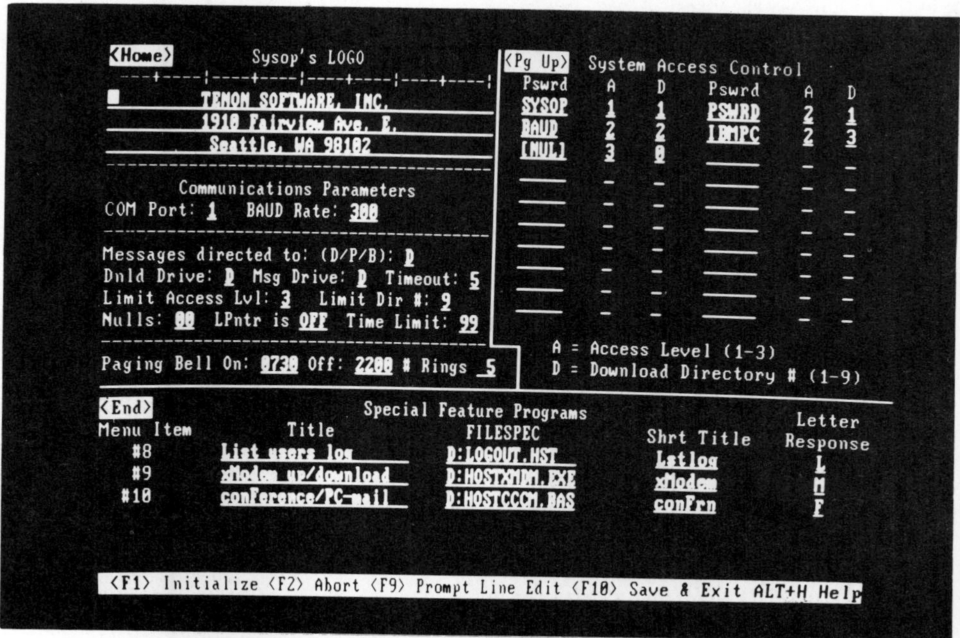

Figure 6-14. Hostcomm configuration screen

uploads and downloads. (*Hostcomm* by itself does not support error correction in file transfers.) The error-correction option costs $80 and includes a few other useful utilities to rearrange disk directories, exclude undesirable callers, and produce statistics.

The most useful *Hostcomm* utilities are PCE-Mail and Conferencing, available for $80 each or $125 for both. PCE-Mail is a true electronic mail system, allowing *Hostcomm* callers to send mail to one another. Messages may be addressed to individuals or to everyone. A two-digit user number is the security system. The *Hostcomm* password controls access to PCE-Mail, and the user number prevents callers from reading other callers' mail.

The **Conferencing** module is surprisingly similar to The Source's Participate. The SYSOP establishes conferences and starts each conference with introductory messages. Conferencing is like a collection of bulletin boards combined on one system. Callers can view a list of conferences, choose one, and then list and read messages and contribute their own. Conferencing uses the same user-number security system that PCE-Mail uses.

Here is some sample dialog from *Hostcomm* Conferencing:

```
    *** WELCOME TO CCC CONFERENCING SYSTEM ***


Hello, DAVE...

If you do not have a USER NUMBER type <N>ew.
If you want to search for your name, type <S>earch.
Type <Q>uit or type <H>elp... otherwise:


ENTER your USER NUMBER -> 46

ENTER your PASSWORD -> .......


Conf# --------Name-------- --Date-- -Msgs-
    1 The Day After        11/29/83   0
    2 PC's for the deaf    11/29/83   1
    3 Pres. nominations    11/29/83   0

Number of conference, <Q> or <D> ->2


The following functions are available:

<R>ead          Read messages from current conference
<C>ontribute    Enter a message
<X>-Expert      Make yourself an expert
<S>can          Scan messages
<Q>uit          Quit and return to HOSTCOMM
<H>elp          Print this message
<D>isplay       Display and choose new conference

R, C, D, X, S, Q, <H>elp?s
```

```
** Scan **

Format = NSDT
F, R, S, Q, <H>elp?h

<F>orward      Scan all messages forward from first available message
<R>everse      Scan all messages backward from last available message
<Q>uit         Quit the scan mode
<S>et          Set the scan format code
               This command allows you to tell the system what to include in
               the scan.  The format consists of a string of characters as
               follows:

                 N - Full name
                 F - First name
                 L - Last name
                 S - Subject
                 D - Date
                 T - Time

               When the system requests format, you would enter the characters
               for the information you wish to see. For instance, to see first
               name, subject and date, enter "FSD". The default is "NSDT".

Format = NSDT
F, R, S, Q, <H>elp?f

Msg # ---------Author--------- -----Subject---- --Date-- -Time-
    1 SYSOP KRUGLINSKI         CBB FOR DEAF     11/29/83  17:01
    2 JOE   SMITH              CAN WRITE        11/30/83  20:05
    3 MARY  JONES              I NEED ONE       11/30/83  21:30

R, C, D, X, S, Q, <H>elp?r

** Read **

Messages 1 thru 3 are available.

F, R, Q, <H>elp, <CR>, Msg #:1

Message: 1
Author: SYSOP KRUGLINSKI
Subject: CBB FOR DEAF
Date: 11/29/83 at 17:01

We are trying to put together a CBB for access by deaf persons with
Baudot terminals.  There are thousands of deaf people who communicate
with one another via small printing terminals.  Communication is point-
to-point without any conferencing or store-and-forward mail functions.
The goal is to create a CBB accessible by the deaf.  This can be used
for both improved communication within the community and for communi-
cation with non-deaf persons.

One approach to this problem is to modify BASIC such that it translates
to and from Baudot and sets the speed properly.  This would enable use
of all standard CBB software including PC - RBBS and maybe HOSTCOMM.
If anyone has any ideas, please contribute.  This is a chance to do some-
thing useful!
            SYSOP

Delete this message? (Y/N) ..

F, R, Q, <H>elp, <CR>, Msg #:h

<F>orward   - sets direction of retrieval to forward (increasing msg numbers).
<R>everse   - sets direction of retrieval to reverse (decreasing msg numbers).
<Q>uit      - quits the read mode
<H>elp      - prints this message.
<CR>        - Pressing <CR> retrieves the next message based on direction.
```

```
Msg #        - Message number to retrieve.

If the Conferencing system detects that you authored a message after it is
read, you will be given the option to delete it.  To delete the message,
type a "Y" followed by <CR>.

The direction will automatically be switched to the opposite direction when
the beginning or end of file is reached.

F, R, Q, <H>elp, <CR>, Msg #:q

Conf# --------Name-------- --Date-- -Msgs-
    1 The Day After        11/29/83    0
    2 PC's for the deaf    11/29/83    1
    3 Pres. nominations    11/29/83    0

Number of conference, <Q> or <D> ->q

Returning control to HOSTCOMM mainline
```

One problem in using *Hostcomm* is that the program will not work with the Hayes 1200B internal modem card, a problem that Hayes is correcting in future models. In addition, the cable used to connect the PC to an external modem requires that pin 22 be connected, a connection that many modem cables do not provide.

Other Bulletin Board Options

You can get around the one-caller-at-a-time limit with a multi-user message system called Qbulletin. It's available from Quantum Software Systems, and it runs with the QNX operating system. The price is $250, exclusive of QNX. You have to learn a new operating system, and you must have extra phone lines and the necessary hardware.

If you depart from the PC, Radio Shack's VIS videotex system may be for you. It runs on the TRS-80 Model 16 with the Xenix operating system. A complete system with an eight-line multiplexer costs about $22,000.

SEVEN

GENERAL-PURPOSE COMMUNICATIONS PROGRAMS

The **special-purpose communications programs** described in Chapter 6 are designed to be used with specific information utilities. You buy *Sourcelink* for use with The Source, *VIDTEX* for CompuServe, *Market Manager* for Dow Jones, and so on. Those programs insulate you from the technical details of data communications and provide special services such as graphics displays, error-free file transfers, and automatic updates of your data files.

General-purpose communications programs are designed to work with a variety of information utilities. Most general-purpose communications programs let you choose services like The Source, CompuServe, or Dow Jones from a menu and allow you to automatically log in to each service at the touch of a key. One program lets remote users dial into your PC, enabling them to run any of your software as if they were typing on your keyboard. General-purpose programs also work with remote mainframes, minicomputers, and other PCs. A general-purpose program is essential for using bulletin boards, doing PC-to-PC file transfers, and using most electronic mail systems.

Which type of communications program should you purchase now, special-purpose or general-purpose? The answer depends on the information utility. A single general-purpose package to handle all your communications tasks is a nice idea; you only need to buy and learn one program. But as personal computers and PCs become more popular, information providers are tailoring their services to take advantage of the intelligence at the remote end of the link and are allowing subscribers to use dedicated, special-purpose programs to take advantage of features like special graphics displays. The Viewtron videotex service described in Chapter 5 is an extreme example. But because general-purpose programs are so useful, you can expect to own both types.

Uses of General-Purpose Communications Programs

Here are some things you can do with a general-purpose communications program. (Note that some programs listed in this chapter cannot do all of them.)

1. Access information utilities such as CompuServe, exercising all system features except graphics displays and error-free file transfers.
2. Connect to most electronic mail services. Telex is included, but services that require specially formatted data, like the U.S. Post Office's E-COM, are not.
3. Use computer bulletin boards (CBBs) that are themselves communications programs that often run on a PC.
4. Exchange microcomputer disk files (programs, text, and data) over phone lines.
5. Exchange files between your PC and a microcomputer that uses an incompatible disk format via a direct cable connection.
6. Turn your PC into an industry-standard terminal with a direct connection or phone hookup to a minicomputer or mainframe.
7. Allow remote access to your PC.

Mailing a Diskette

Before you get too swept away by high technology, consider the problem of sending a PC disk file to another PC owner two states away. You could transfer the program with a communications program via a long-distance phone call. However, at 1200 bps it would take about an hour to transfer an entire diskette. If, on the other hand, you just mail a diskette, the postage costs about $0.50, and the disk arrives in two or three days. For $10 you could use an overnight express service.

Some Real Programs

The programs *COMM.BAS, PC-TALK III, Smartcom,* and *Crosstalk* are presented in this sequence because each succeeding program adds features to the one before it. A feature is explained when it is first introduced; so in order to fully understand the range of features that are available in general-purpose programs, you'll have to read the whole chapter.

COMM.BAS

COMM.BAS is a free program that comes with your DOS disk, and it's documented in the IBM BASIC manual. If you have a serial port and modem you can immediately use *COMM.BAS* to sample CBBs and a few free information utilities or The Source and Dow Jones if you have a subscription. Running *COMM.BAS* is an inexpensive way to become familiar with PC communications, but you'll soon realize that you got what you paid for. *COMM.BAS* makes the PC much like a **dumb terminal**, and dumb terminals provide only the bare essentials for using an information utility.

When you run *COMM.BAS* by entering the command BASICA COMM.BAS, you see a menu with the following choices:

```
1 Description of program
2 Dow Jones/News Retrieval
3 IBM Personal Computer
4 Series/1
5 The Source
6 Other service
7 End Program
```

This is more than a dumb terminal could give you, but it's not all that it appears to be. The program doesn't dial for you or log in to the selected service. Normally, you dial the information utility's local number with your telephone; you can also dial from the PC's keyboard if you have an **autodial modem**, a modem capable of dialing a number when it is sent the proper command. Once you reach an information utility like The Source, you must key in your account number, password, and special codes, as is detailed in the documentation that comes with your subscription. *COMM.BAS* sets the transmission speed and other communications parameters by using preset values for Dow Jones, IBM Series/1, and The Source. You can enter your own values for communicating with another IBM Personal Computer and for using other services.

Chapter 9 will introduce you to the details of communications parameters. For the time being, just remember that the parameters of your PC's serial port have to match those of the remote computer; otherwise your screen will be filled with nonsense. A communications program, even a simple one like COMM.BAS, allows you to preset these parameters for certain services. It's like presetting the stations on your car radio.

Speed is the most obvious parameter. You can choose to communicate at 300 bps or at 1200 bps, depending upon your modem and the system at the other end of the line. Here are some special cases:

1. When you are communicating with a dumb terminal or another PC running *COMM.BAS,* the systems at both ends of the line must be configured to communicate at the same speed.
2. If you are communicating with a PC through a Hayes 1200 bps modem running a communications program like *Smartcom II* or *RBBS,* you can select either 300 or 1200 bps and the other system will adjust. There's no reason not to use 1200 bps if your modem allows it.
3. If you connect to an information utility via Tymnet, you are free to choose your speed. Most Tymnet access numbers automatically adjust for speed. Remember that you pay more for 1200 bps. You'll recall from Chapter 2 that Tymnet and Telenet are nationwide data communications carriers that connect you to your information utility via a local phone call.
4. If you connect to an information utility via Telenet, there are separate access numbers for 300 bps and 1200 bps. Call the appropriate number for the correct speed.
5. The procedures for connecting directly to an information utility vary. You need to read the documentation for the utility you are using.

The parity, the number of data bits, and the number of stop bits can be found by trial and error. Most services will work with

No parity, 8 data bits, 1 stop bit

If you get strange characters on the screen, try

Even parity, 7 data bits, 1 stop bit

That's all there is to it.

When you communicate in **full-duplex**, as you usually will, the characters you type are sent down the wire, and the remote system echoes the same characters back to your screen. You know immediately if you are connected and if the line is good. If you're using a network like Tymnet or Telenet, the character is echoed by the local packet-switching computer, not the information utility's computer. If the remote computer doesn't echo the characters, your PC must display what you type. If not, you're typing "blind." With this **half-duplex** system you never know if your character was transmitted or if it was received correctly. Unfortunately, the telex store-and-forward services operate this way to maintain compatibility with the older Teletype machines.

In any case, the communications program, *COMM.BAS* included, must allow you to select full-duplex or half-duplex. If half-duplex mode is selected with a full-duplex remote computer, you'll see double characters. If full-duplex mode is selected with a half-duplex computer, you won't see anything.

COMM.BAS does allow some limited printing by using some of the functions of DOS. You can print screen images with the PRTSC key, or you can continuously print whatever appears on the screen.

If you want to connect to other services such as CompuServe or your favorite CBB, you can customize *COMM.BAS*, changing the menu choices and the preset parameters. To do this, you need to be familiar with BASIC.

PC-TALK III

PC-TALK III is a Freeware product distributed through an unconventional channel. You can get the program free by downloading it from a CBB or by sending a blank disk to the publisher, Headlands Press. If you like the program you can send $35 to the publisher. The author of the program, Andrew Fluegelman, in a speech at the 1983 San Francisco IBM PC Faire, claimed that 10 percent of *PC-TALK* users had paid for the program, and he speculated that few other software publishers were so fortunate.

PC-TALK is a worthwhile program and certainly a bargain at $35. It can be used for accessing information utilities and for PC-to-PC communications. (However, since *PC-TALK* can only handle communications speeds of up to 1200 bps, you may find its speed restrictive when you are transferring information from one PC to another via a cable connection.) One of *PC-TALK*'s advantages over *COMM.BAS* is its ability to save and transmit data to and from disk files. Another advantage is a **dialing directory** that allows your PC to automatically dial information utilities, CBBs, and other PCs with **autoanswer** modems, modems capable of automatically answering the phone.

PC-TALK is extremely easy to use and works well with the information utilities detailed in Chapter 4. Once you're connected to a utility, the program is "invisible." You enter commands to *PC-TALK* with the ALT key. For example, ALT S (press S while holding down the ALT key) saves the contents of the screen in a disk file called SCRNDUMP.PCT. The HOME key causes a "help menu," a list of PC-TALK's commands, to be displayed, as shown in Figure 7-1. You can display this help menu at any time while communicating and leave the left side of your screen intact.

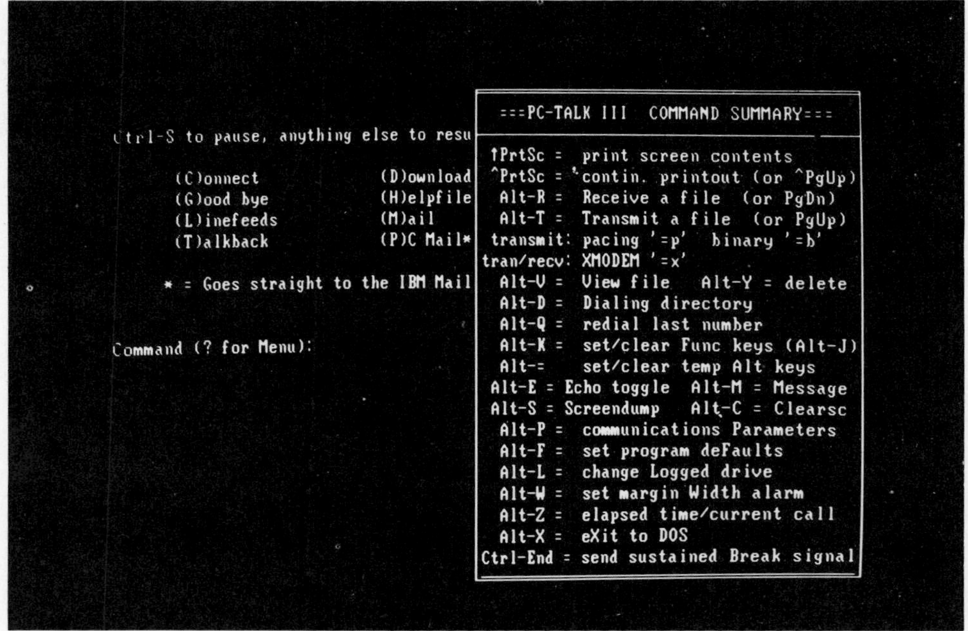

Figure 7-1. PC-TALK III help screen

PC-TALK also displays the **session time** at the bottom of the screen. This is the elapsed time since you were connected to an information utility or CBB. Some CBBs cut you off after a half hour or so, so it's useful to know how much time you have left. If you're using an information utility, the session time helps you know how much money you've spent. Unfortunately, *PC-TALK* sometimes erases the bottom line.

The dialing directory, called up by keying ALT D, is shown in Figure 7-2. The phone numbers and information service names are, of course, entered by you. In this example, typing a 1 causes *PC-TALK* to automatically dial The Source, assuming you have an autodial modem. The cryptic codes in the right-hand columns are the communications parameters you preset for each service. *PC-TALK* allows you to enter as many as 60 directory entries, 15 per page, and it accommodates the use of discount long-distance services like MCI and Sprint.

While *PC-TALK* does dial the number, it does not automatically send your user ID and password. If you do not have an autodial modem, don't worry. It's still helpful to display the phone numbers on the screen with a single command, and *PC-TALK* does set the communication parameters for you.

```
DIALING DIRECTORY  1 ===  Modem dialing command = ATDT
                          Long distance service +# =
                                                -# =
Name                            Phone #   Comm Param  Echo Mesg Strip Pace
1-The Source/Tymnet             2850109   1200-N-8-1   N    N    N     N
2-PC board (Edmonds             7781940    300-E-7-1   N    N    N     N
3------------------------ - --- --- ----   300-E-7-1   N    N    N     N
4------------------------ - --- --- ----   300-E-7-1   N    N    N     N
5------------------------ - --- --- ----   300-E-7-1   N    N    N     N
6------------------------ - --- --- ----   300-E-7-1   N    N    N     N
7------------------------ - --- --- ----   300-E-7-1   N    N    N     N
8------------------------ - --- --- ----   300-E-7-1   N    N    N     N
9------------------------ - --- --- ----   300-E-7-1   N    N    N     N
10----------------------- - --- --- ----   300-E-7-1   N    N    N     N
11----------------------- - --- --- ----   300-E-7-1   N    N    N     N
12----------------------- - --- --- ----   300-E-7-1   N    N    N     N
13----------------------- - --- --- ----   300-E-7-1   N    N    N     N
14----------------------- - --- --- ----   300-E-7-1   N    N    N     N
15----------------------- - --- --- ----   300-E-7-1   N    N    N     N

Dial entry #:            ; or...    Enter: R to revise or add to directory
                                           M for manual dialing
                                       F / B to page through directory
                                           X to exit to terminal
                         ; For long distance service, precede entry # with +/-
```

Figure 7-2. PC-TALK III dialing directory

Like *COMM.BAS*, *PC-TALK* uses the PC's PRTSC key to control printing. While printing is the only way to "capture" data with *COMM.BAS*, *PC-TALK* lets you save data on disk for later editing or printing. However, you should avoid printing while communicating since the printer will slow down the communications process. Capture the data on disk and then use your text editor or word processor program to "clean up" the copy before printing.

PC-TALK's best feature is its ability to save and transmit to and from disk files. The ALT R command allows all data from the remote computer, including echoes of your keystrokes, to be written to the disk file of your choice. Writing to disk is fast except when the drive's head must be moved to a new track. Since a remote computer sends data relentlessly and at a fixed rate, *PC-TALK* uses PC BASIC's **communications buffer** to smooth out the data flow from the serial port to the disk, thus preventing any character loss.

Writing to disk is easy, but transmitting data that is stored on disk is another story. *PC-TALK* can send data at a steady rate, but the information utility on the other end may not be equipped to receive it that fast. *PC-TALK* provides two ways of coordinating the PC's communication with a remote computer. The preferred way is through the use of a protocol called **XON/XOFF**, which works with most remote computers. XOFF and XON are names for two ASCII characters that, by convention, mean "stop sending data" and "start sending it again." When the remote computer can't handle any more characters, it sends an XOFF to the PC and the PC waits. When the remote computer is ready to start receiving again, it sends an XON and the PC resumes sending. XON/XOFF is *PC-TALK*'s default method of sending files.

If the remote computer doesn't follow the XON/XOFF protocol, you can tell *PC-TALK* to use **pacing**. With pacing you either specify a **time delay** of several seconds between transmissions of data or you tell *PC-TALK* to wait for a **prompt**, a special character such as a question mark, before transmitting the next line of data.

Not all the disk file transfer schemes allow for **error-checking**. If an "A" is changed to a "B", you'll never know it. Error rates are usually low enough so there's no problem with text files. A few extra typos won't matter. Programs are a different story. When you download a program, you can't afford to have errors introduced during the transmission. Executable programs are particularly critical; one bad byte and the program may not run at all.

PC-TALK uses the **XMODEM error-checking protocol**, which will be described in Chapter 9 and Appendix D. This protocol enables the PC to detect errors in blocks of received data. You can use the XMODEM protocol to exchange programs with other *PC-TALK* users, most CBBs, and systems running the *Remote Access* program or *Crosstalk XVI* version 3.4 or greater. Here's the procedure for sending a file via modem between two PCs with *PC-TALK*:

1. Set one modem to answer mode and the other to originate mode.
2. Start *PC-TALK* on the answering PC using half-duplex mode (ALT E).
3. Start *PC-TALK* on the originating PC, also in half-duplex mode, and select the proper phone number from the dialing directory.
4. If you are the sending party, press ALT T, enter the name of the file to transmit, and follow it with =x, the special suffix indicating the XMODEM protocol.
5. If you are the receiving party, press ALT R, enter the name of the file to receive, and follow it with =x.
6. File transfer is automatic from this point on, with the remaining transfer time displayed on the screen.

You've just learned about *PC-TALK*'s important features. But there are some other features that make *PC-TALK* pleasant to use. You can display the contents of a disk file at any time, look at a directory, or change the default drive. You can program the PC's function keys and any unused ALT key commands to send words or phrases. For instance, you can store your Source ID and password to partially automate the log-in process. Figure 7-3 shows the default screen. This screen displays the communications parameters and configuration information to allow you to customize *PC-TALK* for your own PC and modem. The default values are set for the Hayes Smartmodem.

PC-TALK is supplied in both BASIC source and compiled object formats. If you have only 64K of memory, you must use the BASIC source version with the BASICA interpreter. If you have 128K or more memory, you can run the more efficient and faster-loading compiled version.

Many people have customized *PC-TALK*, and some CBBs provide a list of changes (called a **merge file**) to make *PC-TALK* run at 450 bps. If you have a BASIC compiler you may recompile the changed version.

Documentation comes in the form of a disk file that is the equivalent of about 70 printed pages. It's clearly written and well organized, but there's no index. However, you could use your word processing program to search the file for key words and phrases.

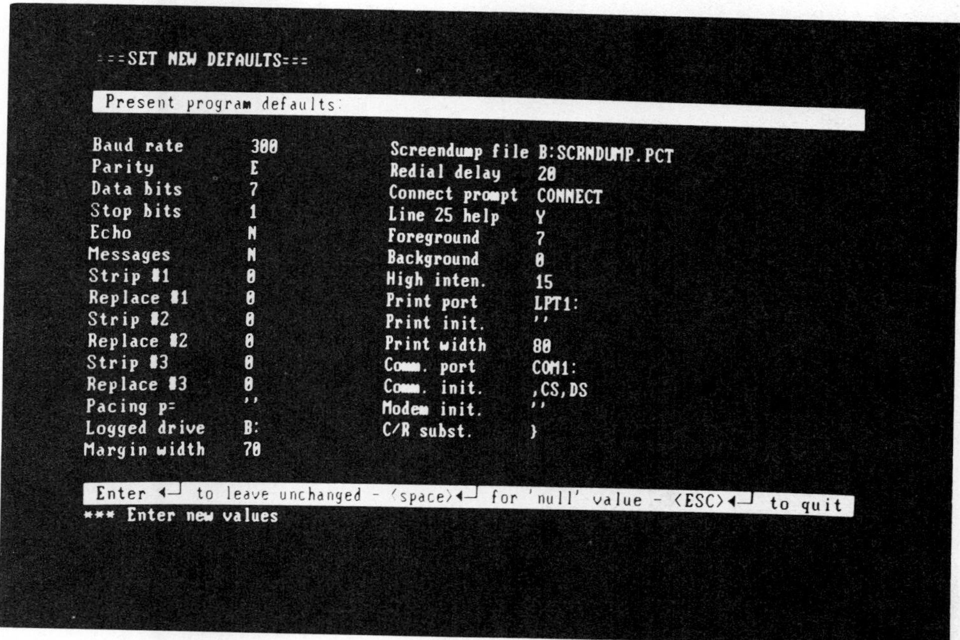

Figure 7-3. *PC-TALK III default screen*

Smartcom II

Smartcom II comes free with the Hayes 1200B circuit card modem. You can buy it for $119 for use with other Hayes modems or Hayes-compatible modems. Because Hayes designed *Smartcom II* specifically for Hayes modems, the supreme test of Hayes compatibility is whether it runs *Smartcom II*.

Smartcom II does everything *PC-TALK* does except support the XMODEM error-checking protocol and display the elapsed session time. You can live without the time display, but you can't upload or download CBB software without the XMODEM protocol. *Smartcom II* does have its own error-correcting protocol, which permits you to exchange files with other *Smartcom* users.

Some of the nice features of *Smartcom II* are **automatic log-in**, **memory capture**, and **remote access** from another system running *Smartcom*. Automatic log in relieves you of the burden of typing your user ID and password each time you connect to an information utility or CBB. Capture to memory allows you to save a copy of the incoming data in the PC's memory, and remote access allows

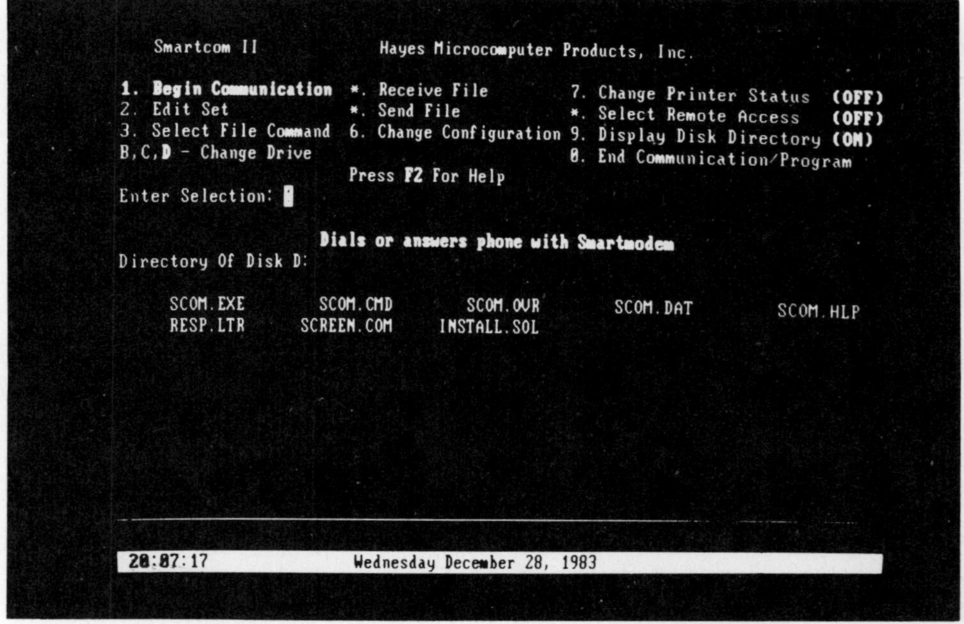

Figure 7-4. Smartcom II main menu

an authorized caller to control file transfers to and from your PC.

Functions aside, *Smartcom II*'s personality comes from the fact that it's menu-driven. *Smartcom*'s menu gives you an efficient, single-keystroke method of getting the job done. It's logical and easy to learn—an ideal program for occasional users.

Figure 7-4 shows the *Smartcom II* main menu along with a disk directory. If you choose item 1, Begin Communication, you will be prompted to select originate or answer mode, and you will see the screen shown in Figure 7-5. Once you select a letter A through Z, the rest is automatic, assuming you've already set up all your phone numbers, IDs, and passwords. Hayes has set up 13 entries for you, but you must customize those 13 with local phone numbers plus your own IDs and passwords.

Once the entries are set up, operation of *Smartcom II* is easy. Figure 7-6 shows the screen after you've logged in to the Dow Jones News/Retrieval Service. The last three lines indicate the name of the network or service, the definition of the four function keys, and the current time and date. The function keys can be redefined to perform a variety of functions.

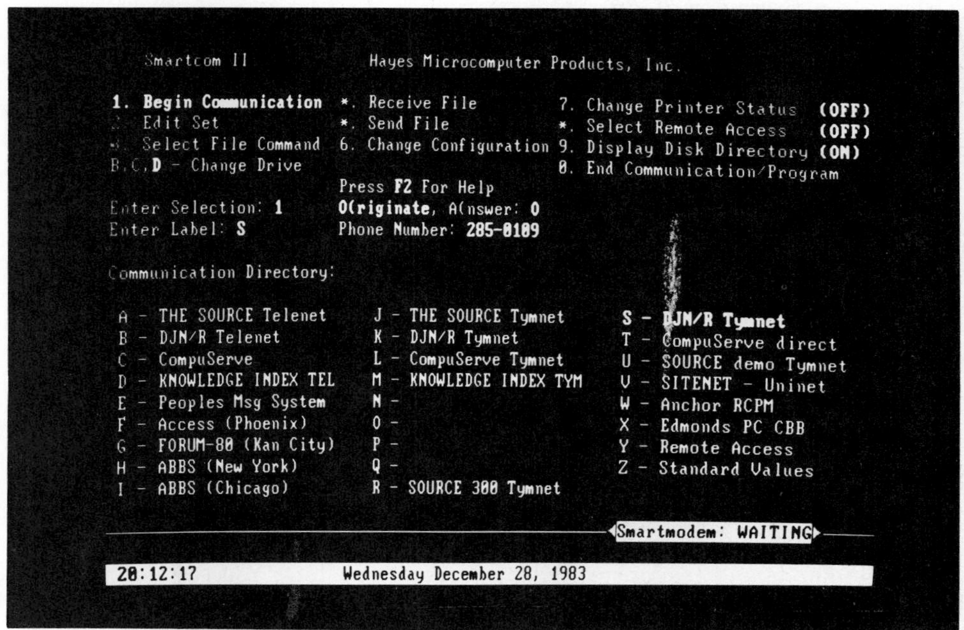

Figure 7-5. Smartcom II communication menu

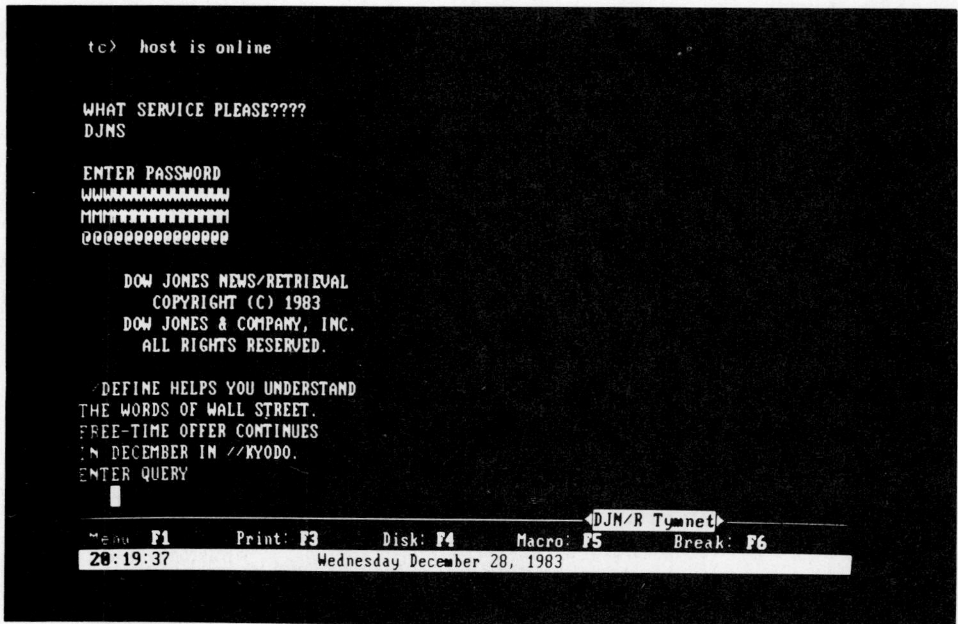

Figure 7-6. Smartcom II after log in

Menu: F1 switches back to the main menu shown in Figure 7-4. The switch to the menu is instantaneous, and the switch back to your original screen is just as quick.

Print: F3 switches the printer on and off. Printer status is shown on the second status line at the bottom of the screen.

Disk: F4 starts data capture to a disk file named TEMP. The ESC key stops the capture and gives you a chance to rename the file. Note that one keystroke starts data capture, so there's no delay if you see something you like. You can think of a file name later.

Macro: F5 lets you execute an automatic dialog (a predetermined sequence of commands and responses) with the remote system. You can define as many as 24 of these sequences, identified by letters A through X, for each service. For example, if you're on CompuServe, you can program a key to get you the local ski report.

Break: F6 sends a break signal to the host system. Break interrupts some host computers, causing them to stop what they're doing and to accept new instructions. Break is seldom used with the information utilities you're likely to encounter.

When two *Smartcom II* systems are connected, there are two levels of interaction. If you originate a call to a friend whose system is set to answer mode, you can send and receive files with an error-correcting protocol called verification protocol. You select the entry Send File, and your friend selects the entry Receive File from the main menu. You may each use a different file name. If both you and your friend select the entry Remote Access, the file transfer process is more automated. Your friend need no longer be at the computer; you can view the disk directory or send and receive files from your own keyboard. The remote computer can be unattended because there is **password protection** to keep intruders out; callers must enter the password you've established in order to gain access to the system.

Smartcom II supplements disk capture with **memory capture**. An area of your system's memory, called a **buffer**, is used to store incoming data. This is automatic—you have no control over it. The HOME key takes you to the top of the buffer so you can read what came in earlier, and you can scroll backward and forward by line or by page. The END key returns you to where you were. Using the HOME and END keys with the buffer is similar to shuffling through a long printout. Memory capture and disk capture are independent; you can't save memory data to disk. After you are disconnected from the remote system, the data remains in memory for viewing or printing with the PRTSC key.

Smartcom allows you to set up parameters and **macros** for each information utility. Figure 7-7 shows the parameter screen accessed from the main menu. You just call up a screen by letter; change the parameters like data rate, phone number, and so forth; and write the parameter values back to disk. All this is done under menu control. Notice the name and phone number entries. The name also appears on the main menu used to select the service. Associated with each parameter screen is a set of macros, as listed in Figure 7-8. These are command sequences to be used with an information utility for logging in, checking your mail, or displaying your favorite stock prices. The parameters, together with as many as 26 associated macros, make up what Hayes calls a **communication set**, diagramed in Figure 7-9.

Figure 7-10 shows a log-in macro for The Source. *Smartcom* waits for the prompt shown in column 2, and then sends the data string shown in column 3 followed by an optional carriage return (column 4). If the prompt is not received within the time-out interval shown in column 1, *Smartcom* moves down to the

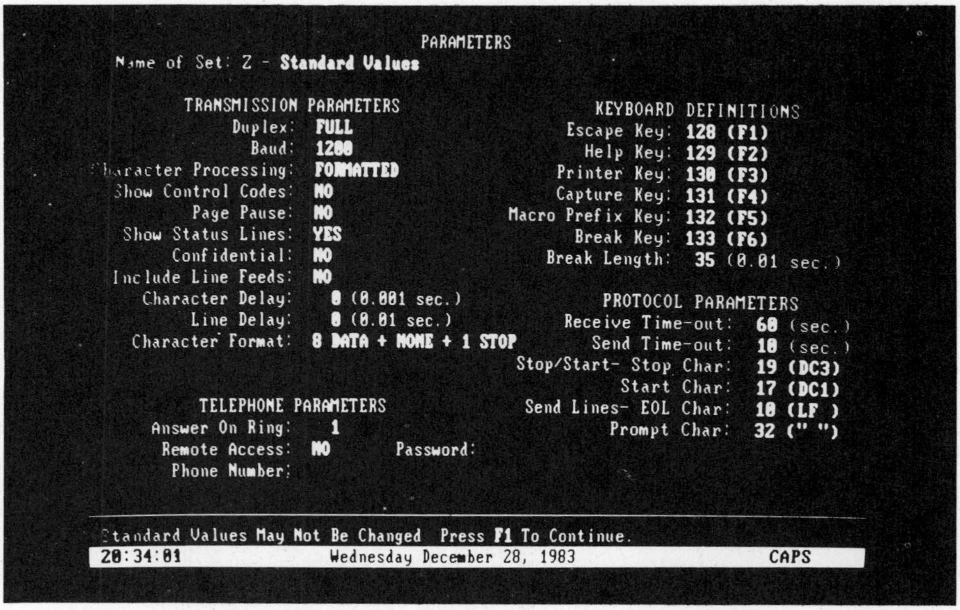

```
                                 PARAMETERS
   Name of Set: Z - Standard Values

          TRANSMISSION PARAMETERS                      KEYBOARD DEFINITIONS
                    Duplex:  FULL                       Escape Key:  128 (F1)
                      Baud:  1200                         Help Key:  129 (F2)
      Character Processing:  FORMATTED                 Printer Key:  130 (F3)
        Show Control Codes:  NO                        Capture Key:  131 (F4)
                Page Pause:  NO                   Macro Prefix Key:  132 (F5)
         Show Status Lines:  YES                         Break Key:  133 (F6)
              Confidential:  NO                       Break Length:   35 (0.01 sec.)
       Include Line Feeds:   NO
           Character Delay:    0 (0.001 sec.)          PROTOCOL PARAMETERS
                Line Delay:    0 (0.01 sec.)      Receive Time-out:   60 (sec.)
          Character Format:  8 DATA + NONE + 1 STOP  Send Time-out:   10 (sec.)
                                          Stop/Start- Stop Char:   19 (DC3)
                                                      Start Char:   17 (DC1)
          TELEPHONE PARAMETERS              Send Lines- EOL Char:   10 (LF )
            Answer On Ring:    1                     Prompt Char:   32 (" ")
             Remote Access:  NO        Password:
              Phone Number:

  Standard Values May Not Be Changed  Press F1 To Continue.
  20:34:01              Wednesday December 28, 1983                   CAPS
```

Figure 7-7. Smartcom II parameter screen

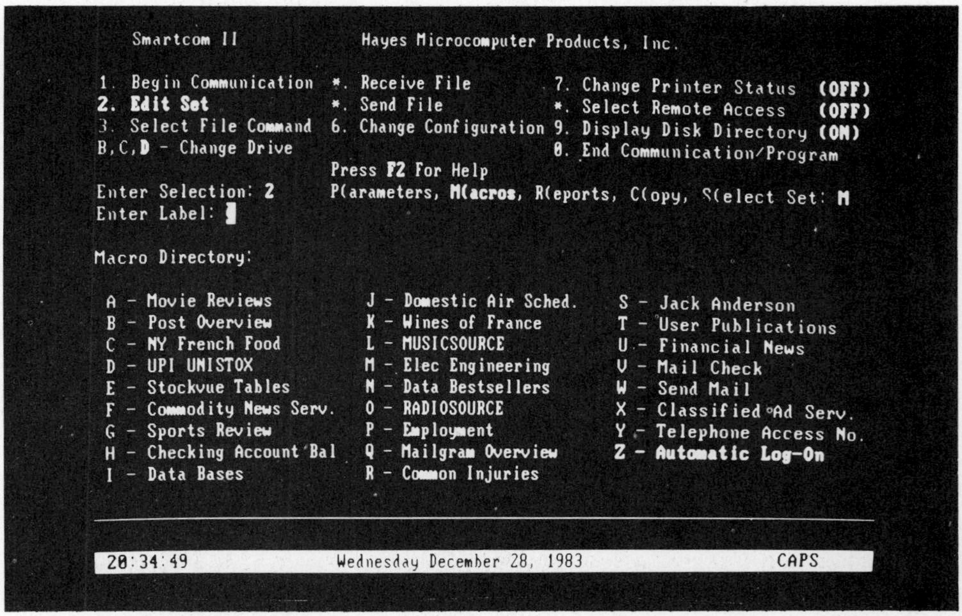

```
   Smartcom II             Hayes Microcomputer Products, Inc.

  1. Begin Communication  *. Receive File        7. Change Printer Status  (OFF)
  2. Edit Set             *. Send File           *. Select Remote Access   (OFF)
  3. Select File Command  6. Change Configuration 9. Display Disk Directory (ON)
  B,C,D - Change Drive                           0. End Communication/Program
                          Press F2 For Help
  Enter Selection: 2      P(arameters, M(acros, R(eports, C(opy, S(elect Set: M
  Enter Label:

  Macro Directory:

   A - Movie Reviews          J - Domestic Air Sched.    S - Jack Anderson
   B - Post Overview          K - Wines of France        T - User Publications
   C - NY French Food         L - MUSICSOURCE            U - Financial News
   D - UPI UNISTOX            M - Elec Engineering       V - Mail Check
   E - Stockvue Tables        N - Data Bestsellers       W - Send Mail
   F - Commodity News Serv.   O - RADIOSOURCE            X - Classified Ad Serv.
   G - Sports Review          P - Employment             Y - Telephone Access No.
   H - Checking Account Bal   Q - Mailgram Overview      Z - Automatic Log-On
   I - Data Bases             R - Common Injuries

  20:34:49              Wednesday December 28, 1983                   CAPS
```

Figure 7-8. Smartcom II macro selection screen

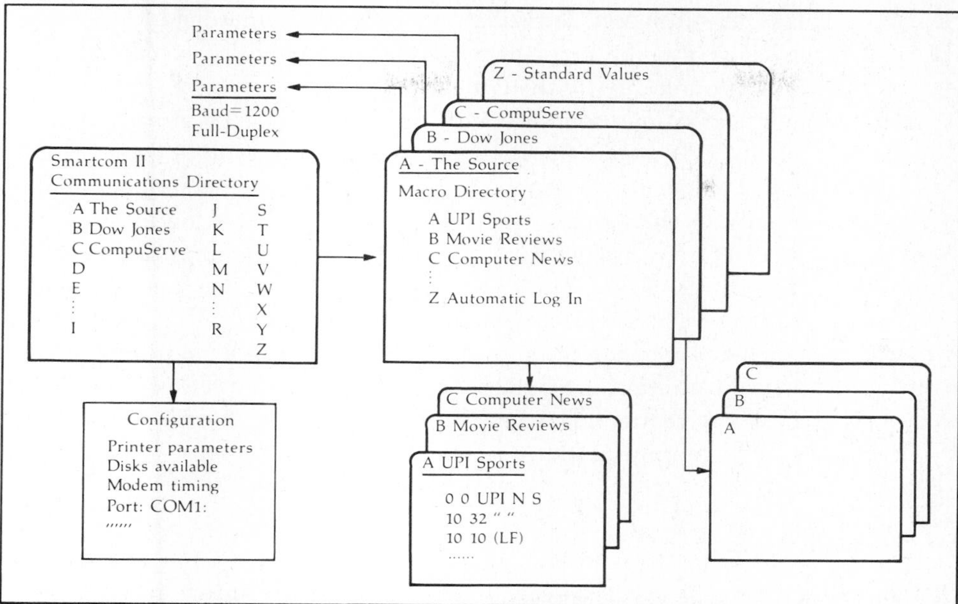

Figure 7-9. Smartcom II communication set diagram

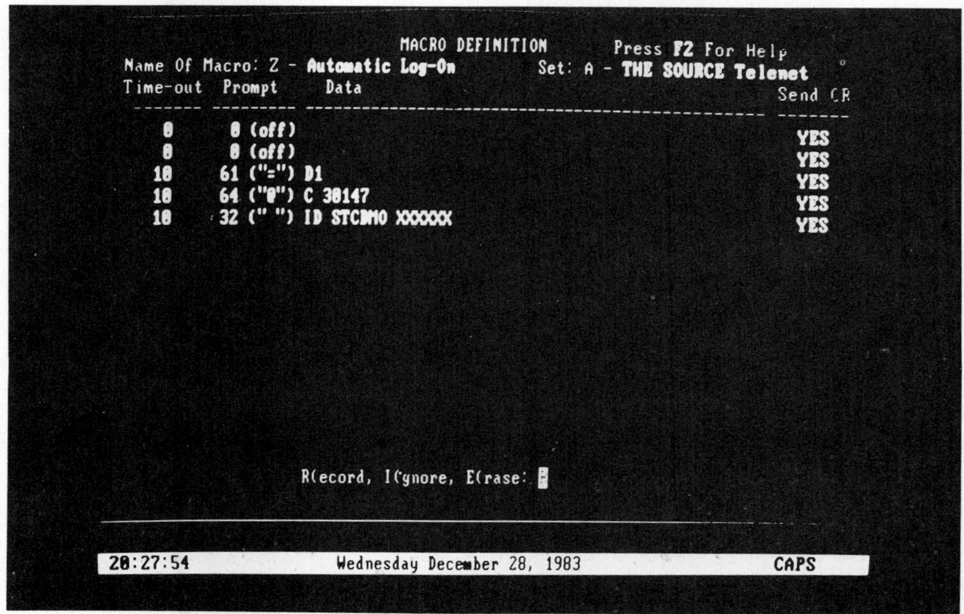

Figure 7-10. Smartcom II macro for Source log in

next line. This is an automated conversation between *Smartcom* and The Source. The "Z" macro is always the log-in macro; it is automatically executed whenever you start communicating with that service.

You can copy communication sets with *Smartcom.* If you've already defined a set in "A" called "THE SOURCE Telenet," you can copy it to "J", renaming it "THE SOURCE Tymnet." You must then change the phone number in the parameter screen and change the "Z" macro for the correct log-in sequence. Note that you can't copy individual macros from one communication set to another.

Hayes provides a very complete user manual with *Smartcom II,* but there's no index. It does include some communication theory along with summaries of the popular information utilities, a troubleshooting guide, and a list of CBBs. The manual is attractively printed in two colors and comes with handy divider tabs. It's a self-contained communications reference.

Crosstalk XVI

Microstuf's *Crosstalk XVI* is everything you always wanted in a general-purpose communications program and is well worth its $195 price. It does everything *PC-TALK III* does and even more, including transferring files using the XMODEM protocol. This feature is a recent addition. For the first-time user, *Crosstalk* isn't as easy to learn as *Smartcom,* but there are many features that make *Crosstalk* ideal for seasoned communications users. If you like the popular database management program dBASE II, you'll love *Crosstalk* because it's command-driven. You'll need to keep the manual by your side for the first week, but you'll soon memorize the two-letter abbreviations of your favorite commands.

Crosstalk connects you to all of the popular information utilities and CBBs, and it works well for transferring files via phone line or direct connection. *Crosstalk* supports speeds of 300 and 1200 bps for modems as well as a searing 9600 bps for direct micro-to-micro file transfers and remote control. *Crosstalk* also allows your PC to emulate five popular video terminals: you attach your PC to a minicomputer or mainframe either directly or via a modem.

Like *Smartcom, Crosstalk* supports memory capture, but it also permits you to search the capture buffer for a specific word or phrase. In addition, *Crosstalk* gives you the option of saving the memory capture buffer to disk. (Be careful, though, because the buffer can be as large as your available memory and possibly larger than the space on your disk.) One nice feature of *Crosstalk,* **retro-capture**, allows you to capture data up to two screens old. A circular buffer always saves the previous 4096 bytes of data, much like the automatic flight recorder in an airplane maintains a recording of the most recent 20 minutes of flight-deck conversation. You can, of course, capture data directly to disk, but retro-capture is a good alternative. Figure 7-11 summarizes *Crosstalk*'s data capture modes.

Crosstalk's most powerful feature is its script language, which you can use to create prearranged conversations with information utilities. You've seen that *Smartcom* allows simple prompt-response sequences, as shown in Figure 7-10. *Crosstalk* carries this further by adding decision-making and looping capabilities. A simple example is the log-in procedure for CompuServe. Sometimes you will see the prompt HOST NAME and sometimes you won't. This would confuse *Smartcom*, but *Crosstalk* handles it with the following script:

```
Wait delay 30                        (ASCII Code 03)
Reply CTL-C
When "HOST NAME" reply CIS¦          (¦ means send a carriage return)
Wait char ":"
Reply 70006,513¦
Wait char ":"
Reply FORCE/DOUBLE¦
```

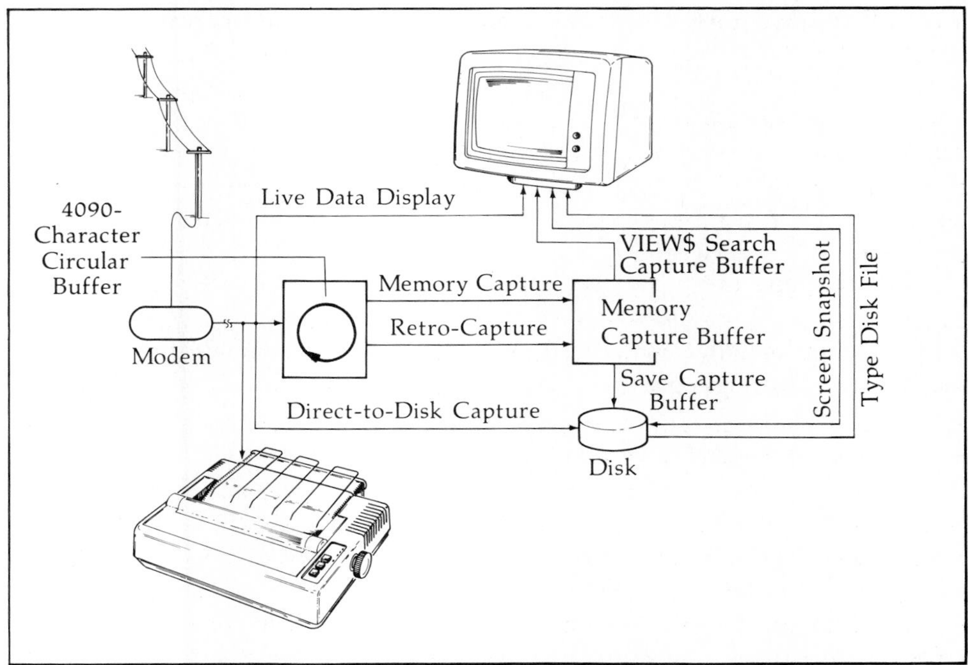

Figure 7-11. Crosstalk XVI data capture modes

The actual log-in sequence goes like this:

```
C
HOST NAME CIS
User ID: 70006,513
Password:                         (not echoed on your terminal)

Consumer Information Service
21:58 PST  Tuesday   22-Nov-83
```

Log-in scripts are easy to write, and the *Crosstalk* manual gives examples. If you write more complex scripts, you need programming skills or access to a programmer. For instance, if you need a script to check your electronic mailbox automatically and retrieve all new messages in sequence, *Crosstalk* can handle it, but not without some programming effort.

What does **terminal emulation** do for you? Suppose your company uses a minicomputer to keep track of inventory. If this minicomputer is like most multi-user systems, a number of terminals are attached to it so many users can access the system concurrently. However, rather than use the terminals, you could use a PC running *Crosstalk* to emulate a terminal, thus giving your PC access to the inventory. *Crosstalk* can emulate or operate like any of the following terminals:

Televideo 910/920

IBM 3101

ADDS Viewpoint

DEC VT-52

DEC VT-100

If the minicomputer can operate with one of these terminals, the inventory program won't even know that you're using a PC, but will work as if you had a terminal.

Crosstalk recognizes the emulated terminal's unique **cursor control sequences**, which allow text to be positioned anywhere on the screen. With the IBM 3101 terminal, for example, if the remote computer sends the character sequence Esc, Y, $, G, the terminal's cursor moves to row 5, column 40, and any following text is displayed starting at that position.

Emulation isn't just for minicomputers, however. Compuserve's *VIDTEX* program (described in Chapter 6) requires a terminal that closely matches the IBM 3101. If you tell *Crosstalk* to emulate the 3101, you will get well-formatted screens in which each page starts at the top of the screen. *Crosstalk* can substitute for CompuServe's own *VIDTEX* program if you don't need graphics and error-free file transfers.

Crosstalk, like *Smartcom,* can be operated remotely from another microcomputer. Another *Crosstalk* user can access your PC (running *Crosstalk*) for error-free file transfers. An earlier version of *Crosstalk* runs on 8-bit machines using the popular CP/M operating system. This system allows you to transfer all your old CP/M WordStar and dBASE II files onto PC disks. Crosstalk permits file transfers using a special character called a wild card. Wild cards allow you to specify a group of files containing the same group of characters in their names. For example, you can specify all of the files on drive B ending with '.CMD' with the file specifier B:*.CMD. Dumb terminals or computers that are not running *Crosstalk* can connect to a *Crosstalk* system only to check directories and list text files. Microstuf's *Transporter* program can dial into *Crosstalk* and exchange files using *Crosstalk*'s data transfer protocol.

How do you get started with *Crosstalk*? As with IBM BASIC, commands can be entered directly from the keyboard, or they can be stored as programs. *Crosstalk* starts up by displaying the screen shown in Figure 7-12. You are prompted

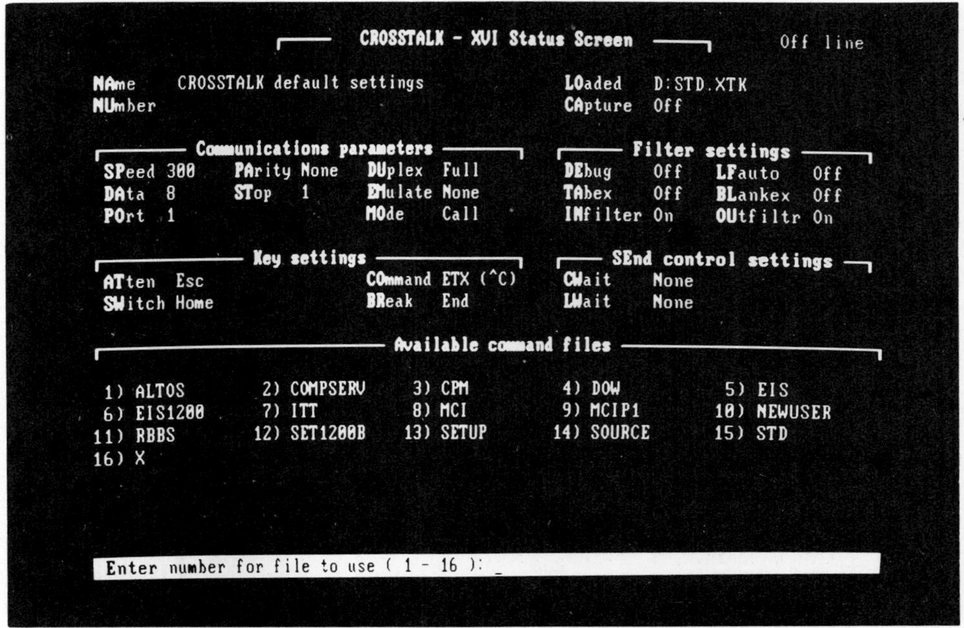

Figure 7-12. Crosstalk XVI startup screen

to select a **command file** by number, and if you've named those command files appropriately (SOURCE, COMPSERV, DOWJONES, and so forth), you'll have an easy time logging in to your service. Once you key in the number of the command file, you're on.

If you haven't defined your command files and scripts, you've got some work to do. If you press the ESC key, you will see the prompt Command? at the lower left of the screen. Entering SP 1200 and PO 2, for instance, set the data rate and serial port number. The DP command tells *Crosstalk* how to dial with your modem, enabling you to use almost any modem available. The SA command writes the communications parameters to a disk file in the form of commands as though you typed them. This command file, named COMPSERV.XTK, is readable by text editors and word processor programs.

When starting *Crosstalk,* you execute command files by typing XTALK COMPSERV, for example, by selecting a numbered .XTK file, as shown in Figure 7-12, or by typing a command like LOad COMPSERV. The command file instructs the PC to dial the number and establish the connection.

The scripts reside in their own files with names ending in .XTS, which you create using a text editor. The log-in script has the same first name as the command file and is automatically invoked as soon as the connection is made. Other scripts may be activated with the DO command. You've already seen an example of the CompuServe log-in script COMPSERV.XTS.

What skills do you need to run *Crosstalk*? While using *Crosstalk* to communicate is easy, writing script files and setting up parameters requires some programming and an understanding of data communications. If you're setting up a local transfer (without modems) from a CP/M machine to a PC, you've got your hands full. Because 8-bit machines have no standard serial port configurations, you must adjust the speed and protocol with the utilities provided by the computer manufacturer. Assuming everything matches and the cable connecting the two computers is wired properly, the sequence necessary to complete the transfer is still fairly complicated.

Transferring files from PC to PC over the phone line is also somewhat involved, requiring both computer operators to coordinate their actions. A simultaneous voice-telephone connection will be helpful.

Crosstalk provides lots of extras, including:

- Programmable function keys. F1 can be programmed to start data capture to a predetermined disk file.
- DOS 2.0 directory change. Files can be sent and received to or from any subdirectory.
- Interactive script debug mode. This mode helps get scripts working.

- Session time display. The status line displays how long you've been connected.
- Automatic answerback. This feature is useful for communicating with telex services.
- Color change. You can select your own color for text, background, and status line.
- Screen snapshot. The current screen is saved to disk or memory.
- Disk file display/erase. You can read or delete files on a disk.
- Sorted disk directory display. A sorted list of files on a disk is displayed.

The documentation is a typeset manual with the commands summarized and cross-referenced alphabetically. An index is not provided, but it is really not necessary.

Remote Access

Both *Smartcom II* and *Crosstalk XVI* offer limited remote access to your PC. Both programs can put the PC into autoanswer mode, allowing remote callers to view your PC's directory and to exchange disk files. Custom Software's *Remote Access* goes one step further. It lets remote callers run PC programs as though they were entering commands from your PC's keyboard.

The *Remote Access* program runs on a PC, but callers don't need PCs; they can use other microcomputers or ordinary terminals. If the calling terminal is a PC, so much the better. The *Remote Access* package includes a communications program called *PC-PHONE*, which is similar to *PC-TALK III*. *PC-PHONE* supports automatic dialing and XMODEM protocol file transfers.

Who can use *Remote Access*? Consider a small freight-forwarding company that uses an IBM PC XT for spreadsheets, word processing, and accounting. Once a month the company sends a barge to Alaska, which requires preparation of about 30 shipping manifests. All the information is accumulated at the dock and must be immediately input to the computer so that freight bills may be sent to the shippers. The shipping clerk could drive across town with all the paperwork and then spend half a day at the XT in the office, but there's a better way. With *Remote Access* running on the XT, the clerk dials into the office XT from another PC at the dock. The clerk enters the manifest information. The freight bills can then be printed and the accounts receivable records updated at the office. All this is done with *Remote Access* plus an ordinary off-the-shelf accounting program with an order entry/invoicing module. No custom programming is required.

This application requires two modems and a PC with one disk drive at the remote end—an expensive setup. One option would be to use a dumb terminal at the dock, but then the keyboard differences would complicate the operation of the accounting software. Alternatively, the clerk could enter the manifests on a stand-alone PC and then send a diskette to the office via courier. This scheme requires some custom programming on the XT in order to merge the external transactions with the local ones. In addition, modems limit *Remote Access*'s speed to 1200 bps, but that speed can be raised to 9600 bps if a cable is connected from the host to the remote PC.

Remote Access makes the PC an inexpensive multi-user system with one main limitation: real multi-user computer systems allow simultaneous access from many terminals, while *Remote Access* allows only one terminal to be connected at a time. All in all, *Remote Access* is a good program to have in your bag of tricks for just the right situation. If you just want to transfer files, use *Smartcom* or *Crosstalk*. If you want to set up a full-scale electronic mail system, use *Hostcom*. But if you want to remotely execute a specific program, consider *Remote Access*.

Remote Access keeps a log of all users by recording user name, date, and time. The XMODEM file transfer module ensures error-free file transfers with many communications programs such as *PC-TALK III* and *Crosstalk*. Optional password protection is provided, but serious hackers could still break in.

When you try to run PC programs from terminals and computers other than the PC, things become complicated. Programs can be divided into three categories with respect to screen access. The first group, including programs like the DOS commands DIR, TYPE, and DEBUG, is easily handled by *Remote Access*. These programs write to the screen one line at a time with the prior data scrolling off the screen. The second class of programs uses operating system routines (BIOS) to write text to certain locations on the screen. IBM's BASIC and dBASE II are prime examples. *Remote Access* handles these programs nicely if you specify the type of terminal that you are using (ADM 3a, Televideo 920, and so forth). The third class includes spreadsheets and word processors. These programs take advantage of the PC's memory-mapped video and treat the screen as a window to a block of memory. Characters are displayed by writing them to specific memory locations. *Remote Access* handles these types of programs with a function called **screen capture**, which transmits the PC's entire screen to the remote terminal. Operation is slow and awkward, so avoid using these types of programs with *Remote Access*.

Remote Access also allows non-PC keyboards to send PC keyboard codes. For example, the ALT A combination can be simulated by a CTRL A followed by an A. This works fine except when you need to send a CTRL A. You can change the key definitions by changing a table, but this gets more and more complex. It is better to use a PC or PC-compatible computer as the remote terminal.

If your remote terminal is a PC and you want to communicate locally at 9600 bps, you must use *Crosstalk* or a similar program on the remote end because *PC-PHONE* is too slow. If you tell *Remote Access* to assume an IBM 3101 terminal, for instance, you must configure *Crosstalk* to emulate the same terminal.

Remote Access is easily configured for your system and comes with a 37-page user's manual suitable for the experienced PC communicator. The price is only $89, and it runs in 64K of memory with DOS 1.1 and 128K of memory with DOS 2.0.

CTTY

CTTY, included with DOS 2.0, purports to offer the same service as *Remote Access*. It does, but in a very limited way. *CTTY* transfers the PC's keyboard and display functions over to a terminal connected to the serial port. It's assumed that the terminal is attached by a cable, as there are no provisions in the program for autoanswer modems. *CTTY* only works with a very limited class of programs: those using the operating system BDOS calls, like the DOS utilities and compiler programs. BASIC won't work at all with *CTTY*, and only parts of dBASE II will work. You could write a program specifically for *CTTY* using a compiled language like C or Pascal, but don't count on using *CTTY* with most application programs that you purchase. When connecting a terminal to the PC, you need to use the null modem cable (described in Chapter 9) because *CTTY* does some strange things with the control lines.

Other Programs

There are many general-purpose communications programs available for the PC. Those described here are typical. While a program like *Crosstalk* is designed to do everything, other programs are better at specific jobs.

VTERM from Saturn Consulting ($125) emulates the DEC VT-100 and VT-52 terminals. Its parameter screen is easier to work with than *Crosstalk*'s, but its main advantage is the status line at the bottom of the screen that closely mimics the DEC terminals' status line. You can easily see whether you're in upper-or lower-case mode and whether the keyboard is in numeric or cursor control mode. The DEC terminals have four programmable LED indicators, which are simulated on the status line. The *VTERM* manual gives full specifications for the DEC terminals including all control sequences. Unfortunately, you can't make working copies of the *VTERM* diskette, but you can load *VTERM* onto hard disk and run it, supplanting the need for the diskette.

Move-It from Woolf Software Systems ($150) is a full-featured communications program that runs at speeds up to 9600 bps. There are 8-bit versions for many CP/M computers, and the file transfer function is easier to use than *Crosstalk*'s. Commands are "symmetrical"; for instance, LDIR gets you a local directory and RDIR gets you a remote directory. There's no special set-up procedure required to transfer files to a remote computer.

Dynamic Microprocessor Associates *ASCOM* ($175) is a command-driven program that offers translation tables to convert a character to any other character on both input and output. It has its own file transfer protocol, but it doesn't have a dialing directory.

EIGHT

ASYNCHRONOUS MODEMS

A modem is an electronic device connecting your PC's serial port to a phone line. It is two devices in one—a **modulator** for converting serial output pulses into tones and a **demodulator** for converting incoming tones into pulses. You must have a modem in order to use information utilities and to communicate with any computer beyond the reach of a direct cable.

There are four questions to ask yourself when you are selecting a modem:

- Do you want a 300 bps modem, or do you want a combination 300 and 1200 bps modem?
- Do you want your computer to dial telephone numbers and answer calls automatically, or are you content to dial and answer manually?
- Do you want a separate external modem, or do you want your modem on a circuit card inside your PC?
- Will you be using your modem with a particular communications program? If so, are they compatible?

This chapter will help you answer these questions, and it will help you select, operate, and understand your modem.

Modem Standards

In the early 1960s AT&T held a monopoly on data communications, dictating that only equipment manufactured by the Bell System could be connected to Bell phone lines. Two types of modems that AT&T developed were the 103 and the 212A. Later, other manufacturers sold their own modems and set their own standards, but because there were so many Bell modems installed, most of the non-Bell modems were designed to be Bell-compatible. The 103 modem set the standard for 300 bps, and the 212A set the standard for 1200 bps. The 212A allowed communication at 300 bps as well as at 1200 bps and was thus compatible with 103 modems.

The 103 and 212A standards refer only to the frequencies and timing of the tones used in communication. They don't address features like automatic dialing and automatic answering. With respect to these features, modem manufacturers have developed their own standards, and Hayes Microcomputer Products, Inc., is considered a leader. Several other companies have adopted the standard set by Hayes, advertising their modems as "Hayes-compatible." However, any two 212A-type modems can communicate with each other regardless of whether they operate like the Hayes version.

Modems to Avoid

Another 1200 bps modem standard used on some mainframe computers and networks is the Racal-Vadic VA3400. You should buy a Racal-Vadic VA3400 modem only if your host computer accepts no other. Most 1200 bps host computers allowing Racal-Vadic VA3400 connections also support the Bell 212A standard. The 202A, yet another Bell standard, permits 1200 bps communications in half-duplex mode, but it is not used by services offered to PC users.

All modern modems allow for **direct connection** to the telephone line via the same modular plugs and jacks used between the telephone and the wall connector (see Figure 8-1). Many older modems are **acoustically coupled**, requiring the telephone handset to be inserted into a pair of rubber cups. Acoustically coupled modems were originally introduced to circumvent restrictions on what could and could not be connected to the Bell phone line. Use an acoustically coupled modem only if you must communicate from places where you absolutely cannot connect the PC directly to the wall jack. Multi-line office phones also present problems, but later in this chapter you will see how to connect the PC directly to a multi-line phone jack. If you have an old phone without modular jacks, you can obtain conversion parts from your local electronics store or phone company.

Figure 8-1. Connecting a modem to the phone line

You should avoid modems that are optimized for use with dumb terminals. Many of these modems have features like built-in dialing directories, alternate number dialing, and even message storing. The PC's communications program, not the modem, should take care of all the intelligent features. Besides, the Federal Communications Commission (FCC) has rules concerning the number of times a modem may automatically redial a number; communications programs are not bound by those rules.

Originate Versus Answer

The modem provides a two-way communications path between two computers. Since there is only one telephone circuit for sending messages in two directions, the two directions must be differentiated through the use of different signaling frequencies. In the 103 standard, the two frequency bands are

1070-1270 Hz and 2025-2225 Hz. Which computer gets which frequency band? By convention, the 1070-1270 Hz band is the **originate** channel used by a remote terminal (or PC) to send data to an information utility or another host system. The 2025-2225 Hz band is the **answer** channel used by the information utility to send data back to the terminal.

If you did nothing but communicate with an information utility, your modem would transmit only at 1070-1270 Hz and receive only at 2025-2225 Hz, making it an **originate-only** modem. Indeed, most early modems were originate-only because of component costs. But two PC owners with originate-only modems cannot communicate with each other. At least one person must have an **originate/answer** modem, and fortunately, almost all available modems for the PC are originate/answer.

When you dial up an information utility like The Source, your modem must be in originate mode, but when you set up your PC as a bulletin board, your modem must be in answer mode in order to receive messages. If you and a friend are exchanging data between two PCs, you will have to decide who will operate in originate mode. Some modems will automatically select originate or answer mode for you.

300 Versus 1200 bps

A 300 bps modem (103 standard) allows communication at speeds of about 30 characters per second (cps). Bulletin board users have successfully pushed the 30 cps limit to 45 cps, but 30 cps is the low-speed standard used by information utilities. A 1200 bps modem (212A standard) allows communication at 120 cps, four times faster than a 300 bps modem.

More and more communication is happening at 1200 bps, and the new graphics videotex services demand 1200 bps. If you can afford it, buy a 1200 bps modem. Remember that with most 212A-type modems, you will be able to communicate at 300 bps and at 1200 bps.

Autodial, Autoanswer, or Manual

If your modem has a feature called **autodial**, you can dial phone numbers from your PC's keyboard and eliminate the need for a telephone on the line. Better still, your communications program can dial the number and follow up by logging you onto an information utility. The **autoanswer** feature allows your PC to answer the phone, letting remote users call your PC.

If you have a manual modem, you must dial the number on your telephone. You must also switch on the modem to answer a call and hang up when the call is complete. Communications programs allow for manual modems, but they are designed specifically for automatic modems. It's sometimes difficult to make a manual call with a high-powered communications program.

Freestanding Versus Circuit Card Modems

You can buy a freestanding modem (Figure 3-6) or a plug-in circuit card modem (Figure 8-2). Both are roughly equivalent, but they differ in a few ways:

Freestanding modem

Can be used with other computers, including the PCjr.

May have indicator lights to show you if a signal is being received.

Requires a serial port on the PC, but that port may also be used for a printer or local computer.

Usually requires a cable.

May require switches to be set when different programs are used.

Circuit card modem

Fits entirely within the PC for portability and security.

May or may not supply a standard connector for a serial printer or local computer.

Does not require additional serial port hardware.

More must be said about serial ports. If you have a freestanding modem, you must have serial port hardware: either the IBM Asynchronous Communications Adapter or a multi-function board manufactured by Quadram, AST, or others. If you have a circuit card modem, you don't need serial port hardware; but unless your circuit card modem has an appropriate connector, you won't be able to attach a serial printer or a local computer to the serial port. Even if you bought a circuit card modem equipped with the proper connector, such as a Ven-Tel or Quickcom, you can't simultaneously use the modem and a serial printer; there's only one serial port to be shared. In other words, you may need both the circuit card modem and a serial port card.

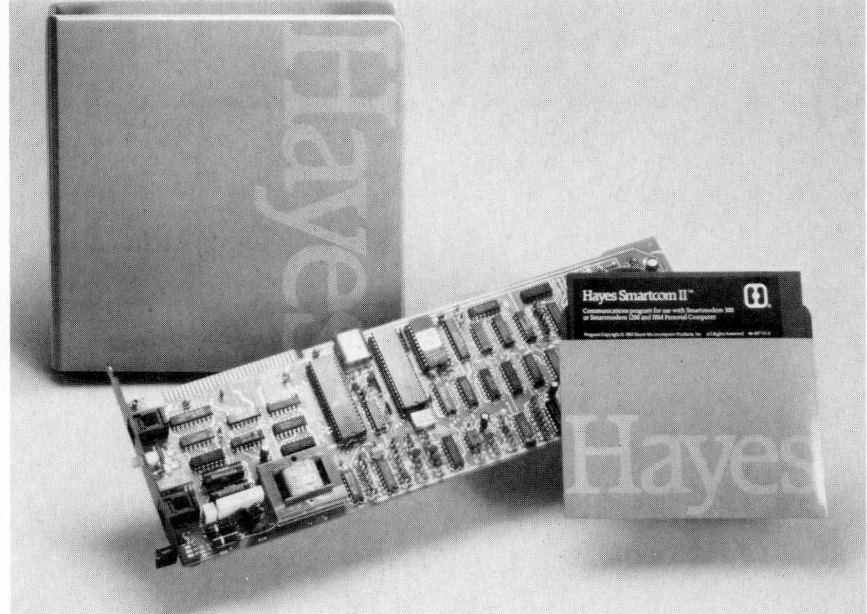

Photo courtesy of Hayes Microcomputer Products, Inc.

Figure 8-2. Hayes 1200B plug-in circuit card modem

Program Compatibility

Just as the IBM PC has emerged as the standard in personal computers, the Hayes modem has become the standard in personal computer modems. Just as there are IBM-compatibles, there are Hayes-compatibles, and there are different levels of compatibility.

Many programs, including Hayes' *Smartcom II*, the *Dow Jones Market Analyzer*, and CompuServe's *VIDTEX* program, require a Hayes or Hayes-compatible modem. In particular, *Smartcom II* demands that the modem be very Hayes-compatible. If there's any doubt about a particular program working with a modem, ask to see a demonstration.

Choosing a Modem

In choosing a modem, here are some facts to consider:

- Most 1200 bps modems have standard autodial and autoanswer features.

- The cost of automatic 1200 bps modems is coming down; the cheapest is already less than $300.
- The average 300 bps automatic modem costs about $100 less than the cheapest 1200 bps modem.
- There are few 300 bps modems available on PC circuit cards.
- The cheapest freestanding 300 bps manual modems sell for less than $80.

Now there are only four reasonable choices:

1. 300 bps manual, freestanding
2. 300 bps automatic, freestanding
3. 1200 bps Hayes-compatible, freestanding
4. 1200 bps Hayes-compatible, circuit card.

Choice 2 is not cost-effective. There are, however, many automatic 300 bps modems in use today. Choices 3 and 4 are equivalent from the viewpoint of software. The Anchor 300 bps freestanding Volksmodem and the Hayes 1200B circuit card modem, described in the next sections, represent opposite ends of the spectrum.

The Anchor Volksmodem

This is a "plain vanilla" 300 bps manual modem. You should buy it if you have a tight budget or if you won't be communicating very often. This modem, shown in Figure 8-3, comes in a small plastic case with an internal 9-volt battery. The list price is $79.95 and a cable costs $12.95. It's the least expensive there is, but it does everything a manual 300 bps modem is supposed to do. The Anchor Volksmodem is Bell 103-compatible, it operates in originate and answer mode, and a TALK/DATA switch disconnects it from the phone circuit when you want to talk.

Switching between originate and answer is automatic. If there's an answer signal or no signal on the other end of the line, the Volksmodem goes into originate mode. If there's an originate signal, the Volksmodem goes into answer mode. If there is a Volksmodem at each end of the line, the first one switched to DATA is the originate modem.

PC-Talk III is an ideal communications program for the Volksmodem because of its low price and because it adapts easily to manual modems. You bring up *PC-Talk* and then use your phone to dial the number with the Volksmodem set to VOICE. After you hear the carrier tone from the other end of the line, you switch the modem to DATA, hang up the phone, and let *PC-Talk* take over.

Photo courtesy of Anchor Automation, Inc.

Figure 8-3. Anchor Volksmodem

Don't forget to switch the modem back to VOICE when you're finished communicating, or the modem will be "off hook," tying up the line.

The Volksmodem, like many modems, comes with a subscription to The Source (the Source manual is $20 extra). If you're faced with paying $100 for a Source subscription, buy a Volksmodem instead.

The Hayes 1200B Smartmodem

The Hayes 1200B is a modem and serial port on a plug-in circuit card that works with most communications programs, including *PC-Talk III, Smartcom II,* and *Crosstalk.* The Hayes 1200B requires one expansion slot in the PC, but it is thick enough to require two slots in the XT. It does not have an RS-232C connector.

With a manual modem, you must set switches in order to control the way the modem operates. In 1980 Bizcomp improved on that by allowing the computer or terminal to send commands to the modem via the same link used for the data. Hayes now pays royalties to Bizcomp to make these "smart" modems, but the command formats that Hayes uses aren't the same as Bizcomp's.

Normally, you don't need to worry about how the Hayes commands work because the communications program will take care of commands for you. But for those who want to know, here's how the Hayes Smartmodem commands work. Suppose you're running the simple terminal program listed in the IBM BASIC manual, Appendix F. If you type

ATDT1-206-555-1212

the modem dials the phone number 206-555-1212 and lets you listen in via its built-in speaker. AT means "attention, modem," DT means "dial with tones instead of pulses," and 1-206-555-1212 is the phone number with the long-distance prefix (1) required by many telephone companies.

Once the phone connection is established, the remote computer will send an answer tone (carrier). The Smartmodem detects this tone, responds with its own originate tone, and sends the message CONNECT back to the PC. In addition to sending the CONNECT message, the modem activates a line called Carrier Detect (CD) to signal the PC that the connection is established. The modem then switches from **command mode** to **on-line mode**, and the actual data communication begins.

Here are a few more examples of Smartmodem commands. Suppose you want the Smartmodem to answer an incoming call automatically. To do this you would type the command

ATS0=1

to force the modem to answer on the first ring. As before, the command AT means "attention." The Smartmodem has 18 internal registers (storage locations), S0 through S17, used to control the operation of the Smartmodem. Register S0 controls the number of rings before an automatic answer. The default value of S0 is 0, meaning the modem will never answer the phone. The command S0=1 stores a "1" in register S0, which causes the modem to answer after one ring.

How does the Smartmodem know when to hang up once the modem is in on-line mode? First you need to type the sequence +++ (three pluses) with a pause before and after it to put the modem back into command mode. Then you can type the command

ATH0

which causes the modem to hang up. While the ATH0 command is one way to force the Smartmodem to hang up, many communications programs will manipulate a signal, called Data Terminal Ready (DTR), on the serial port to cause the modem to hang up. This will be explained more fully in Chapter 9.

The Smartmodem hangs up by itself if the connection is broken for more than 0.6 second. This time interval may be changed with a command. When the connection is broken, a condition called **loss of carrier**, the modem sends a NO CARRIER message to the PC and deactivates the Carrier Detect line.

What about speed? The Smartmodem can communicate at both 300 and 1200 bps. How does it know which speed to use? When the PC sends the command prefix AT for attention, the Smartmodem examines the signal carefully to determine the proper data rate, parity, and number of stop bits to use. In other words, on originating calls the Smartmodem automatically determines the proper speed and format based on the signals it receives from the PC.

When the Smartmodem answers the phone, it must first determine the speed of the incoming message and then set its speed accordingly. This gets tricky, demanding some intelligence in the communications program, since the PC must accept calls at either 300 bps or 1200 bps. The Smartmodem answers the phone, determines the caller's speed, and sends the PC a result code. That result code indicates the new speed. The communications program then sets the speed of the serial port to the new rate. All communication is now at the new data rate.

Now you've seen how the Smartmodem can dial a call, answer a call, hang up, and change speed. That's about all an automatic modem needs to do, and that's what most communications programs expect from a modem. Redialing the same number and hanging up in the absence of a carrier are tasks the communications program can handle. The Smartmodem isn't smart enough to recognize a dial tone or a busy signal, but its speaker will let you monitor what's happening while the connection is being made. The program dials the number and then waits for a fixed length of time, say, 30 seconds. If a carrier signal is not detected for whatever reason, the program can hang up, dial an alternate number, or redial the first number.

In summary, the Hayes Smartmodem 1200B is reliable, easy to install, well documented, and loaded with features. The $599 price includes the *Smartcom II* communications program. Owning a Hayes modem gives you guaranteed access to all programs advertising "Hayes compatibility."

Other 1200 bps Modems

The Hayes 1200 is the freestanding version of the Hayes 1200B. The only functional difference is the 1200's LED indicator and some switches that control the Smartmodem 1200's operating characteristics. The 1200B uses commands in place of the 1200's switches. The 1200 has a switch to ignore the DTR signal from the PC, which lets the 1200 work with a number of communications programs written in BASIC including *Hostcomm.* The 1200B won't work with some communications programs written in BASIC because of the way BASIC manipulates the DTR line, causing the modem to hang up. The Hayes company is working on a modification to allow the 1200B to ignore the DTR line.

Anchor Automation sells a 1200 bps freestanding modem that consumes very little power and can operate from a battery. The Signalman Mark XII sells for $399, and Anchor claims it's compatible with over 50 Hayes-oriented communications programs including *Smartcom II.* The Signalman Mark XII doesn't have a speaker, but it displays the status of the communications line on the screen.

Qubié Distributing has announced a 1200 bps circuit card modem priced at $299. This modem uses a new technology that sidesteps Bell's 212A patents. Instead of using hard-to-tune analog filters, the modem processes incoming signals digitally. Hayes compatibility is claimed, and the card is thin enough to fit in a single XT slot. An RS-232C connector is available for $20 extra.

Bizcomp's 2120 PC:IntelliModem is another circuit card modem. Its uniqueness lies in its programmable telephone handset jack, which allows you to switch between voice and data communication. The $499 price includes a communications program called *PC:IntelliCom.* Here's how the modem works: assume each of two people has an IntelliModem, the *IntelliCom* software, and a telephone handset plugged into the modem. Once a connection is made, the PC's F2 function key can allow both parties to switch between voice and data communication. Each person must switch modes within 20 seconds of the other in order to maintain the connection.

There are many other stand-alone and plug-in circuit card modems available for the PC. Two cards already mentioned are the Quickcom from Wolfdata and Ven-Tel's PC Modem Plus. Both feature RS-232C connectors, and the Ven-Tel uses the PC's speaker instead of an on-board speaker. The latest version of the Ven-Tel is sufficiently Hayes-compatible to work with *Smartcom II.*

Connecting a Freestanding Modem to Your PC

If you have a freestanding modem, you need a cable to connect it to your PC's serial port. Figure 8-4 shows a typical modem-to-PC connection. Your dealer can supply the proper cable if you specify which modem and serial port you have. Chapter 9 tells you how to build your own cable.

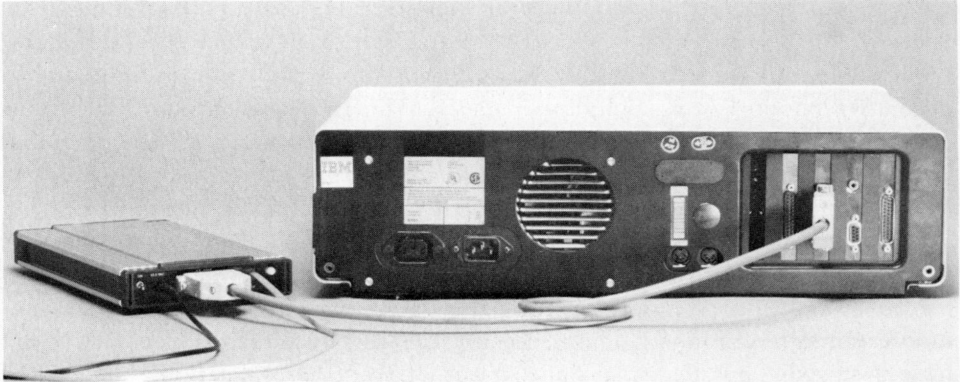

Figure 8-4. Connecting a freestanding modem to the PC

Connecting Your Modem To the Phone Line

Connecting the modem to the phone line depends on the type of modem that you have. All modems provide for one of three types of phone connections:

1. Two modular jacks (Hayes 1200B)
2. One modular jack, one attached telephone cable with a modular plug
3. One modular jack (Hayes 1200, 300).

Types 1 and 2 are almost the same. You could buy a modular phone cable with a plug on each end from Radio Shack or another supplier, plug one end into the modem, and turn a type 1 modem into a type 2. Most type 1 modems come with this cable.

If you have a standard desk telephone that plugs into a modular wall jack with an RJ11 modular plug (as shown in Figure 8-1), connecting the modem is easy. If your modem is type 1 or 2, you simply transfer the telephone cable from the wall jack to the modem's "jack" or "line" connector and then plug the phone into the "phone" connector. When the modem goes on-line, it disables the phone. When the modem is off-line, the phone works normally; the phone and the modem don't interfere with each other. If the modem is capable of automatically dialing a number, you can remove the phone completely. Figure 3-7 illustrates the phone line connections for a Hayes 1200B modem.

If your modem is a type 3 and has only one phone jack, you can connect it directly to the phone line and get rid of the telephone. If you also need to use the phone, you must buy a "Y" adapter from an electronics store. Figure 8-5 shows the connections.

Be aware that "Y" adapters and extension phones can cause voice/data conflicts. A phone connected either way will interfere with the modem if someone intrudes while you are communicating. Conversely, someone will get an earful of noise if you try to use the modem while he or she is talking.

If your PC is located in an office, you may have difficulty connecting it to the office phone system. The phone company will install the required modular plugs and jacks, but that will probably cost over $100. Don't try to install the modular plugs and jacks yourself unless you have some telephone system experience. If you do attempt the job yourself, you'll need a "test set"—a telephone with a special cable that allows you to access the phone signals easily. The phone line consists of a pair of wires, one called **tip** and the other called **ring**. The easiest way to find the tip and ring signals is to probe the telephone junction box with the test set's red and green wires. Once you've found the pair of wires that work with the phone, identify the line by calling in from another

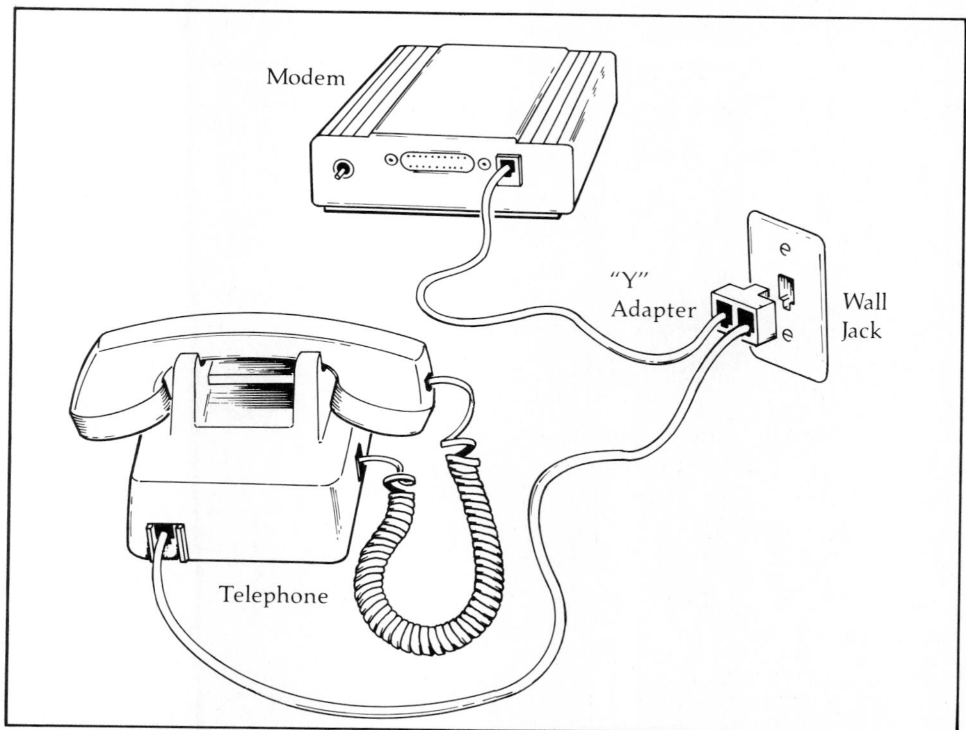

Figure 8-5. Connecting a modem to the phone line with a "Y" adapter

phone; then connect the red and green wires to a modular jack (available at Radio Shack). Now you can connect the modem, as shown in Figure 8-1 or Figure 8-4.

Hayes modems have a special switch setting for multi-line modular jacks designated RJ12 and RJ13. You must find out whether your jack is an RJ11, RJ12, or RJ13 and set the modem accordingly.

Establishing a Connection

Accessing a CBB or an information utility like Dow Jones is easy with a communications program that can log on for you. Your communications program dials the number, logs on, and then you are ready to use it. If you have a manual modem, you start the communications program, dial the number, wait for a connection, and then type your ID and password when prompted.

Exchanging files with another PC owner is more complicated. It's difficult to establish a connection with only one phone call unless both parties have manual modems. In that case, make a normal voice call, then put your modem on-line and have your correspondent do likewise. Then set one modem to originate

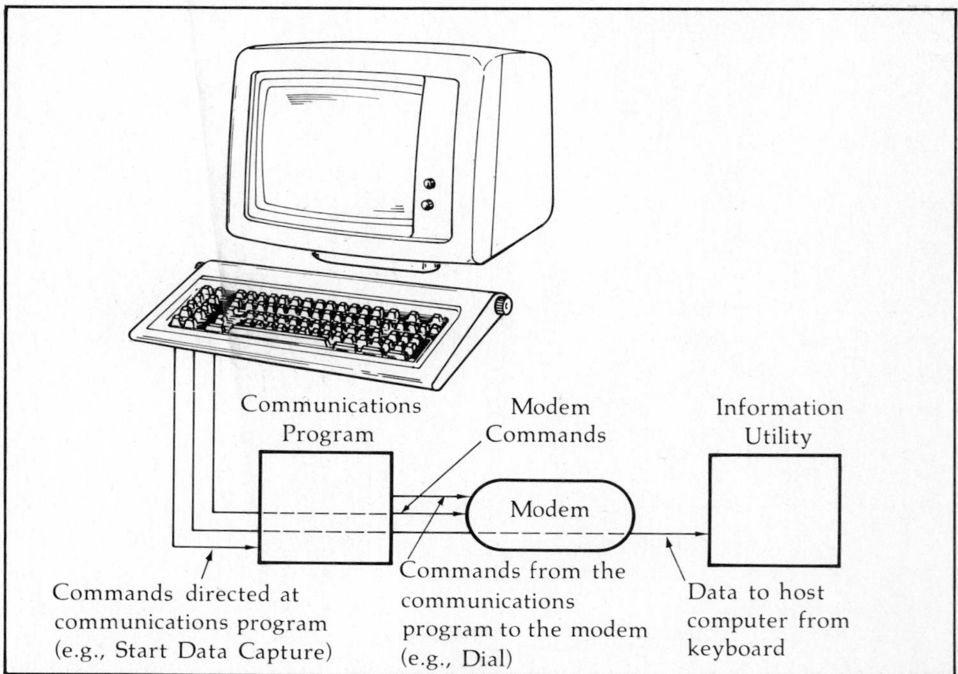

Figure 8-6. Communications programs, modems, and information utilities

and the other to answer. (Anchor Volksmodems automatically select originate/answer.) Each person hangs up the telephone, and the communications program takes over.

If both of you have automatic modems, you must first make a voice call to plan the transfer. One of you must set your system for autoanswer, and the other must originate the call. (Invariably, an insurance salesperson will call the instant you set the modem switch to autoanswer—but that's life.) If each of you is in an office with two phone lines, your job is easier; there's always a voice line available to coordinate the transfer.

Once you have established a connection, it is hard to keep track of your keystrokes. At times you will be sending commands to the modem; at other times you will be sending commands to the communications program; and ultimately, you will be entering the actual data to send to a remote computer or information utility. The relationship of your communications program, your modem, and the remote computer is shown in Figure 8-6.

New Modem Developments

No faster modems are about to be released, but there are some exciting new products in modem technology. The CoSystem from Cygnet Technologies is a good example. This product, shown in Figure 8-7, is a combination telephone, modem, and computer designed to work in tandem with the PC. Think of it as a super-intelligent modem with a handset and touchtone dialing capabilities.

To appreciate the CoSystem, imagine that you have on your desk a PC, an automatic modem, and a telephone. With them you can easily get stock quotes from CompuServe, send and receive MCI mail, run Multiplan or WordStar, and make ordinary voice calls.

Integrating a microprocessor with a modem and a telephone, the CoSystem allows its own brand of electronic mail to be received, even if the PC is turned off, by flashing a light as messages come in. The CoSystem also allows you to insert a bookmark into any PC program. The bookmark lets you interrupt what you are doing in order to process the incoming "screen mail" and then return to where you left off. All modern telephone features such as speed dialing, last-number redial, conferencing, and speakerphone are supported. PC programs that are integrated into the CoSystem package include a personal calendar and a 650-name phone directory. In addition, the CoSystem keeps a record of each voice and data call made. Data from 160 calls is stored in battery-operated memory and then dumped to a PC data disk for off-line analysis.

Cygnet is a start-up company founded by Federico Faggin, former R&D

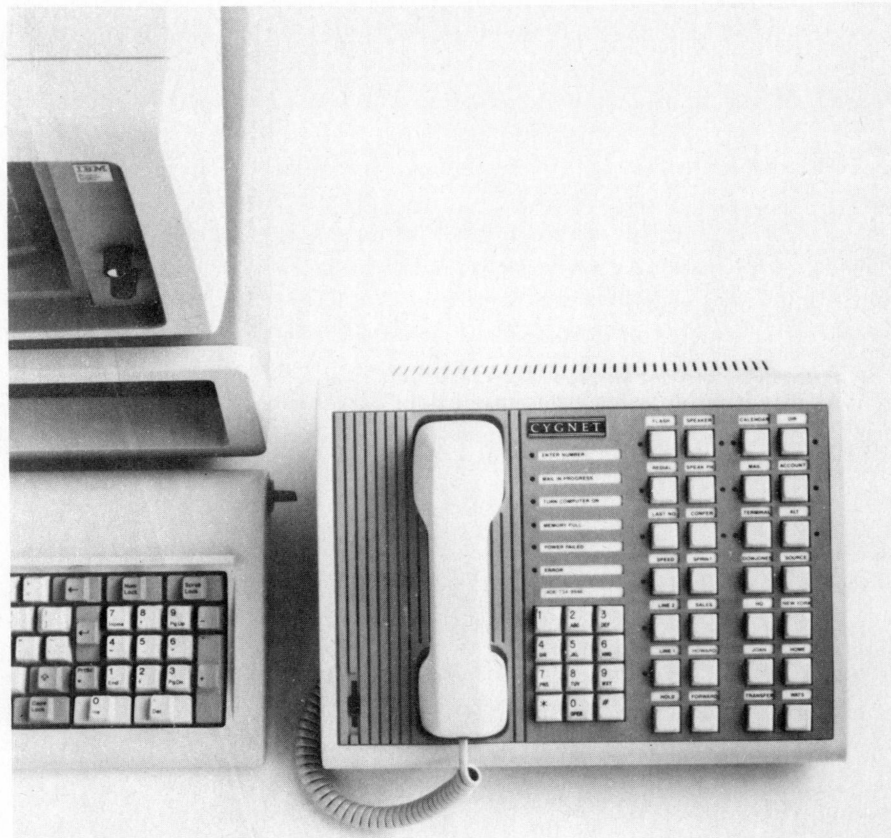

Photo courtesy of Cygnet Technologies, Inc.

Figure 8-7. Cygnet CoSystem

manager at Intel and cofounder of Zilog. Cygnet is breaking new ground by selling telephone equipment through computer stores as well as pursuing sales through telephone system channels. Cygnet has as much optimism as it has venture capital; but if the CoSystem is popular, there'll be competition. The PC and the CoSystem are an attractive alternative to the PC/modem/telephone combination. At $1845, the CoSystem does not cost much more than a 1200 bps modem, software, and a sophisticated two-line telephone. Office productivity could be doubled if the whole staff were outfitted with CoSystems and were committed to using screen mail. It's the paperless office everyone's been talking about.

Technical Details

Chapter 3 gave you a head start in understanding the 300 bps 103 modems, showing you how frequency modulation or frequency shift keying (FSK) converts digital marks and spaces to tones of 1270 and 1070 Hz for the originate channel and 2225 and 2025 Hz for the receive channel. All modems operating on the public-switched telephone network must use frequencies normally found in the human voice. This range of frequencies is called the **voice bandwidth**, and it spans the frequencies 300-3100 Hz.

Figure 8-8 shows the distribution of frequencies, called the **frequency spectrum**, used by a 103-type modem. Note that the originate and answer bandwidths are each about 500 Hz wide, or about 1.5 times the 300 bps data rate. If the 103 modulation technique were used at 1200 bps, a bandwidth of 1200 × 1.5 × 2, or 3600 Hz, would be required—more than the telephone channel offers. Therefore, at 1200 bps a more sophisticated scheme called **phase shift keying** (PSK) is used to pack more information into a limited bandwidth.

The 212A standard groups pairs of data bits into units called **dibits** that are used to modulate the phase of the carrier signal (1200 Hz for originate, 2400 Hz for answer). Figure 8-9*a* shows four variations of the 2400 Hz signal, each at a different phase corresponding to the four dibits. The bit pattern "001001", made up of dibits "00", "10", and "01", generates the signal shown in Figure 8-9*b*.

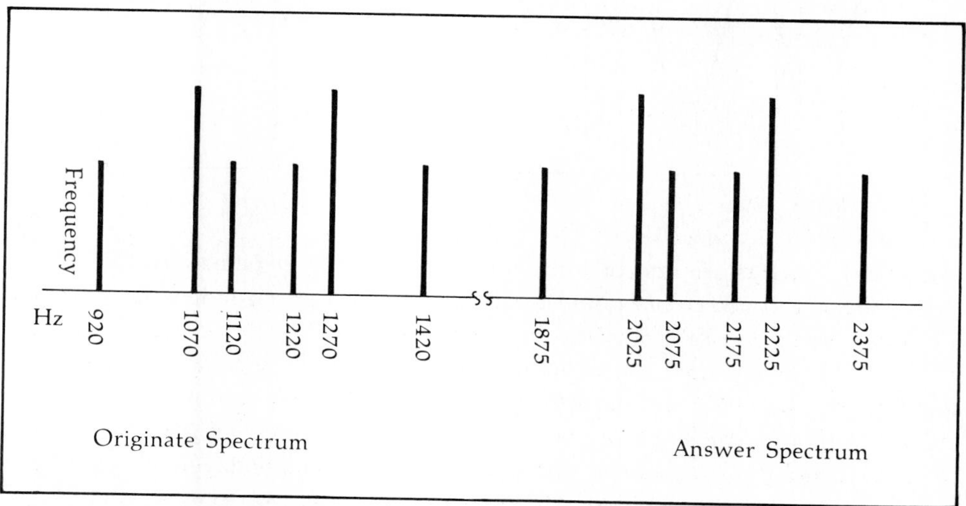

Figure 8-8. Frequency spectrum of a 103-type modem

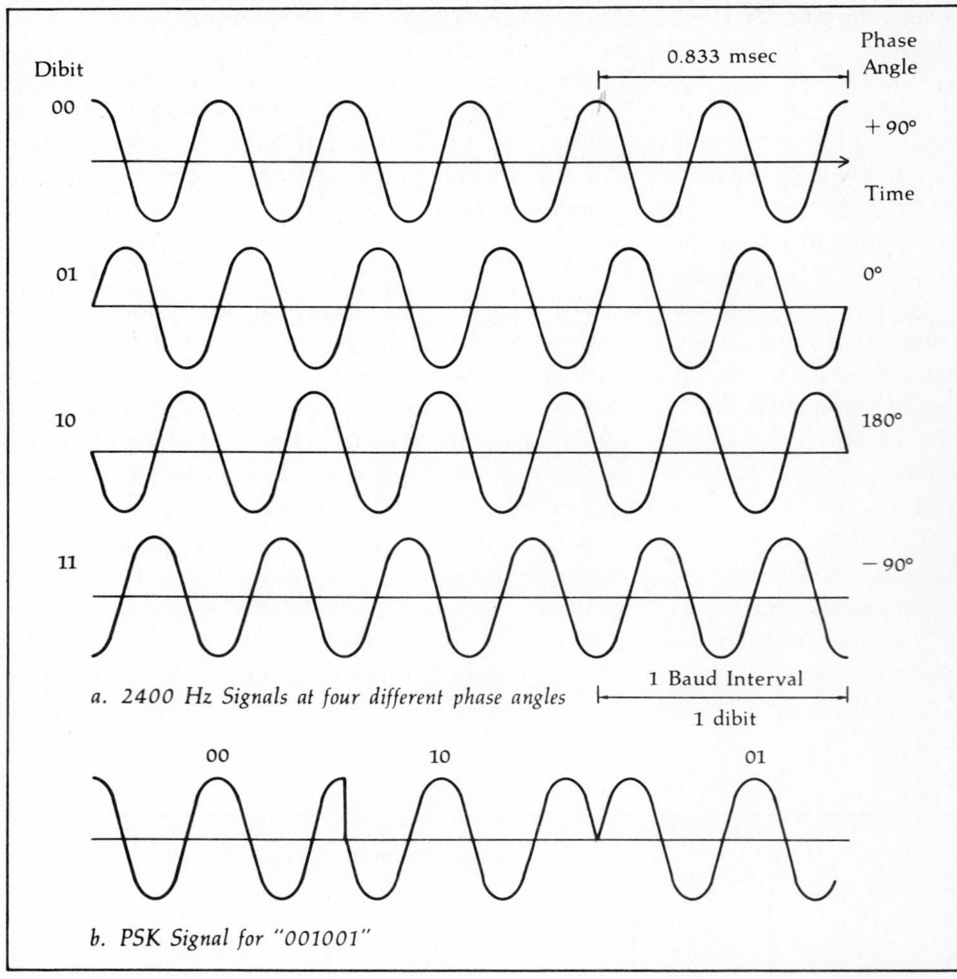

Figure 8-9. Phase shift keying

Note that two bits are encoded into a single state. Since the **baud rate** is determined by the number of potential state changes per second, your 1200 bps modem is really operating at 600 baud.

If you thought your 1200 bps modem was too expensive, consider this: for a 1200 bps transmission to work properly, each transmitted dibit has to be the same length, and the length must be exactly related to the carrier frequency. In other words, a dibit is two cycles long in originate mode and four cycles long in answer mode. Since your serial port isn't synchronized with your modem, whole stop bits must be added or deleted to even the flow. The receiver also needs a steady reference signal to compare against the changing phase. This is derived from the incoming signal, which is really 1200 Hz (originate) with some momentary aberrations. Regular patterns found in data transmissions may upset the reference signal, so the transmitting modem scrambles the bits according to a formula spanning a number of bytes. The receiving modem unscrambles the bits according to the reverse formula. Because of the scrambling, a single bit error at 1200 bps can wipe out three characters.

The 212A modems actually use a synchronous data transmission scheme with an asynchronous interface on both ends. Some 212A modems provide an external synchronous interface, but most units available for the PC do not.

NINE

ASYNCHRONOUS COMMUNICATION THEORY

In this chapter you'll learn about the PC's serial port (the RS-232C serial interface), cables, the DB-25 connector, and the 8250 UART chip. In addition, you'll see how to use IBM PC BASIC to communicate with the serial ports. Finally, you'll learn how to do some simple troubleshooting when things don't work. If you aren't technically inclined, you may want to look over this chapter briefly; you can always come back to it when you've learned a little more.

The serial port is the main subject of this chapter. Fortunately, serial ports for the PC are generic; the port on the IBM Asynchronous Communications Adapter card is almost the same as the port on a multi-function card or the built-in port on an IBM-compatible micro.

The RS-232C Serial Interface

RS-232C is an electrical interface standard for connecting system components such as modems, printers, and computers. The standard was established by the Electronic Industries Association (EIA), an industry trade organization.

RS-232C defines a 25-wire signal path that establishes 18 circuits with a return through ground. The standard also defines the voltages—the ranges for a logical "0" and a logical "1"—used in all circuits. Note that no physical damage results from a short circuit within the cables or connectors; this means you can't hurt anything while experimenting.

Why does RS-232C need 25 wires? The standard was defined by a committee, and the resulting interface had to satisfy an entire industry. The IBM PC serial port at most uses only 9 wires and can often get by with 3. Only the 9 signals used by the PC will be described here; if you need to know about the others, consult the references in Appendix F.

The logic signals inside the PC conform to what are called "TTL levels," a de facto standard for interconnecting integrated circuit chips. A voltage between 2 and 5 volts is a logic "1", and a voltage between 0 and 0.8 volt is a logic "0". These levels are not used outside of the PC because they don't provide enough immunity from electrical noise. Instead, the scheme shown in Figure 9-1 is used. Note that the voltage thresholds at the receiving end are different from those at the sending end to allow for degradation of the signal in the cable. Remember that it is voltage that defines the logical state of a circuit, not the presence or absence of current as it is in telegraph systems.

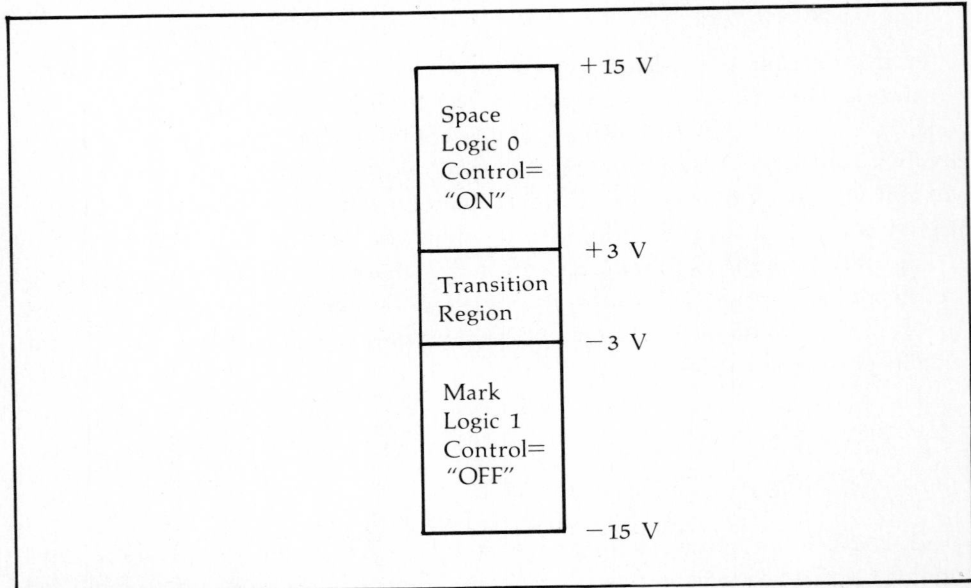

Figure 9-1. RS-232C voltage levels

The PC and most communications equipment output signals of plus and minus 12 volts. However, an input of plus or minus 3 volts is enough to define the logic state. Figure 9-2*a* shows a clean signal going into a 100-foot cable. The noisy signal emerging from the other end is shown in Figure 9-2*b*, and the signal as it appears inside of a receiving PC is shown in Figure 9-2*c*. Remember that the RS-232C signal in the cable is reversed in polarity from the TTL signal in the PC; a 3 volt TTL logic "1" is equivalent to a minus 12 volt logic "1" or mark.

Wires lead to connectors, but the actual physical connector isn't defined in the standard. Connectors have pins, and the pins are numbered 1 through 25. The RS-232C standard refers to pin numbers. The RS-232C pins that are available in a typical PC serial port are defined in Table 9-1. IBM's Asynchronous Communications Adapter uses four additional pins for a **current loop interface** for Teletype machines. Teletypes are outmoded now, but if you have one, see the IBM Personal Computer Technical Reference manual for details on how to hook it up.

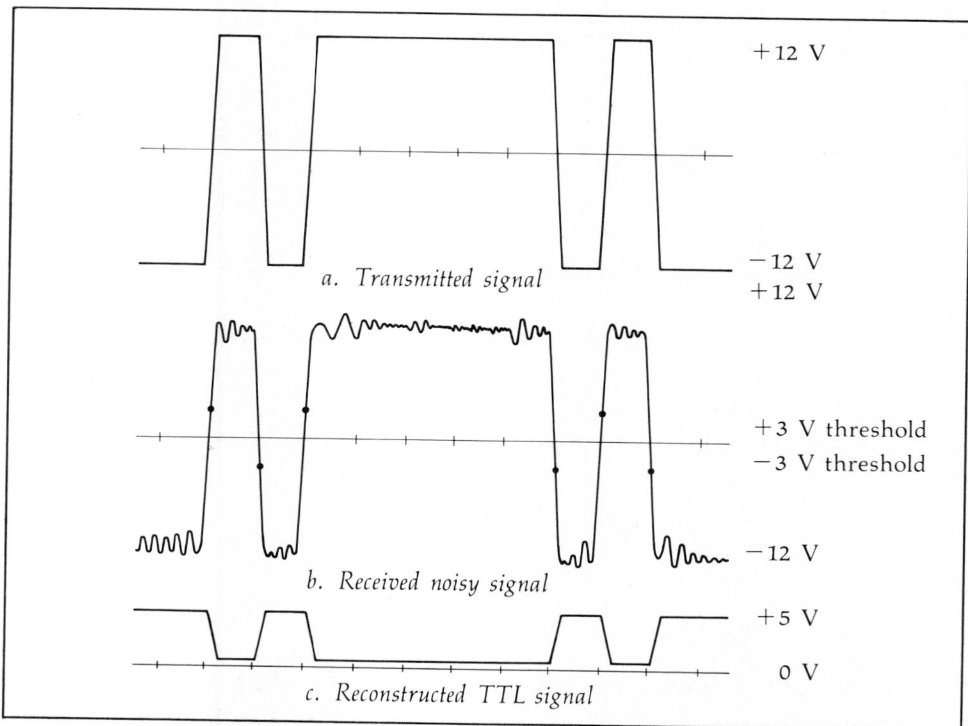

Figure 9-2. The effects of noise

Table 9-1. PC Serial Port RS-232C Pin Definitions

Pin	*Signal*	*Description*
2	Transmit Data	Data out from PC
3	Receive Data	Data into PC
4	RTS	Request to Send, set by PC when it wants to send data
5	CTS	Clear to Send, received by PC when device is ready for data
6	DSR	Data Set Ready, received by PC when modem is powered on and connected
7	Ground	Signal ground
8	CD	Carrier Detect or Received Line Signal Detect received by PC when modem detects carrier
20	DTR	Data Terminal Ready, set by PC whenever data communication is active
22	RI	Ring Indicator, received by PC when modem is receiving a ring signal (answer mode only)

Most data communication tasks don't use all the circuits shown in Table 9-1. The most important circuits are **Transmit Data** and **Receive Data**, pins 2 and 3. These are the two wires over which serial data is simultaneously sent and received. The remaining circuits, with the exception of ground (pin 7), are **control circuits**.

If you're looking for a systematic definition of the control circuits, you won't find it. On the PC, those signals are completely under software control, and as usual, every programmer does things differently. The control signals RTS and CTS aren't used as much as the others, having been designed to control half-duplex communication. Some PC programs, such as *CTTY*, use the RTS line unpredictably, but a special cable (called the null modem cable) sidesteps the problem. Serial printers often use the control circuits to indicate that the printer is busy or off-line. Appendix B gives you more details.

Cables— DTE Versus DCE

The simplest communication scheme is the direct hookup of two PCs using the connections shown in Figure 9-3*a*. Pin 2 of PC 1 is connected to pin 3 of PC 2, and pin 2 of PC 2 is connected to pin 3 of PC 1. None of the other pins are

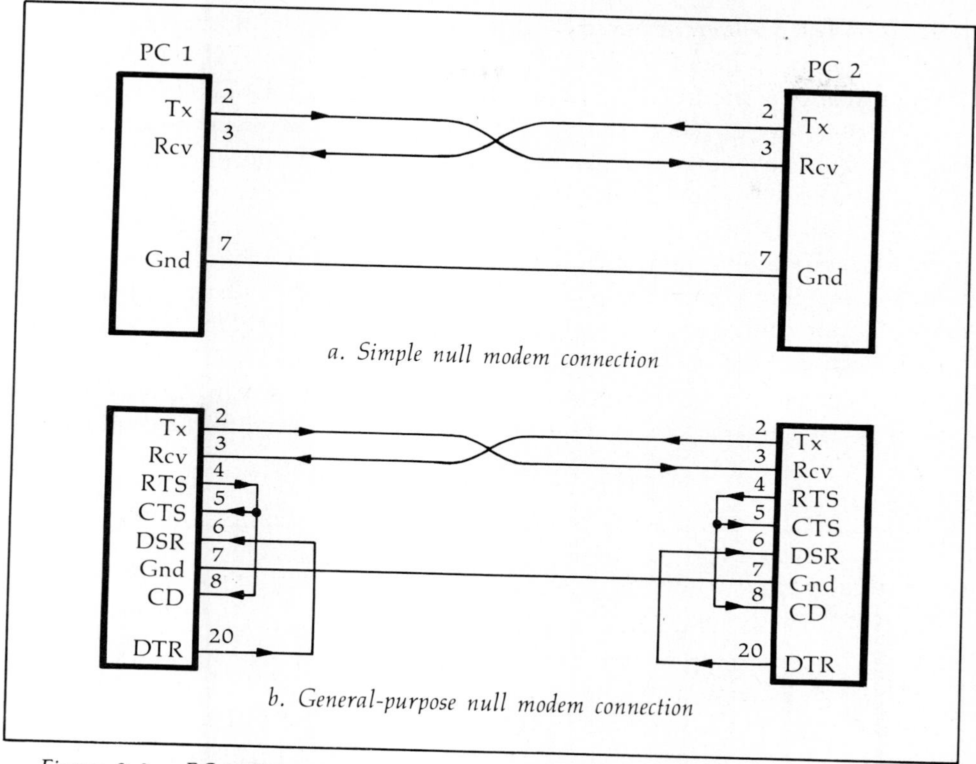

Figure 9-3. PC-to-PC connections

connected except ground, pin 7, the common return for both the transmit and receive circuits. A three-wire cable could handle the job, and it would work well with many communications programs such as *Crosstalk,* but not with all programs. Some programs monitor the CTS, CD, and DSR lines and won't function unless one or all of these signals are logic "0" or ON. You can, however, fool the program by connecting CTS and CD to RTS and by connecting DSR to DTR, as shown in Figure 9-3*b*. One drawback to this connection is that neither PC knows whether the other is ready to communicate. But what difference does this make? If PC 2 isn't ready, PC 1's operator will find out when no data moves across the line.

When the PC is connected to a modem, the control signals are more important. The modem must know that the PC is ready before it automatically answers a call, and the PC must know if the modem is switched on and if it is receiving a carrier signal from the remote system. The simplest modem hookup, used with the *Smartcom* program and the Hayes modems, is shown in Figure 9-4*a*. Pins 2 and 3 handle the data as usual and are connected straight across. DTR on pin 20 is the PC's means of activating the modem, and CD on pin 8 is the modem's way of telling the PC that a connection has been made. The PC has no way of knowing whether the modem is powered on prior to making a call. A general-purpose PC-to-modem cable is shown in Figure 9-4*b*. You can't do any better than this because you're using all of the signals on the PC's serial port. Most communications programs don't use all the control circuits anyway; *Crosstalk* uses only CTS, DSR, CD, and DTR. Be aware that some PC-to-modem cables do not connect pin 22 (RI), a signal that is required for some bulletin boards such as *Hostcomm*.

You may have noticed that pins 2 and 3 were reversed in Figure 9-3 and connected straight across in Figure 9-4. That's because RS-232C interfaces

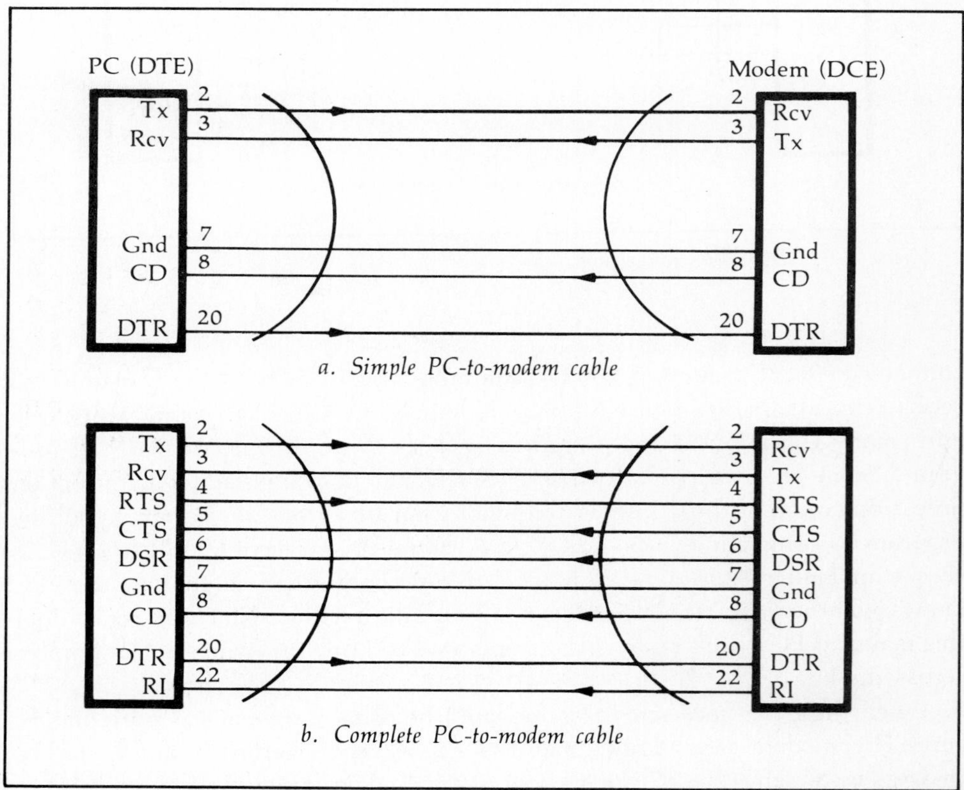

Figure 9-4. PC-to-modem connections

come in two "electronic sexes," **data terminal equipment (DTE)** and **data communications equipment (DCE)**. The PC is a DTE, transmitting data on pin 2; and a modem is a DCE, transmitting data on pin 3. If a DTE is connected to a DCE, the wires go straight across. If two DTEs or two DCEs are connected, the data lines (pins 2 and 3) must be "crossed." In some cases certain control lines must also be crossed. Cables connecting DTEs or DCEs, as shown in Figure 9-3, are called **null modem** cables.

Two PCs connected together require the null modem cable. What about other micros and minis? Some common microcomputers are listed here, along with their electronic sex:

Altos	DCE	TRS-80 II,12	DTE
Northstar	DCE	Vector	DCE
Osborne	DCE	Xerox 820	DTE
Superbrain	DTE	Zenith	DCE
Televideo 801	DCE	Eagle I-IV, 1600	DCE
Televideo 802	DTE	Kaypro	DTE

A cable connecting the PC with a DCE is shown in Figure 9-66.

DB-25 Connectors

Even though the RS-232C standard specifies pin numbers, it doesn't specify a connector. The usual connector is commonly referred to as a DB-25 connector, and it is available in male and female "genders," the DB-25P and the DB-25S, as shown in Figure 9-5. The IBM Asynchronous Communications Adapter comes with a male DB-25P, in contrast to the female DB-25S used by the parallel printer port in the IBM Monochrome Display and Printer Adapter. Be careful not to plug a "live" RS-232C male connector into the parallel port connector as the parallel port is not guaranteed against damage in such a situation.

The connector's gender has nothing to do with a device being a DTE or a DCE. It's obvious, though, that you can plug only male and female DB-25s together. Modems and the serial ports of almost all other computers have female connectors, so a cable connecting a PC with one of those devices must be male on one end and female on the other. An alternative is a standard male-to-male cable with a female-to-female adapter on the PC end. It's like plumbing.

Multi-function boards have unique connector layouts. A popular board such as Quadram's Quadboard contains both a serial and a parallel port. Unfortunately, there's not enough room on the adapter card to mount two DB-25s, so

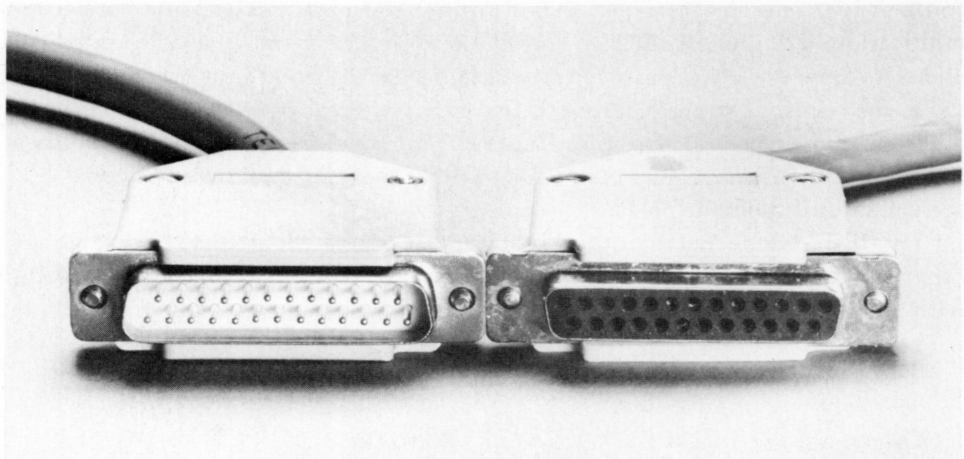

Figure 9-5. DB-25 connectors, male (left) and female (right)

the parallel port connector must be mounted separately with a small ten-conductor adapter cable. The Quadboard II, with two serial ports, has one DB-25 mounted on the card and a second attached to a cable with a mounting plate designed to fit in the back end of an unused card slot. The DB-25 connector for the serial port is mounted on the rear of the AST multi-function board.

IBM-Compatible Computers

Many of the serial ports found on IBM-compatible computers are built into the main circuit board instead of on a separate adapter card. While the IBM PC Asynchronous Communications Adapter provides a male DB-25 connector, many of the serial ports on IBM-compatible computers come with a female DB-25 connector. In many cases, the serial port connectors of an IBM-compatible computer, while being different in gender, are wired identically to the PC's connector. In those cases where the serial connector is wired as a DCE, you will need to use the cables shown in Figure 9-6. If you are in doubt as to whether a certain communications program will run on an IBM-compatible, run the program on the machine before you buy it.

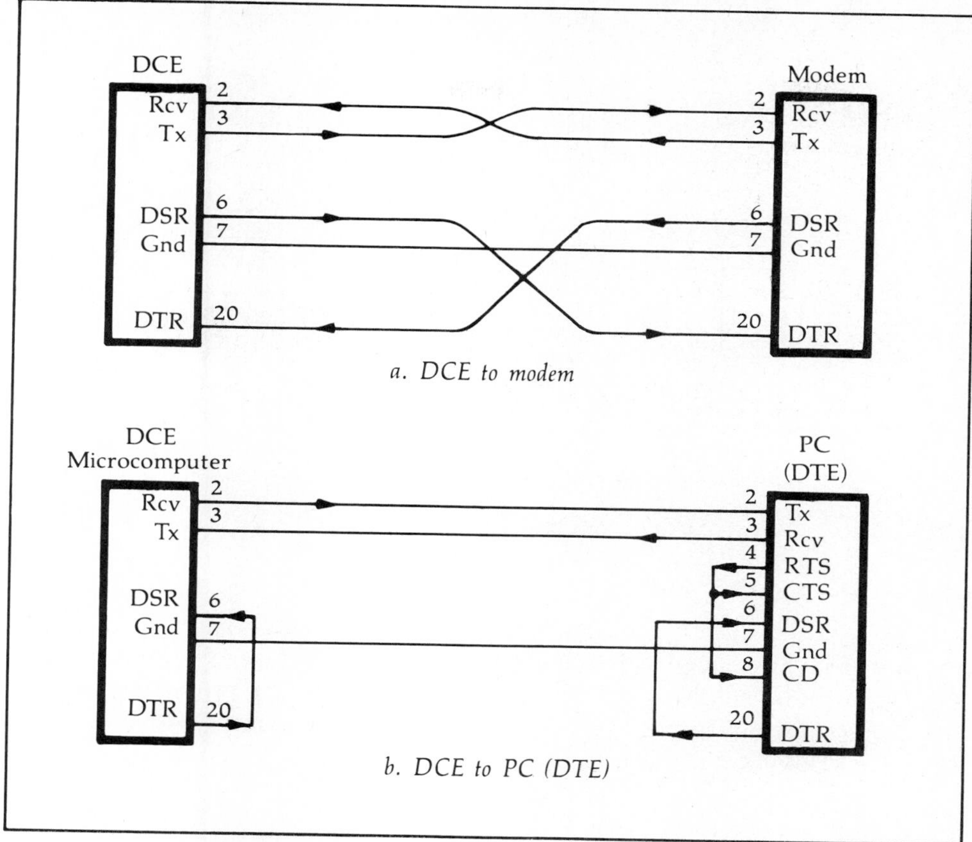

Figure 9-6. Cables for DCE microcomputers

Building Your Own Cables

If you build your own cables to save money, here's a tip for you. Buy the DB-25 connectors without the gold-plated pins and sockets installed (Amphenol parts 205207-1 and 205208-1). Get the pins and sockets separately, solder them to the cable conductors, and then use long-nosed pliers to insert them into the connector body. If you try to solder directly to a DB-25, you'll make a mess of it.

For long cable runs or electrically noisy environments, use shielded cable, and use twisted pairs for the signal lines (2 and 3). Figure 9-7 shows a null modem cable using twisted-pair cable for the signals on pins 2 and 3. The shield

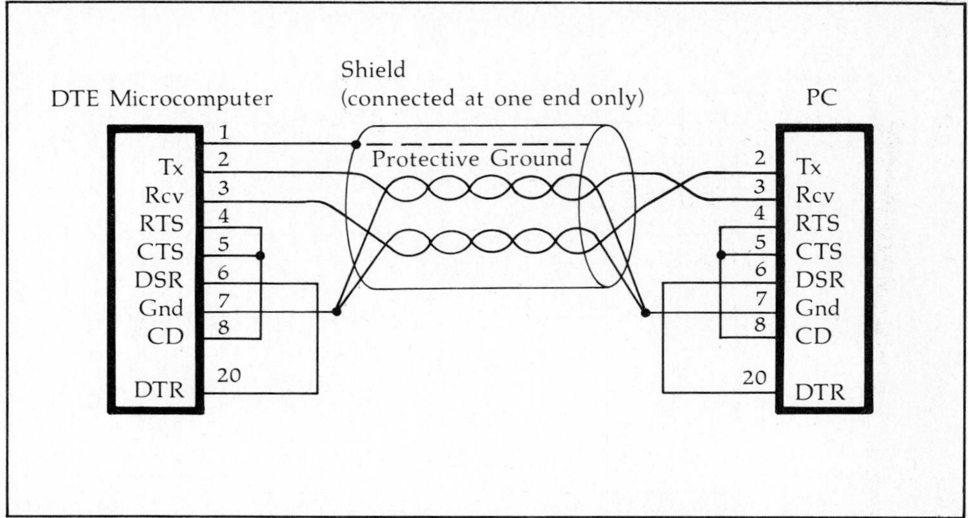

Figure 9-7. Shielded, twisted-pair null modem cable

should attach to ground only at one end to prevent unwanted current from flowing in the shield. Normally the shield would connect to **protective ground**, pin 1, but that pin is not connected in the Asynchronous Communications Adapter. A 100-foot run will support 9600 bps.

The Inner Workings Of a Serial Port

Up to now you've been looking at signals on pins outside the PC. Now you'll find out how the serial port card creates and processes those signals. The Asynchronous Communications Adapter and most multi-function boards use an integrated circuit known as the 8250 **universal asynchronous receiver/-transmitter (UART)**. You feed the 8250 the ASCII code for an "A" and it produces a waveform, as shown in Figure 9-8, the TTL equivalent of the signal that is sent out over the cable. An 8250 at the other end of the line converts the waveform back into an "A".

Data moves 8 bits at a time within the PC along a path called the **data bus**. Eight conductors on the system board link the 8088 CPU, main memory, and all the expansion slot connectors. Each plug-in adapter card can send and receive data over the data bus. Data flows back and forth between the CPU and memory, between the CPU and the input/output (I/O) ports, and between

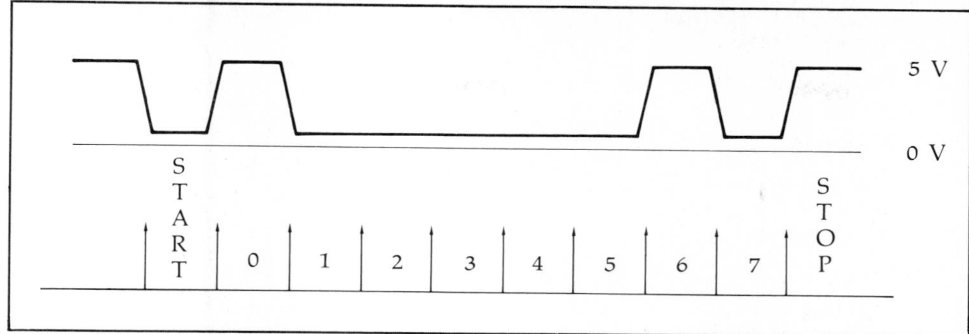

Figure 9-8. TTL output waveform from the 8250

memory and the I/O ports. One group of seven I/O ports is devoted to each 8250.

Please note that an I/O port is not the same as a serial port. An **I/O port** is an 8-bit window into the PC that can be read from and written to like memory. The 8088 CPU can address as many as 64K distinct I/O ports by using special input and output instructions to read and write data. The **serial port** *is* the Asynchronous Communications Adapter card—the 8250, the DB-25 connector, and the intervening circuitry. The seven I/O ports allow you to access the ten storage locations (registers) inside of the 8250 chip.

Figure 9-9 shows the 8250 register layout, and Appendix H describes the registers in detail. The 8088 CPU accesses the 8250 to perform three functions: initialization, sending data, and receiving data. Initialization sets the data rate and other communication parameters including the state of the DTR line. Transmitting data requires the CPU to check the line status register to see if the 8250 is ready to accept new data. If the 8250 is ready, the CPU writes the next byte into the transmitter holding register. The line status register also indicates whether data has been received. If a byte of data is ready, the CPU reads the newly arrived byte from the receiver buffer register.

How does the 8250 generate serial pulses? Outgoing data is stored in the **transmitter shift register**. The least significant bit of that register is tied to the serial output line and the register is shifted right, one bit at a time at the baud rate, as shown in Figure 9-10. Start and stop bits are added as required.

Incoming data is shifted through the receive shift register until all eight bits are accumulated, and then the byte is moved to the receiver buffer register. The process begins on the leading edge of the start bit, as shown in Figure 9-11. The 8250 waits half a bit and then proceeds to sample the input at 1-bit intervals. If the first sample doesn't show a space, there is a **false start**, and the 8250 waits

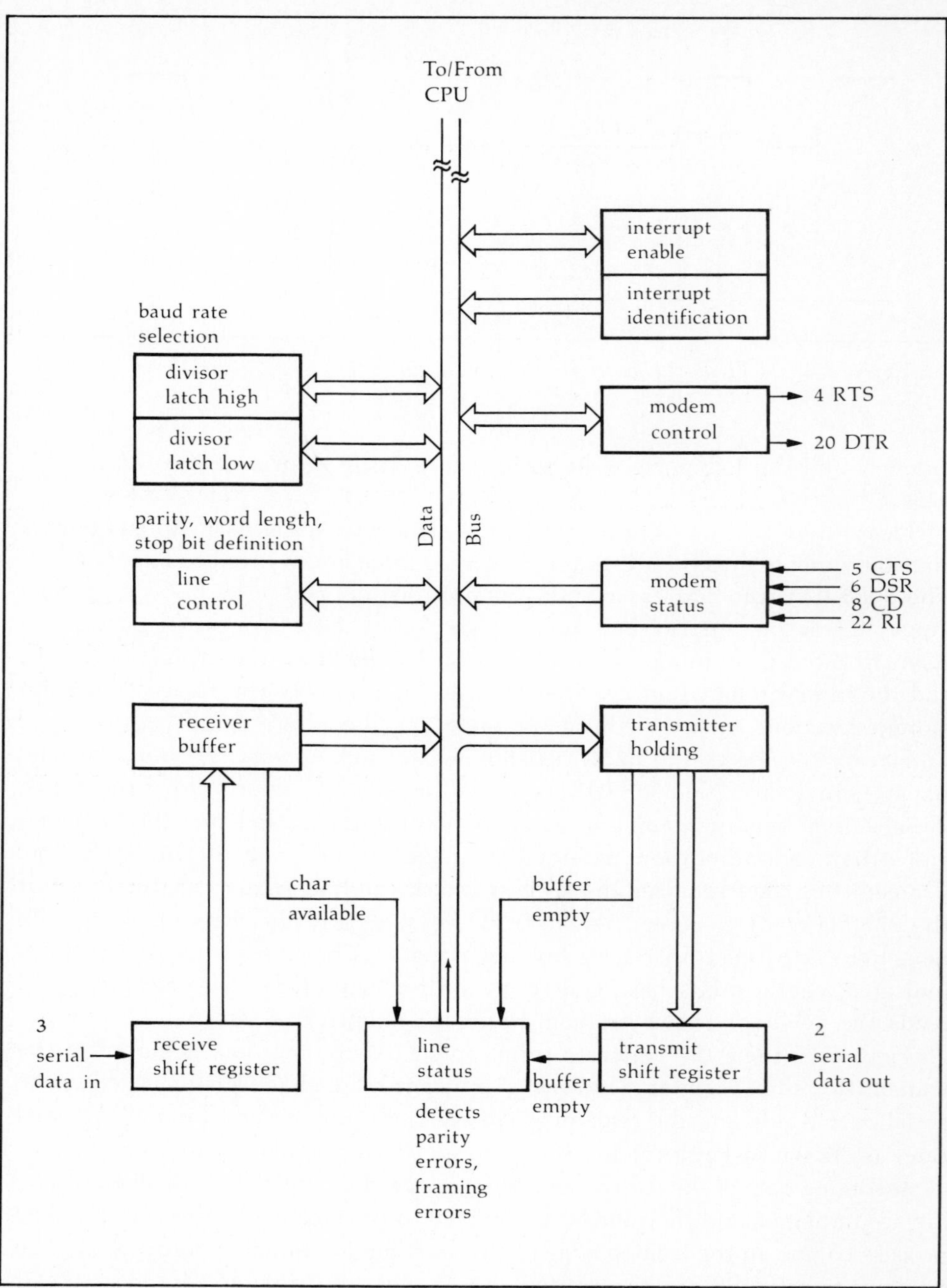

Figure 9-9. 8250 register layout

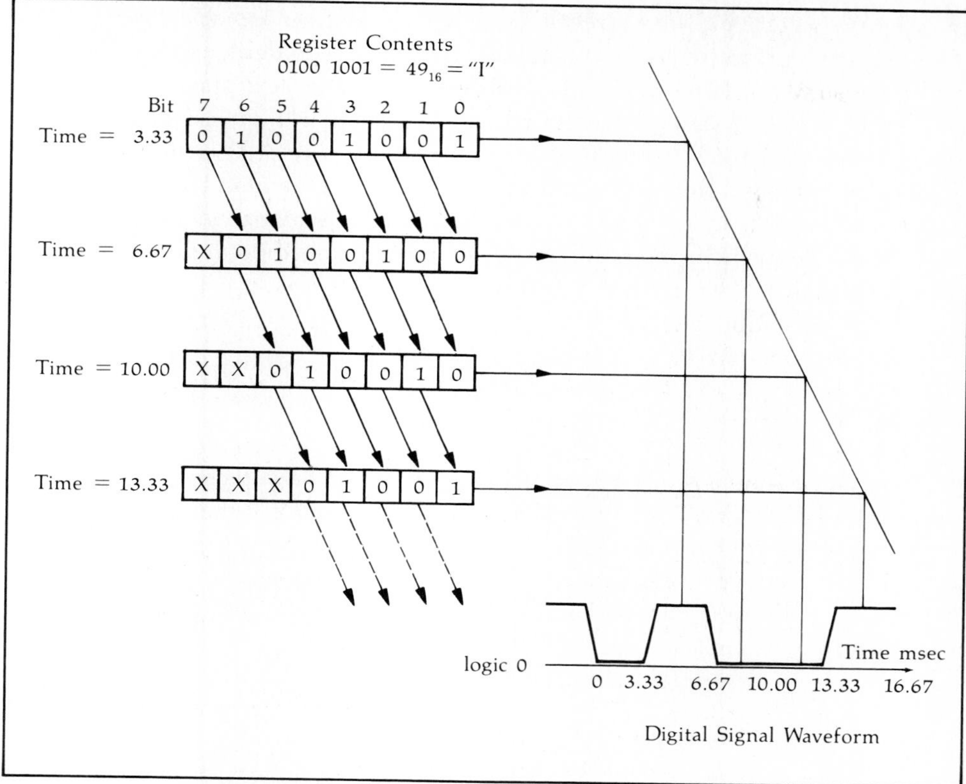

Figure 9-10. 8250 transmitter shift register

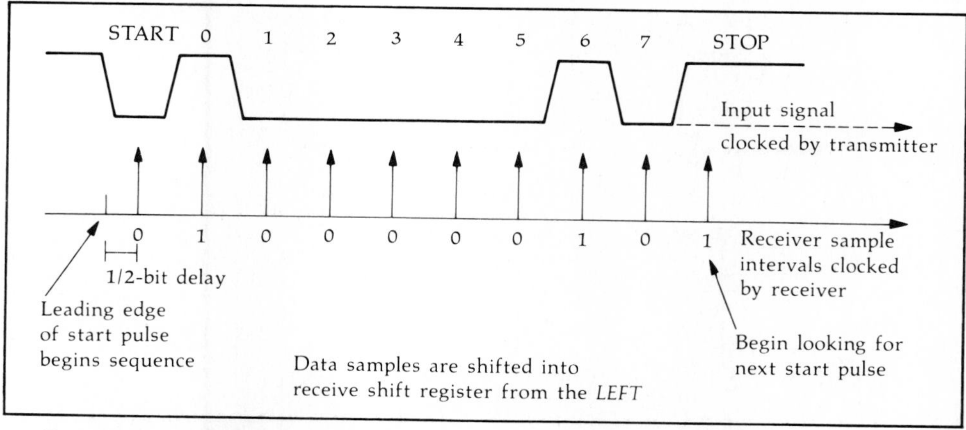

Figure 9-11. Serial-to-parallel conversion

for the next start bit. If the tenth sample doesn't show a mark (stop bit), the 8250 reports a **framing error**. Once a stop bit has been detected, the 8250 can immediately begin looking for the leading edge of the next start bit.

Figure 9-12 shows an input signal running about 5% slow. Notice that the receiver can still track it because the sample points are still within the proper window. Therefore, the error is not carried over into the next byte. If the input signal was more than 10% fast or slow, the sampling scheme would fail and data would be lost. Asynchronous communication is so named because the transmitters and receivers don't need to be synchronized.

The information you need to program the 8250 in assembly language is included in Appendix H.

Parity

Parity is a simple scheme that allows an error to be detected in a stored or transmitted data character. If you've expanded your PC's memory by adding chips, you may have wondered why you needed nine chips for each 64K 8-bit byte. The ninth chip stores the **parity bit**, one for each memory byte. The parity bit is a "1" if there is an odd number of "1"s in the byte, and a "0" otherwise. Here are four examples:

memory byte	parity (even)
00000000	0
00000001	1
00000011	0
01000001	0

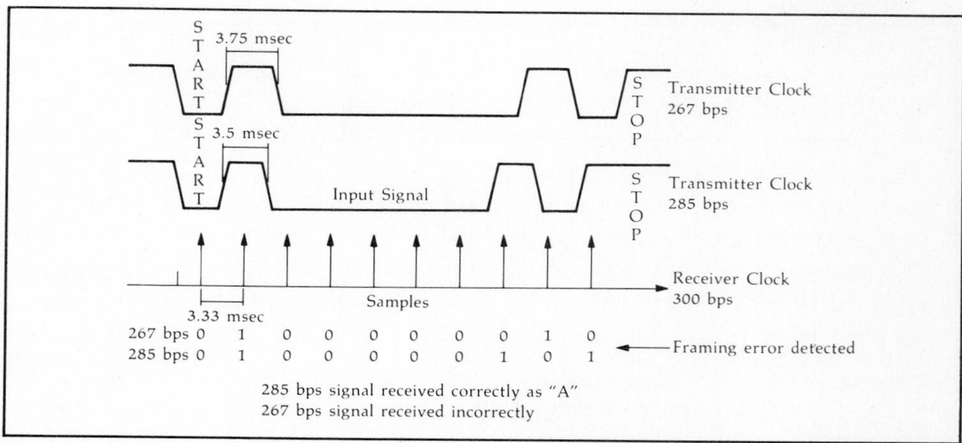

Figure 9-12. Slow input signal

If a single bit, either the parity bit itself or one of the data bits, goes bad, a special circuit notes that the parity no longer matches and causes an error message to be displayed. If two bits go bad, the error will not be detected.

Parity works very well for memory error checking in the PC because the memory is organized so that adjacent bits are on different chips. An error in one chip is not related to an error in another chip. If there is a 0.0001 chance of any bit going bad (modern RAM chips do better than that), there is a 0.0000005 chance of two bits going bad in the same byte—an error rate small enough to be ignored.

Parity checking is also used in serial communications, but it's not very effective. The noise on the data lines almost always lasts more than a 1-bit duration, causing errors to go undetected 30% of the time.

Some information utilities demand parity bits, but few PC communications programs take action once the 8250 UART detects a parity error. Since bits are invariably sent in groups of eight, the existence of a parity bit leaves room for only 7 data bits. While standard ASCII characters can be represented in 7 bits, special graphics characters and *WordStar*'s control characters cannot.

Most information utilities don't use parity, so you can normally set your communications program for 8 data bits, no parity, one stop bit. If this doesn't work, try 7 data bits, even parity.

Advanced Error-Correction Schemes

If you are transferring text files, you can live with an occasional error. Executable programs, graphics files, and important numerical data are another story. You must achieve error-free transmission, and there are better alternatives than parity checking. The simplest method is the **checksum** or **longitudinal redundancy check (LRC)** as used in the Christensen XMODEM protocol, a protocol system used on computer bulletin boards. The transmitting PC sends data in 128-byte blocks, followed by a 1-byte checksum. This byte is the lower-order 8 bits of the sum of the preceding data bytes. If the received checksum doesn't match the checksum calculated by the receiving PC, the receiving PC knows there's been an error and requests the transmitting PC to send the block again. The details of the XMODEM protocol are shown in Appendix D.

While *PC-TALK* and a few other communications programs use the XMODEM protocol, other programs use an even more sophisticated scheme called **cyclic redundancy checking (CRC)**. Here the check character is 2 bytes, calculated by a complex formula that minimizes undetected errors. This CRC method gives 100% protection against error bursts of 17 or fewer bits. *Crosstalk* and *Smartcom* both use CRC methods for data transfers between microcomputers, but these methods are proprietary; you can't write your own program to exchange data with these products.

Up to now, information utilities have not provided for error detection and correction, but the CompuServe *VIDTEX* program does provide for error-free data exchange between a PC and CompuServe utility. The packet-switched networks are planning similar protocols in the links between PCs and network nodes. Note that transmission within the packet-switched networks is always error-free.

A block-by-block error-correction scheme, often called ACK-NAK, is shown in Figure 9-13*a*. In practice, this scheme is slow because the transmitting computer sends a block of data and then must wait for an acknowledgment (ACK) before sending the next block. If a negative acknowledgment (NAK) is received, the block must be retransmitted. Using the ACK-NAK protocol with a satellite link introduces a one-second delay between blocks. **Windowing**, as shown in Figure 9-13*b*, is an improved method of data transmission. Here a sequence of

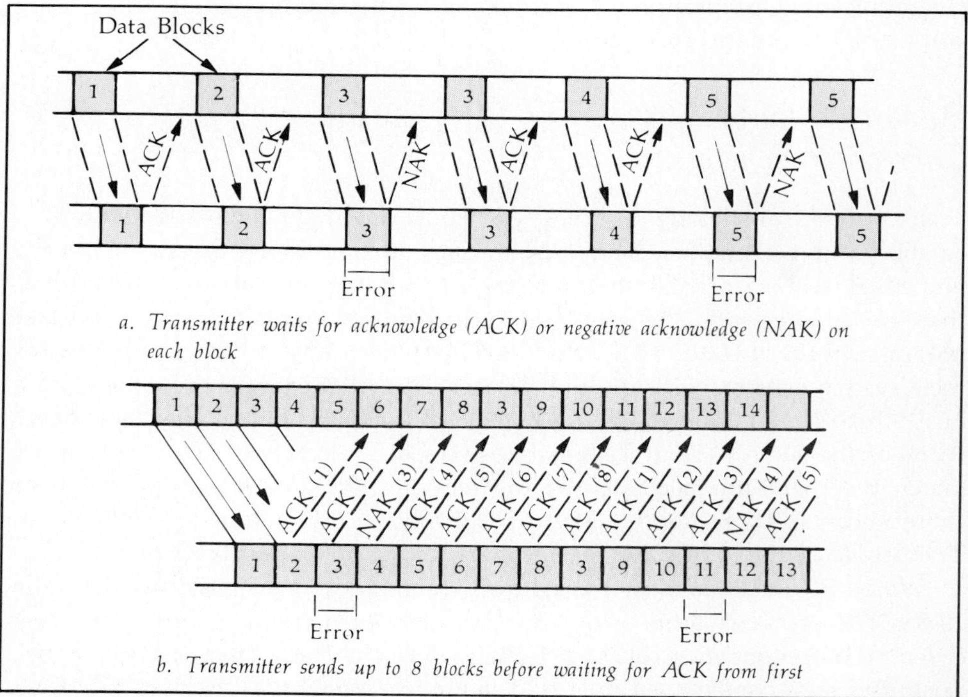

a. Transmitter waits for acknowledge (ACK) or negative acknowledge (NAK) on each block

b. Transmitter sends up to 8 blocks before waiting for ACK from first

Figure 9-13. Error-correction methods

eight blocks is sent without waiting for an acknowledgment. A negative acknowledgment for any one block causes only that block to be retransmitted, mixed in with new blocks. A maximum of eight blocks, forming a sliding window, can be "pending" at any given time.

Communications Programming in BASIC

Microsoft's BASIC for the IBM PC and PC-compatibles broke new ground by allowing you to do your own communications programming. Because the earlier 8-bit microcomputers all had non-standard serial port arrangements, there were no BASIC statements specifically for communication. That has changed, and there are statements now available to **open** a port and to **read** from and **write** to that port as though it were a file.

Data comes in over the communication line in a never-ending stream that the PC can't always turn on and off. A communications program must catch every character; it can't afford to lose or throw characters away just because it is busy doing something else, such as writing to disk. For that reason there is a **communications buffer** built into BASIC that is designed to smooth the flow of data to a program. Incoming characters generate **interrupts**. When an interrupt occurs, the PC momentarily suspends whatever it is doing in order to read a character from the port and to store the received character in the buffer. The BASIC program can withdraw characters from the buffer at its leisure and can even interrogate the buffer for a count of the remaining characters.

IBM's BASIC manual explains the communication statements very well. To summarize, the OPEN "COM.. statement initializes the serial port with proper speed and control parameters, assigning it to a logical file number. The INPUT statement reads characters from an input buffer, and the PRINT statement writes a character to an output buffer. If the output buffer is full, the system waits until there is room. The LOC function returns the number of characters in the input buffer, and the LOF function returns the number of bytes remaining. The size of the communications buffer, typically 4096 bytes, is set when BASIC is invoked. Appendix F in the IBM BASIC manual is devoted to communications and shows a sample program that turns the PC into a dumb terminal.

BASIC can handle serial data efficiently at speeds of up to 1200 bps, the highest speed of most modems for the PC. Compiled BASIC programs are more efficient than interpreted programs, but you won't notice any difference at 300 bps. Because of space and language limitations, most popular communications programs are written in assembler or a language like C. *PC-TALK III* shows how far you can go with BASIC. It does a lot, but not as much as *Smartcom* or *Crosstalk*.

IBM's PC BASIC handles all of its own communications input and output directly when addressing the I/O ports and processing interrupts; neither DOS nor BIOS is used. Thus, any attempts to redirect communications input and output won't work. This defeats the purpose of an operating system, but there's nothing you can do about it.

Troubleshooting

What do you do when nothing works? First, make sure the computer and modem are plugged in and switched on. If that's not the problem, then you've got work to do. An ideal but inexpensive troubleshooting tool for serial communication is the Line Status Indicator from Electro Service Company, shown in Figure 9-14. This is a straight-through cable with a DB-25 connector on each end, one male and the other female, designed to be inserted into a serial line. Built into one connector are 7 two-color LEDs, each monitoring an important

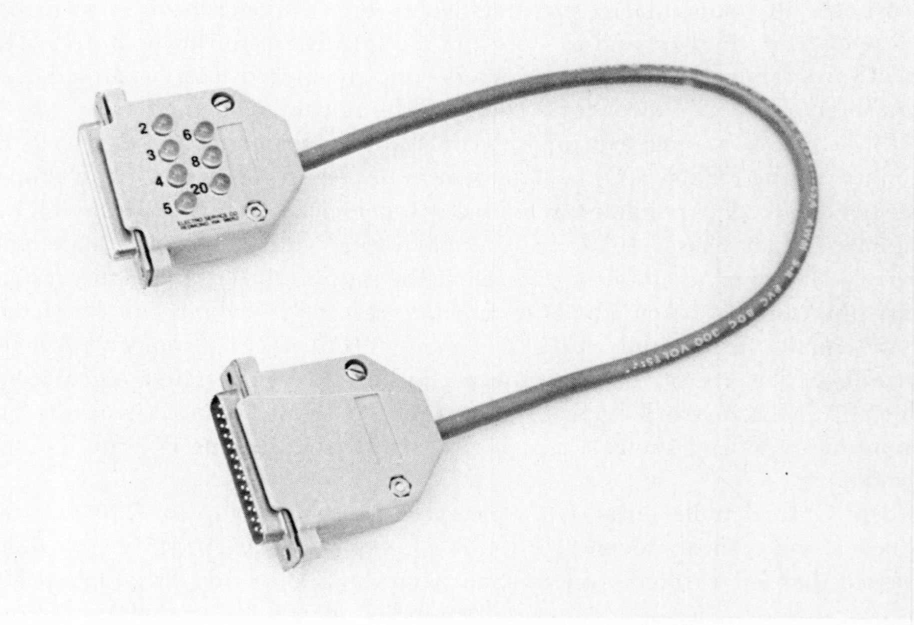

Photo courtesy of Electro-Service Co.

Figure 9-14. RS-232C Line Status Indicator

RS-232C line. Red indicates a space, or +12 volts; and yellow indicates a mark, or −12 volts. If the transmit or receive line is passing data, the corresponding LED flickers.

You can tell at a glance which control lines are active, and you can tell if and in which direction data is being sent. Plugging the one end of the Line Status Indicator into a device will quickly determine if it is a DTE or a DCE. A quiescent DTE will cause pin 2's LED to be yellow; a DCE will cause pin 3's LED to be yellow.

Communications problems may be caused by the following:

- The speeds of the transmitting and receiving devices are not matched.
- One device expects parity, and the other doesn't provide it.
- One device expects a control signal such as DTR, DSR, or CD, and the other device doesn't provide it.
- The cable is wired improperly.
- The communications program is addressing the wrong serial port.

If you need to measure data rate or otherwise examine an incoming signal, you can use an oscilloscope on the received data line (pin 3). This is not usually necessary, but it *is* educational.

TEN

CONNECTING PCS TO IBM MAINFRAMES

If you need to connect your PC to an IBM mainframe, the information in Chapters 3 through 9 will not directly apply. The technology is completely different, the communications protocols are different, and the hardware and software products are different. This chapter explains the products and techniques you will utilize to connect to a mainframe. As you read this chapter, you will often see the number 3270 and the word synchronous. The **3270** refers to a series of IBM terminal products. IBM 3270 terminals (Figure 10-1) communicate with IBM mainframes using **synchronous** communications techniques. The PC can imitate, or emulate, a 3270 terminal with the addition of hardware and software that allow the PC to communicate using a synchronous protocol.

Even though you will be using synchronous communications, the concepts used in asynchronous communications are still important. Many 3270 emulation products use the same elements that are employed in asynchronous communication: serial ports and asynchronous modems. Some IBM systems directly support asynchronous terminals through a software product called Time Sharing Option (TSO). All of the asynchronous modems, ports, and communications

Reprinted with permission of International Business Machines Corporation

Figure 10-1. IBM 3270 terminal

programs will work with TSO. However, this chapter has been written for common IBM operating systems that support on-line synchronous terminals.

Uses for 3270 Emulation Products

If you modify your PC to emulate a 3270 terminal, what can you do with it? In addition to replacing an actual 3270, you can use the PC to transfer files between a PC and a mainframe, share data with a mainframe database, and set up dedicated transaction processing systems.

Direct Replacement of 3270 Terminals

The most obvious and widespread use of 3270 emulators is to replace (or avoid the purchase of) an IBM 3270 terminal. You can use your desktop PC as a full-function personal computer and as a terminal. With some configurations, you can have the 3270 on-line with a mainframe while you are using the PC to run a program like *VisiCalc*.

File Transfers Between PCs and Mainframes

A PC imitating a 3270 terminal saves space and money. But you can also transfer data files back and forth between the PC and the mainframe. Most emulation products allow you to save a copy of the 3270 screen on the PC's disk. Other products come with software tools for sending entire files back and forth. A menu lets you specify the name of the file on the mainframe (called a data set name), the PC disk file name, and the transfer direction.

One way to use a micro-to-mainframe file transfer is to enter files of data while you are off-line. You can then transmit a "batch" of files to a mainframe during the night. This way you don't need to wait for a slowly responding mainframe, and your daytime computer resources are conserved. A common use of a mainframe-to-micro transfer is retrieving reports for off-line editing with a PC word processor program or calculating with a spreadsheet. With both types of transfers, you take advantage of the PC's processing power. In the second case, you use programs that are usually better than their mainframe equivalents.

Intelligent Data Sharing

For most file transfer applications you need special programs for both the PC and the mainframe. Programming is expensive and time-consuming, so it's better to buy "off-the-shelf" software. There is at least one commercially available package that allows intelligent data sharing between the PC and a mainframe. That package, *Executive Peachpak II,* is, unfortunately, tied to a specific mainframe application package, MSA accounting software. (The program is described later in this chapter.) If you already use that package, you can easily transfer data into several spreadsheets, graphics packages, and word processors with no programming.

Special Applications

The PC can accept data from the mainframe, process it in some unique way, and then send it back again. An electronic funds transfer network, for example, could use a PC to control the encryption of data. The encryption programs could be stored in the PC's read-only memory (ROM) and would be less susceptible to alteration than programs stored in the mainframe's alterable random-access memory (RAM). When the mainframe sent a number to the PC, the PC would encrypt it and send it back to the mainframe. To the mainframe, the operation would be the same as if a human operator on a 3270 terminal had seen the original number on the screen and then calculated and sent the encrypted value back to the mainframe.

The Multi-Layer Model for Data Transfer

The ideal data processing environment would allow data to flow freely between micros and mainframes and be limited only by security factors. Such a situation is difficult to achieve because the micro and mainframe's software are each independent and oblivious to the other's needs. Fortunately, computer scientists are working on the problem, and they've proposed a **multi-layer model** for data transfer software. The names of the layers and even the number of layers are different depending on whom you listen to. Many previously published explanations of these layers have been difficult to understand, so here's a simplified explanation built around a four-layer model.

What's a **layer**? You have to know something about computer programming to appreciate layered software development. It's not realistic for a programmer, starting with an "empty machine," to write, for example, a complete on-line accounts payable system including all the low-level instructions for communication with the terminals. Normally, an **applications programmer** writes the accounts payable programs in a high-level language such as COBOL, and a **systems programmer** writes the low-level communications software in assembly language. This low-level software is often supplied by the computer manufacturer and comes with extensive documentation that defines an "interface" for the applications programmer. The interface allows the applications programmer to use instructions like GET and PUT in a COBOL program to exchange data with the remote terminal. Thus there are separate applications and communications layers.

Communication Link Control Layer

The communications layer consists of three layers, as shown in Figure 10-2. At the lowest level, the **communication link control** layer controls the actual movement of bits and bytes on the communications line. Here is where you'll find the synchronous protocol, called **SDLC** (Synchronous Data Link Control). The signals electronically follow the RS-232C standard with respect to pin numbers and voltages. The similarity to asynchronous communications ends there, however. The start and stop bits are gone and are replaced by a new technology. SDLC's job is to transmit **message units**, or blocks of data, from

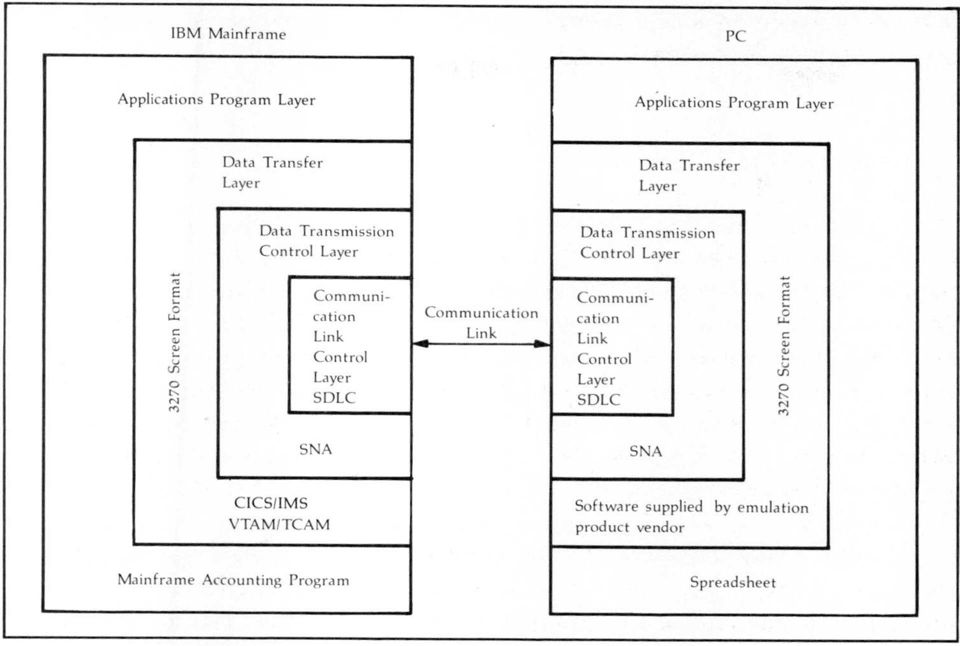

Figure 10-2. The four-layer model for data transfer

one place to another in the network. Errors are transparently corrected if possible, and if not, the next layer up is notified of the problem.

Data Transmission Control Layer

Immediately above the communication link control layer is the **data transmission control** layer. This layer is included entirely within IBM's **SNA** (Systems Network Architecture). If you're interested, IBM will supply a foot-high stack of manuals that tell you more than you ever wanted to know. SNA establishes communication among **logical units**, typically IBM mainframe applications programs and 3270 terminals. The applications program isn't concerned with the physical location or characteristics of the logical unit. The applications program accesses a terminal using a **network name**, not caring whether the terminal is in the computer room or across the country. SNA takes care of all the details, translating the network name to a **network address**. If one circuit (path) fails during communication, SNA automatically switches to a new one. Not only does SNA handle mainframe-to-terminal communication, but it also links one mainframe to other mainframes and is thus the backbone of a **distributed processing system** — a system that integrates several computers into what appears to be one large system.

Data Transfer Layer

The **data transfer** layer, the next step up, is the least defined of all the layers. Ideally, there would be one standard interchange format for data on the order of the DIF format established for use with the *VisiCalc* spreadsheet program. Any program — mainframe accounting system or PC spreadsheet — would store all its data in this format. Information exchange between programs would be easy. Unfortunately, a national data standard is nowhere in sight, but curiously, the 3270 terminal itself has introduced a standard in the form of an 80-character by 24-row screen. The mainframe program stores data into a screen at one end, and the PC program retrieves it at the other.

The 80 × 24 screen is an easy-to-understand data standard, but the programs are far more complex. On the mainframe end, there's a **transaction processor**, usually CICS or IMS, which includes database management functions. Below that there's the **access method** — VTAM or TCAM. The SNA umbrella includes components "inside of" CICS, IMS, VTAM, and TCAM. See your systems programmer for details.

PC data transfer software is supplied by the manufacturers of 3270 emulation products. The 80 × 24 screen is accessed either by BASIC subroutines or through tables.

The Applications Program Layer

The top layer, **applications programs**, speaks for itself. Applications programs are those written for a specific business task such as accounting, but productivity tools like *Multiplan* and *Lotus 1-2-3* also qualify. Enabling all these programs to talk to each other through the exchange of data is a major goal of the computer industry.

3270 Terminals And IBM Software

On-line computer software has evolved into two distinct branches: minicomputer/microcomputer and mainframe. A terminal connected to a multi-user minicomputer or to a single-user microcomputer communicates with its own private application program or program copy. That program accepts individual keystrokes, often echoing them back to the terminal. The mini/micro program writes characters to the screen and can manipulate the screen in other ways. Mainframe software utilizing 3270s, on the other hand, is geared to move entire 80 × 24 screens back and forth between the terminal and the mainframe. Figure 10-3 shows a data entry screen for an employee master record. The 3270 operator fills in all the blanks, or **fields**, and is free to move around the screen and make changes as necessary. The screen data is stored in the terminal until the TRANSMIT key is pressed. All the employee data is then sent to the mainframe in one burst where it's processed as a **transaction**. The mainframe application program, which may be handling transactions from a dozen terminals, processes the screen and sends back an acknowledgment or error messages.

It's easy to understand the 3270 data transfer layer if you imagine two 80 × 24 screens, one in the terminal and one in the mainframe. The mainframe software and the 3270 are constantly striving to keep the two screens exactly in sync. If the terminal operator makes a change and transmits a screen, that change must be made in the mainframe's screen. The software is smart enough not to send all 1920 characters each time one field changes; it sends only the updated data. Look at Figure 10-3 again. Notice the **tags** such as "CLOCK NUMBER:" and "SS NUMBER:". The mainframe program sends these tags to the 3270. The operator can enter data only in the fields; the tags are **protected** from being modified and there's no point in sending tags back to the mainframe.

How are some screen areas protected and others not? **Attributes** make the difference. The PC has a "shadow screen" containing one hidden character for

```
BIG-TIME CORP.              EMPLOYEE MASTER MAINTENANCE              PAYROLL
DATE: 12/12/83                     SCREEN PR22-5                 TIME: 11:36

CLOCK NUMBER:____                        SS NUMBER: ___-__-____

LAST NAME: ______________                FIRST NAME: _____________

MARITAL STATUS: _                        NUMBER OF EXEMPTIONS: __

HOURLY RATE: _______.__                  UNION CODE: __

DEDUCTION 1 DESCRIPTION: ______________  RATE: __.__

DEDUCTION 2 DESCRIPTION: ______________  RATE: __.__

DEDUCTION 3 DESCRIPTION: ______________  RATE: __.__

DEDUCTION 4 DESCRIPTION: ______________  RATE: __.__
```

Figure 10-3. 3270 data entry screen showing fields and tags

each one you see. Those hidden characters, called attributes, determine whether the corresponding character is displayed with underline, reverse video, bright video, blink, and color (if there's a color monitor). The PC's video memory (in 24 × 80 text mode) contains 3840 characters: 1920 displayable characters and 1920 attributes.

The original 3270s had room for only 1920 characters, so the attributes had to occupy space on the screen. Notice the blanks between tags and fields in Figure 10-3. Current 3270s have a shadow screen that provides one attribute per character. To preserve compatibility, the newer 3270s have the original **field attributes** as well as the added **character attributes** and **extended field attributes**, which shadow the field attributes. Field attributes allow protected fields and invisible fields as well as numeric-only and alpha-only fields to be defined. A field attribute applies to all of the subsequent text characters up to the next attribute. Character attributes determine characteristics like color, underline, and so on.

Suppose your PC is emulating a DEC terminal connected to a VAX computer running UNIX. Once you're logged in, you can stop the emulator program and even turn off the PC; you're still logged in. The 3270, in contrast, must constantly maintain contact with the system to remain connected. The 3270 is connected to a controller which sends **poll commands** to the terminal several times a second. If the terminal doesn't respond, the communications session ends. Some 3270 emulators can answer the polls even when the PC is busy doing other tasks; others can't.

The PC uses the ASCII character set shown in Appendix A. Standard ASCII includes 128 characters as defined by the low-order seven bits of an 8-bit byte. The PC uses the remaining 128 characters for special graphics symbols. IBM mainframes have traditionally used the 8-bit **EBCDIC** (Extended Binary Coded Decimal Interchange Code). Most 3270 terminals operate with EBCDIC, but it is possible for a 3270 to use ASCII.

Programmers of IBM on-line applications are thoroughly familiar with the 3270 screen and its attributes. Until recently, all of the programming was done on the mainframe since the 3270 terminals couldn't be programmed in the usual sense of the term. The PC has changed all that. Some of the 3270 emulation products allow the emulated 3270 to be programmed at the PC end. Since both PC and mainframe programmers are faced with the same 24 × 80 screen and the same attributes, the job of creating an on-line applications program is somewhat easier. Don't worry though; you won't need to pay two programmers. Others have done the programming for you. If their programs fit your application, you're in luck.

Executive Peachpak II

Management Science America (MSA), owner of Peachtree Software, markets one of the very few integrated micro/mainframe software products available. *Executive Peachpak II*'s cornerstone is *Peachlink,* the software that transfers data from MSA accounting programs running on mainframes to PCs. Other components are *PeachCalc,* a version of the *SuperCalc* spreadsheet program; *PeachText,* formerly the Magic Wand word processer; and *Business Graphics.* There's also a list manager and asynchronous telecommunications software. The entire package costs $6000 for each PC, but there are "stripped down" versions costing as little as $1500. Remember also that you need some special hardware, which typically costs $1195 for each PC. *Peachpak* requires either an IRMA board or a Renex protocol converter. Both of these are described later in this chapter.

What can you do with *Peachpak?* Nothing, unless you have MSA mainframe on-line accounting software. What is MSA software? It's the large-system equivalent of *Peachtree* PC accounting modules, a program capable of running a company the size of General Motors. Included are general ledger, payroll, accounts payable and receivable programs, and more. *Peachpak* lets you extract data from your MSA files and manipulate it with your PC. You can use *PeachCalc* and *Business Graphics,* and you can also use *Lotus 1-2-3* and *VisiCalc.* Figure 10-4 shows an MSA-generated salary report and a *PeachCalc* budget forecast using an across-the-board six percent salary increase. Figure 10-5 shows a mainframe departmental overtime report and a bar chart generated on the PC by the *Business Graphics* program.

Some MSA software uses database technology, thereby allowing users to enter queries for specific information. *Peachpak* supports this with **database sharing**. For example, you can extract the balances for accounts with a greater-than-50% change since the last period. Once you get these figures into your PC, you can work with them in a spreadsheet or include the list in a memo. Currently, only general ledger and accounts payable support database sharing.

How does it all work? Recall the *Dow Jones Market Manager* described in Chapter 6. That program dialed Dow Jones and extracted information, since it knew exactly what to expect from the Dow Jones service. *Peachpak* does the same thing with your mainframe, except it uses 3270 technology instead of asynchronous terminal technology. The MSA programs are unaware of *Peachpak*'s existence, just as the Dow Jones service is not aware that you're using *Market Manager.* Both act as though a human operator is making queries.

```
SALARY REPORT                 GATEWAY ENERGY                      REPORT NO    16
REFINERY DIV                REFINERY DIVISION                     PAGE          3
DEPT    EMPLOYEE     REVIEW      SUPERVISOR      BASE
CODE     NUMBER       DATE          NAME        SALARY
ADMN      136467    01/01/83    M WALTERS     15,000.00
ADMN      368724    02/01/83    M WALTERS     16,000.00
ADMN      683421    08/01/83    M WALTERS     22,000.00
ADMN      036214    11/01/83    M WALTERS     30,000.00
**  TOTALS FOR DEPARTMENT    ADMN             83,000.00
 QC       532146    02/01/83    S JONES       35,000.00
 QC       345962    05/01/83    S JONES       40,000.00
 QC       046132    09/01/83    S JONES       26,000.00
**  TOTALS FOR DEPARTMENT     QC             101,000.00
TECH      136487    04/01/83    W SMITH       24,000.00
TECH      365982    05/01/83    W SMITH       18,000.00
TECH      013211    05/01/83    W SMITH       27,000.00
**  TOTALS FOR DEPARTMENT    TECH             69,000.00
**  TOTALS FOR DIVISION      RFNY            253,000.00
* * * * * * * * * * * * * * * * * * * * * * * * * * * * * * * * * * * * * * *
SCREEN: M7
KEY INFO: L1: AT   L2: LA EMP NO:                  3
ACTION: ____
```

a. MSA salary report in 3270 format (reprinted with permission of MSA)

```
                              GATEWAY ENERGY
                   1983 BUDGET FORECAST-REFINERY DIVISION

ANNUAL    ANNUAL      MONTHLY NUMBER OF  ANNUAL    ANNUAL
REVIEW     BASE         6%    MONTHS AT FORECAST    TOTAL
 DATE     SALARY       INCR   INCREASE  INCREASE  BUDGETED
01/01/83       15000      75        12       900     15900
02/01/83       16000      80        11       880     16880
08/01/83       22000     110         5       550     22550
11/01/83       30000     150         2       300     30300
    TOTAL BY DEPARTMENT     ADMN            2630     85630
02/01/83       35000     175        11      1925     36925
05/01/83       40000     200         8      1600     41600
09/01/83       26000     130         4       520     26520
    TOTAL BY DEPARTMENT      QC             4045    105045
04/01/83       24000     120         9      1080     25080
05/01/83       18000      90         8       720     18720
05/01/83       27000     135         8      1080     28080
    TOTAL BY DEPARTMENT     TECH            2880     71880

 TOTAL BY DIVISION RFNY                     9555    262555
```

b. PeachCalc spreadsheet after salary data is downloaded to PC

Figure 10-4. Peachpak—MSA salary report and PeachCalc spreadsheet

Peachpak is completely menu-driven, so operation is easy. Look for similar products from vendors of other mainframe software soon.

IBM's Jigsaw Puzzle

There are many ways to attach a 3270 terminal to an IBM mainframe. Actually, there's no such thing as a 3270. That number refers to a class of terminals

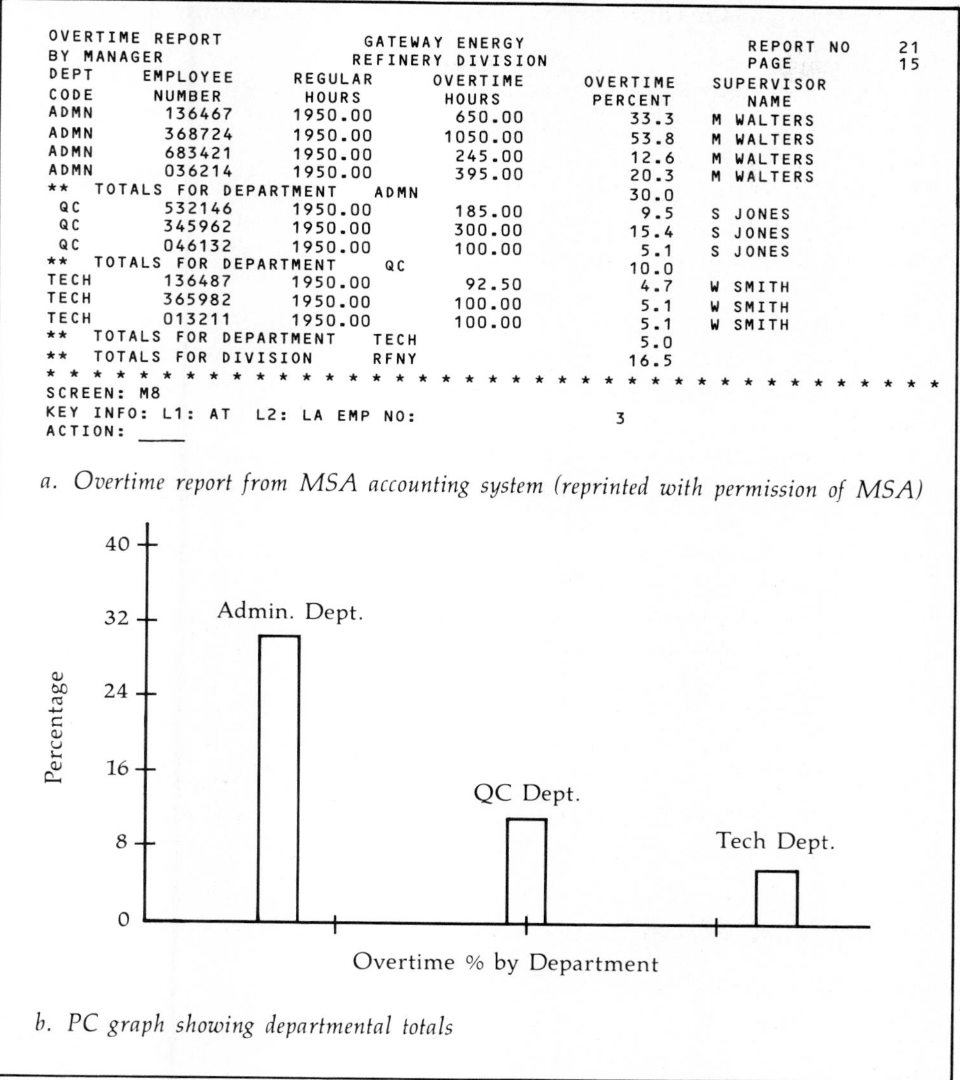

OVERTIME REPORT BY MANAGER — GATEWAY ENERGY REFINERY DIVISION — REPORT NO 21, PAGE 15

DEPT CODE	EMPLOYEE NUMBER	REGULAR HOURS	OVERTIME HOURS	OVERTIME PERCENT	SUPERVISOR NAME
ADMN	136467	1950.00	650.00	33.3	M WALTERS
ADMN	368724	1950.00	1050.00	53.8	M WALTERS
ADMN	683421	1950.00	245.00	12.6	M WALTERS
ADMN	036214	1950.00	395.00	20.3	M WALTERS
** TOTALS FOR DEPARTMENT		ADMN		30.0	
QC	532146	1950.00	185.00	9.5	S JONES
QC	345962	1950.00	300.00	15.4	S JONES
QC	046132	1950.00	100.00	5.1	S JONES
** TOTALS FOR DEPARTMENT		QC		10.0	
TECH	136487	1950.00	92.50	4.7	W SMITH
TECH	365982	1950.00	100.00	5.1	W SMITH
TECH	013211	1950.00	100.00	5.1	W SMITH
** TOTALS FOR DEPARTMENT		TECH		5.0	
** TOTALS FOR DIVISION		RFNY		16.5	

* *
SCREEN: M8
KEY INFO: L1: AT L2: LA EMP NO: 3
ACTION: ____

a. Overtime report from MSA accounting system (reprinted with permission of MSA)

b. PC graph showing departmental totals

Figure 10-5. Peachpak—MSA overtime report and PC graph

and equipment. Here is a breakdown:

- 3278 A monochrome display and keyboard terminal with a coaxial cable connection.
- 3279 The color equivalent of the 3278. There's an option for graphics.

- 3274 A **cluster controller** capable of controlling as many as thirty-two 3278s or 3279s.
- 3276 A combination cluster controller and keyboard display. This product is no longer manufactured.

The IBM 3278 and 3279 terminals cannot attach directly to most IBM mainframes; they must connect to the mainframe via a 3274 cluster controller. However, some IBM 4300 series mainframes do have built-in 3274 capabilities and thus can connect directly to 3278 and 3279 terminals.

If the distance is short, the 3274 cluster controller (or 3276) can connect to the mainframe directly via a high-speed data channel. Otherwise, it must connect to the mainframe via another device called the 3705 communications controller.

The 3705 **communications controller** provides a number of RS-232C serial ports that use synchronous protocol and are capable of speeds up to 56,000 bps. Figure 10-6 shows a mainframe with some local terminals and a batch of remotes. Notice that the 3274 and 3705 are connected via high-speed modems and dedicated phone lines.

How the PC Fits In

You've seen how a PC emulation of a 3270 terminal is a more intelligent and software-flexible terminal than the 3270 itself. Now you'll see how the PC can give you more options for connecting to the mainframe. There are five ways to set up the PC for use with a mainframe.

Coax-connected 3270 Card

Imagine all of the electronics in a 3279 terminal on a PC-compatible plug-in circuit card. Everything is included except the CRT screen and the keyboard. This is the most popular way to emulate a 3270. The card plugs into the PC, the coax cable plugs into the 3274 cluster controller, and special software is loaded into the PC. The card contains its own microprocessor and a 1920-character screen buffer. As long as the PC's power is on, the 3270 card responds to commands exactly as a 3270 terminal responds, even if the PC is idle or running another program. When the special PC software is loaded, the screen buffer is displayed on the PC's monitor and the keyboard is activated. Since the screen buffer exists independently of the PC, programs can be written to access that buffer and to simulate keystrokes from the 3270's keyboard.

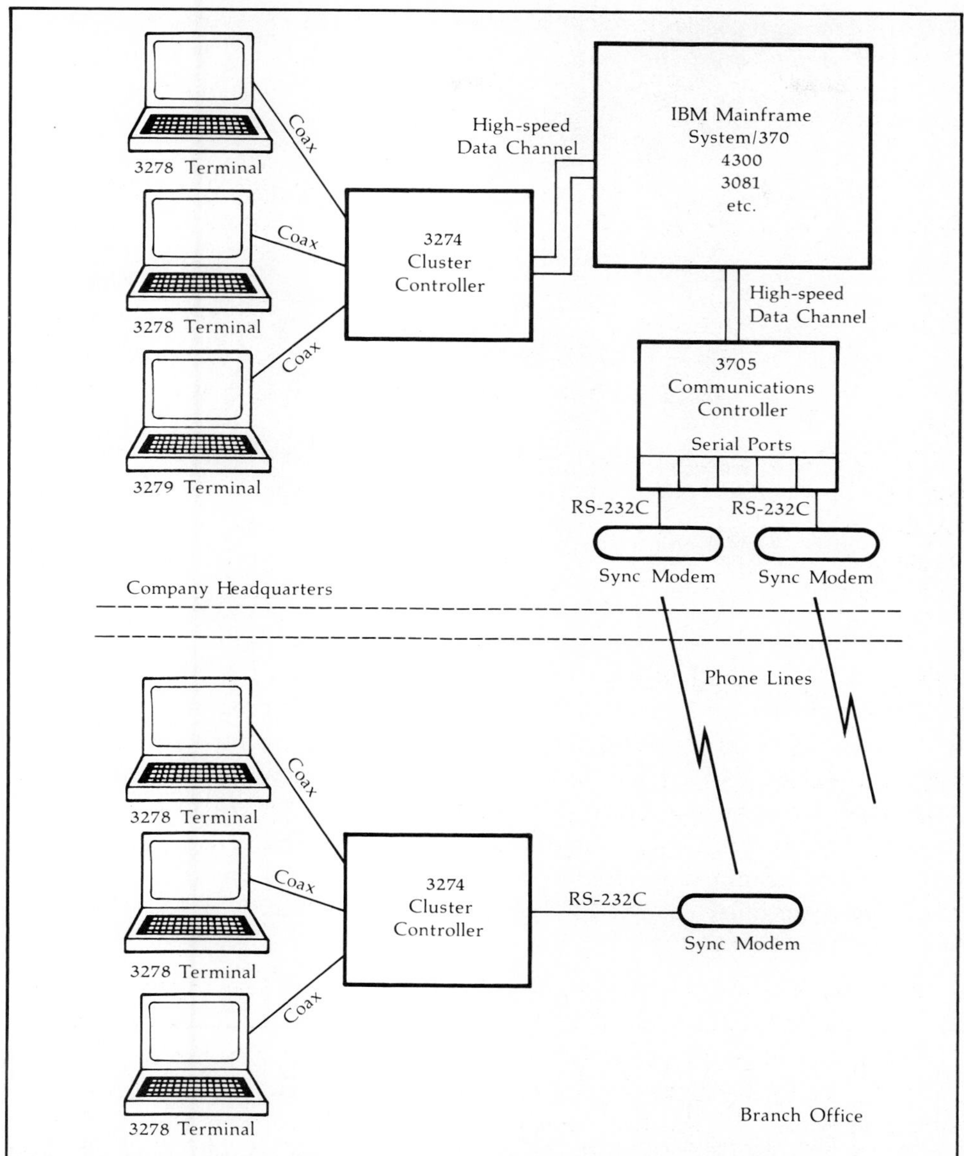

Figure 10-6. IBM mainframe with attached terminals

The IRMA board from DCA, Inc. (formerly TAC) is one of the leading coax-connected 3270 cards. IRMA's proper name is Decision Support Interface, Model PC/3278, but she's happy if you call her by her first name. Figure 10-7 is

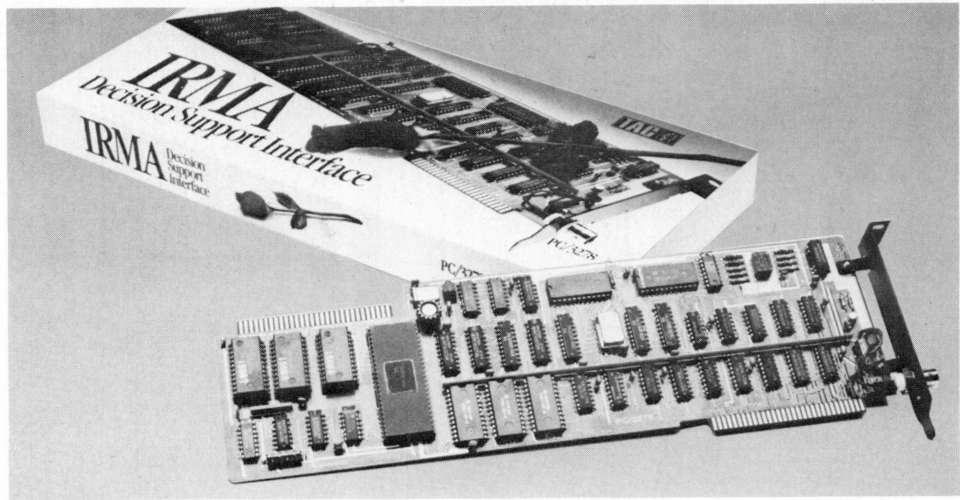

Photo Courtesy of DCA

Figure 10-7. IRMA card

a photo of the card. Note the coax connector at the lower right. This connector is accessible at the back of the PC when the card is installed. IRMA costs $1195, software included, and it supports the *Executive Peachpak II* program. DCA claims that IRMA will display seven colors on the IBM Color Monitor while emulating a 3279. A set of BASICA subroutines is included to allow BASIC programs to access the screen buffer and to simulate the keyboard. Figure 10-8 shows how the PC's keyboard is used to simulate the 3270's keyboard. The 3270 terminals contain 24 programmed function keys (PF1, PF2, and so on). In order to simulate these keys, you must use the PC's ALT key in conjunction with the designated key.

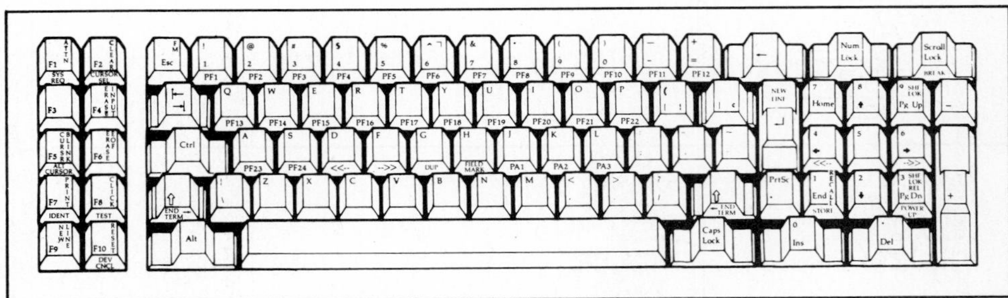

Figure 10-8. IRMA keyboard map

Another coax card is the PCOX card from CXI. This card is sold directly by CXI and is also being sold under a private label by AST Research, Inc. The PCOX card sells for the same price as IRMA, but offers a table-driven screen interface in lieu of the BASIC subroutines. Four colors are supported in 3279 mode. CXI claims that its direct memory access (DMA) hardware implementation makes the board perform better than IRMA. Figure 10-9 shows how the IRMA or PCOX cards fit into the IBM puzzle.

RS-232C Synchronous Adapter Card

While the coax card allows a PC to connect directly to a 3274 cluster controller, a synchronous adapter card connects the PC to a 3705 communications controller with or without intervening modems. Chapter 9 described the asynchronous adapter with its 8250 UART chip. That chip is incapable of synchronous communication, so it won't work with a 3705. A synchronous adapter

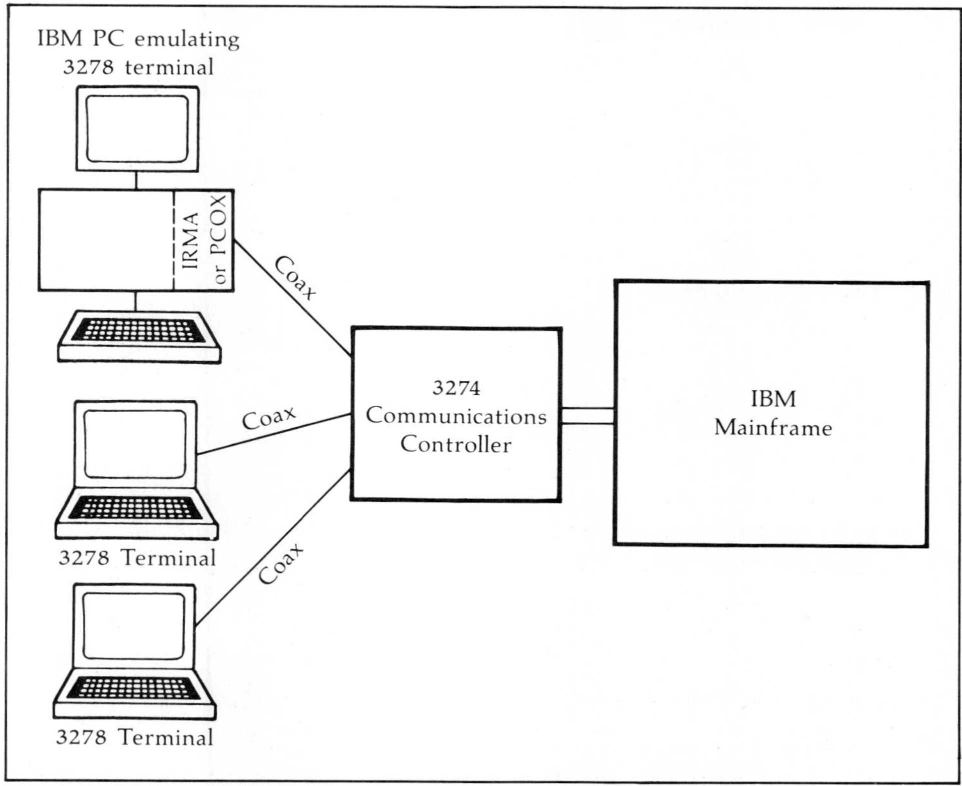

Figure 10-9. IRMA/PCOX cards in an IBM network

card is required along with special emulation software. The software, running on the PC's 8088 processor, assumes most of the communications burden. A dedicated chip on the adapter card handles most of the details of the SDLC communications protocol, but the emulation software implements SNA and manages the 3270 screen and keyboard. All of the protected and special fields must be simulated in software. The software bottleneck limits communications to 9600 bps and precludes most custom programming.

IBM makes an SDLC Adapter Card that sells for $300. The IBM 3270 emulation software costs $700 a copy. The card is built around the 8273 SDLC protocol control module, a very sophisticated communications processor on a chip. AST Research sells a combination synchronous card and emulator program for $895. That card uses the Zilog SIO chip, which can handle several synchronous protocols as well as asynchronous communication. The same card is used with AST's bisync, 3780, and 5251 software.

Another card, PC Express, from Intelligent Technologies offers more features than the IBM and AST cards. PC Express is a combination synchronous/asynchronous adapter with a built-in automatic 300 bps asynchronous modem. Not only can you use it for normal asynchronous communication, but you can also emulate a 3270 with automatic dialing. Most synchronous modems don't dial automatically, but PC Express's built-in modem can bypass the synchronous modem long enough to dial a call. Universal Data Systems (UDS) makes a 4800 bps synchronous modem that sells for $1750. PC Express can use this modem for a 3270 link or for PC-to-PC file transfers. The fully-configured PC Express card costs $1295. Figure 10-10 shows a 3270 emulation setup with a PC, two UDS modems, and a PC Express card.

Intelligent Technologies is introducing a product called Cluster-Net that allows you to attach as many as 12 PCs to a PC that is designated as the "cluster controller." Each satellite PC connects to the cluster controller using twisted-pair cable and an asynchronous interface. The PC acting as the controller requires an $1100 card and may not act as a terminal. The other PCs require the $895 standard version of PC Express.

AST and Information Technologies, Inc., report they are building "intelligent" communications processors that connect to a synchronous RS-232C line. These cards contain their own microprocessor chips and screen buffers and are capable of communicating at speeds of up to 56,000 bps.

3274-attached Protocol Converter

Here's a way to emulate a 3270 with an asynchronous interface at the PC. DCA's IRMALINE (Figure 10-11) connects via coax to a 3274 port. An asynchronous modem such as a Hayes 1200 connects to IRMALINE via an RS-232C

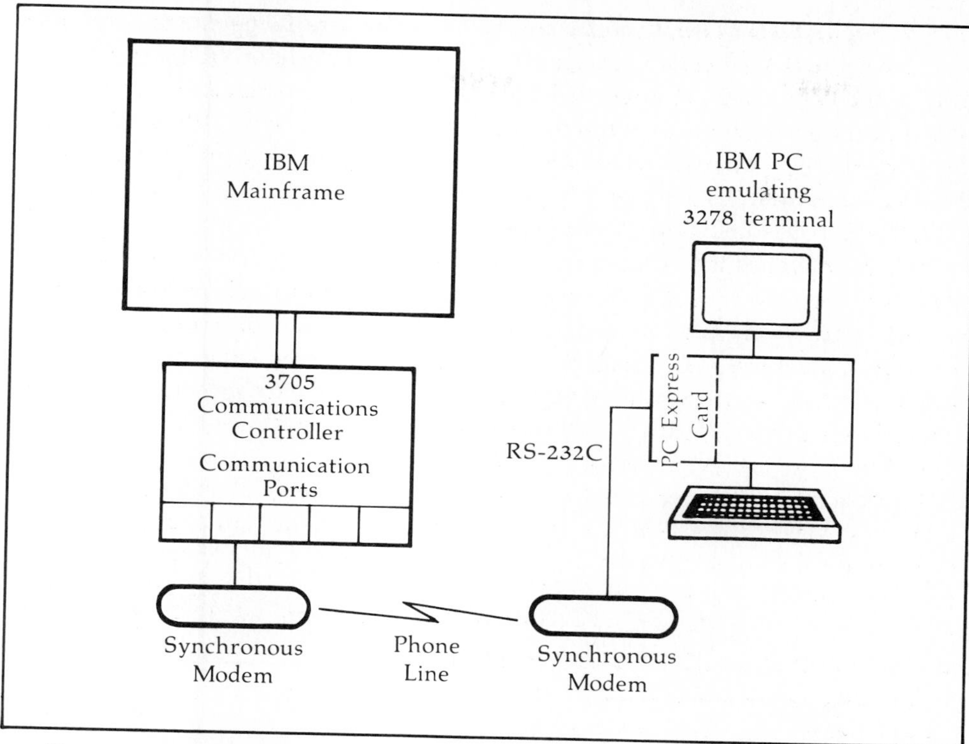

Figure 10-10. PC Express with modems

Photo Courtesy of DCA

Figure 10-11. IRMALINE

connection. At the PC end there's another modem, a serial port, and some software to emulate a standard asynchronous terminal such as a DEC VT-100 or IBM 3101. IRMALETTE, an asynchronous interface card from DCA, plugs into the PC and permits you to use DCA's file transfer software. IRMALINE costs $1395 and IRMALETTE costs $325, software included. Figure 10-12 shows an IRMALINE/IRMALETTE hookup.

IRMALINE is known as a **protocol converter** because it converts 3274 coax signals to standard asynchronous RS-232C signals. There's a danger in using any protocol converter; errors can be introduced in the asynchronous link. Synchronous protocols have built-in error checking and error correction. Some asynchronous links use error-correcting protocols, but since IRMALINE is designed to work with ordinary terminals as well as with the PC, there is no error checking. Be careful.

3705-attached Protocol Converter

Another type of protocol converter simulates a 3274 cluster controller. The 3274 has coax connections and uses a unique protocol, but this protocol converter has asynchronous RS-232C connections. As many as 32 asynchronous

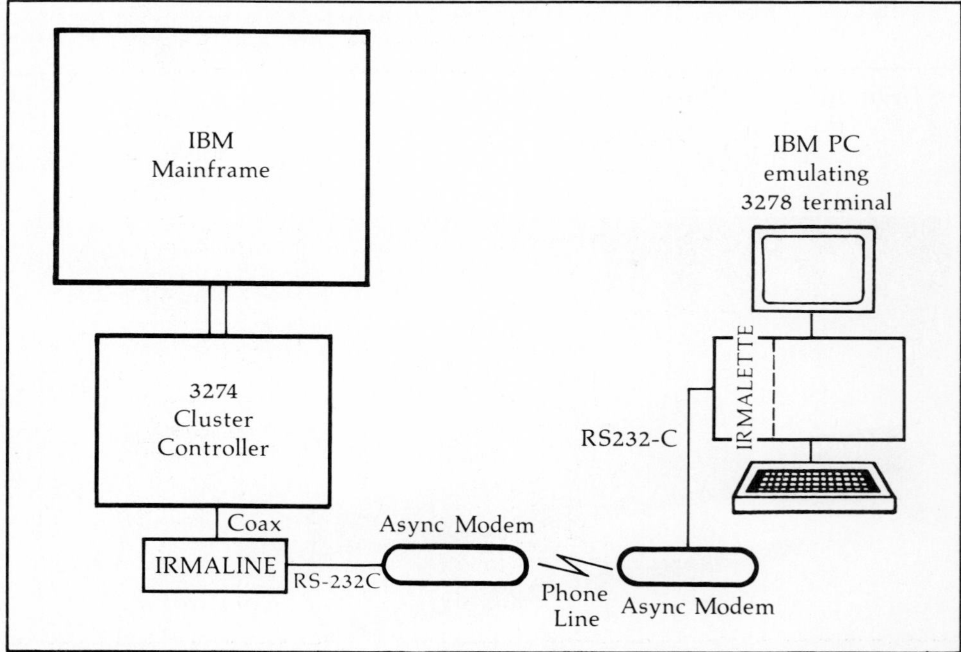

Figure 10-12. Diagram of IRMALINE/IRMALETTE connection

terminals or 32 PCs may be connected either directly or via modems. Figure 10-13 shows two protocol converters connected to one 3705. One converter is located in the computer room and connects via asynchronous modems to PCs in different locations. The second converter serves a group of PCs in a branch office and is connected to the 3705 with one pair of synchronous modems. The PCs are directly attached with RS-232C serial cables. Connected PCs can run

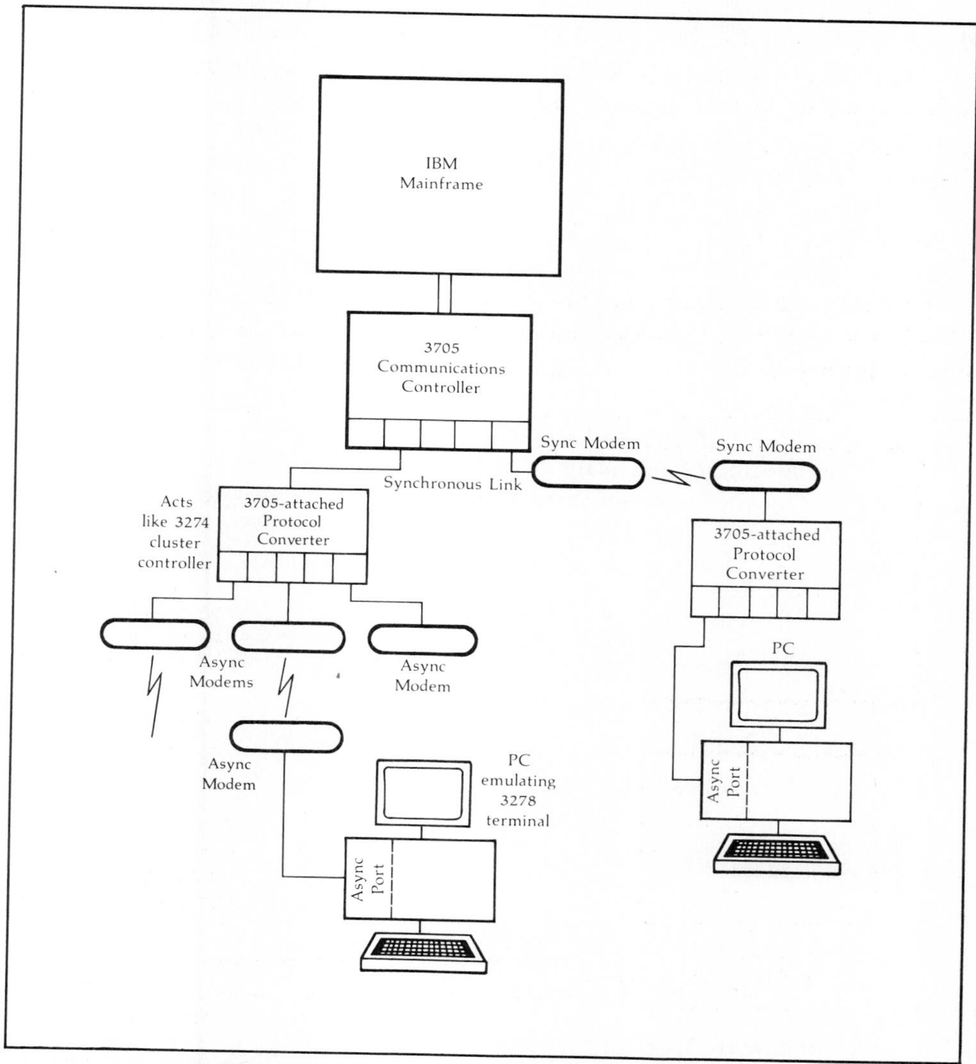

Figure 10-13. Diagram of 3705-attached protocol converter

ordinary emulation programs such as *Crosstalk XVI,* or they can run special-purpose programs. A version of *Executive Peachpak II* supports the Renex Corporation's protocol converter, which costs between $8000 and $16,000, depending on the number of ports.

The 3270-PC

You may feel that the 3270-PC is not a product for the PC. Well, you can always trade your PC for the 3270-PC, knowing that *it* will run all your PC software. Think of the IBM 3270-PC as an IBM PC XT with an IRMA card, a new 122-key keyboard, an enhanced color/graphics adapter, and window software. The window software is the most impressive feature. IBM's windows weren't in production at the time of this book's preparation, but neither were anyone else's.

The 3270-PC Control Program gives you seven windows for seven concurrent tasks. Four of those windows can be separate, interactive 3270 sessions, two can be local notepad operations, and one can be a standard PC DOS 2.0 session. The 3270-PC is IBM's first serious attempt to combine all the features of the PC and the 3270 in an integrated way. Even the keyboard includes all of the PC's and the 3270's keys.

Why not just forget about PCs and XTs? You may already have an office full of them, and you might not want to spend the extra money for the 3270-PC. Also, you may want to use modems and protocol converters to set up remote terminals; the 3270-PC must be coax-connected to a 3274 cluster controller or equivalent. Here are the prices for the 3270-PC:

Standard Model 2

System unit with 256K of memory

One double-sided disk drive

Enhanced display adapter

Keyboard

3270 coax adapter for connection to 3274

List Price: $4290

Standard Model 4

System unit with 320K of memory

Two double-sided disk drives

Enhanced display adapter

Keyboard

3270 coax adapter for connection to 3274

Parallel printer adapter

List Price: $5319

Standard Model 6

System unit with 320K of memory

One double-sided disk drive

10 MB fixed disk

Enhanced display adapter

Keyboard

3270 coax adapter for connection to 3274

Parallel printer adapter

List Price: $7180

Items Priced Separately

5272 color display monitor: $995

3270-PC Control Program: $300

File Transfer Program: $600

A Glimpse Into The World Of SNA and SDLC

Many programmers make a very nice living writing programs to support IBM's complex communications protocols. Reading this section won't guarantee you a high-paying job, but it will give you some background for understanding the link between an IBM mainframe and a 3270.

The simplified four-layer data transfer model shown in Figure 10-2 separated SNA and SDLC, but the SNA standard technically includes the SDLC protocol. SDLC is the lowest of seven SNA layers defined in IBM's documentation.

Synchronous Data Link Control (SDLC)

Asynchronous communication, as you recall, provided for point-to-point communication, forced each character to have a start bit and one or more stop bits, and included no standards for effective error detection and correction. The maximum realistic data rate was 9600 bps and 1200 bps with modems. SDLC overcomes all these limitations.

SDLC allows a message to be sent by one **primary station** to several **secondary stations**, as shown in Figure 10-14. This is called **multipoint communication**. The primary station's message is electrically conveyed to all the secondaries, but it is addressed to only one. The addressed station, having gained permission to use the link, responds to the master station. SDLC allows both half- and full-duplex communication. When the PC acts as a 3270 terminal, however, communication is point-to-point half-duplex; the 3705 is the primary station, and the PC is the one and only secondary station.

To understand SDLC, you must first understand **synchronous** communication. Recall the multiplex telegraph and the time-division multiplex systems from Chapter 2. Each of those used a rotating distributor at each end of the communications link, and those distributors were kept synchronized—a tricky process. When the transmitter was sending bit 1 of channel 3, the receiver had

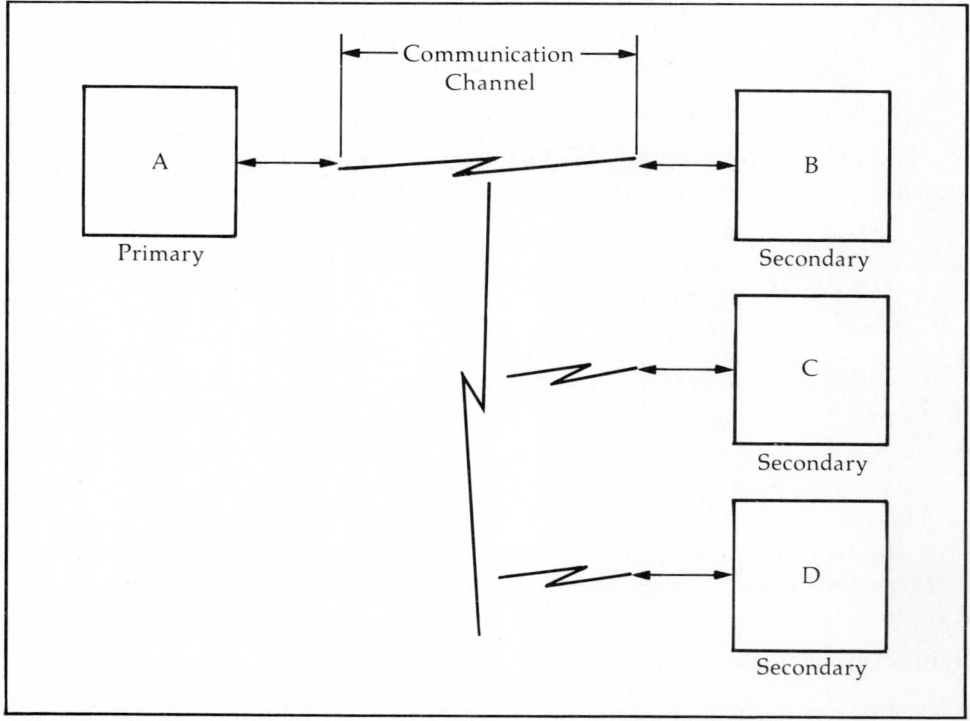

Figure 10-14. Multipoint SDLC communication

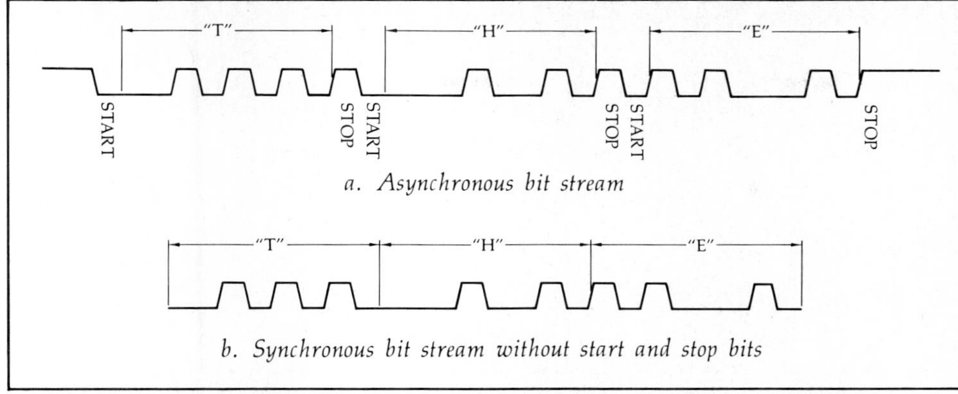

Figure 10-15. Asynchronous and synchronous bit streams for the word "THE"

to pick up the same bit and send it to the proper printer. Modern synchronous data communication does not have to interleave characters from different messages, but it does have to keep the bits straight. Bit 1 must always end up as bit 1.

Figure 10-15*a* shows an asynchronous bit stream for the word "THE". The character boundaries are easily distinguished by the start and stop bits. Figure 10-15*b* shows the same characters transmitted synchronously—without start and stop bits. How does the receiver stay synchronized? One way is to send a **synchronizing signal** through an adjacent channel, as shown in Figure 10-16. If the transmitter and receiver are synchronized at the beginning of the message, they will stay in sync for the duration; the receiver looks for a data bit every

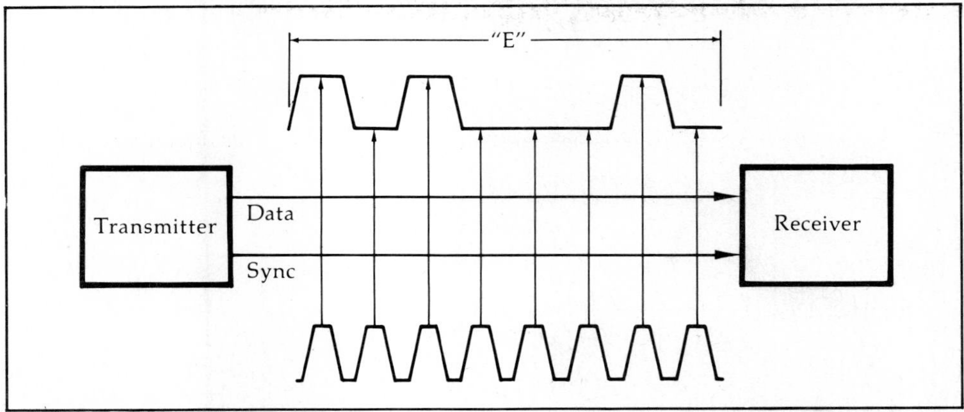

Figure 10-16. Synchronizing signal sent through adjacent channel

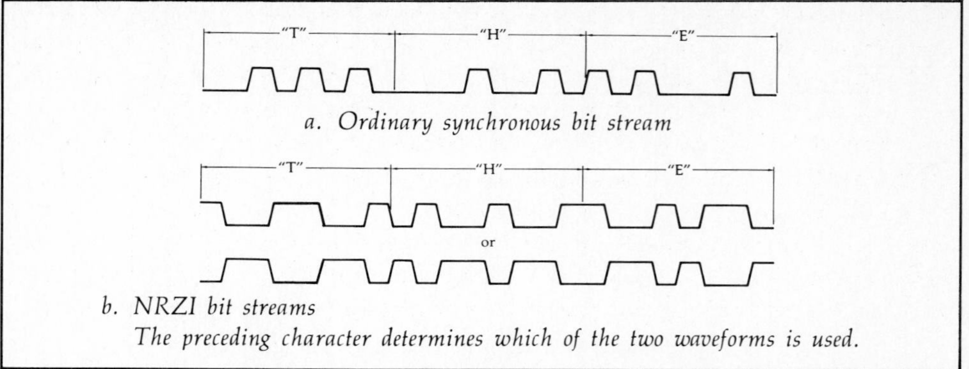

Figure 10-17. Non-return-to-zero coding

time it receives a pulse. Synchronization begins with a special **sync character** preceding the message.

An external sync signal is practical only with direct connections—it won't pass through a modem. There are several schemes for achieving self-synchronization. SDLC uses a scheme called **zero-bit insertion** and a coding method called **Non-Return to Zero Inverted** (NRZI). This method guarantees enough zero/one transitions so that the electronics in the receiver can "lock" onto the incoming signal. Figure 10-17 shows how it works. An ordinary synchronous waveform is shown in Figure 10-17*a*. The voltage is high for a one and low for a zero. The corresponding NRZI waveform is shown in Figure 10-17*b*. Here the voltage *changes* for every zero. If a string of five or more ones comes along, an extra zero is inserted, preventing extended periods of unchanged voltage. Those extra zeroes are removed on the receiving end.

Figure 10-18 shows an **SDLC frame,** which is used to send a message unit over a data link. The leading and trailing **flags** are represented by the bit

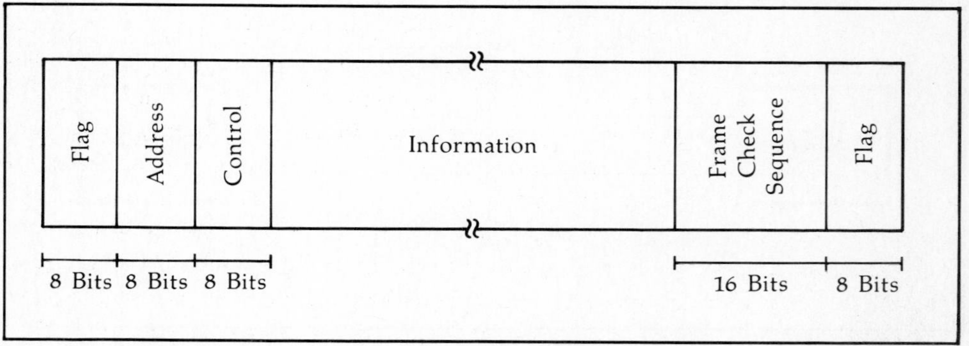

Figure 10-18. SDLC frame

sequence "01111110" which, you may notice, breaks the rule stating that a zero must be inserted in a string of five or more. This is how the receiver recognizes the boundaries of the frame. The **address field**, with only 8 bits, is the destination address if the frame is being sent to a secondary, or link-controlled, station. The address is the source address if the frame is being sent to the primary, or link-controlling, station. The **control field**, also 8 bits, is used to number the frames in sequential order. The **information field**, which may be of any length (multiple of 8 bits), contains the data to be transferred on the link. The **frame check sequence** is a 16-bit cyclic redundancy check (CRC) used for error checking as it is in the asynchronous schemes described in Chapter 9.

Systems Network Architecture (SNA)

IBM's documentation says "SNA is a comprehensive specification for distributed data processing networks. It defines the message formats used within a network, and it defines the rules governing the interaction among components of the network." Most SNA installations aren't true distributed processing systems, but rather groups of terminals connected to mainframes. Today the PC is being used as an intelligent terminal, capable of processing data off-line. Soon it may be used as part of a true distributed processing network.

The network is a collection of components, each connected by links over which formatted message units are sent. Physically, there are central processing units (CPUs), communications controllers, cluster controllers, and terminals. Logically, there are **network addressable units** (NAUs), defined as SNA programs providing services to network users and operators. There are three types of NAUs: the **logical unit** (LU), the **physical unit** (PU), and the **system services control point** (SSCP).

The logical unit is the easiest to understand. It is an SNA program that acts as a bridge between the end user and the network. The end user may be an operator at a terminal, an application program controlled by an operator, or an application program running in batch mode. The end user communicates with the LU, and the LU communicates with the network. Each LU has a unique **network name** that is translated to a **network address**. There may be several end users attached to one LU. An operator can, for example, have a payroll window and a customer inquiry window open at the same time. Those windows are each given distinct network addresses but are served by the same LU.

The physical unit is a program similar to the LU except that it doesn't interact with an end user; instead it interacts with the physical hardware in which it is included. Each terminal, controller, and processor contains a PU. The PU receives messages ordering the startup, testing, or shutdown of the corresponding device. If a new program is to be sent to a programmable cluster controller, for example, the program is sent "in care of" the PU.

The system services control point controls the network. Usually there is only one SSCP, but there could be more in large networks. The SSCP allows the human operator to start up and shut down the network, and it also establishes and terminates communication between other NAUs.

Any NAU is allowed to communicate with another NAU by means of a **session.** Two logical units engaged in this relationship are called **session partners**. Typically, a 3270 operator is connected through the LU in the 3274 and the LU in the mainframe to an applications program. The LU-LU session is usually initiated by one of the LUs, but it could be initiated by some other LU or by the network operator through the SSCP. In any case, the SSCP is involved in setting up the session. An SSCP-PU session can gather error statistics from a 3274 and accommodate newly-connected 3278s. **Parallel sessions** permit concurrent communication by several end users as in the multi-window example described previously.

Figure 10-19 shows a typical SNA network with a PC attached. Note that a PC attached to a 3705 has both an LU and PU within the emulation software.

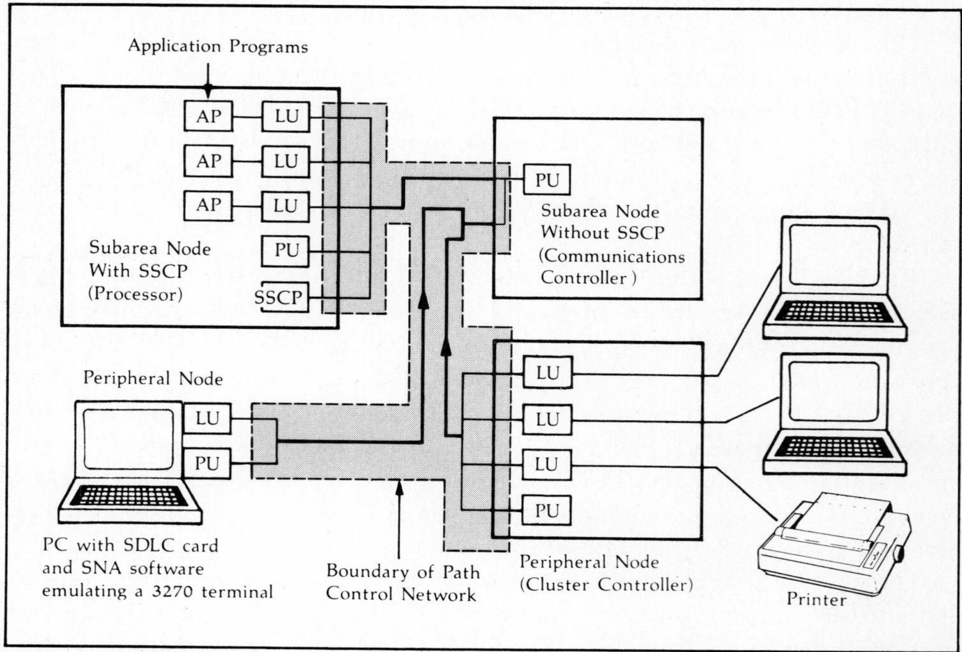

Figure 10-19. SNA network diagram

PCs attached to a 3274 need neither LU nor PU because those functions are included in the cluster controller. The dotted line shows the boundary of the SNA **path control network,** which is the balance of SNA software not included in the NAUs. Figure 10-19 illustrates the hierarchical nature of SNA geography. Notice that the processor and communications controller and PC are called **peripheral nodes**. The **node** is a physical location where SNA components reside. Some subarea nodes have SSCPs; others do not.

Don't forget that SNA nodes can be located at opposite ends of the country. In that case there may be several parallel communication links between each node, as shown in Figure 10-20. Data traffic is distributed over the links and is processed in the correct sequence at the receiving end. The parallel channels act as a single, high-capacity link, usually at a lower cost. Don't confuse the parallel link with the parallel session. The former spreads a single session across several physical links.

Each type of SNA session—and there are hundreds—is carefully "scripted." The IBM manuals provide charts showing the sequences of requests and responses. SNA's message units fit inside the information fields of the SDLC frame and are subdivided into **transmission headers** (THs), **request/response headers** (RHs), and **request/response units** (RUs). The contents of the THs, RHs, and RUs depend on the message's role in the session. RUs usually contain user data.

Binary Synchronous Communication

Binary Synchronous Communication, known as **bisync** or **BSC**, is the predecessor to SDLC/SNA. It's still used in many IBM systems and where PCs are

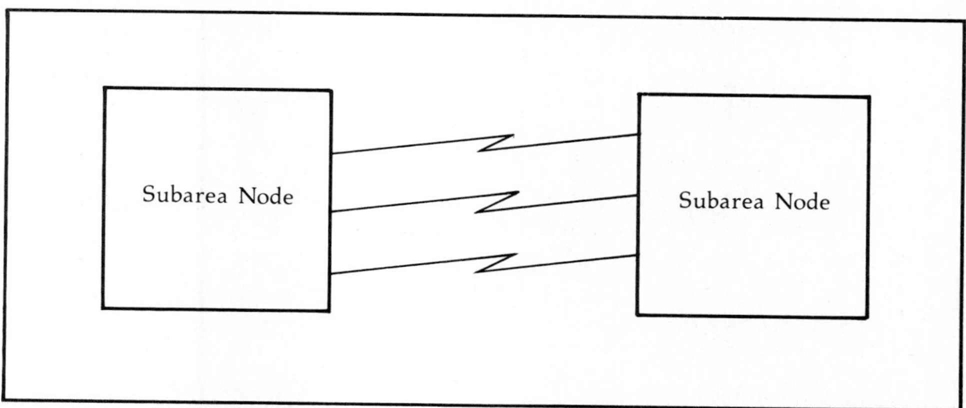

Figure 10-20. SNA parallel links

called upon to emulate the older bisync 3270 terminals. Bisync is definitely a synchronous protocol, but it's different from SDLC. SDLC makes no assumptions about character length, but bisync assumes 8-bit characters. All bisync message blocks are preceded by sequences of special header characters, and special sync characters are inserted periodically to maintain synchronization. If there's no data to be sent, these sync characters are sent continuously. Communication is always point-to-point half-duplex, and there is no attempt to route messages dynamically, support parallel links, or do any of the fancy SNA stuff. The mainframe-to-3270 protocol is cut-and-dried, though, and easy to emulate on the PC.

IBM makes a $300 Binary Synchronous Communication Adapter card for use with the $700 Binary Synchronous 3270 Emulation program. This connects the PC to the RS-232C interface on a properly configured 3705 communications controller. AST Research makes an equivalent hardware/software product for $895. There is no bisync equivalent to the SNA coax-connected products.

ELEVEN

THE FUTURE

The future is easy to predict if you assume there'll be no unexpected developments. In 1970 no one could have predicted the current personal computer boom because the microprocessor chip hadn't been invented. In 1980 people were predicting that some form of Digital Research's CP/M operating system would always be the microcomputer standard. All that was changed with IBM's introduction of the PC with Microsoft's operating system.

It may be easy to draw a curve plotting the falling prices of computers, but it's not easy to predict how easily people will accept the new videotex communications medium or what they'll use it for. Notice how the word "videotex" appeared in place of the more general "PC communications." The color/graphics videotex described in Chapter 5 is the mature form of the new medium that will either live or die in the marketplace. A hundred thousand Source subscribers aren't as important as 10 million videotex subscribers.

Recall the AT&T radio station, WEAF, in Chapter 2. Today videotex is at the same point radio was in 1923. Viewtron is a modern WEAF. Just as there were only a few radio receivers and a small number of stations in 1923, there are only a few videotex terminals and only one videotex service now. Contemporary videotex programming is at the same level as WEAF's song singing and 15-minute real estate commercials. Radio was quite mature in 1949, 16 years after WEAF. What will videotex be like in 16 years—in the year 2000?

Sure Bets

No one will dispute the fact that computers will continue to become cheaper and more powerful. We've already seen computers for $50, although Texas Instruments would rather that we hadn't. Is it not unreasonable to expect a $50 Sceptre terminal and a $200 PC by the year 2000?

Learning from history is both fun and inexpensive. Figure 11-1 is a graph of the historical growth of five major electronic media: the telephone, AM radio, television, cable TV, and color TV. The vertical axis shows the percentage of market penetration achieved by each of the three media. One hundred percent means all households can access the medium. The horizontal axis shows years.

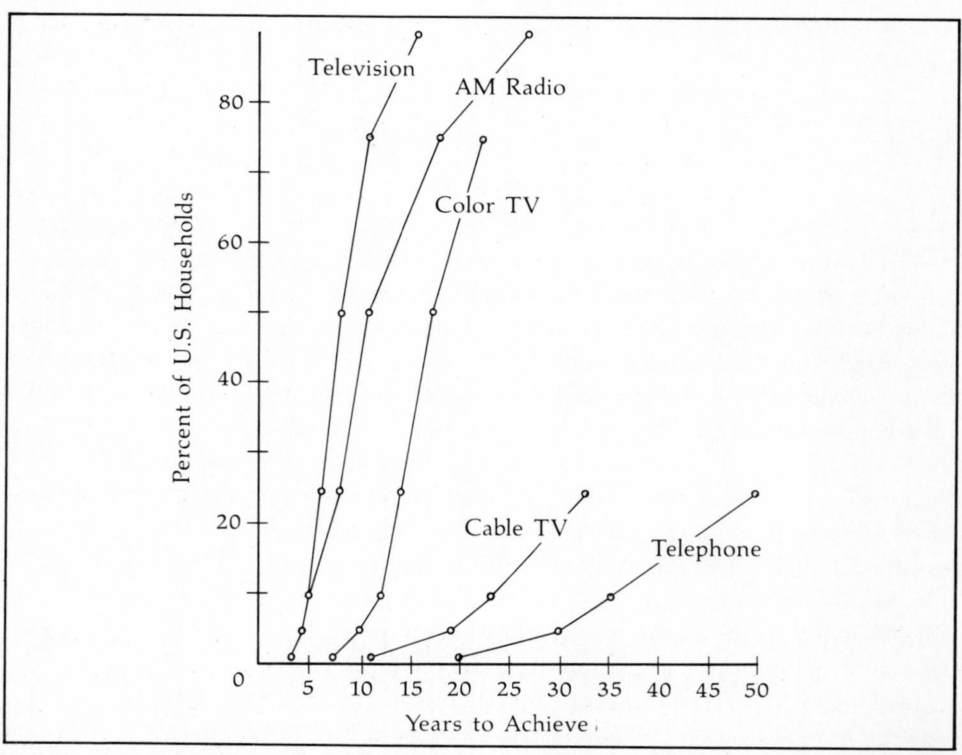

Figure 11-1. Historical growth of media in the United States

The telephone needed 50 years to achieve 25 percent penetration, but radio and television took only five years. Notice that all the curves are somewhat S-shaped. There's a period of slow growth followed by a period of constant growth followed by another period of slow growth as the market saturates. What will the line for videotex be like? Your guess will be as good as any expert's.

Big business exists to make money, and the lower its costs, the more money it makes. One way of lowering costs is to automate, and banks have taken the lead. In California, Bank of America is supplementing branch offices with automatic teller machines and videotex bank-at-home services. It may eventually be cheaper to do business directly with a computer than through a human intermediary. This is why the telephone system started to automate in the 1920s. Once videotex is established, it will be cheaper for stores to sell merchandise electronically than it will be to sell through salespersons and expensive shopping mall locations. Sooner or later, you'll pay a premium to go to a store, a bank, or a travel agent.

The direct access LADT used by Viewtron and Southern Bell will probably be the communications standard in 16 years. The 500-character-per-second data rate is more than sufficient for videotex as we know it today, and the simultaneous phone capability is a bonus. The LADT makes maximum use of the 1890s-style two-wire local telephone circuit, a circuit which today comes under the domain of the local telephone operating companies. Short-distance data traffic will probably be handled by the local operating companies because they own the local telephone exchanges, but long-distance data traffic will be handled by AT&T and other telecommunications companies.

Currently, about 30 percent of the population has one-way cable TV. Two-way systems are technically possible but costly and difficult to standardize. Individual fiber optic cables replacing phone lines are the ideal, and the technology is here. However, the cost of replacing the entire country's telephone lines is staggering.

Scenario 1 — Videotex Fails

Imagine it's the year 2000. Viewtron went bankrupt in 1986 because nobody understood it, and no other company dared make another try for the mass videotex market. Business users and hobbyists were still enthusiastic about personal computers, but home users became bored quickly and moved to hologram video games — the less thinking the better. Nevertheless, the PC communications community grew, and The Source, CompuServe, and Dow Jones flourished. Inexpensive NAPLPS-compatible computers were developed so most information utilities offered a color/graphics option but continued to serve owners of the old terminals and computers. A few old-timers even kept their Apple IIs on-line.

All growth in the information industry was directed to business. Researchers found information retrieval systems an absolute necessity because of the volume of published material, and executives liked the pretty colored stock charts. Videotex technology was used to sell electronics parts and industrial equipment.

LADTs died out because there wasn't enough traffic to support them, and conventional packet-switched networks persevered. Communication costs dropped a little as competition increased. The X.PC standard (Appendix E) caught on, and multiple-session communication became popular along with window-oriented personal computer software.

Scenario 2 — Videotex Takes Off

It's the year 2000 again, but this time it's a different world. During Viewtron's first year, IBM announced that the PCjr had been made Viewtron-compatible, thereby striking a blow at its old rival AT&T. There were videotex services in all major cities by 1986, and competition within cities had produced an incredible array of services. The Source, CompuServe, and Dow Jones quickly adopted the NAPLPS standard and stressed the national scope of their services, lowering their rates at the same time. The BRS and Dialog services retained their text format but reduced their prices substantially because of the wide subscriber base.

The same electronics revolution that reduced the PC's price to $200 also reduced the price of system operators' computers. A desktop system with the power of a 1984 top-of-the-line VAX cost only $5000, and that price included a 1000-megabyte disk. Now anyone with $5000 could be a national publisher; no costly printing and distribution were required. This resulted in information availability that was unimaginable in 1984. The tables had been turned on Big Brother because the people now had more information than the government had. Information utilities were no longer just easy-access backups to printed publications. Much of the printed word was obsolete because most information was strictly electronic.

Social Implications

The really poor people will never have access to videotex, no matter how cheap it is. However, the majority of citizens can afford $12-per-month subscriptions and $50 terminals. At that price videotex is cheaper than cable TV. The biggest problem is getting people to understand what videotex is and how it can be used. Until videotex achieves the same penetration as radio and TV, there will be two classes of people, the "information haves" and the "information have-nots." The haves will get ahead and the have-nots will fall behind. The have-nots might even lose their option of buying a newspaper or magazine. Maybe the schools could push people into the have category, but there has been criticism of their ability even to teach children to read and write. One good sign that schools are up to the challenge is the fact that teachers and students are becoming more involved with personal computers.

Videotex poses some threats to personal privacy. It's possible for certain employees of the videotex service to read any and all messages. Police agencies could search message files for words like "Communist," "bomb," and "revolution," and hackers could break in. It's even possible for someone to monitor exactly which electronic publications you read every day. The science of cryptography allows theoretically unbreakable codes for data transmission, but the National Security Agency (NSA) is trying to prevent the use of any codes it can't decipher.

Videotex's dark side — the segmentation of society and the potential violation of privacy — must be dealt with by industry and by government. Videotex's benefits far outweigh its disadvantages, and the primary benefit is easy public access to the medium. Viewtron is already working with community groups to provide neighborhood news and communication. Fortunately, we don't have to depend solely on the existing videotex system operators to "give" us access to information because anyone will be allowed to start his or her own service through the LADT. What a contrast to radio, television, and cable, where big business has locked up all the frequencies and franchises.

APPENDIX A

ASCII CHARACTERS

Table A-1 lists the ASCII codes used in the PC. The decimal values are shown in the first column and the hexadecimal values in the second column. The next column lists the control characters used in some communications protocols; note that only decimal codes 0 through 31 have control character equivalents. The last column shows the character that is displayed on the PC's screen when the corresponding ASCII code is used in text mode.

Table A-1. ASCII Codes for the PC

Decimal Value	Hexadecimal Value	Control Character	Character
0	00	NUL	Null
1	01	SOH	☺
2	02	STX	☻
3	03	ETX	♥
4	04	EOT	♦
5	05	ENQ	♣
6	06	ACK	♠
7	07	BEL	Beep
8	08	BS	◘
9	09	HT	Tab
10	0A	LF	Line-feed
11	0B	VT	Cursor home
12	0C	FF	Form-feed
13	0D	CR	Enter
14	0E	SO	♫
15	0F	SI	☼
16	10	DLE	►
17	11	DC1	◄
18	12	DC2	↕
19	13	DC3	‼
20	14	DC4	¶
21	15	NAK	§
22	16	SYN	▬
23	17	ETB	↨
24	18	CAN	↑
25	19	EM	↓
26	1A	SUB	→
27	1B	ESC	←
28	1C	FS	Cursor right
29	1D	GS	Cursor left
30	1E	RS	Cursor up
31	1F	US	Cursor down
32	20		Space
33	21		!
34	22		"

Table A-1. ASCII Codes for the PC (continued)

Decimal Value	Hexadecimal Value	Control Character	Character
35	23		#
36	24		$
37	25		%
38	26		&
39	27		'
40	28		(
41	29		)
42	2A		*
43	2B		+
44	2C		,
45	2D		-
46	2E		.
47	2F		/
48	30		0
49	31		1
50	32		2
51	33		3
52	34		4
53	35		5
54	36		6
55	37		7
56	38		8
57	39		9
58	3A		:
59	3B		;
60	3C		<
61	3D		=
62	3E		>
63	3F		?
64	40		@
65	41		A
66	42		B
67	43		C
68	44		D
69	45		E

Table A-1. ASCII Codes for the PC (continued)

Decimal Value	Hexadecimal Value	Control Character	Character
70	46		F
71	47		G
72	48		H
73	49		I
74	4A		J
75	4B		K
76	4C		L
77	4D		M
78	4E		N
79	4F		O
80	50		P
81	51		Q
82	52		R
83	53		S
84	54		T
85	55		U
86	56		V
87	57		W
88	58		X
89	59		Y
90	5A		Z
91	5B		[
92	5C		
93	5D		]
94	5E		^
95	5F		_
96	60		‘
97	61		a
98	62		b
99	63		c
100	64		d
101	65		e
102	66		f
103	67		g
104	68		h

Table A-1. ASCII Codes for the PC (continued)

Decimal Value	Hexadecimal Value	Control Character	Character
105	69		i
106	6A		j
107	6B		k
108	6C		l
109	6D		m
110	6E		n
111	6F		o
112	70		p
113	71		q
114	72		r
115	73		s
116	74		t
117	75		u
118	76		v
119	77		w
120	78		x
121	79		y
122	7A		z
123	7B		{
124	7C		¦
125	7D		}
126	7E		~
127	7F		⌂
128	80		Ç
129	81		ü
130	82		é
131	83		â
132	84		ä
133	85		à
134	86		å
135	87		ç
136	88		ê
137	89		ë
138	8A		è
139	8B		ï

Table A-1. ASCII Codes for the PC (continued)

Decimal Value	Hexadecimal Value	Control Character	Character
140	8C		î
141	8D		ì
142	8E		Ä
143	8F		A
144	90		É
145	91		æ
146	92		Æ
147	93		ô
148	94		ö
149	95		ò
150	96		û
151	97		ù
152	98		ÿ
153	99		Ö
154	9A		Ü
155	9B		¢
156	9C		£
157	9D		¥
158	9E		Pt
159	9F		ƒ
160	A0		á
161	A1		í
162	A2		ó
163	A3		ú
164	A4		ñ
165	A5		Ñ
166	A6		ª
167	A7		º
168	A8		¿
169	A9		⌐
170	AA		¬
171	AB		½
172	AC		¼
173	AD		¡
174	AE		«

Table A-1. ASCII Codes for the PC (continued)

Decimal Value	Hexadecimal Value	Control Character	Character
175	AF		»
176	B0		░
177	B1		▒
178	B2		▓
179	B3		│
180	B4		┤
181	B5		╡
182	B6		╢
183	B7		╖
184	B8		╕
185	B9		╣
186	BA		║
187	BB		╗
188	BC		╝
189	BD		╜
190	BE		╛
191	BF		┐
192	C0		└
193	C1		┴
194	C2		┬
195	C3		├
196	C4		─
197	C5		┼
198	C6		╞
199	C7		╟
200	C8		╚
201	C9		╔
202	CA		╩
203	CB		╦
204	CC		╠
205	CD		═
206	CE		╬
207	CF		╧
208	D0		╨
209	D1		╤

Table A-1. ASCII Codes for the PC (continued)

Decimal Value	Hexadecimal Value	Control Character	Character
210	D2		╥
211	D3		╙
212	D4		╘
213	D5		╒
214	D6		╓
215	D7		╫
216	D8		╪
217	D9		┘
218	DA		┌
219	DB		█
220	DC		▄
221	DD		▌
222	DE		▐
223	DF		▀
224	E0		α
225	E1		β
226	E2		Γ
227	E3		π
228	E4		Σ
229	E5		σ
230	E6		μ
231	E7		τ
232	E8		Φ
233	E9		θ
234	EA		Ω
235	EB		δ
236	EC		∞
237	ED		∅
238	EE		ϵ
239	EF		∩
240	F0		≡
241	F1		±
242	F2		≥
243	F3		≤
244	F4		⌠

Table A-1. ASCII Codes for the PC (continued)

Decimal Value	Hexadecimal Value	Control Character	Character
245	F5		J
246	F6		÷
247	F7		≈
248	F8		°
249	F9		•
250	FA		·
251	FB		√
252	FC		n
253	FD		2
254	FE		■
255	FF		(blank 'FF')

APPENDIX B

COMMUNICATING WITH SERIAL PRINTERS

Printers come in two "flavors," parallel and serial, as determined by the electrical interface. The most common are the parallel printers that communicate with the PC via an 8-bit parallel connection. The characters are sent to the printer over a set of eight wires, and the printer sends back "ready," "paper out," and "off-line" signals over different wires. The serial printer, on the other hand, uses the same RS-232C interface used with modems and local computers. You need a serial port, either the IBM Asynchronous Communications Adapter or a multi-function board from another manufacturer.

Many printer manufacturers make both serial and parallel versions of the same printer. The serial printer has the familiar DB-25 connector, and the parallel printer has a 36-pin Centronics connector. You need a parallel printer cable to link the parallel printer's Centronics connector with the female DB-25 printer connector on the IBM Monochrome Display Adapter or multi-function board. You need a serial cable to link a serial printer's female DB-25 connector with the male DB-25 on the IBM Asynchronous Communications Adapter or multi-function card.

Most PCs use IBM's standard printer, manufactured by Epson. As a consequence, the software you buy always works with the IBM parallel printer. PC DOS accommodates most serial printers, but some software packages, such as the Dow Jones *Market Manager,* will not work with any serial printers.

Why buy a serial printer at all? Perhaps you own one already, or perhaps your PC and another computer must share a printer. You may be surprised to know that the PCjr's "standard" printer is serial, although it can accommodate a parallel printer. The biggest advantage to owning a serial printer is that cable runs can be longer—100 feet or more. If you need a switch box for printer sharing, a serial box will be cheaper than a parallel box because it has fewer wires to switch.

Serial Printer Protocols

A printer prints a limited number of characters per second depending on the speed of the print head and how many line feeds and form feeds there are. While the speed of a printer may nominally be listed as 80 cps or 120 cps, it's usually slower. Both the PC and most serial printers may be set to any data transmission rate up to 9600 bps. The faster the transmission speed, the more efficient the data transfer because most printers hold or buffer 2000 or more characters. Whatever transmission speed is used, the printer must be able to tell the PC, "Stop sending until I catch up!" and "Okay, I'm ready for some more data."

The method used to do this varies from printer to printer. Some printers use a control signal on the RS-232C interface (called **hardware handshaking**); others use a software protocol that sends a special character out over the data line when the printer's buffer becomes full.

Newer printers allow you to select a protocol by setting small switches on the back of the printer. Cable connections depend upon the protocol used. The following sections describe three protocols and three cable hookups. Use these as guidelines or "starting points." You should count on doing some troubleshooting with each different printer you connect.

Hardware Handshaking

Hardware handshaking has some variations, but in general "one cable fits all." Normally the RTS line indicates whether the printer is busy or ready to accept data, and the DTR line indicates whether the printer is connected and switched on-line. Some printers monitor the CD, CTS, and DSR lines from the PC, but you can always fool the printer into thinking the PC is on-line. After all, if the PC isn't on-line, the printer can't print anything. Most software that runs under PC DOS will work with serial printers that use hardware handshaking if you give the PC the command

MODE LPT#:=COMn

where

is a logical printer number, usually 1
n is the serial port number, 1 or 2.

Don't forget to use the MODE command to set the PC's data rate to match the printer's.

Figure B-1*a* shows the cable connections if RTS is used. Sometimes signaling is done only with DTR, in which case Figure B-1*b* applies. These cables assume that the printer sends nothing to the PC on the received data line (pin 3) since that wire is not connected.

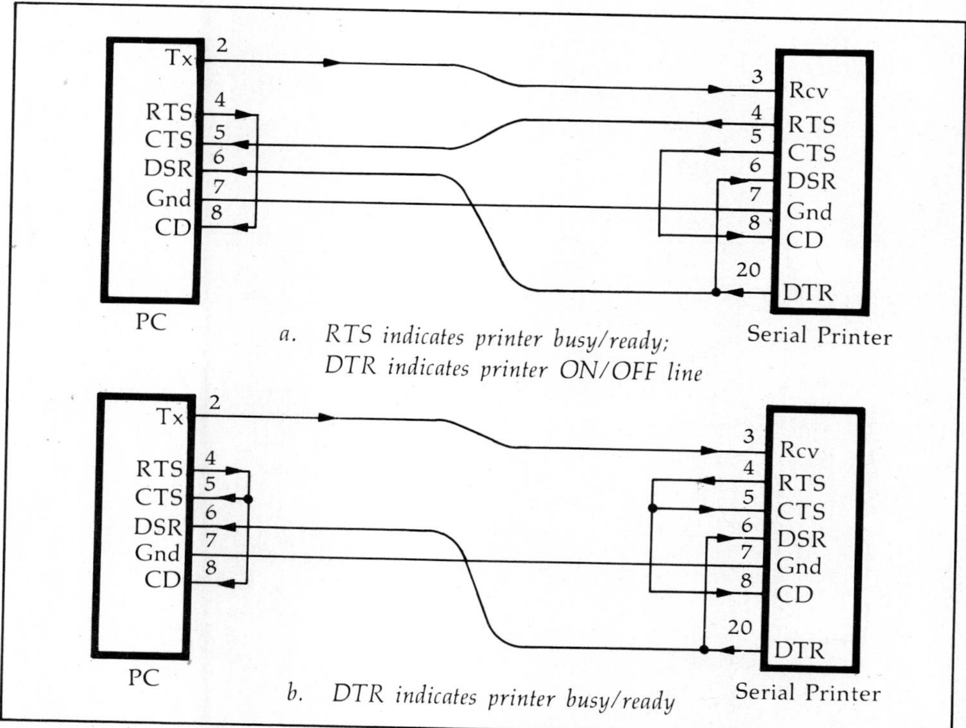

Figure B-1. Serial printer cables for hardware handshaking

XON/XOFF

The XON/XOFF protocol is used by printers designed for remote use with modems. The Texas Instruments 820 is an example. Since the modem can't pass the RTS or DTR signals, the printer must send an XOFF (ASCII 19) character to the PC to suspend data transmission. An XON (ASCII 17) restarts the transmission. The DTR signal is still used to indicate that the printer has gone off-line. Figure B-2 shows a cable for this type of printer. If the printer doesn't use DTR, you can use the null modem cable shown earlier in Figure 9-3*b*.

PC DOS can't deal directly with a printer that uses XON/XOFF unless you reduce the data rate so that the printer buffer never fills up. You can write a BASIC program to transmit a disk file to the printer, but you can't always expect that someone else's software will print correctly. There is hope, however. The print spooler software included with AST Inc.'s multi-function boards will allow full use of an XON/OFF printer.

ETX/ACK

The earlier NEC Spinwriters used ETX/ACK protocol. However, avoid this if possible because it leads to severe complications. With this protocol the PC transmits data in small blocks of, say, 128 characters followed by an ETX (ASCII

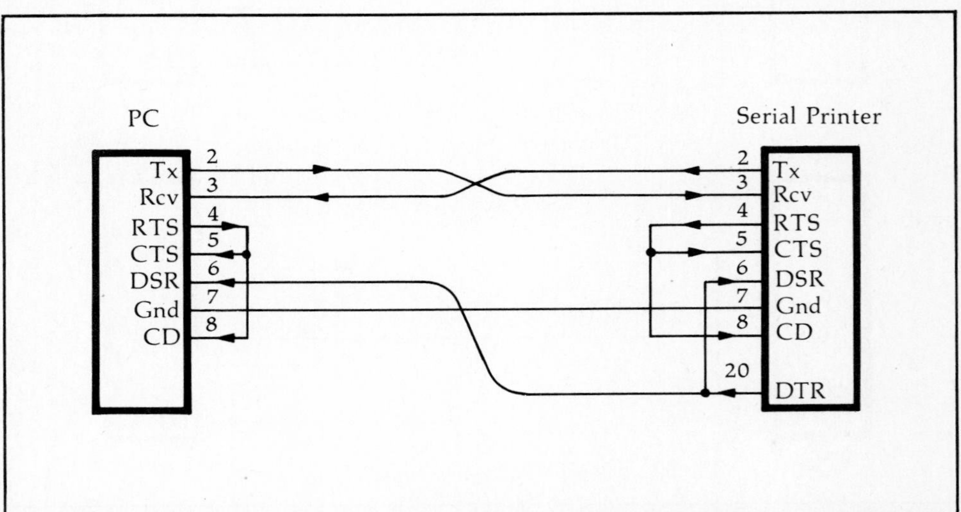

Figure B-2. Serial printer cable for XON/XOFF, ETX/ACK

3) character. When the printer is ready for another block, it sends the PC an ACK (ASCII 6). Word processing programs use escape sequences to control printer characteristics like pitch, subscripting, font, and so forth. If the escape sequence is interrupted by an ETX, some printers will not operate correctly. To get around this problem, the ETX character could be sent before the ESC, but this would require some extra program intelligence. AST's spool software handles ETX/ACK, but its ability to handle escape sequences correctly wasn't tested. The cables used with the XON/XOFF protocol will work with an ETX/ACK printer.

APPENDIX C

STOCK AND COMPANY INFORMATION

This appendix presents all stock and company information from The Source, CompuServe, and Dow Jones. One company, IBM, is featured throughout, but Apple is also included. If you're a stock watcher, this information will help you decide which service or services to subscribe to.

The Source

For stock quotes through The Source, you must select one of about 100 reports made available throughout the day. Here's a partial list:

```
      help reports

         DATA REPORTS IN ALPHABETICAL ORDER
         ----------------------------------

4:23 PM       050      AMEX 4PM MOST ACTIVES
4:16 PM       148      AMEX 4PM STOCK & BOND PRICES
7:40 PM       035      AMEX CLOSING 50-SELECTED LIST
5:00 PM       183      AMEX CLOSING STOCK & BOND PRICES
5:35 PM       090      AMEX CLOSING STOCK & BOND PRICES
                        .........
```

```
7:00 PM        031      GAMBLER'S CORNER
9:58 PM        175      GUN NAVAL STORES
12:25 PM       021      JOLIET LIVESTOCK
6:00 PM        083      KANSAS CITY CASH GRAIN
2:28 PM        082      KANSAS CITY LIVESTOCK
7:10 PM        005      LATE DIVIDENDS
6:00 PM        056      MARKET INDEXES
4:23 PM        121      MARKET TRENDS
6:00 PM        063      MARKETS AT A GLANCE
                         ..........
4:00 PM        138      NYSE 4PM STOCK PRICES
11:20 AM       091      NYSE 500 AND AMEX 50 SELECTED STOCKS
11:45 AM       152      NYSE BOND PRICES
1:45 PM        155      NYSE BOND PRICES (RATINGS & YIELDS)
2:22 PM        156      NYSE BOND PRICES (RATINGS & YIELDS)
3:22 PM        157      NYSE BOND PRICES (RATINGS & YIELDS)

-> UNISTOX

...UPI UNISTOX...ARE ON-LINE

WHICH REPORT? 138
```

You've selected the "nyse 4pm stock prices."

```
ENTER KEYWORDS, ONE PER LINE, AND PRESS RETURN TWICE,
OR PRESS RETURN ONCE FOR THE ENTIRE REPORT.
IBM

FRI, NOV 25 1983
```

These numbers must be decoded using the manual.

```
 IBM     3.80    14 5485 121 3-4 120 7-8 p121 +  1-8

-> STOCKVUE

           MEDIA GENERAL
             STOCKVUE

ENTER STOCK SYMBOLS, GROUP NUMBERS, OR FILE NAMES.
(TYPE "SYMB" TO FIND SYMBOLS OR "HELP" FOR ASSISTANCE.)
! IBM
! AAPL
!
```

You can process several stocks at a time.

Now you can view up to 12 predefined "screens."

```
SCREEN  1 - "LOCATOR"  - SHOWS STOCK NAME, SYMBOL,
             INDUSTRY GROUP, EXCHANGE, AND A
             DESCRIPTION OF THE INDUSTRY GROUP.

DATA FOR WEEK ENDING 11/25/83   1 - "LOCATOR"

STOCK            STK   IND                    INDUSTRY
NAMES            SYM   GRP EXCH             DESCRIPTION

INTL BUS MACH    IBM    71  NY    COMPUTERS
APPLE COMPT      AAPL   71  OTC   COMPUTERS

SCREEN  2 - "INDUSTRY GROUPS" - FOR ANY GIVEN GROUP NUMBER,
             SHOWS STOCK NAME, SYMBOL, EXCHANGE, CURRENT PRICE,
             AND % CHANGE THIS WEEK FOR EACH STOCK.

DATA FOR WEEK ENDING 11/25/83   2 - "INDUSTRY GROUPS"

STOCK            STK         CURR      % CHANGE
NAMES            SYM   EXCH  PRICE $   THIS WK


INDUSTRY GROUP # 71    COMPUTERS
APPLE COMPT      AAPL   OTC    20.50     -0.6
INTL BUS MACH    IBM    NY    121.00     -2.0

SCREEN  3 - "PRICE CHANGE & RANGE" - SHOWS
             WEEKLY HIGH LOW CLOSE $ AND % CHG, 200 DAY
             MOVING AVG AND 52 WEEK HIGH & LOW.
```

DATA FOR WEEK ENDING 11/25/83 3 - "PRICE CHANGE & RANGE"

STK SYM	------WEEKLY-------- HIGH	LOW	CLOSE	CHANGE ($)	(%)	200 DAY AVG	52 WEEK HIGH	LOW
AAPL	21.50	20.00	20.50	-0.13	-0.6	39.43	62.75	17.25
IBM	125.63	120.00	121.00	-2.50	-2.0	117.00	134.25	82.00

SCREEN 4 - "PERIODIC PRICE CHANGE (%)" - SHOWS % CHANGE IN LAST TRADE WEEK, LAST 4, 13 AND 52 WEEKS AND YEAR TO DATE.

DATA FOR WEEK ENDING 11/25/83 4 - "PERIODIC PRICE CHANGE (%)"

STK SYM	IND GRP	LAST WEEK(%)	4 LAST WKS(%)	LAST 13 WKS(%)	LAST 52 WKS(%)	YEAR TO DATE(%)
AAPL	71	-0.6	-1.8	-33.6	-29.3	-31.4
IBM	71	-2.0	-5.5	2.7	45.1	25.7

SCREEN 5 - "PRICE EARNINGS RATIOS" - SHOWS CURRENT AND 5 YEAR AVG HIGH AND LOW P/E RATIOS, AND 5 YEAR HIGH LOW AND CURRENT PRICE.

DATA FOR WEEK ENDING 11/25/83 5 - "PRICE EARNINGS RATIOS"

STK SYM	IND GRP	P/E RATIO--------- CUR-RENT	5 YEAR AVG HIGH	LOW	5 YEAR PRICE HIGH	LOW	CURR. PRICE
AAPL	71	16.0	36.8	19.3	62.75	10.75	20.50
IBM	71	14.3	13.4	9.3	134.25	48.38	121.00

SCREEN 6 - "RELATIVE PRICE/ACTION" - SHOWS MARKET VALUE AS % OF REVENUE, % OF MKT. NORM, % OF IND. NORM, PRICE EQUITY RATIO, REL. PRICE INDEX, EARNINGS YIELD, UP BETA AND DOWN BETA.

DATA FOR WEEK ENDING 11/25/83 6 - "RELATIVE PRICE/ACTION"

STK SYM	IND GRP	CURR PRICE	%/MKT TO REV	%/MKT NORM	%/IND NORM	PRICE/ EQUITY	%/REL INDEX	EARN YIELD	BETAS UP	DOWN
AAPL	71	20.50	123	174	130	456.00	801	6.3	4.07	1.46
IBM	71	121.00	214	191	142	365.00	286	7.0	1.23	-0.08

SCREEN 7 - "TRADING VOLUME" - SHOWS SHARES TRADED, VOL. AS % OF SHRS OUTSTANDING, WEEKLY DOL. VALUE OF SHRS., LIQUID. RATIO AND ON-BAL. INDEX.

DATA FOR WEEK ENDING 11/25/83 7 - "TRADING VOLUME"

STK SYM	IND GRP	SHARES TRADED (00)	(%) SHARES OUT.	VALUE TRADED $ 000	LIQUID. RATIO $ 000	OBV INDEX
AAPL	71	16154	2.75	33990	4894.8	73
IBM	71	40957	0.67	500635	161645.4	62

SCREEN 8 - "TREND TO MARKET" - SHOWS 200 DAY PRICE INDEX VS MKT AND VS IND, PRICE TREND VS MKT LAST 30 & LAST 5 DAYS, VOLUME TREND VS MKT LAST 30 & LAST FIVE DAYS.

DATA FOR WEEK ENDING 11/25/83 8 - "TREND TO MARKET"

STK SYM	IND GRP	200 DAY PRICE VS/MKT	INDEX VS/IND	PRICE TREND (%) PER DAY LAST 30	LAST 5	VOLUME TREND (%) PER DAY LAST 30	LAST 5

```
AAPL  71    39    38       -0.12   -0.94      -1.93   -3.31
IBM   71   110   109       -0.20   -1.04      -1.89   11.51

SCREEN  9 - "EARNINGS PER SHARE" - SHOWS
             EPS LAST 12 MOS AND LAST FISCAL YEAR,
             PERCENTAGE CHANGE LAST YEAR, FY TO DATE AND LAST
             12 MONTHS, AND 5-YEAR GROWTH RATE.


DATA FOR WEEK ENDING 11/25/83    9 - "EARNINGS PER SHARE"

           LAST   LAST      PERCENTAGE  CHANGE     5 YEAR
STK  IND   12 MO  FISC    YTD VS THIS FY  LAST     GROWTH
SYM   GRP    $     YR $     LYTD   VS LFY 12 MO    RATE %

IBM   71   8.48N   7.39      22      20       23       13
AAPL  71   1.28F   1.28      21      20       21       63

SCREEN 10 - "REVENUES AND RATIOS" - SHOWS
             LAST FISCAL YEAR REVENUE AND EARNINGS, PROFIT
             MARGIN, RETURN ON EQUITY, DEBT TO EQUITY RATIO,
             AND CURRENT RATIO.

DATA FOR WEEK ENDING 11/25/83    10 - "REVENUES AND RATIOS"

             LAST FISCAL    PROF RETURN  DEBT    CUR-
STK   IND  REVENUE  EARN    MARG ON COM   TO     RENT
SYM   GRP   (S)MIL ($)MIL   (%)  EQTY %   EQ.%   RATIO

IBM   71 34364.0  4409.0   12.8  22.1     14     1.6
AAPL  71   982.8    76.7    7.8  23.8      1     3.7

SCREEN 11 - "SHAREHOLDINGS" - SHOWS MARKET VALUE,
             LAST OUT. SHARES, INSIDER NET TRADE, SHORT
             INTEREST 000, SHORT INTEREST RATIO AND FISCAL
             YEAR ENDING DATE.

DATA FOR WEEK ENDING 11/25/83    11 - "SHAREHOLDINGS"

            MARKET    LATEST    INSIDER   SHORT      SHORT       FISC
STK  IND     VALUE    SHARES    NET TRD  INTEREST   INTEREST     YEAR
SYM  GRP    $ 000     OUT/000    000       000     RATIO/DAYS    E/MO

IBM    71  73513550   607550        -9   1294.3        1.1      12/82
AAPL   71   1204601    58761      -103      0.0        0.0      09/83

SCREEN 12 - "DIVIDENDS" - SHOWS CURRENT DIVIDEND RATE
             AND YIELD, CURRENT AND FIVE YR AVG. PAYOUT,
             AND LATEST EX-DIVIDEND DATE.

DATA FOR WEEK ENDING 11/25/83    12 - "DIVIDENDS"

            CURRENT RATE      PAYOUT       LAST
STK   IND    AMT    YIELD    LAST LAST   X-DIVDND
SYM   GRP    ($)     (%)     FY % 5YR%     DATE

IBM    71   3.80    3.1       47   55    11/ 2/83
AAPL   71   0.00    0.0        0    0
```

CompuServe

CompuServe offers an impressive amount of stock information, most of which is available on both CIS and EIS. Most information requires a premium of, typically, $0.25 cents per company accessed. Here is a sample:

```
CompuServe
                                                Page IQ-1
INVESTMENTS & QUOTES

 1 Ticker Retrieval Reports          7 Banking Services
 2 Expert Investor                   8 Brokerage Services
 3 Current-Day Pricing               9 Portfolio Reporting
 4 Historical Pricing               10 Download Data
 5 Ann & Qtr Financial Rpts         11 File Management
 6 Estimates & Projections          12 Ticker & CUSIP Look Up
                                    13 User Information


Enter a ticker (ie, HRB), a cusip (ie, 09367110), or
an asterisk followed by the beginning of a company's
name (ie, *BLOCK).  Type /M to exit or /HELP for cost
information and instructions.
Company: *INTERNATIONAL B
10 issues found for INTERNATIONAL B.
Do you want to list them? Y
    Ticker Company Name                         Issue
    ------ ------- ----                         -----
  1 IBM    INTERNATIONAL BUSINESS MACHS
  2 IBK    INTERNATIONAL BANKNOTE INC
  3 IBKW   INTERNATIONAL BK WASH D C
  4 IBKWA  INTERNATIONAL BK WASH D C            CLASS A
  5 IBM 86 INTERNATIONAL BUSINESS MACHS         NT 9.50% 10/01/1986
  6 IBM 04 INTERNATIONAL BUSINESS MACHS         DEB 9.375% 10/01/04
  7 IBK P  INTERNATIONAL BANKNOTE INC           PREF CONV $0.40
  8 INBS   INTERNATIONAL BANCSHARES CO
  9 IBCA   INTERNATIONAL BROADCASTING

Company: IBM

INTERNATIONAL BUSINESS MACHS  (IBM)      Cusip:  45920010
                                         Exch:   N

  Date       Time    Volume     High      Low      Last    Change
--------   -----  ---------  -------  -------  -------  -------
11/25/83   FINAL    548,800  121 3/4  120 7/8  121       +0 1/8

1 S&P synopsis 5/04/83
2 Price history thru 11/25/83
3 Dividends through 11/02/83    9 Annual financial stmt 12/82
4 Price stats, last 52 weeks
5 Detailed issue description   11 IBES/Value Line forecasts
6 Bonds issued, appx 2

Last menu page. Key digit or M for "Company:" prompt


1 S&P synopsis 5/04/83


INT'L BUSINESS MACHINES
Cusip# 45920010
Last updated 07/22/83
S&P Industry 4201
SP RANK: A+           EXCHANGE: NYS
SALES($M)            34364.00
NET($M)               4409.00
1982 EPS EST($)          9.00
12 MONTH EPS($)          8.09
1981 EPS($)              7.39
1980 EPS($)              5.63
1979 EPS($)              5.72
EPS 5-YR GROWTH(%)       9.00

YEAR END MONTH: DC
```

```
 Summary IBM is the world's largest manufacturer of computers and
information processing equipment and systems. A good earnings gain is
expected for 1983, aided by continued strong demand for information
processing, a better ratio of sales to rentals, and wider margins
attributable to higher volumes and productivity improvements.
 Important Developments Jul. '83- In releasing second-quarter results,
IBM said that demand for large-scale processors and disk drives
remained strong, both domestically and overseas; display products,
including the newer 3178, also did well, and IBM Personal Computer
sales continued to exceed expectations. It also noted some improvement
in orders for the smaller general purpose business computers, such as
the System 36.
 Business Summary IBM is primarily involved in information-handling
systems, equipment and services.

Product lines table
Gross
revenues
(U.S.
only)                  1982 1981
Processors/periphera    52%  50%
Office products         19%  20%
Programs/maint./othe    24%  25%
Federal systems          5%   5%

 Office-Armonk, New York 10504. Tel-(914) 765-1900. Stockholder
Relations Dept-590 Madison Ave., NYC 10022. Tel-(212) 407-4000. Chrmn &
CEO-J. R. Opel. Pres-J. F. Akers. Secy-J. H. Grady. Treas-J. W.
Rotenstreich. Investor Contact-J. M. Heatley. Dirs-J. F. Akers, S. D.
Bechtel, Jr., G. B. Beitzel, H. Brown, J. E. Burke, F. T. Cary, W. T.
Coleman, Jr., P. R. Harris. C. A. Hills, A. Houghton, Jr., J. N. Irwin
II, N. deB. Katzenbach, R. W. Lyman, J. G. Maisonrouge, M. McK. Moller,
W. H. Moore, J. R. Munro, J. R. Opel, D. P. Phypers, P. J. Rizzo, W. W.
Scranton, I. S. Shapiro, C. R. Vance, T. J. Watson, Jr. Transfer
Agents-Company's NYC & Chicago offices. Registrars-Morgan Guaranty
Trust Co., NYC; First National Bank, Chicago. Incorporated in New York
in 1911.


INTERNATIONAL BUSINESS MACHS

2 Price history thru 11/25/83

(D)aily, (W)eekly, (M)onthly? : D
Starting date :   11/18/83
Ending date   :   11/25/83
                INTERNATIONAL BUSINESS MACHS

Cusip: 45920010    Exchange: N    Ticker: IBM

  Date         Volume         High/Ask     Low/Bid     Close/Avg
-----------------------------------------------------------------
11/18/83      818,100         123.750      122.000      123.500

11/21/83      778,000         125.500      123.125      125.250
11/22/83      985,000         125.625      122.625      123.000
11/23/83    1,784,000         123.375      120.000      120.875
11/24/83            0          HOL          HOL          HOL
11/25/83      548,800         121.750      120.875      121.000

Prices Available: 12/31/73 through 11/25/83

INTERNATIONAL BUSINESS MACHS

3 Dividends through 11/02/83

Starting date :   01/01/80
Ending date   :   11/25/83
                INTERNATIONAL BUSINESS MACHS

Cusip: 45920010    Exchange: N    Ticker: IBM
```

Rate	Type	Ex-Date	Record	Payment
$ 0.860	Cash	2/06/80	2/13/80	3/10/80
$ 0.860	Cash	5/08/80	5/14/80	6/10/80
$ 0.860	Cash	8/07/80	8/13/80	9/10/80
$ 0.860	Cash	11/05/80	11/12/80	12/10/80
$ 0.860	Cash	2/05/81	2/11/81	3/10/81
$ 0.860	Cash	5/07/81	5/13/81	6/10/81
$ 0.860	Cash	8/06/81	8/12/81	9/10/81
$ 0.860	Cash	11/04/81	11/10/81	12/10/81
$ 0.860	Cash	2/04/82	2/10/82	3/10/82
$ 0.860	Cash	5/06/82	5/12/82	6/10/82
$ 0.860	Cash	8/05/82	8/11/82	9/10/82
$ 0.860	Cash	11/04/82	11/10/82	12/10/82
$ 0.860	Cash	2/03/83	2/09/83	3/10/83
$ 0.950	Cash	5/05/83	5/11/83	6/10/83
$ 0.950	Cash	8/04/83	8/10/83	9/10/83
$ 0.950	Cash	11/02/83	11/09/83	12/10/83

INTERNATIONAL BUSINESS MACHS

4 Price stats, last 52 weeks

INTERNATIONAL BUSINESS MACHS

11/26/82 - 11/25/83
(7 holiday dates included)

	High/Ask	Low/Bid	Close/Avg
11/26/82	83.625	83.000	83.375
11/25/83	121.750	120.875	121.000
Pct Change	45.590%	45.633%	45.127%

	Value	Date
High High	134.250	10/10/83
High Close	134.250	10/10/83
Low Low	82.000	11/29/82
Low Close	82.500	11/29/82
High Volume	2,098,000	9/26/83
Low Volume	373,100	7/01/83

	Average	Standard Dev
High	113.162	12.484
Low	111.111	12.533
Close	112.166	12.578
Volume	879,078	309,204

Total Volume: 223,285,900
Beta factor: 0.913 Beta centile rank: 72

INTERNATIONAL BUSINESS MACHS

5 Detailed issue description

CUSIP#	Ticker	Class	SIC	Beg Hist	Last Update
45920010	IBM	EQUITY	3573	12/31/73	11/25/83

Exchange Code: N -- NEW YORK
Co & Issue: INTERNATIONAL BUSINESS MACHS
Issue Type: COMMON MARGINABLE
Issue Status: ACTIVE - NO SPECIAL STATUS APPLIES

Earnings Date	12 mo EPS	I.A. Dividend	Yield	Shares Outstanding
9/30/83	$8.480	$3.800	3.140%	607,550,000

```
E.P.S. Footnote:       PRIMARY EPS (COMPANY REPORTED)
I.A. Div. Footnote:    REGULAR RATE
Shares Out Footnote:   ACTUAL SHARES OUT. -- NO EQUIVALENTS INCLUDED

L-P Date        Volume            High       Low        Close       P/E
--------     ------------      --------   -------    -------     -------
11/25/83         548,800       121 3/4    120 7/8    121           14.26

52 Week High :   134 1/4    on: 10/10/83
         Low :    82        on: 11/29/82
Trading Type (Status) : REGULAR TRADING
S & P  Rating : A+
Beta Factor :    .913    Beta Centile :    72

Dividend History Begins:  2/05/68   and Ends: 11/02/83

  Rate        Dividend Type        Ex-date       Record      Payable
---------   ---------------     ---------     --------    --------
$    .9500  Cash Dividend        11/02/83      11/09/83   12/10/83

Codes: PM=  1     PO=  1     TB=  1     BC= 0     TC= 0     LRC= 0

INTERNATIONAL BUSINESS MACHS

6 Bonds issued, appx 2

Ticker    Cusip        Issue Identifier        Yield     Coupon
------  ---------   --------------------    ---------  ------
No bonds available for

INTERNATIONAL BUSINESS MACHS

9 Annual financial stmt 12/82



           INT'L BUSINESS MACH.
             Income Statement
                               12/81      12/82
                            ---------  ---------
Gross Revenues              29070.00   34364.00
  Cost of Goods Sold         8687.00   10126.00
  Selling & Admin Exp       11027.00   12620.00
  Depreciation, Amort        3329.00    3562.00
  Total Interest              407.00     454.00
  Unconsolidated Subs           0.00       0.00
  Other Income                368.00     328.00
  Other Expenses                0.00       0.00
  Minority Interest             0.00       0.00
                            ---------  ---------
Pretax Income                5988.00    7930.00

  Total Taxes                2680.00    3521.00
  Special Items                 0.00       0.00
                            ---------  ---------
Net Income Before Ext        3308.00    4409.00
  Extraordinary Items           0.00       0.00


           INT'L BUSINESS MACH.
              Balance Sheet
                               12/81      12/82
                            ---------  ---------
Cash & Equivalents           2029.00    3300.00
Accounts Receivable          4792.00    5433.00
Inventories                  2805.00    3492.00
Other Current Assets          677.00     789.00
                            ---------  ---------
Total Current Assets        10303.00   13014.00
```

Gross Plant	30136.00	30767.00
Accum Depreciation	12858.00	13204.00
Net Plant	17278.00	17563.00
Long-Term Investments	0.00	0.00
Deferred Charges	2005.00	1964.00
Intangible Assets	0.00	0.00
Other Long-Term Asset	0.00	0.00
Total Assets	29586.00	32541.00

Balance Sheet (cont.)

	12/81	12/82
Notes Payable	615.00	387.00
Accounts Payable	872.00	983.00
Taxes Payable	2412.00	2854.00
Other Current Liab	3263.00	3843.00
Deferred Taxes	252.00	323.00
Minority Interest	0.00	0.00
Long-Term Debt	2827.00	2993.00
Other Long-Term Liab	1184.00	1198.00
Total Liabilities	11425.00	12581.00
Preferred Stock	N/A	N/A
Common Stock	4389.00	5008.00
Additional Capital	N/A	N/A
Retained Earnings	13772.00	16259.00
Total Equity	18161.00	21267.00

INT'L BUSINESS MACH.
Sources & Uses

	12/81	12/82
Cash Flow	6637.00	7971.00
Property Sales	1255.00	1642.00
Common Financing	423.00	613.00
Preferred Financing	0.00	0.00
Long-Term Debt Financ	751.00	480.00
Other Sources	-433.00	152.00
Capital Spending	6845.00	6685.00
Other Investments	0.00	0.00
Common Retired	0.00	0.00
Preferred Retired	0.00	0.00
Debt Retired	181.00	298.00
Common Dividends	2023.00	2053.00
Preferred Dividends	0.00	0.00
Add'l Working Capital	-416.00	1822.00

INT'L BUSINESS MACH.
Key Ratios

	12/81	12/82
Earnings Per Share	5.63	7.39
Price/Earnings Ratio	10.29	9.39
Return on Equity	18.21	20.73
Return on Assets	11.18	13.55
Dividends Per Share	3.44	3.44
Dividend Yield	5.94	4.96
Sales / Assets	0.98	1.06
Market/Book Value	1.89	2.09
Current Ratio	1.41	1.59
Quick Ratio	1.02	1.16
Times Interest Earned	15.71	18.47
Beta	N/A	1.00
Common Shares	592.29	602.41
Net Avail for Common	3308.00	4409.00

INTERNATIONAL BUSINESS MACHS

11 IBES/Value Line Forecasts

1 Value Line 3- to 5-year
2 Expanded IBES consensus as of 11/08/83
3 Brief IBES consensus as of 11/08/83

1 Value Line 3- to 5-year

INT'L BUSINESS MACH.
Value Line Forecasts
3 - 5 Year Projection

Forecast period falls between 1986-1988

Shares Outstanding	650.00
Sales	64025.00
Earnings Per Share	15.50
Dividends Per Share	7.60
Book Value Per Share	75.85
High Target Price	305.00
Low Target Price	250.00
% Appreciation High	145.00
% Appreciation Low	100.00
Estimated EPS For 12-Month Per Ending 6 Months Hence	9.08
Estimated Dividends Per Share Next 12 Months	4.30

2 Expanded IBES consensus as of 11/08/83

I/B/E/S Earnings Estimate Report
INTERNATIONAL BUSINESS MACHS
Current price (11/25/1983): 121.00
Latest EPS (9/30/83): 8.48 Latest actual P/E: 14.27

	Current fiscal yr ending 12/83				Next fiscal yr ending 12/84		Long term growth %
	11/22	Nov	11/08	11/01	11/22	Nov	Nov
# of estimates	36	36			36	36	16
# revised upward	0	5	2	0	0	1	
# revised downward	0	9	2	1	0	6	
Mean estimate	8.91	8.91	8.92	8.91	10.34	10.34	15.70
% change in mean		-0.10					
Median estimate	8.94	8.94	8.00	8.00	10.27	10.27	16.00
Highest estimate	9.10	9.10			11.10	11.10	17.00
Lowest estimate	8.50	8.50			9.98	9.98	13.00
Coeff of variation %	1.23	1.23				2.51	8.28
Naive estimate	8.09	8.09			8.86	8.86	
Implied PE ratio	13.81	14.00			11.90	12.07	

3 Brief IBES consensus as of 11/08/83

```
        I/B/E/S Mean EPS Estimates
       INTERNATIONAL BUSINESS MACHS

Current Fiscal Year ending 12/83
--------------------------------
Weekly update of 11/22                8.91
Last monthly estimate on 11/16        8.91
Weekly update of 11/08                8.92
Weekly update of 11/01                8.91

Next Fiscal Year ending 12/84
-----------------------------
Weekly update of 11/22               10.34
Last monthly estimate on 11/16       10.34

Long Term Growth(%)
-------------------
Last monthly estimate on 11/16  15.70
```

CompuServe can extract stock prices, volumes, and so forth into a file for processing within CompuServe or for downloading to your PC. You can then operate on this data with a program or spreadsheet. Error-free file downloads are possible with the *VIDTEX* communications program described in Chapter 6.

CompuServe allows you to store a portfolio of your stocks with the number of shares and their cost. You can then evaluate your portfolio against current stock prices.

Dow Jones

Shown here is the "raw" output from Dow Jones. Programs like the *Market Manager* (Chapter 6) reformat the news and current quotes, making them easier to read.

The news about IBM shows the most recent headline page.

```
//DJNEWS
  .IBM 01

N  IBM        01/14
FR 11/25 TAIWANESE APPLE COMPUTER
 (WJ) COPIES STOPPED BY U.S. CUSTOMS
FQ 11/25 SHAKEOUT OF PERSONAL COMPUTER
 (WJ) PRODUCERS -2-
FP 11/25 SHAKEOUT OF PERSONAL COMPUTER
 (WJ) PRODUCERS MAKES BUYERS NERVOUS
FO 11/23 IBM RESTRUCTURES CIRCUITS AND
 (DJ) SEMICONDUCTOR PARTS UNITS
FN 11/23 HITACHI STOCK FALLS IN JAPAN
 (WJ) ON PRESS REPORTS OF IBM PACT
FM 11/21 COMPUTER RETAILING SHAKEOUT
 (BN) SEEN SOON -2-
FL 11/21 COMPUTER RETAILING SHAKEOUT
 (BN) SEEN SOON AS BUSINESS GROWS
FK 11/22 WYLY CORP. UNIT SIGNS
 (DW) MARKETING PACT WITH IBM
FJ 11/22 VISICORP IN DISTRIBUTION PACT
 (DJ) WITH IBM UNIT
FI 11/22 IBM BOOSTS STAKE
 (DW) IN INTEL TO 16.28%
```

```
FH 11/22 ITT TO UNVEIL SMALL COMPUTER
 (WJ) PRICED 5% BELOW IBM'S PC
```

You can read a story by typing its code (FR, FQ, FP, etc.).

How about a current quote?

```
   IBM
STOCK       BID        ASKED
            CLOSE      OPEN       HIGH       LOW        LAST       VOL(100'S)
IBM         120 7/8    121 1/8    121 3/4    120 7/8    121        5488

   //HQ

HISTORICAL QUOTES  BEING ACCESSED
ENTER QUERY
   1IBM P1
```

Ask for most recent 12 days.

```
STOCK 1IBM

 DATE         HIGH        LOW       CLOSE        VOL(100/S)
11/09/83    123 5/8    122 3/8    123 5/8        6782
11/10/83    125 3/4    124        125 3/4        9402
11/11/83    127 1/4    125 1/8    127            6467
11/14/83    128 1/4    127        127 1/8        8950
11/15/83    127 5/8    124        124 5/8       11519
11/16/83    125 1/2    123 3/4    124 3/8        8968
11/17/83    124 1/2    122 7/8    123 1/4        6606
11/18/83    123 3/4    122        123 1/4        5749
11/21/83    125 1/2    123 1/8    125 1/4        6969
11/22/83    125 5/8    123        123            8439
11/23/83    123 1/4    120        120 7/8       14522
11/25/83    121 3/4    120 7/8    121            4614


DOW JONES HISTORICAL
STOCK QUOTE REPORTER SERVICE


STOCK 1IBM

    1982  QUARTERLY SUMMARY
              HIGH        LOW       CLOSE        VOL(100/S)
FIRST         64 1/2     55 3/4     59 5/8       409183
SECOND        66 1/8     57 5/8     60 5/8       327579
THIRD         77 5/8     59 3/8     73 1/2       510010
FOURTH        98         73 1/4     96 1/4       532805

STOCK AAPL

    1983  MONTHLY SUMMARY
 DATE         HIGH        LOW       CLOSE        VOL(100/S)
01/83         41         27 1/2                  221638
02/83         48 1/8     41 5/8                  140772
03/83         46 5/8     41 3/8                  118229
04/83         52 1/8     39 3/8                  149055
05/83         60 3/8     48 3/8                   93054
06/83         62 5/8     46 3/4                  125334
07/83         49 1/4     34                      138294
08/83         37 1/8     30 1/4                  136676
09/83         39 3/8     22 3/4                  354536
10/83         23         19 1/4                  224191
11/83         23 1/2     17 3/4                  173667

   //EARN

  CORPORATE EARNINGS ESTIMATOR
 ZACKS INVESTMENT RESEARCH INC.
        CHICAGO, ILL.
THIS WEEKLY DATABASE PROVIDES
CONSENSUS FORECASTS OF EARNINGS
PER SHARE FOR 3,000 COMPANIES
BASED ON ESTIMATES PROVIDED BY
```

```
1,000 RESEARCH ANALYSTS AT MORE
THAN 60 MAJOR BROKERAGE FIRMS.
FOR CONSISTENCY, ESTIMATES ARE
CONVERTED TO PRIMARY EARNINGS
BEFORE EXTRAORDINARY ITEMS.
------------------------------
PLEASE ENTER DESIRED STOCK
SYMBOL AND PRESS RETURN    IBM

IBM
--FISCAL YEAR ENDS  12/83

EARNINGS PER SHARE ESTIMATES
--MEAN     8.89
--HIGH     9.10
--LOW      8.50
NUMBER OF ANALYSTS  28
P/E RATIO (ESTIMATED EPS)  13.88
PAST EARN PR SH ESTIMATES (MEAN)
--WEEK AGO     8.89
--13 WEEKS AGO   8.86
--26 WEEKS AGO   8.68
------------------------------
PRESS RETURN FOR NEXT PAGE

IBM
--FISCAL YEAR ENDS  12/84

EARNINGS PER SHARE ESTIMATES
--MEAN   10.32
--HIGH   11.10
--LOW     9.90
NUMBER OF ANALYSTS  26
P/E RATIO (ESTIMATED EPS)  11.95
PAST EARN PR SH ESTIMATES (MEAN)
--WEEK AGO   10.32
--13 WEEKS AGO  10.33
--26 WEEKS AGO  10.07


//DSCLO

DISCLOSURE II
COPYRIGHT (C) 1983
DISCLOSURE INC.

FINANCIAL AND MANAGEMENT
INFORMATION ON PUBLIC
CORPORATIONS BASED ON REPORTS
FILED WITH THE SECURITES AND
EXCHANGE COMMISSION
--------------------------------

   IBM

COMPANY NAME:        INTERNATIONAL BUSINESS MACHINES CORP

ENTER    FOR

 1      CORPORATE PROFILE
 2      BALANCE SHEETS FOR 2 YEARS
 3      INCOME STATEMENTS FOR 3 YEARS
 4      QTRLY INC STATEMENTS (CUR FY)
 5      LINE OF BUSINESS DATA
 6      5-YR SUMMARY DATA (REVS, INCOME,
           EPS)
 7      FULL FINANCIAL DATA (2 THRU 6)
 8      OFFICERS AND DIRECTORS
 9      OWNERSHIP AND SUBSIDIARIES
10      OTHER CORPORATE EVENTS
11      MANAGEMENT DISCUSSION
```

There's an extra charge of $2 or $4 each time you inquire about a company.

```
12      CORPORATE RECORD (1 THRU 10)
13      FULL CORPORATE RECORD (1 THRU 11)
14      2-YR LIST OF REPORTS ON FILE
            WITH THE SEC
99      HOW TO ORDER FULL TEXT OF SEC
            REPORTS
    1

DISCLOSURE CO NO:    I510600000
COMPANY NAME:        INTERNATIONAL BUSINESS MACHINES CORP
CROSS REFERENCE:     NA
ADDRESS: NA
ARMONK
NY
10504
TELEPHONE: 914-765-1900
INCORPORATION: NY
EXCHANGE: NYS
TICKER SYMBOL: IBM
FORTUNE NUMBER: 0006
CUSIP NUMBER: 0004592002
D-U-N-S NO: 00-136-8083
SIC CODES: 3573 3572 3579 3679 3861 7379
PRIMARY SIC CODE: 3573
DESCRIPTION OF BUSINESS:
MANUFACTURES DATA PROCESSING MACHINES AND SYSTEMS, TELECOMMUNICATIONS
SYSTEMS AND PRODUCTS, INFORMATION DISTRIBUTORS, OFFICE SYSTEMS,
ELECTRIC AND ELECTRONIC TYPEWRITERS, COPIERS, DICTATION EQUIPMENT,
EDUCATIONAL AND TESTING MATERIALS, AND RELATED SUPPLIES AND SERVICES.

CURRENT OUTSTANDING SHARES:    605,550,159 (SOURCE: 10-Q      06/30/83)
SHARES HELD BY OFF & DIR:        2,775,383
SHAREHOLDERS:                      725,745
EMPLOYEES:                         364,796
FISCAL YEAR END: 12/31
AUDITOR CHANGE: NA
AUDITOR: PRICE WATERHOUSE
AUDITOR'S REPORT: UNQUALIFIED

    2

          BALANCE SHEET ASSETS
     FISCAL YEAR ENDING:        12/31/82         12/31/81
CASH                         405,000,000      454,000,000
MRKTABLE SECURITIES        2,895,000,000    1,575,000,000
RECEIVABLES                4,976,000,000    4,382,000,000
INVENTORIES                3,492,000,000    2,803,000,000
RAW MATERIALS                         NA               NA
WORK IN PROGRESS                      NA               NA
FINISHED GOODS                        NA               NA
NOTES RECEIVABLE                      NA               NA
OTHER CURRENT ASSETS       1,246,000,000    1,095,000,000
TOTAL CURRENT ASSETS      13,014,000,000   10,309,000,000
PROP, PLANT & EQUIP       30,767,000,000   29,301,000,000
ACCUMULATED DEP           13,204,000,000   12,504,000,000
NET PROP & EQUIP          17,563,000,000   16,797,000,000
INVEST & ADV TO SUBS                  NA               NA
OTH NON-CUR ASSETS                    NA               NA
DEFERRED CHARGES           1,964,000,000    2,001,000,000
INTANGIBLES                           NA               NA
DEPOSITS, OTH ASSETS                  NA               NA
TOTAL ASSETS              32,541,000,000   29,107,000,000


          BALANCE SHEET LIABILITIES
     FISCAL YEAR ENDING:        12/31/82         12/31/81
NOTES PAYABLE                529,000,000      773,000,000
ACCOUNTS PAYABLE             983,000,000      872,000,000
CUR LONG TERM DEBT                    NA               NA
CUR PORT CAP LEASES                   NA               NA
```

ACCRUED EXPENSES	6,697,000,000	5,291,000,000
INCOME TAXES	NA	NA
OTHER CURRENT LIAB	NA	390,000,000
TOTAL CURRENT LIAB	8,209,000,000	7,326,000,000
MORTGAGES	NA	NA
DEFERRED CHARGES/INC	323,000,000	252,000,000
CONVERTIBLE DEBT	NA	NA
LONG TERM DEBT	2,851,000,000	2,669,000,000
NON-CUR CAP LEASES	NA	NA
OTHER LONG TERM LIAB	1,198,000,000	1,184,000,000
TOTAL LIABILITIES	12,581,000,000	11,431,000,000
MINORITY INT (LIAB)	NA	NA
PREFERRED STOCK	NA	NA

BALANCE SHEET LIABILITIES

FISCAL YEAR ENDING:	12/31/82	12/31/81
COMMON STOCK NET	5,008,000,000	4,389,000,000
CAPITAL SURPLUS	NA	NA
RETAINED EARNINGS	16,259,000,000	13,909,000,000
TREASURY STOCK	NA	NA
OTHER LIABILITIES	-1,307,000,000	-622,000,000
SHAREHOLDER'S EQUITY	19,960,000,000	17,676,000,000
TOT LIAB & NET WORTH	32,541,000,000	29,107,000,000

3

INCOME STATEMENT

FISCAL YEAR ENDING:	12/31/82	12/31/81	12/31/80
NET SALES	34,364,000,000	29,070,000,000	26,213,000,000
COST OF GOODS	13,688,000,000	11,737,000,000	10,266,000,000
GROSS PROFIT	20,676,000,000	17,333,000,000	15,947,000,000
R & D EXPENDITURES	3,042,000,000	2,451,000,000	2,287,000,000
SELL GEN & ADMIN EXP	9,578,000,000	8,583,000,000	8,094,000,000
INC BEF DEP & AMORT	8,056,000,000	6,299,000,000	5,566,000,000
DEPRECIATION & AMORT	NA	NA	NA
NON-OPERATING INC	328,000,000	368,000,000	430,000,000
INTEREST EXPENSE	454,000,000	407,000,000	273,000,000
INCOME BEFORE TAX	7,930,000,000	6,260,000,000	5,723,000,000
PROV FOR INC TAXES	3,521,000,000	2,650,000,000	2,326,000,000
MINORITY INT INCOME	NA	NA	NA
INVEST GAINS/LOSSES	NA	NA	NA
OTHER INCOME	NA	NA	NA
NET INC BEF EX ITEMS	4,409,000,000	3,610,000,000	3,397,000,000
EX ITEMS & DISC OPS	NA	NA	NA
NET INCOME	4,409,000,000	3,610,000,000	3,397,000,000
OUTSTANDING SHARES	602,406,128	592,293,624	583,806,832

4

INCOME STATEMENT

QUARTERLY REPORT FOR:	03/31/83	06/30/83
NET SALES	8,287,000,000	9,590,000,000
COST OF GOODS	3,269,000,000	3,814,000,000
GROSS PROFIT	5,018,000,000	5,776,000,000
R & D EXPENDITURES	786,000,000	855,000,000
SELL GEN & ADMIN EXP	2,457,000,000	2,541,000,000
INC BEF DEP & AMORT	1,775,000,000	2,380,000,000
DEPRECIATION & AMORT	NA	NA
NON-OPERATING INC	105,000,000	137,000,000
INTEREST EXPENSE	94,000,000	95,000,000
INCOME BEFORE TAX	1,786,000,000	2,422,000,000
PROV FOR INC TAXES	810,000,000	1,079,000,000
MINORITY INT INCOME	NA	NA
INVEST GAINS/LOSSES	NA	NA
OTHER INCOME	NA	NA
NET INC BEF EX ITEMS	976,000,000	1,343,000,000
EX ITEMS & DISC OPS	NA	NA
NET INCOME	976,000,000	1,343,000,000
OUTSTANDING SHARES	604,808,564	607,550,159

6

```
           FIVE  YEAR  SUMMARY
                SALES           NET INCOME                EPS
 1982   34,364,000,000     4,409,000,000              7.39
 1981   29,070,000,000     3,610,000,000              6.14
 1980   26,213,000,000     3,397,000,000              5.82
 1979   22,863,000,000     3,011,000,000              5.16
 1978   21,076,000,000     3,111,000,000              5.32

COMMENTS:
OTHER LIABILITIES IS TRANSLATION ADJUSTMENTS
1981 FINANCIALS AND 1980 INCOME STATEMENT ARE RESTATED DUE TO CHANGE
IN METHOD OF ACCOUNTING FOR FRGN. CURRENCY TRANSLATION
```

8

```
OFFICERS (NAME/ AGE/ TITLE/ REMUNERATION):
OPEL, JOHN R./ 58/  CHAIRMAN OF THE BOARD, CHIEF EXECUTIVE OFFICER
(PRX 03-16-83)  / $1,267,405
CARY, FRANK T./ 62/  CHAIRMAN OF THE BOARD, RETIRED (PRX 03-16-83)  /
$1,169,537
RIZZO, PAUL J./ 55/  VICE CHAIRMAN OF THE BOARD (PRX 03-16-83)  /
$930,465
BEITZEL, GEORGE B./ 54/  SENIOR VICE PRESIDENT (PRX 03-16-83)  /
$817,353
PHYPERS, DEAN P./ 54/  SENIOR VICE PRESIDENT (PRX 03-16-83)  /
$808,387
AKERS, JOHN F./ 48/  PRESIDENT / NA
MAISONROUGE, JACQUES G./ 58/  SENIOR VICE PRESIDENT, SUBSIDIARY
OFFICER / NA CASSANI, KASPAR V./ 54/  SENIOR VICE PRESIDENT,
SUBSIDIARY OFFICER / NA
KATZENBACH, NICHOLAS DEB./ 61/  SENIOR VICE PRESIDENT, LEGAL COUNSEL
/ NA
KUEHLER, JACK D./ 50/  SENIOR VICE PRESIDENT / NA
PFEIFFER, RALPH A., JR./ 55/  SENIOR VICE PRESIDENT, SUBSIDIARY
OFFICER / NA ROGERS, CLARENCE B., JR./ 53/  SENIOR VICE PRESIDENT /
NA
        .............

DIRECTORS/NOMINEES (NAME/ AGE/ TITLE/ REMUNERATION):
 PROXY: 03/16/83

AKERS, JOHN F./ 48/  PRESIDENT, NOMINEE / NA
BECHTEL, STEPHEN D./ 57/  NOMINEE / NA
BEITZEL, GEORGE B./ 54/  SENIOR VICE PRESIDENT, NOMINEE / $817,353
BROWN, HAROLD/ 55/  NOMINEE / NA
BURKE, JAMES E./ 58/  NOMINEE / NA
CARY, FRANK T./ 62/  CHAIRMAN OF THE BOARD, RETIRED, NOMINEE /
$1,169,537

        ...............
```

9

```
OWNERSHIP:
TYPE           DATE(Q,M)  OWNERS    CHANGE (000S) HELD   %OWN
INVEST. COS.   06/30/83(Q)                0            0  0.00
INSTITUTIONS   06/30/83(Q)  556      -1,837      297,584 49.30
5% OWNERS      07/31/83(M)    0          NA            0  0.00
INSIDERS       07/31/83(M)   76          NA        2,225  0.36
% OWNED MAY TOTAL ABOVE 100% DUE TO OVERLAPPING HOLDINGS REPORTS

SUBSIDIARIES:
IBM CREDIT CORP.
*IBM CREDIT OVERSEAS N.V.
INFORMATION SATELLITE CORP.
IBM EXPORTS SALES CORP.
IBM INSTRUMENTS, INC.
INTERNATIONAL VIDEO DISK CORP.
*DISCOVISION ASSOCIATES, 50%
```

SCIENCE RESEARCH ASSOCIATES, INC.
*SCIENCE RESEARCH ASSOCIATES PTY. LIMITED
*SCIENCE RESEARCH ASSOCIATES (CANADA) LIMITED
*SCIENCE RESEARCH ASSOCIATES LIMITED (UNITED KINGDOM)
IBM WORLD TRADE CORP.

....

**IBM SINGAPORE PTE LTD.
**IBM TAIWAN CORP.
**IBM THAILAND COMPANY LIMITED
**IBM DEL URUGUAY, S.A.
**IBM DE VENEZUELA, S.A.
***IBM DE EXPORTACION Y SERVICIOS, S.A.

END OF SECTION. MAKE ANOTHER MENU SELECTION, OR ENTER COMPANY STOCK SYMBOL TO VIEW MENU AGAIN.

10

OTHER CORPORATE EVENTS:
NA

11

MANAGEMENT DISCUSSION:
(From Annual Report to Shareholders 1982)
Results of Operations

The results of operations for the current year were outstanding, as reported in the Letter of Stockholders.

Gross income totaled $34.4 billion, an increase of 18.2 percent over 1981. Gross income from U.S. operations increased by 26.1 percent while gross income from non-U.S. operations increased by 9.7 percent.

Net earnings for the year were $4.4 billion, up 22.1 percent over 1981. Net earnings from U.S. operations increased by 33.4 percent over 1981 and from non-U.S. operations by 7.0 percent.

Gross income from sales increased by 30.3 percent over 1981. In 1982, the percent of gross income derived from sales amounted to 48.9 percent, compared to 44.4 percent in the prior year. Purchase of equipment previously on rent grew by 29.2 percent, and purchase of newly manufactured equipment grew by 36.0 percent. In the U.S., purchase of equipment previously on rent grew by 50.3 percent, compared to a modest non-U.S. growth of 6.9 percent. The increase in the proportion of gross income from the purchase of products reflects a trend in customers' choice of the method of acquisition toward outright purchase or sales type leases. Accordingly, we saw a modest growth of 2.6 percent in rental revenue over 1981.

....

During this past year, IBM has positioned itself for continued growth. IBM's advanced technology large-scale processors and the family of high-performance direct access storage devices were exceptionally well received this past year. These high technology products contributed significantly to the excellent incoming order flow across our worldwide operations. Reflecting the effects of the recession, the company experienced a softening in orders for mid-range systems in the third and fourth quarters of 1982. Orders for office systems and low-end processors, including the Personal computer, remained strong throughout the year. Despite continuing economic uncertainty, management believes the economic pace will quicken in 1983, and expects the company to continue the trend of sustained growth and profitability.

14

FILINGS: (with the Securities Exchange Commission)

10-Q 06/30/83
10-Q 03/31/83

```
PROXY           03/16/83
ARS             12/31/82
10-K            12/31/82
10-Q            09/30/82
NYL             09/07/82
PRSPCT          07/21/82
REGST S03 A00   07/19/82
8-K 57          07/12/82
REGST S03       07/01/82
10-Q            06/30/82
PROXY           06/07/82
NYL             05/17/82
REGST S08       04/29/82
REGST S08       04/29/82
10-Q            03/31/82
PROXY           03/17/82
8-K 5           01/31/82
ARS             12/31/81
10-K            12/31/81

//MEDGEN

    MEDIA GENERAL-FINANCIAL
         SERVICES, INC.
MARKET AND FUNDAMENTAL DATA ON
COMMON STOCKS AND RELATED
SUMMARY MATERIAL ON INDUSTRY
GROUPS, COPYRIGHT (C) 1983.

   IBM/P

INTERNATL BUSINESS MACH
-PRICE & VOLUME- 11/25/83  (170)

PRICE CHANGE       (1)
-LAST TRDNG WK -2.0%
-LAST 4 WKS -5.5%
-LAST 13 WKS 2.7%
-LAST 52 WKS 45.1%
-YR TO DATE 25.7%
CHANGE VS. S & P 500
-LAST TRDNG WK 97%
-LAST 4 WKS 92%
-LAST 13 WKS 100%
-LAST 52 WKS 117%
-YR TO DATE 106%


PRICE RANGE        (2)
-LAST CLOSE $121.00
-52 WEEK HIGH $134.25
-52 WEEK LOW $82.00
-5 YEAR HIGH $134.25
-5 YEAR LOW $48.38
RELATIVE PRICE
-P/E RATIO CURRENT 14.3
-P/E RATIO 5 YR AVG HI 13.4
-P/E RATIO 5 YR AVG LOW 9.3
-PRICE TO COMMON EQUITY 336%
-PRICE TO REV PER SHARE 192%
-RELATIVE PRICE INDEX 137%


PRICE ACTION       (3)
-BETAS UP 1.00
-BETAS DOWN 0.76
VOLUME
-THIS WK SHRS 4,096,000
-THIS WK DOLLAR $500,635,000
-THIS WK % SHRS OUTSTND 0.67%
```

```
-LIQUIDITY RATIO 61,645,000
-ON BALANCE INDEX 62

   IBM/F

INTERNATL BUSINESS MACH
-FUNDMNTL DATA- 11/25/83    (170)
REVENUE            (1)
-LAST 12 MOS $38,357 MIL
-LAST FISCAL YEAR $34,364 MIL
-PCT CHANGE LAST QTR 15.1%
-PCT CHANGE YR TO DATE 17.1%
EARNINGS 12MOS $5,122.0N MIL
EARNINGS PER SHARE
-LAST 12 MONTHS $8.48
-LAST FISCAL YEAR $7.39
-PCT CHANGE LAST QTR 22.3%
-PCT CHANGE FY TO DATE 22.3%
-PCT CHANGE LAST 12MOS 23.3%
-FIVE YR GROWTH RATE 13.0%
DIVIDENDS          (2)
-CURRENT RATE $3.80
-CURRENT RATE YIELD 3.1%
-5 YR GROWTH RATE 9.7%
-PAYOUT LAST FY 47%
-PAYOUT LAST 5 YEARS 55%
-LAST X-DVD DATE 11-02-83
RATIOS
-PROFIT MARGIN 13.4%
-RETURN ON COMMON EQUITY 23.6%
-RETURN ON TOTAL ASSETS 15.7%
-REVENUE TO ASSETS 118%
-DEBT TO EQUITY 14%
-INTEREST COVERAGE 18.4
-CURRENT RATIO 1.6
SHAREHOLDINGS      (3)
-MARKET VALUE $73,514 MIL
-LTST SHR OUTSTND 607,550,000
-INSIDER NET TRADING -10,000
-SHORT INTEREST RATIO 1.1 DYS
-FISCAL YEAR ENDS 12 MOS
```

APPENDIX D

THE XMODEM ERROR-CHECKING PROTOCOL

The XMODEM protocol, developed by Ward Christensen, is illustrated in Figure D-1. As you can see from that figure, XMODEM does not begin the transfer of data until the receiving computer signals the transmitting computer that it is ready to receive data. The Negative Acknowledge (NAK) character is used for this signal and is sent to the transmitting computer every 10 seconds until the file transfer begins. If the file transfer does not begin after nine NAKs are sent, the process has to be manually restarted.

After a NAK is received, the transmitting computer uses a Start of Header (SOH) character and two block numbers (a true block number followed by a 1's complement of the number) to signal the start of a 128-byte block of data to be transferred. It then sends the block followed by an error-checking checksum. The checksum is calculated by adding the ASCII values of each character in the 128-character block; the sum is then ANDed with 255, and the result is retained as the checksum. After each block of data is transferred, the receiving computer computes its own checksum and compares the result to the checksum received from the transmitting computer. If the two values are the same, the receiving

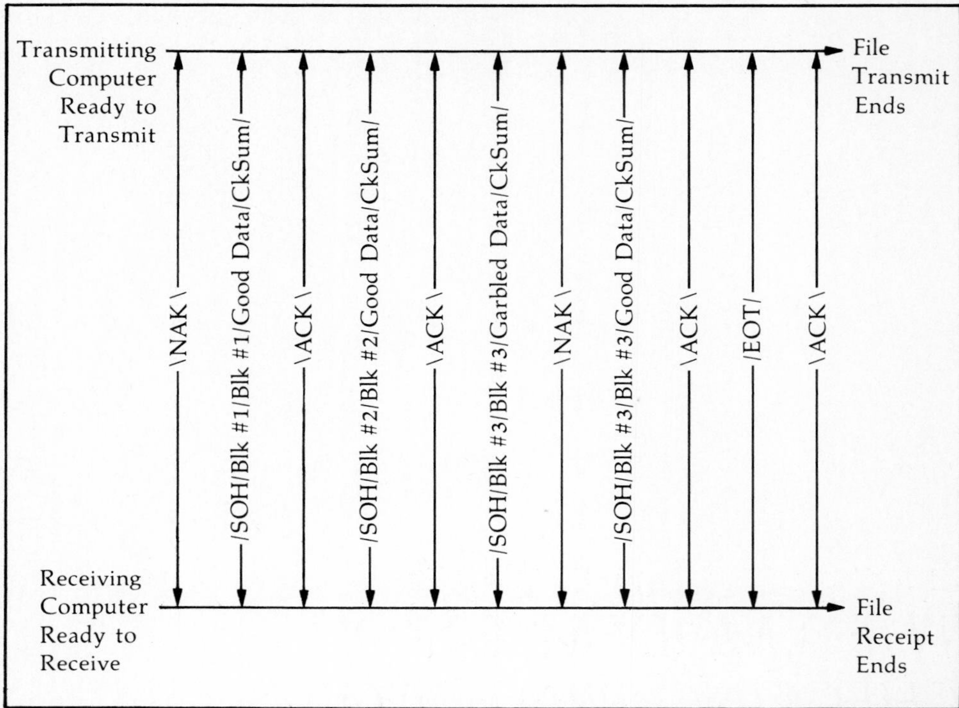

Figure D-1. XMODEM protocol file transfer

computer sends an Acknowledge (ACK) character to tell the receiver to send the next sequential block. If the two values are not the same, the receiving computer sends the transmitter a NAK to request a retransmission of the last block. This retransmission process is repeated until the block of data is properly received or until nine attempts have been made to transmit the block. If the communications link is noisy, resulting in improper block transmission after nine attempts, the file transfer is aborted.

XMODEM uses two block numbers at the start of each block to be sure the same block is not transmitted twice because of a handshake character loss during the transfer. The receiving computer checks the transmitted block to be sure that it is the one requested. Blocks that are retransmitted by mistake are thrown away. When all data has been successfully transmitted, the transmitting computer sends the receiver an End of Transmission (EOT) character to indicate the end of file.

APPENDIX E

PACKET-SWITCHED NETWORKS AND THE X.25 PROTOCOL

Chapter 2 explained that **packet switching** is your PC's path to the national information utilities. When you dial your favorite information utility, you are connected to a local number via a normal telephone circuit. There's a path between you and the local network node that no one else can use. A computer at the node converts your incoming and outgoing data to **packets** and transfers them to the host computer through a network. Your packets are mixed in with everyone else's, but the network is clever enough to send each one to the right place. As far as you're concerned, you have a circuit straight through to the host computer. It's not a real circuit, but rather a **virtual circuit**.

At the beginning of 1984, the PC wasn't actually participating in packet-switching protocol, but rather the local node computer converted the PC's standard asynchronous protocol to a packet protocol suitable for the network. This may change as soon as network operators take advantage of the PC's intelligence. In the meantime, it's useful to understand what happens to your data after it gets past an information utility's local number.

Packet-Switching Standards

The packet-switched network industry is growing quickly. System operators are faced with a choice of three national networks (The Source, CompuServe, Dow Jones) and more are on the way. Because system operators attach directly to the networks, there must be a national standard for these connections just as there is a standard for connecting PCs to modems. With such a standard, system operators can buy low-cost communications hardware and software, knowing that they can use it to connect to any packet-switching network, public or private.

In this age of non-standard worldwide communications networks, we are fortunate to have a strong international standard for packet switching called **X.25**. This user-network interface standard was first ratified in 1976 by the CCITT, an international organization with strong leadership from Great Britain, France, Canada, and the United States. The standard was refined in 1980, but it is subject to ongoing enhancements.

Actually, X.25 is only one of a group of standards. X.25 is a protocol defining the logical interface between host computers and the network; it corresponds in many ways to IBM's SNA/SDLC. As a matter of fact, X.25's lowest level is almost identical to SDLC. The electrical interface is a step up from RS-232C, however. There are two options, X.26 and X.27, that correspond to two Electronic Industries Association (EIA) standards, RS-423A and RS-422A. Both of these standards employ special techniques to reduce noise. This means that data rates up to 100,000 bps are allowed, but 56,000 bps is the usual maximum imposed by the networks. Another network component, the packet assembler/disassembler (PAD) conforms to standards X.28 or X.29. The PAD, located at your local network office, accommodates PCs and asynchronous terminals. Another protocol, X.75, is used for exchanging data between networks. Figure E-1 shows the entire system.

The X.25 Standard

Look back to Figure 10-18. This SDLC frame is almost identical to the X.25 high-level data link control (HDLC) and the advanced data communications control procedure (ADCCP) frame. The control field is a little different; the address field is used only between the DTE and DCE, thus allowing multi-point communication. The information field is unique to X.25. The entire frame is called a **packet**, and there are two basic types. The **call-request packet** initiates a communication session between two points on the network. Once the call has started, **data packets** convey the information.

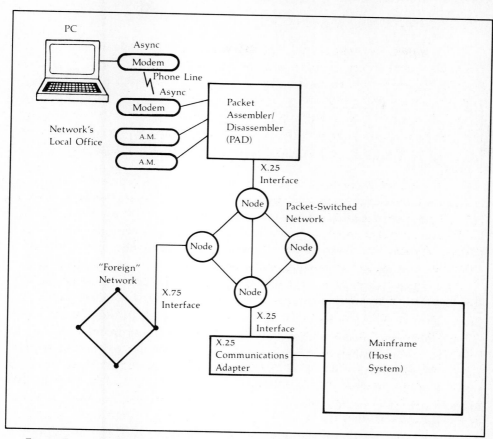

Figure E-1. The components of a packet-switched network

Figure E-2 shows a simplified diagram of the call-request packet. The important fields are the logical channel identifier (LCI) and the called and calling addresses. The addresses are the physical addresses of network users and can be as many as 60 bits long. The LCI is a 12-bit data flow identifier. If you've ever written a computer program that used disk files, you'll be familiar with logical file numbers. You open file ABC.DAT on channel 1 and file XYZ.DAT on channel 2. All future reads and writes are to or from channel numbers, not file names. The X.25 works the same way. The network user opens a communications channel with a call-request packet, gets an LCI number, and then sends and receives with data packets referencing the same LCI number. Thus it is possible to maintain up to 4096 simultaneous conversations with other network users.

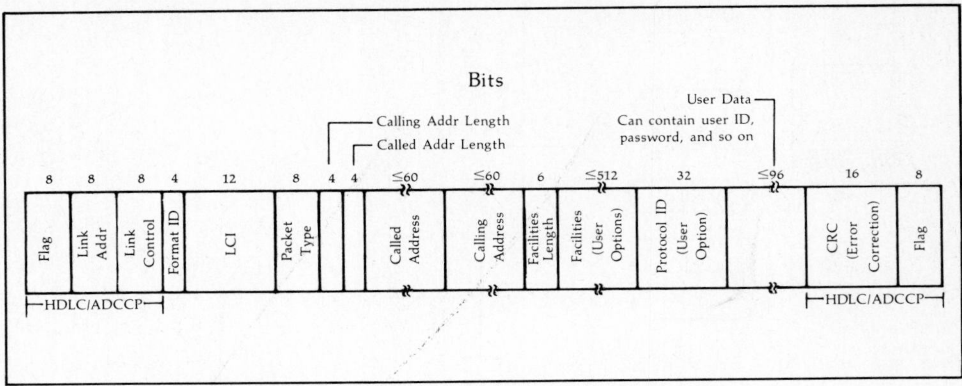

Figure E-2. X.25 call-request packet format

Figure E-3 shows the data packet. Note the send and receive packet sequence numbers. These numbers ensure that the packets will be received in the correct sequence with no omissions or duplications. A windowing scheme much like that shown in Figure 9-13 allows the network to "hold" a predetermined number of undelivered packets. This is called **flow control**.

There are a number of special-purpose packets similar to the call-request packet. These tell the host if (1) a new call is coming in, (2) there's been a network error, (3) the caller has hung up, (4) the caller is calling at 1200 bps, and so forth. The X.25 standard clearly defines the format of each of these packet types.

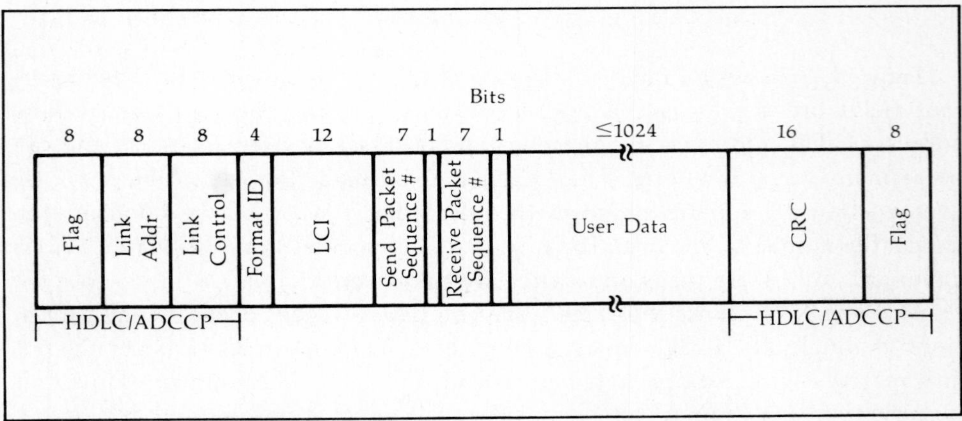

Figure E-3. X.25 data packet format

Public Packet-Switched Networks

The X.25 standard defines the users' interface to the network, but it says nothing about how data is sent within the network. In fact, the public packet-switched networks operate in entirely different ways. Telenet's internal protocols evolved from ARPANET, making Telenet a classic virtual-circuit-based packet-switching network. Packets contain from 1 to 1000 data characters and pass through 56,000 bps lines.Two packets contained in the same message may reach their destination by completely different routes, but they are reassembled in the correct order. Telenet was designed for sporadic communication, such as that encountered in PC-host dialogues, as well as for high-volume inter-mainframe data transfers. Users are charged by the packet regardless of how full it is. Billing for a line of text is the same as it is for a one-character response to a menu prompt. Don't worry, this charge is usually included in your information utility's hourly connect charge.

If you establish a connection through Tymnet, you are guaranteed that all packets will follow a fixed route unless part of the network fails during the session. A centralized network controller is aware of each new connection, and it sends messages to set up all switching nodes to route that call's data through the network. User data is grouped into logical records that, in turn, are combined with other logical records into physical records. It's like cars in a freight train. Users are charged by the character, making Tymnet well suited for economical PC-host communications.

X.PC

X.PC extends the X.25 network right into the PC. It's a new standard being introduced by Tymnet for enhanced PC communication. Principal advantages are error-free data transfer and multiple sessions. You can establish simultaneous virtual circuits to several hosts on the same network, and some of those hosts can be other PCs. X.PC fits in with the new window software. Imagine being able to transfer a file to your friend in Omaha while simultaneously viewing Dow Jones news. You're paying standard Dow Jones connect charges, but your file transfer costs far less than the long-distance call equivalent. High-level protocol is the same as X.25 except that a four-bit logical channel identifier (LCI) allows only 16 parallel sessions. Low-level protocol is asynchronous RS-232C. Tymnet is making this standard public in the hope that other networks will adopt it.

X.PC's competitor is a new protocol from Microcom, Inc., called MNP. Microcom's protocol has been adopted by IBM for use with the PCjr and also for the

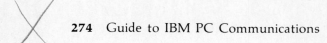

PC. Telenet, Dow Jones, and a number of other companies have chosen MNP because Microcom supplies technical details and a license for a reasonable fee. MNP is not as sophisticated as X.PC; it's similar to the protocols used by *Smartcom* and *Crosstalk*.

APPENDIX F

PC COMMUNICATIONS ANNOTATED BIBLIOGRAPHY

The following list of additional resource material will help you find out more about data communications and your IBM PC.

Brooks, John. *Telephone: The First Hundred Years.* New York: Harper and Row, 1976.

Although the author claims to be independent, this book is regarded as the "official" history of AT&T. The story is thorough and readable, and the business aspect is emphasized.

Cane, Mike. *The Computer Phone Book.* New York: Plume/New American Library, 1983.

Descriptions of all information utilities and CBBs with *Computer Phone Book* (CPB) reference numbers.

Glossbrenner, Alfred. *The Complete Handbook of Personal Computer Communication.* New York: St Martin's Press, 1983.

A thorough description of the available on-line services accessible to any personal computer or terminal. Special emphasis is given to The Source, CompuServe, and Dow Jones.

Hiltz, Starr R., and Turoff, Murray. *Network Nation: Human Communication Via Computer*. Reading, Mass.: Addison-Wesley, 1978.

This "classic" book describes the EIES computer conferencing system.

International Business Machines. *IBM Synchronous Data Link Control: General Information*. GA27-3093-2. Research Triangle Park, N.C.: IBM, 1979.

An overview of SDLC written in a manner that is not too technical.

———. *Systems Network Architecture: Concepts and Products*. GC30-3072-0. Research Triangle Park, N.C.: IBM, 1981.

A good introduction to IBM's Systems Network Architecture.

Jordan, Larry, and Churchill, Bruce. *Communications and Networking for the IBM PC*. Bowie, Md.: Robert J. Brady/Prentice-Hall, 1983.

A good discussion of Local Area Networks for the IBM PC.

Marland, E.A. *Early Electrical Communication*. New York: Abelard-Schuman, 1964.

A British history of the telegraph with emphasis on Cooke and Wheatstone's contributions. Some discussion of Samuel Morse's work in America is included.

Martin, James. *Telecommunications and the Computer*. Englewood Cliffs, N.J.: Prentice-Hall, 1976.

A readable yet technical description of all types of transmission and switching technologies. This book also presents a thorough explanation of packet-switched networks.

Nichols, Elizabeth A., Nichols, Joseph C., and Musson, Keith R. *Data Communications for Microcomputers*. New York: McGraw-Hill, 1982.

Because of its emphasis on RS-232C asynchronous communications and protocols, this book will be of interest to readers with technical or engineering backgrounds. Descriptions of RS422 and RS423 interfaces are included.

Rosner, Roy D. *Packet Switching: Tommorrow's Communications Today*. Belmont, Calif.: Wadsworth, Lifetime Learning Publications, 1982.

A good introduction to packet switching and X.25. With excellent drawings and graphs, the book presents easily understood communications traffic and queuing theory as well as descriptions of real networks. Additional packet-switching articles and papers are referenced.

Shiers, George. *The Electric Telegraph: An Historical Anthqlogy*. Salem, N.H.: Ayer Company (Arno Press), 1977.

Reproductions of the original articles and drawings by the originators of the telegraph from its beginnings through 1944.

Vallee, Jacques. *Network Revolution: Confessions of a Computer Scientist*. Berkeley, Calif.: And/Or Press, 1982.

The author, a co-founder of the Notepad computer conferencing system, describes his early, unappreciated computer programs and relates some negative aspects of computer communications. The overall tone of the book is optimistic, however.

APPENDIX G

PC COMMUNICATIONS PRODUCT LIST

This list contains PC-related data communications products (hardware and software) and services.

SNA 3270
RS-232 3270 emulator

AST Research, Inc.
2372 Morse Ave.
Irvine, CA 92714
(714) 863-1333

TLX-A-SYST
Telex communication program

American Intl. Communications
4745 Walnut
Boulder, CO 80301
(303) 444-6675

Signalman/Volksmodem
Modem

Anchor Automation
6913 Baljean Ave.
Van Nuys, CA 91406
(213) 997-6493

BRS After Dark On-line database service (encyclopedic)	Bibliographic Retrieval Services 1200 Rte. 7 Latham, NY 12110 (518) 783-1161
PC: IntelliModem 1200 baud internal modem with software	Bizcomp 532 Weddell Dr. Sunnyvale, CA 94086 (408) 745-1616
SmarTelex Telex communication program	Cappcomm Software, Inc. One World Trade Center #1453 New York, NY 10048 (212) 938-5702
Desk Top Broker Stock buy and sell program	C.D. Anderson & Co. 300 Montgomery St. Suite 440 San Francisco, CA 94104 (800) 822-2222 (415) 433-2120
PCOX PC-to-host coax connection	CXI 3606 W. Bayshore Rd. Palo Alto, CA 94303 (415) 424-0700
CIS/EIS Information utility	CompuServe 5000 Arlington Centre Blvd. Columbus, OH 43220 (800) 848-8199
Plato Homelink On-line education system	Control Data Publishing Co. 4455 Eastgate Mall San Diego, CA 92121 (800) 233-3784 (800) 233-3785

Product	Vendor
Remote Access Communication program for remote access of PC	Custom Software P.O. Box 1005 Bedford, TX 76021 (817) 282-7553
CoSystem Intelligent telephone that works with PC	Cygnet Technologies 1296 Lawrence Station Rd. Sunnyvale, CA 94089 (800) 331-9116 (800) 331-9113
IRMA 3270 Coax emulator	DCA 303 Technology Park Norcross, GA 30092 (800) 241-4762
Dialog/Knowledge Index Information utility	Dialog Information Services, Inc. 3460 Hillview Ave. Palo Alto, CA 94304 (800) 227-5510 (415) 858-3796
MAIL-COM Software for E-COM	Digisoft Computers, Inc. 1501 Third Ave. New York, NY 10028 (212) 734-3875
Dow Jones News/Retrieval Service Information service and intelligent communications program	Dow Jones & Co., Inc. P.O. Box 300 Princeton, NJ 08540 (609) 452-2000
ASCOM Communication program	Dynamic Microprocessor Associates 545 Fifth Ave., #602 New York, NY 10017 (212) 687-7115
Line Status Indicator RS-232C cable male-female with bipolar LEDs	Electro-Service Co. 5702 154th Ave. N.E. P.O. Box 92 Redmond, WA 98052 (206) 881-0709

Telenet Packet-switched network	GTE Telenet Communications 8229 Boone Blvd. Vienna, VA 22180 (800) 336-0437 (800) 572-0408
Smartcom II Communication program for Hayes Smartmodems	Hayes Microcomputer Products, Inc. 5923 Peachtree Industrial Blvd. Norcross, GA 30092 (404) 449-8791
Smartmodem 1200B 1200 baud modem	Hayes Microcomputer Products, Inc. 5923 Peachtree Industrial Blvd. Norcross, GA 30092 (404) 449-8791
Timetran Microcomputer-Telex link	ITT Worldcom 67 Broad St. New York, NY 10004 (800) 424-1170
Linkup Synchronous communications board; does not contain a modem	Information Technologies, Inc. 7850 East Evans Rd. Scottsdale, AZ 85260 (602) 998-1033
PC Express Communication card with internal 300-baud modem, serial interface to external modems	Intelligent Technologies Intl. 151 University Ave. Palo Alto, CA 94301 (415) 328-2411
Hostcomm Communications program	Janadon, Inc. P.O. Box 2462 Fairfax, VA 22031 (703) 978-0866
MCI Mail Electronic mail with optional post office delivery	MCI Mail 2000 M St. NW Washington, DC 20036 (800) 624-2255

Product	Vendor
Executive Peachpak II Micro-mainframe software link	MSA Software Co. 3445 Peachtree Rd. NE Atlanta, GA 30326 (800) 554-8900 (404) 239-2000
Nexis On-line database	Mead Data Central P.O. Box 1830 Dayton, OH 45401 (800) 227-4908
ERA 2 1200 bps modem on a card with special protocol for Telenet	Microcom 140A Providence Hwy. Norwood, MA 02062 (800) 322-3722 (617) 762-9310
Microstar NAPLPS for the PC	Microstar Software Ltd. 687 Mansfield Ave. Ottawa, ON K2A2T (613) 722-7426
Transporter Communication program for PC-to-PC unattended operation	Microstuff, Inc. 1845 The Exchange, #140 Atlanta, GA 30339 (404) 952-0267
Crosstalk Communication program	Microstuff, Inc. 1845 The Exchange, #140 Atlanta, GA 30339 (404) 952-0267
TELigraph NAPLPS system for PC	Microtaure, Inc. P.O. Box 6039, Station J Ottawa, ON K2A1T (613) 745-6661
NewsNet On-line newsletter service	NewsNet, Inc. 945 Haverford Rd. Bryn Mawr, PA 19010 (800) 345-1301 (215) 527-8030

Colorplus Color graphics adapter	Plantronics/Frederick Electronics 7630 Hayward Rd. P.O. Box 502 Frederick, MD 21701 (301) 662-5901
Qbulletin Multi-user bulletin board and message system	Quantum Software Systems, Inc. 7219 Shea Ct. San Jose, CA 95139 (408) 629-9402
212A Modem Circuit-card 1200 bps Hayes-compatible modem with optional RS-232C connector	Qubié Distributing 4809 Calle Alto Camarillo, CA 93010 (805) 482-9829
Telex communications Microcomputer-telex link	RCA Global Communications 60 Broad St. New York, NY 10004 (212) 806-7000
Protocol Converter Translator	Renex Corporation 6901 Old Keene Mill Rd. Springfield, VA 22150 (703) 451-2200
VTERM Terminal emulator VT100, VT52	Saturn Consulting Group, Inc. 147 West 26th St. New York, NY 10001 (212) 675-7753
The Source Data communications service	Source Telecommunications 1616 Anderson Rd. McLean, VA 22102 (703) 734-7500
Telelearning Computer-aided instruction with intelligent communications interface	Telelearning 505 Beach St. San Francisco, CA 94133 (415) 928-2800
PC-Talk III Communication program	The Headlands Press, Inc. P.O. Box 862 Tiburon, CA 94920 (415) 435-9775

Tymnet Packet-switched network	Tymnet, Inc. 2710 Orchard Pkwy. San Jose, CA 95134 (408) 446-7000
Uninet Packet-switched network	United Telecom Communications, Inc. 10951 Lakeview Ave. Lexana, KS 66219 (913) 541-4400
208 A/B synchronous modem 4800-bps half- or full-duplex, manual dial, answer	Universal Data Systems 5000 Bradford Dr. Huntsville, AL 35805 (205) 837-8100
PC Modem Plus 300 bps circuit card modem with 1200 bps option	Ven-Tel, Inc. 2342 Walsh Ave. Santa Clara, CA 95051 (800) 538-5121 (408) 727-5721
Viewtron Videotex service	Viewdata Corp. of America 1111 Lincoln Rd. 7th fl. Miami Beach, FL 33139 (305) 674-3457
Westlaw Legal information service	West Publishing Co. 50 W. Kellog Blvd. P.O. Box 3526 St. Paul, MN 55165 (612) 228-2500
EasyLink Microcomputer-telex service	Western Union Telegraph Co. One Lake St. Upper Saddle River, NJ 07458 (201) 825-5000
NAPLPS decoder software Not ready yet	Wolfdata 187 Billerica Rd. Chelmsford, MA 01824 (617) 250-1500

APPENDIX H

8250 UART Registers

This appendix* describes the registers of the 8250 UART chip used on the serial port of the IBM PC. The 8250's registers are accessed by reading or writing to input/output ports 3F8-3FF (COM1) or ports 2F8-2FF (COM2). Registers that can be read from as well as written to are listed as read/write (R/W); those only read from are listed as read-only (R/O); and those only written to are listed as write-only (W/O).

Line Control Register (LCR) 3FB R/W

LCR specifies character format and controls access to other registers as defined in Table H-1.

LCR Bit Map

7	6	5	4	3	2	1	0
DLAB	SET BREAK	STICK PARITY	EPS	PEN	STB	WSL1	WSL0

* Reprinted, by permission of Hayes Microcomputer Products, from the *Hayes 1200B Hardware Reference Manual*, 4-2-4-9.

Table H-1. Line Control Register Bit Definitions

Bit	Name	Function
0	Word Length Select Bit 0 (WLS0)	Sets length of each character.
1	Word Length Select Bit 1 (WLS1)	Bit 1 / Bit 0 / Word Length: 0 0 5 bits 0 1 6 bits 1 0 7 bits 1 1 8 bits At least 7 bits are required for ASCII characters.
2	Number of Stop Bits (STB)	1 2 stop bits per character (1 1/2 for 5-bit words only). 0 1 stop bit per character.
3	Parity Enable (PEN)	1 Enables parity generation or checking. 0 Disables the same.
4	Even Parity Select (EPS)	1 Even parity. 0 Odd parity. Bit 3 must be logic 1.
5	Stick Parity	Not commonly used.
6	Set Break	1 Causes a modem to transmit a continuous break signal. 0 Stops the break signal.
7	Divisor Latch Access Bit (DLAB)	1 Enables access to the Divisor Latches of the Baud Rate Generator during a read or write operation. 0 Enables access to the Receiver Buffer, Transmitter Holding Register, and Interrupt Enable Register.

Divisor Latch (DLL)
3F8 R/W (least significant byte)

DLL contains the lower eight bits of the baud rate divisor used to set the Baud Rate Generator. The most significant byte is contained at the next address. Together, both addresses must contain the hex equivalent of the divisor predetermined to generate the desired baud rate. The hex value to enter is as follows:

For 110 bps *enter* 17 hex
300 bps 80 hex
1200 bps 60 hex.

Note that to access this register, DLAB of LCR must equal 1.

Divisor Latch (DLM) *3F9 R/W (most significant byte)*

DLM contains the upper eight bits of the baud rate divisor. Complete the divisor with the appropriate value:

For 110 bps	*enter* 4 hex
300 bps	1 hex
1200 bps	0 hex.

The divisor table is reproduced in the IBM *Technical Reference* manual. The divisor for selecting another baud rate (within the modem's range) may be obtained by computing the formula

$$\text{Divisor} = \frac{115{,}200}{\text{Baud Rate}}$$

Note that to access this register, DLAB of LCR must equal 1.

Line Status Register *(LSR) 3FD R/O (bit 0, R/W)*

LSR provides status information (shown in Table H-2) about data transfer and associated error conditions. The conditions signaled by bits 0-5 produce an interrupt, provided that the interrupt is enabled (*see* "Interrupt Enable Register").

LSR Bit Map

7	6	5	4	3	2	1	0
—	TSRE	THRE	BI	FE	PE	OE	DR

Modem Control Register *(MCR) 3FC R/W*

MCR manages the interface with the modem. The bits of the MCR are defined in Table H-3.

MCR Bit Map

7	6	5	4	3	2	1	0
—	—	—	LOOP	OUT 2	OUT 1	RTS	DTR

Table H-2. Line Status Register Bit Definitions

Bit	*Name*		*Function*
0	Data Ready (DR)	1	Indicates that a character has been received and is being held in the Receiver Buffer Register (*see* "Receiver Buffer Register"). Reset to 0 by CPU when data is read; may also be written to under program control.
1	Overrun Error (OE)	1	Indicates that character in Receiver Buffer Register was not read before next character was received; previous character was destroyed. Reset to 0 whenever Line Status Register is read.
2	Parity Error (PE)	1	Indicates that parity of character received does not match that specified by EPS of Line Control Register. Reset to 0 whenever Line Status Register is read.
3	Framing Error (FE)	1	Indicates that character received lacks a valid stop bit. Reset to 0 whenever Line Status Register is read.
4	Break Interrupt (BI)	1	Indicates that a break signal has been received; does not indicate when break signal ends. Reset to 0 whenever Line Status Register is read.
5	Transmitter Holding Register Empty (THRE)	1	Indicates that the UART is ready to accept a new character for transmission. Reset to 0 when Transmitter Holding Register is loaded (*see* "Transmitter Holding Register").
6	Transmitter Shift Register Empty (TSRE)	1	Indicates that the last character in Transmitter Shift Register has been transmitted. Reset to 0 upon data transfer from Transmitter Holding Register to Transmitter Shift Register.
7	—		Unused; always 0.

Table H-3. Modem Control Register Bit Definitions

Bit	*Name*	*Function*
0	Data Terminal Ready (DTR)	1 Enables modem operation. 0 Disables modem (i.e., modem neither accepts commands nor auto-answers, and if on-line, modem disconnects).
1	Request to Send (RTS)	Action depends on modem.
2	Output 1 (OUT 1)	User-designated output.
3	Output 2 (OUT 2)	User-designated output.
4	LOOP	1 Activates loopback feature for diagnostic testing of the UART. 0 Setting for normal operation.
5–7	—	Unused; always 0.

Modem Status Register (MSR) 3FE R/O

MSR provides the current status of control signals from the modem as defined in Table H-4. Whenever bit 2 or 3 is logic 1, a Modem Status interrupt is generated if it is enabled (*see* "Interrupt Enable Register").

MSR Bit Map

7	6	5	4	3	2	1	0
RLSD	RI	DSR	CTS	DRLSD	TERI	DDSR	DCTS

Receiver Buffer Register (RBR) 3F8 R/O

RBR contains the character just received. The character is received serially with the least significant bit (bit 0) received first. Note that to access this register, DLAB of LCR must equal 0.

Table H-4. Modem Status Register Bit Definitions

Bit	*Name*		*Function*
0	Delta Clear to Send (DCTS)		Always 0.
1	Delta Data Set Ready (DDSR)		Always 0.
2	Trailing Edge Ring Indicator (TERI)	1	Indicates that Ring Indicator (bit 6) has changed from logic 1 to logic 0. Reset to 0 when MSR is read.
3	Delta Received Line Signal Detect (DRLSD)	1	Indicates that Received Line Signal Detect has changed states. Reset to 0 when MSR is read.
4	Clear to Send (CTS)		Always 1.
5	Data Set Ready (DSR)		Always 1.
6	Ring Indicator (RI)	1	Indicates that the modem detects a ringing signal on the telephone line.
7	Received Line Signal Detect (RLSD)	1 0	Indicates that the modem detects a carrier signal on the telephone line. Indicates absence of a carrier signal.

Transmitter Holding Register (THR) 3F8 W/O

THR contains the next character to be transmitted serially. The least significant bit (bit 0) is transmitted first. Note that to access this register, DLAB of LCR must equal 0.

Interrupt Enable Register (IER) 3F9 R/W

IER enables the interrupt sources to activate the interrupt output signal. The bits of the IER are defined in Table H-5.

IER Bit Map

7	6	5	4	3	2	1	0
—	—	—	—	EDSSI	ELSI	ETBEI	ERBFI

Table H-5. Interrupt Enable Register Bit Definitions

Bit	*Name*	*Function*
0	Enable Received Data Available Interrupt (ERBFI)	1 Causes the UART to generate an interrupt whenever Data Ready (DR) of Line Status Register becomes logic 1.
1	Enable Transmitter Holding Register Empty Interrupt (ETBEI)	1 Causes the UART to generate an interrupt whenever THRE of Line Status Register becomes logic 1.
2	Enable Receiver Line Status Interrupt (ELSI)	1 Causes the UART to generate an interrupt whenever an overrun error, parity error, framing error, or break interrupt occurs; see Line Status Register.
3	Enable Modem Status Interrupt (EDSSI)	1 Causes the UART to generate an interrupt whenever RI or RLSD of Modem Status Register becomes logic 1.
4-7	—	Unused; always 0.
Note that to access this register, DLAB of LCR must equal 0.		

Interrupt Identification Register (IIR) 3FA R/O

IIR stores information indicating that a prioritized interrupt is pending. The bits of the IIR are defined in Table H-6.

IIR Bit Map

7	6	5	4	3	2	1	0
—	—	—	—	—	Interrupt ID	Interrupt ID	Interrupt Pending

Table H-6. Interrupt Identification Register Bit Definitions

Bit	*Name*	*Function*			
0	Interrupt Pending	0 Indicates that an interrupt condition has occurred.			
1-2	Interrupt ID	Indicates priority of interrupt condition.			
		Bit 2	Bit 1	Priority	Interrupt Source
		1	1	1 (highest)	Overrun Error (OE) or Parity Error (PE) or Framing Error (FE) or Break Interrupt (BI) (see Line Status Register)
		1	0	2	Data Ready (DR) (see Line Status Register)
		0	1	3	Transmitter Holding Register Empty (THRE) (see Line Status Register)
		0	0	4 (lowest)	Ring Indicator (RI) or Received Line Signal Detect (RLSD) (see Modem Status Register)
3-7	—	Unused; always 0.			

Note that the information contained in bits 0 to 2 is always available even if the interrupt capability has not been enabled by the Interrupt Enable Register (IER).

INDEX